The Market Power of Multinationals

John M. Connor

FOREWORD
Willard F. Mueller

The Praeger Special Studies program, through a selective worldwide distribution network, makes available to the academic, government, and business communities significant and timely research in U.S. and international economic, social, and political issues.

The Market Power of Multinationals

A Quantitative Analysis of U.S. Corporations in Brazil and Mexico

PRAEGER SPECIAL STUDIES IN INTERNATIONAL BUSINESS, FINANCE, AND TRADE

Praeger Publishers   New York   London

Library of Congress Cataloging in Publication Data

Connor, John M
    Market power of multinationals.

    (Praeger special studies in international business,
finance, and trade)
    Bibliography: p.
    Includes index.
    1. International business enterprises. 2. Indus-
trial concentration. 3. Corporations, American—Brazil.
4. Corporations, American—Mexico. I. Title.
HD2755.5.C638   1977   338.8'8   77-14302
ISBN 0-03-023036-5

PRAEGER SPECIAL STUDIES
200 Park Avenue, New York, N.Y., 10017, U.S.A.

Published in the United States of America in 1977
by Praeger Publishers,
A Division of Holt, Rinehart and Winston, CBS, Inc.

789   038   987654321

Printed in the United States of America

For Ulla

Although much of the vast literature on multinational corporations (MNCs) discusses the market power held—or not held—by these global enterprises, there has been precious little empirical work on the subject. This void stems not from a lack of interest but a lack of reliable data to test the basic hypotheses of the sources and consequences of market power. Because of its interest in this subject, the Senate Subcommittee on Multinational Corporations, chaired by Senator Frank Church, developed a rich body of data that for the first time permitted a comprehensive quantitative analysis of the roots and fruits of U.S. MNCs' market power in Brazil and Mexico. The subcommittee commissioned two studies based on these data; John Connor participated in both of these.

Drawing from this prior work and expanding on it, Connor uses the theory of industrial organization as his frame of reference in examining the market power of U.S.-based MNCs operating in Brazil and Mexico. This framework has been used widely in researching the competitive performance of industries in the United States and in other more economically advanced market-oriented economies. My colleague, Professor Leonard Weiss, recently reviewed what he characterized as the "massive effort" to test industrial organization theory, that the competitive characteristics of the markets in which firms operate influence, significantly, the degree of their market power. After reviewing the evidence of studies of United States, British, Canadian, and Japanese industries, Weiss concluded, "In general the data have confirmed the relationship predicted by theory even though the data are very imperfect, and almost certainly biased toward a zero relationship."

Connor's work makes a strong case for adding Brazil and Mexico to Weiss' list. Using data superior to that of most studies of American industries, he confirms that the structural variables found to be significant in the more developed nations are also significant determinants of power in Brazil and Mexico, specifically, the level of market concentration, the relative dominance of individual firms, and the height of the entry barriers confronting new competitors.

Despite differences in the historical paths of development, differences in the institutional environment in which MNCs operate, and dif-

Willard F. Mueller is William F. Vilas Research Professor in the departments of Agricultural Economics, Economics, and the Law School.

ferences in the relative importance of U.S. MNCs' participation in their economies, the similarities in structure and performance of MNCs in the two countries far outweigh the differences. This indicates that there exist powerful economic forces determining how markets are structured and how MNCs perform in them. This study has not uncovered all of these forces; but it goes far in explaining and quantifying the market power that results from the existing structures.

Serious students of the place of the multinational corporation in world affairs will welcome the new light Connor sheds on this dimension of MNCs operating in these two large developing nations. Policy makers in the United States and host nations cannot ignore these findings. Perhaps most important, the findings indicate that the state of competition in a market does indeed make a big difference in the market power of firms. In some industries host nation policy makers may therefore be faced with a trade-off between less competition and greater efficiency. Connor has not measured the magnitude of the efficiency gains associated with great market power. This determination probably will require an industry-by-industry analysis. But in industries where the major source of power appears to be advertising-created barriers to entry the trade-off less often involves efficiency considerations.

After spending many years attempting to formulate and implement policies designed to cope with the market power problem within the United States, I am reluctant to recommend how Brazil and Mexico should deal with the problem. Advising other nations as to how to solve their problems is always hazardous at best. This is especially true when those dispensing advice base it largely on American experience. Our nation has struggled with its own market power problem for over a century, employing a blend of policies including procompetition efforts as embodied in our antitrust laws, regulation of natural monopolies with independent regulatory commissions, periodic experiments with voluntary and compulsory price controls, and even occasionally creating publicly owned enterprises. But our lackluster record in coping with entrenched market power does not provide a strong recommendation for exporting to less developed countries (LDCs) the American model for the social control of corporate power. U.S. foreign policy makers therefore should be tolerant of other nations' experiments in dealing with a problem that Americans have themselves not successfully dealt with at home.

ACKNOWLEDGMENTS

This book has had a long, perhaps tortuous evolution. I have benefited at several stages from the suggestions and criticism of others.

My foremost debt is to Willard F. Mueller. As both mentor and colleague, he provided me with generous measures of intellectual stimulation, guidance, and encouragement for this study. His detailed comments on the bulk of the material in this book have greatly improved both the style and the substance of the text at several points. Indeed, his magisterial influence is so pervasive that I am tempted to hold him responsible for any shortcomings that may remain.

Other economists at the University of Wisconsin have also contributed in various ways. Leonard Weiss gave me very meticulous comments on several chapters of an earlier version of this book. Aaron Cobe Johnson was quite helpful in resolving some sticky statistical problems. Peter Dorner and John Strasma read an early draft of this work and prompted me to consider some policy and institutional aspects of the study that might otherwise have gone unexamined. And finally, only brief mention will be made of several teachers who have influenced my thinking on the problems of economic development: W. W. McPherson, Donald Harris, Marvin Mircale, Don Kanel, and Jeffery Williamson.

Financial support for this study was garnered from several sources. The major portion came from the Graduate School and the Vilas Fund of the University of Wisconsin at Madison. Both financial and clerical aid was received from the U.S. Senate Subcommittee on Multinational Corporations (now renamed the Subcommittee on Foreign Economic Policy). Also, all the members of the University of Wisconsin team that processed the special questionnaire survey used in this study deserve special praise for their intense dedication, drive, and attention to detail; I particularly wish to thank Richard Newfarmer and Mary Bishop in this connection.

Karen Isensee was responsible for the preparation of the final draft of the manuscript and performed that onerous task outstandingly. Earlier drafts were typed by Joanne Schmit and Marie Jacobsen.

CONTENTS

LIST OF TABLES AND FIGURES

Multinational corporations (MNCs) are vast reservoirs of capital, technical, and managerial resources. Some have grown larger than many nation-states and possess great potential economic and non-economic power. In their quest for profitable ventures they have pervaded the global economy. Their superior access to technological know-how and their undisputed capability for transferring it have made them appear indispensable to most nations favoring the capitalist market economy model of development. Even socialist nations, including the USSR, see MNCs as useful instruments for economic growth.

Yet the very characteristics responsible for the modern MNC's omnipresence and success in world affairs often have triggered tensions and hostility. Many of the world's most difficult economic problems have been laid, like unwanted foundlings, at the doorstep of the MNCs. Some of these difficulties first appeared at the same time as MNCs began their phenomenal growth; many other economic conundrums have persisted in regions where MNCs had only recently begun operations on a large scale. Whether these patterns are merely concurrent or whether the two are causally connected remains in most cases an empirically open question. But, fairly or not, the MNC is often a convenient and tempting target for numerous accusations.

There are several important economic issues or conflicts linked by one writer or another to the MNC. These seem to arise from what may be an inherent juxtaposition of the private decision-making standards of the firm and the norms of social welfare. Although not all of these issues are adequately addressed in this book, it is instructive to delineate the main pressure points, roughly in order of their appearance as public concerns.

1. The Balance of Payments and Trade. This concern arose initially in the capital-exporting countries. During the 1960s in particular, large outflows of capital occasioned by activities of MNCs may have led to some worsening in their home country's balance of payments. Second-round effects included underinvestment, lower exports, and rising unemployment in the home country. In the capital-receiving countries (especially the less developed ones), the initial reaction to rising foreign direct investment (FDI) was "the more the better." Dismay later set in as the amounts of foreign exchange required to service dividend, interest, and royalty remissions rose precipitously. Moreover, it became increasingly clear that MNCs were relying primarily

on local sources of savings rather than international transfers of financial capital. The trend toward net positive balance of payments effects of FDI for the donor countries has been evident for some years for petroleum and mining ventures, but has been apparent in the manufacturing sector only recently. Another unexpected effect of manufacturing FDI is that it often generates greater demand for imported inputs than it does for exports of finished goods.

2. National Planning and Macroeconomic Goals. Most countries desire high levels of growth, employment, real investment, monetary stability, and a reduction in regional development disparities. The developed countries are worried that outgoing FDI may lower labor productivity and labor's share in the national income. To the extent that MNCs may act in concert when shifting their sizable liquid funds in anticipation of exchange-rate changes, their actions can precipitate foreign-exchange crises and exacerbate inflationary tendencies. The patent flexibility that MNCs have to shift funds internationally by means of internal accounting procedures ("transfer pricing") opens them to the charge of massive tax avoidance (if not tax evasion). The less developed recipients of FDI have also become somewhat disenchanted. The rate of employment generation has been disappointing: MNCs typically require a total investment of more than $10,000 to create one manufacturing job. Not only transfer pricing, but also disastrous competitive bidding among countries for certain prestigious investments, has resulted in an erosion of potential tax benefits. Moreover, MNCs have generally contributed to growing regional imbalances within the host nations by investing in the prime metropolitan areas. Finally, planners fret over the implications for steady growth in the face of the decidedly footloose capacity of MNCs.

3. Technology Transfer. Perhaps the preeminent argument in favor of MNCs, their efficiency in internationally conveying more productive means of production, has also come under increasing scrutiny. The more advanced countries worry about the depletion of their stock of commercially valuable knowledge and the consequent erosion of their advantages in international trade. But the concerns of the less industrialized countries are somewhat broader. They are worried that MNCs may choose techniques that are outdated or inappropriate for local resource endowments. Furthermore, there is the possibility that MNCs for reasons of business strategy may restrict the benefits or raise the costs of transfer to them. In particular, if either the output markets or the market for the technology itself is imperfectly competitive, many external benefits can be made internal to the firm and the rents to the firms can be quite high. Finally, in such a situation, MNCs may be in a position to restrict the future capacity of the host country to develop its own inventive capabilities.

4. Denationalization. Perhaps the most basic tension, underlying many of the rest, is the suspicion that foreign ownership in key

sectors or in critical proportions portends a loss of economic sovereignty. Thus, this issue is intimately intertwined with overtly sociopolitical considerations. In its most basic form, this source of tension arises because MNCs are perceived by the host country as an alien institution, not an entirely rational business unit. That is, MNCs are thought to carry with them indelible national characteristics and to act as agents of their home country in political matters. More subtle perhaps is the allegation that MNCs tend to create or reinforce class divisions within host countries by supporting conservative or capitalist interest groups. By extension, it would be in the interest of MNCs as a group to divide the capital-importing countries by favoring those with predominantly capitalist ideologies over those with socialist ones. Of course, if MNCs do behave in this manner, their effectiveness would be enhanced if it were accompanied by significant economic power as well.

    5. <u>Monopolization</u>. Many of the doubts expressed about MNCs on other grounds are clearly reinforced by noncompetitive behavior. For while purely competitive firms are completely passive to their environments, monopolists typically engage in strategies that will restructure their surroundings more to their liking. The history of international business is replete with examples of cartels, price-fixing schemes, divisions of markets, and other restrictive or corrupt business practices. Monopolistic conditions give rise to large pools of liquid funds distributed among relatively few firms; this in turn makes bribery and other forms of concerted political meddling more likely. Monopoly profits also contribute to greater inequality of both wages and investment income. Perhaps the most insidious effect of market power is the ability of firms to orchestrate consumer demand. In the less developed countries this generally implies a shift from more traditional and basic goods to the high income, "international" goods that MNCs often produce. Even the food and health products introduced into low income countries by MNCs often do not improve the nutritional and health conditions of the majority (Griffin 1977).

    This book addresses most directly the issues raised under the last two categories—monopolization and denationalization. It focuses on the measurement of the relationship between the market structures of two highly relevant test cases (Brazil and Mexico) and the profit performance of affiliates of U.S. MNCs. It uses the traditional oligopoly theories of economics and an established statistical test of market power to identify and quantify the exercise of market power by MNCs in two important less industrialized countries.

    Thus, in a sense, this is new wine in old bottles. But in several respects this study can claim to be a departure from the ton of the previously published literature on multinational corporations. For one thing, it is explicitly based on a <u>single branch of economics</u> known as industrial organization (IO) theory. Most previous studies of MNCs have employed a more eclectic framework, combining elements of business management, international trade and finance, managerial and behavioral theories of the firm, and imperfect competition theories. By adopting a particular theoretical stance we are able to draw conclusions about both the impetus behind FDI and its welfare effects upon the country. It seems to me that most of the present scholarship is artificially divided between studies that consider only the causes of FDI and those that focus on impacts.

This book also emphasizes the actions of MNCs in the context of their <u>industries</u>. In this it differs from the typical business school studies, which are typically built upon numerous company case studies or interviews with managers of MNCs. By focusing on the industry as the basic unit of analysis, the present study avoids the excessive reliance on highly aggregated national data characteristic of many other studies. Another limitation of much of the published literature on the MNC is a tendency to try to generalize from predominantly vertical investments, namely, those in petroleum, mining, and agriculture. To redress this balance the analysis in this book has been used on data about manufacturing enterprises. Data on this sector have been historically more difficult to obtain, especially in the less developed areas, even though it is in recent years the most dynamic sector.

A final distinctive feature of this book is its decidedly <u>empirical</u> bent. Within the limits imposed by the data base, hypotheses are stated and then tested against a large sample of observations. Unlike most previous works in this area, a questionnaire was designed with the specific purpose of applying statistical tests to certain notions of industrial organization theory. Even the policy discussion is generally related back to the empirical results.

The depth of the empirical investigation was made possible by access to an especially rich body of data derived from a special questionnaire survey commissioned by the U.S. Senate Subcommittee on Multinational Corporations. After completing a well-known series of hearings in March 1973 on the ITT-Chile affair, the subcommittee was convinced that it needed a detailed and definitive report on the economic role of U.S. MNCs in the less developed areas. It soon thereafter commissioned Richard Newfarmer and Willard F. Mueller to do such a study. They designed a survey questionnaire and sent it to more than two hundred large MNCs with significant manufacturing operations in either Brazil or Mexico. The questionnaire requested information on ownership, lines of business, market positions, and a great deal of basic financial and trade data for each of their subsidiaries.

My involvement with the Wisconsin research team began in early 1974, just as the first responses started to arrive from the subcommittee offices. The progress of the study was followed throughout with great interest by such trade magazines as <u>Business Latin America</u>. Many MNCs had clearly expended a great deal of time and care in obtaining the requested data. On the whole, the response of the companies was very gratifying (see Appendix A), and this can be mainly attributed to the tough reputation of the subcommittee staff and its chairman, Senator Frank Church, as well as to our persistence in contacting the companies for clarifications. However, several firms completed the forms and sent them to their legal departments, where they awaited a subpoena that never came.

It was during this time that I conceived the idea of a second report to the subcommittee, one that would quantify and substantiate the existence of multinational market power that the first study could only claim was potential. This second study was written during 1975 after my position as consultant had been briefly extended by the subcommittee. The report was completed in the spring of 1976, and my dissertation somewhat later. The spring of 1977 was spent updating and revising the earlier publications; Chapters 3, 5, and 6 were heavily reworked.

The text comprises six chapters. I will briefly outline the contents of each. In addition, I will attempt to alert the reader to some features of the study that may prove to be original contributions to our knowledge of multinational corporations.

The first chapter reviews the several definitions and alternative economic theories that have been applied to the MNC. While it serves as a defense of the particular approach adopted here, the chapter also suggests how certain aspects of the other theories may be incorporated into the industrial organization framework.

Chapter 2 examines the positions of Brazil, Mexico, the United States and various regions in the world economy. The topics covered include growth, trade, industrialization, and national economic development policies.

Chapter 3 discusses foreign (especially U.S.) direct investment in Brazil and Mexico and its relation to their industrial market structures. It is here that I first exhibit some of the basic findings of the special survey. There is also an analysis that demonstrates the high degree of correspondence among several elements of the market structures of my three case studies. While such parallelisms have been suspected by researchers, this is the first solid confirmation of the phenomenon.* Since the data used are restricted to industries in which

---

*John Dunning, for example, in a paper on the relation of MNCs to market structures put forward the following unsupported proposition: "The market structure of investing firms is often exported" (Dunning 1974d: 597).

MNCs participate, these results suggest that the observed market structure parallelisms are at least in part due to the restructuring activities of MNCs in their host economies. Another discovery, rather surprising to me, was the remarkably similar extents of denationalizationin Brazil and Mexico. Despite their dissimilar histories, levels of development, sizes, and proclaimed attitudes toward foreign investment, both the aggregate levels and industrial distributions of foreign ownership are extremely close.

Chapter 4 is a digression of sorts—a necessarily detailed, technical survey of previous empirical market structure-profit studies. That survey serves primarily as an introduction to the statistical testing of the next chapter.

If this book can be said to have a core, Chapter 5 is very likely it. It is always gratifying for a social scientist to see his theories confirmed by a careful test using good data, and I am no exception. A major lesson to me was how close the estimated profit-structure relationships in Brazil and Mexico came to previous estimates made from U.S. data. Equally important is the fact that it seems to make no difference where the subsidiaries are located; any country-specific characteristics are overwhelmed by market structures when it comes to their effects on performance. Finally, there are some econometric details that may interest other researchers. The special treatment of variables (like the R&D-to-sales ratio) that have many observations close to zero is a problem not highlighted in most econometric texts. The use of a group F test (instead of a "t" test) for polynomial expressions of the same variable is another modest innovation. Lastly, the use of a sigmoidal approximation for the concentration-profits relationship is one that has been long suggested by theory.

The final chapter contains a summary of the first five chapters and an extensive discussion of public policy options. The policy alternatives presented include those available to both the home and host countries and to supranational organizations, but focus especially on those policies that may restore workable competition.

1

THEORETICAL APPROACHES TO THE MULTINATIONAL ENTERPRISE

It is the task of this chapter to relate the tenets of economic theory to the primarily empirical purposes of this work. And since there are several branches of economic theory that claim to explain the behavior and effects of the multinational corporation (MNC), this chapter also serves as a defense of the particular theoretical model adopted here. As will be shown, the economic literature analyzing the phenomenon of the MNC is inextricably bound up with theories of private foreign direct investment (FDI). As Vaitsos (1974) has pointed out, one broad area of this literature deals primarily with the causes that prompt the flow of capital and other resources across national boundaries; the other portion of writings concerns mainly the effects such flows have on the host or donor economies.* That is, analyses of FDI tend to divide along microeconomic (including general equilibrium) versus macroeconomic lines, though clearly there are many interrelationships and a few studies have attempted to evaluate the social benefits and costs of multinational projects using microeconomic techniques. In this chapter, more attention will be given to studies in the former category than the latter. Furthermore, the discussion will confine itself to works in the non-Marxian, orthodox tradition in economics.

---

*There have also been a few studies of the effects of FDI on the donor-country economies. A good example is a recent study covering the United States by Musgrave (1975). Earlier studies can be found in Mikesell (1962), Task Force on the Structure of Canadian Industry (1968), Finance Committee, U.S. Senate (1973a), Dunning (1970), Hymer (1970b), Kemp (1962), MacDougall (1960), Cohen (1975), Bos (1974), Reuber (1973), Hirshman (1969), May (1970), Streeten (1971), Caves (1974b, 1974c), Safarian (1968), Meissner (1969), and ECOSOC (1974).

The plan of the chapter is as follows. In the first section, a few definitions and distinctions are made concerning some basic terms used throughout the study. Next, a list will be provided of some general and distinctive features of FDI and the MNC that any economic theory must endeavor to encompass and explain. The third and major section attempts to survey the various theoretical approaches that have been taken to model the behavior of MNCs. Work in this area is generally quite recent, and there remains a great deal of controversy over which path will prove the most illuminating. Some effort is made to synthesize and evaluate the contending schools of thought.

DEFINITIONS OF TERMS

In practice, it is difficult to distinguish the ordinary operations of the modern multinational corporation (MNC) from private foreign direct investment (FDI); several eminent authorities consider the two topics equivalent (Kindleberger 1969; Dunning 1971b). The MNC, then, is virtually the sole institution that makes new private foreign direct investments and manages old ones, though there are markets and other institutions involved for other types of international transfers of capital.

Private foreign direct investment is defined, simply, as international investment in which the investor retains some form of continuing control over it. "Direct investment and management go together" (Södersten 1970: 444-45). The "private" qualification (hereafter understood) distinguishes FDI from "official" grants or loans that are most often made bilaterally (government to government) but sometimes are made multilaterally through an international agency such as the International Bank for Reconstruction and Development (IBRD). The "direct" qualification differentiates FDI from international portfolio investment, which has been defined by Dunning (1970: 2) as "the acquisition of securities by individuals or institutions issued by foreign institutions, without any associated control over, or participation in their management."* Typically, portfolio investments take the form of bonds, whereas FDI involves some equity participation.

There is not quite as much agreement among the authorities on what distinguishes multinational from national corporations (NCs). One difficulty is that minority ownership often shades into portfolio types of investment. Moreover, intention or attitude on the part of a

---

*Therefore, some public international investment (for example, U.S. ownership of the Panama Canal) is of the direct rather than portfolio type.

firm's top management is often held to be crucial for the true MNC.* Finally, a truly multinational character is often held to be necessary for the proper MNC; some may view a U.S. firm with subsidiaries only in Canada as not global enough to qualify as an MNC—though many Canadians might not agree.

It is Aharoni (1971) who has provided us with the most thoughtful discussion of the nature of the MNC. He argues that the MNC has several dimensions, and that more than one of these is necessary to capture the essence of the phenomenon. First, MNCs have certain "structural" characteristics. The one feature that most writers have stressed is actual managerial interests in productive units in several countries. Legally, the MNC is an immortal person of one nationality who is able to produce an indefinite number of offspring of dual nationality (Vernon 1971). Some writers have suggested that transnational ownership of stock in the parent corporation is a prerequisite, but Aharoni notes that only a very few commonly regarded MNCs are yet multinational in this sense. A final structural quality that has been suggested is the firm's organizational structure. The first MNCs formed an "international division" within the company as soon as their international activity warranted it; more recently most large and diversified MNCs have reorganized on a global, product-group basis, but some prime MNCs (such as IBM) have retained the older international specialist division structure. Hymer (1970a), for one, argues that the MNC represents the highest stage of historical development of the firm: from the workshop to the factory to the (Marshallian) national corporation to the multidivisional corporation to the MNC.

Second, those of a behavioral persuasion are convinced that an MNC is a firm that "thinks multinationally," that is, one that always weighs alternative investments on a global basis. Perlmutter (1970), for example, is convinced that a firm's headquarters orientation toward foreign people, ideas, and resources is a necessary criterion of an MNC. In his experience, senior executives of MNCs believe that a certain degree of multinationality is essential for the secular survival of their firm and that the MNC is "a new type of industrial social arthitecture particularly suitable for the latter third of the twentieth century" (p. 68). The authors of Global Reach also concur that the MNC's "most revolutionary aspect . . . is not its size but its worldview" (Barnet and Müller 1974: 15). Intuitively appealing as it is, this dimension borders on the tautological, is hardly operational, and may be ultimately vague. Conceivably, a company could be thus oriented and still decide on a strategy that involves no foreign operations.

---

*A firm that came by ownership of one foreign subsidiary unintentionally as a result of a domestic merger would probably not be classified as an MNC by most researchers in the field.

Third, many writers on the subject have advocated the application of "performance" criteria, i.e., some absolute or relative size of sales, assets, work force, or earnings derived from foreign operations. The sales criterion is somewhat arbitrary because of decisions regarding exports, distribution subsidiaries, and so forth. Earnings may be the most questionable measure because of wide cyclical swings and the divergence between actual and reported earnings. Aharoni (1971) opts for assets, noting that this measure may quickly capture firms at an early stage in overseas expansion. The choice of a significant foreign percentage remains somewhat arbitrary, however, so he suggests simply grouping MNCs into categories of degrees of foreign involvement. He also advocates grouping by type of overseas operations (vertically integrated, horizontal manufacture, transporters, traders, and so forth).

Thus, there is some agreement among writers on the subject of the MNC that it is an institution involving the central control of a certain minimum number of foreign subsidiaries of substantial asset size and extent of geographical (that is, cross-national) spread. Aharoni (1972) suggests that a minimum of five different countries of operation ought to be adopted as a cutoff; Vernon (1971) used six countries for the Harvard study. For empirical studies, minimum-size constraints have been imposed for selecting MNC samples, but this condition is more for statistical convenience than strict necessity, for in recent years more "medium size" firms (for example, in the United States those below the Fortune 1,000) have begun foreign operations. Indeed, according to a recent study by Tsurumi (1976), most Japanese MNCs are quite small by anyone's standards.

DISTINCTIVE FEATURES OF FDI AND THE MNC

The validity of an economic theory is best established by its ability to "predict" (sometimes using historical data associated with the phenomenon) or explain measurable variables related to the phenomenon under study.* But when the phenomenon is new and rival tests are not available for a comparison of predicted with actual levels attained, other criteria are often applied to competing theories in order to assess their likely authenticity. Internal logic and consistency with received bodies of theory are two such criteria; an additional standard is the appropriateness of the assumption, that is, are the as-

---

*This is indeed the purpose of Chapter 5, but there are too few alternative tests of other theories to judge the relative predictive values of various theories.

sumptions "realistic abstractions of reality?" If a scientific theory is to be useful for policy prescriptions, then it is desirable to have one that provides valid explanations as well as accurate predictions.

It is the intent of this section to list briefly the basic features of FDI and the MNC upon which there is a fairly high degree of consensus. In the next section the ability of the several theories to conform to these salient facts will be examined.

Since the late nineteenth century, and particularly since 1930, foreign direct investment (typically by corporations) has come to replace international, private capital flows of the portfolio type (ordinarily by individuals through financial intermediaries). It is useful to contrast these two types of international investment flows because in much of the theoretical literature on FDI the two are often equated. In 1914 nearly 90 percent of all international capital flows took the portfolio form, but by the 1950s nearly three-fourths of all private flows from the developed countries were of the direct type (Södersten 1970). Nearly all authorities agree that a necessary condition for portfolio investment is an environment practically free from risk. Thus, the major flows of portfolio capital terminated in territories with great political stability (Canada, Australia, and other safe dominions in the case of the United Kingdom) and the transactions were free from exchange risk. The onset of World War I and the collapse of both world trade and the gold standard contributed to the decline in international bond sales. During 1930–39 there was a net repatriation of portfolio investments, whereas at the same time direct overseas investments actually increased slightly (Dunning 1970). With the increased convertibility of many major world currencies since 1955, there has been a resurgence of international bond markets.

In a world with perfectly competitive markets for all goods and factors, no transactions or information costs, and an absence of political or monetary risks, direct foreign investment cannot exist (Kindleberger 1969). All international capital movement in such a world (which was approximated by the late nineteenth century) would be portfolio capital, and its flow would be adequately explained by a slightly amended version of Ricardo's international trade theory. Capital would flow from capital-abundant countries to capital-scarce economies in response to slight differences in interest rates. The existence of large and growing amounts of FDI stocks is evidence of the failure or imperfect functioning of product or input markets. Much of the more recent economic literature on FDI has attempted to identify or evaluate the relative importance of various "market failures" as determinants of the level and direction of FDI flows.

What are the "distinctive features" of FDI that any comprehensive economic theory must endeavor to explain? First, almost all

modern FDI is carried out by <u>corporations</u> rather than individuals.*
And these corporations, in turn, have certain common characteristics
that will be outlined below.

Second, somewhat like portfolio capital, the flows of FDI have
historically been highly <u>concentrated</u>, both in terms of geography and
by industry and at both the investor and receptor poles. Geographically, the ownership of global stocks of FDI is highly skewed toward
only a few large, high-income countries. Moreover, each investing
country has, whether by accident or design, tended to direct the major
part of its FDI to only a very few receiving countries; in fact, the patterns of global distribution of FDI have been highly similar to historical relationships based on colonial ties or other forms of political
hegemony. Thus, U.K. firms have tended to locate their subsidiaries
in former British Empire territories while U.S. MNCs have traditionally placed their foreign investments in Canada or Latin America
(Dunning 1970; Newfarmer and Mueller 1975). Of course, such patterns have been interpreted as evidence of the creation of newer, more
subtle forms of economic colonialism (Baran 1957), or as a device for
the strengthening of capitalist class interests and the weakening or
dividing of labor and popular power (Hymer 1972).[†] Viewed industrially,
for any given country, FDI generally comes from less than four or
five out of twenty or so major industry groups and flows into those
same industries in the receptor country (Dunning 1971b). That is, in
recent decades most FDI has been intraindustry even where the industry definitions used are fairly narrow.

A third general attribute of FDI is that it has <u>evolved by type</u>
over time. Prior to World War I a crude but valid generalization
would be that a large part of FDI was in the service sector of the host
economy (particularly transportation, power, communication, and
trading) while most of the rest was of the "backward vertical integra-

----

*The identity is not complete, however. A negligible amount of
stock is bought by persons, governments, or their agents on foreign
exchanges. Further, given the large size of corporations with stock
traded internationally, stock purchase rarely leads to significant management control. Two recent exceptions are the partial purchases of
Krupp Steel (West Germany) by Iran and of Fiat (Italy) by Libya. Con-
trarywise, corporations, particularly European MNCs, often buy large
shares in companies abroad simply for portfolio purposes and not for
any management control.

[†]These historical, "center-periphery" patterns in FDI have tended
to disperse in the last decade or more (Vaitsos 1975). Moreover, it
has always been something of an artificial exercise to demonstrate such
patterns for countries with no historical empire or political hegemony:
Sweden, Germany, and Switzerland, for example.

tion" type. These latter, mostly raw materials ventures remained important through World War II, but have declined relatively since then. During the interwar period, most of the currently largest manufacturing MNCs made their initial foreign investments, but these "horizontal" or market-extension types of investments have now become the major category (Wilkins 1970, 1974). Forward vertical extensions (that is, sales subsidiaries owned by manufacturers) have tended to decline relatively in importance, and purely conglomerate extensions remain quite rare (Caves 1971).

The fourth recognized characteristic of manufacturing FDI is that it originates in industries that are technologically intensive, "skill-oriented," or progressive (Vernon 1971). In addition, the FDI-prone industries are typically more concentrated (Wolf 1971), have higher advertising outlays per unit of sales, and exhibit above-average export propensities.* Most studies have found that at least since 1960 MNCs have had higher group profits than non-MNCs, and Newfarmer and Mueller (1975) have calculated returns on foreign investment by U.S. MNCs at over 50 percent higher than on their domestic investment. In short, the industries from which FDI tends to originate display many characteristics associated with oligopoly.

In contradistinction to bonds, a fifth general trait of modern FDI is that of interpenetration, at least between two net exporters of industrial capital (Hymer 1960). That is, no matter how narrowly defined the industry, between two developed, donor countries, FDI flows simultaneously in two directions (Kindleberger 1969). This was never true of portfolio capital flows. However, it should be noted that this phenomenon does not exist to a measurable degree between any investing country and a less developed country (LDC); exports of capital from LDCs are almost exclusively of the portfolio type (Södersten 1970).

---

*The Harvard multinational corporation project compared its sample of 187 MNCs with the other 313 Fortune 500 firms in 1967 and concluded that for the MNCs (1) the weighted, four-firm, five-digit Standard Industrial Classification (SIC) "concentration index" was higher (43.2 versus 38.0 percent); (2) advertising intensity was greater (2.5 versus 1.7 percent on sales); (3) more output was exported (6.9 versus 4.6 percent); (4) profits on sales were higher (7.2 versus 5.9 percent); and (5) more R&D was performed (2.5 versus 0.6 percent on sales) (Vernon 1971). Further confirmation of these relationships can be found for 500 U.S. manufacturing subsidiaries in the United Kingdom (Dunning 1973) and for 99 MNCs in Denmark, The Netherlands, and Israel (Hirsch 1973). See also Chapter 3.

The last universal property of FDI, perhaps the most crucial, was recognized only recently by economists, probably because traditional trade theory has generally formulated its models in terms of a single factor of production when capital flows are analyzed.* However, true FDI is really a package of complementary inputs, a "collective flow" of both tangible and intangible assets and services. (The most extensive discussion is in Vaitsos 1974: 8-18, 27-30). A typical foreign direct investment consists of a bundle of inputs, both of money and in kind; not only are equity capital and long-term funds provided by the investing corporation (this is the component of FDI that comes closest to the classical notion), but also technical and managerial services, capital equipment and intermediate inputs, and legal rights to patented or secret products, processes, or trademarks (Kindleberger 1969). Thus, all possible forms of capital (financial, physical, human, and intangible), as well as current inputs, are typically transferred. Moreover, most of the transfer takes place completely within the firm and outside of ordinary, functioning markets (Dunning 1971b). In addition to the inputs offered by the investor, transfer of the package is often made conditional upon the securing of local financing. It has become known that only a minor part of subsequent operating funds originates from the investor country (Vernon 1971, Newfarmer and Mueller 1975). The bundle of collective inputs, even when transferred to a wholly owned subsidiary, is typically "tied together" by contractual agreements that often contain highly restrictive covenants (Vaitsos 1974). One effect of this feature of FDI is to make the investment package of each MNC completely unique or differentiated from that of any other offering by an MNC.

These six prime features of twentieth century, and particularly manufacturing, foreign direct investment are consistent with the empirical facts that have been collected in the last decade or more. A similar effort has been made to collect information on the MNCs themselves, though more is known about U.S.-based international corporations than those headquartered in other nations. Many of the distinctive traits of MNCs are simply firm-level reflections of the industry or national-level characteristics of FDI already outlined above. Moreover, MNCs resemble national corporations of some types.[†] The in-

---

*That is, most formal trade models have assumed one mobile factor of production ("capital") and one immobile factor ("labor"). (See Corden 1974.)

[†]The MNC is not an entirely new institution. Indeed, there are compelling reasons to regard the modern MNC as the lineal descendant of those intrepid, often hugely profitable, seventeenth century trading firms, the archetype of which is England's East India Company (De Jong

ternational trading firm distributes output among sovereign economic units, but unlike the MNC it has no trade in inputs and all sales are "arm's length." Too, there is the NC which exports some of its factor inputs, such as some advertising, consulting, or construction firms; but here the product is owned by another person, and, more important, no package of inputs is offered (Dunning 1974b). The most apt analogy may be the multiplant, multiregional NC; though the regions are not sovereign, transport costs are conceptually close to institutional and informational barriers (Caves 1971). Dunning (1974c) also believes that the concept of the multiplant NC, adjusted for greater risk levels and the international advantages of intrafirm trade, is the closest MNC antecedent.

The basic features of the MNC may be treated rather briefly. First, the modern MNC is a very <u>large, complex organization.</u> In the Harvard multinational corporation survey, the 187 MNCs were more than three times larger than the remaining Fortune 500 firms, as measured by 1967 sales (Vernon 1971). In the Newfarmer-Mueller study (1975), the average assets of 179 manufacturing MNCs were $1.2 billion worldwide in 1972; mean employment was 43,000 workers.* Because of joint ventures, MNCs actually control much more in assets than they own; in 1967 the net book value of U.S. MNC-controlled foreign assets was about $110 billion, of which half was "relatively liquid" (Vernon 1971). These firms are complex because they own many subsidiaries (34 in 15 countries on average in the special survey) and produce a wide array of products (22 five-digit SIC product groups on average in the Harvard survey). Usually highly detailed controls and numerous channels of communication must be maintained in order to ensure that global objectives are the aims of all MNC units (Brooke and Remmers 1970).

A second feature of MNCs is a strong tendency to be producing <u>differentiated, technologically intensive products in relatively concentrated industries.</u> In terms of skilled manpower and R&D outlays per unit of sales, more than two-thirds of the products sold by the 187 MNCs in the Harvard sample were above average (Vernon 1971). Advertising intensities of the firms were also higher than those of the other Fortune 500 firms. Industries in which the sales of MNCs con-

---

1973). Though no longer officially granted sovereign rights, the present-day MNC has instead been bestowed with immortality (Ball 1970).

*The Newfarmer-Mueller (1975) report was largely based on data collected in a special questionnaire survey sponsored by the U.S. Senate Subcommittee on Multinational Corporations. Information on this special survey is contained in Appendix A.

stituted more than half of total U.S. sales in 1967 were: electrical machinery, rubber and plastics, chemicals and drugs, petroleum, fabricated metals, and transportation equipment. Those industries in that list not characterized by differentiation or skill orientation are still at least moderately concentrated owing to scale economy barriers or to control of sources of foreign raw materials.

A final basic trait of MNCs is their high rates of performance, as measured both by profits and by growth. In the special survey, the after-tax net earnings of MNCs on their FDI only were 16.1 percent in 1972; consolidated domestic plus foreign earnings for the same MNCs were only 12.7 percent, while all U.S. manufacturing corporations with more than $100 million in assets earned only 10.6 percent on stockholders' equity (Newfarmer and Mueller 1975). Moreover, much of the growth of the special-survey MNCs could be attributed to the growth of their foreign assets; during 1960-72, overseas manufacturing assets of U.S. MNCs grew more than 15 percent (geometrically) per year. An econometric examination of the growth of the 500 largest U.S. manufacturing firms during 1957-67 concluded that roughly 25 percent was determined by overseas expansion (Rowthorn 1971).

Before examining the theories of FDI, the "causes" of overseas investment mentioned by MNC managers or revealed from case studies should be listed. There have been numerous surveys of managerial motives, with remarkably consistent results (for example, Behrman 1962a, Gaston 1973). Typically, in opinion surveys of this kind the maintenance or increase of the firm's market share was given as a prime reason; related to this was an expressed concern over the moves of a rival firm, an old customer, or an optimistic assessment of growth in a national market formerly served by exports. A second motive given revolved around specialized inputs; sometimes these were essential raw materials and at other times the investment was for components manufacture. A third consideration was government policies, either increased trade barriers or investment inducements of various kinds (local content rules, tax holidays, and so forth). Finally, lower labor costs were infrequently mentioned and in almost all cases were not regarded as decisive.* Profit enhancement was one of the least often mentioned, though it is clear that all of these

---

*Clearly, labor costs are the primary determinant of "platform production" investments like those in Mexico's "border industrialization" program; under U.S. Tariff Items 807.00 and 806.30, tariffs are collected only on the value added of materials (not labor) for products exported and reimported to the U.S. (Helleiner 1973). Many investments by Japanese MNCs in neighboring Asian nations have been of this kind (Tsurumi 1976).

reasons can translate fairly directly into greater long-run profits after a lag of some years (Kindleberger 1969).

There have been only very few, somewhat primitive statistical
studies of the causes of FDI by MNCs (Horst 1972a; Stevens 1969;
Orr 1975; Caves 1974b). However, an OECD (Organization for Economic Cooperation and Development) sponsored, comparative study of
80 different investments of MNCs made in several LDCs was recently
published (Reuber 1973). A major conclusion was that "both the quantitative evidence and the qualitative evidence emanating from this survey support the proposition that profitability is a fundamental determinant of foreign direct investment," but that "in most cases investing firms were responding to threats to existing business operations"
(Reuber 1973: 109-10). Thus, the immediate cause of an FDI decision
is due to the thrust of some rival MNC or a likely change in the host
country's commercial policy; the sine qua non for the investment
riposte was, however, profitability. The calculation of ex ante profits and risks, Reuber emphasizes, brings in a host of "strategic factors," the most important of which are (1) likely future host-country
demand conditions and (2) the likely export or counterinvestment response of the firm's main rivals. Of secondary importance is the
exploitation of the marketing advantages of an advanced or differentiated
product. Relatively unimportant factors are political instability, ownership restrictions, antitrust legislation, the absence of local capital
markets, competition from local firms, and host-country investment
incentives or subsidies. The Reuber study's emphasis on long-run
profit maximization subject to several potential sources of uncertainty
is basically the same conclusion reached by several other seasoned
observers (for example, Vernon 1971; Diaz-Alejandro 1970; Horst
1974a; Dunning 1974a).

SURVEY OF ALTERNATIVE THEORIES

The literature on private foreign direct investment and its prime
conduit the MNC was dominated, until the middle 1960s, by two relatively isolated camps, the "business school" writers and the Marxist
theorists (CTC 1976). The first set of writings has mainly dealt with
the financial management, labor relations, and internal organization
of MNCs (for example, Lall 1975: 84-106). Marxist and neo-Marxist
writers have tended to study the MNC's wider social and political ramifications and have generally concluded that it is a new institution for
fostering economic "dependence" or colonial ties among nations and
reinforcing class divisions within the host nations (see, for example,
Jalée 1968; Baran 1957; Frank 1969; Rhodes 1970b; Hymer 1972).
Both types of literature are indispensable for understanding the nature

of the international corporation and the reaction it often evokes among
host-country intelligentsia. But the works of neither of these schools
will be included in my survey, the one because it is too narrow in
scope, the other because it is too general.

The focus of the present synopsis is on economic theories of the
MNC that relate the decisions of the firm to its economic environment,
its industry, its factor markets, and the policies of its home and host
governments. These theories appear to divide into five fairly distinct
bodies of thought. The first, descended from international financial
theory, sees FDI as most closely analogous to portfolio capital, which
dominated the international capital markets of the nineteenth century.
A second, closely related stream views FDI as a special form of pure
trade. The third approach seeks to develop predictive models of the
MNC by adapting one version or another of the theory of the national
firm or aggregate investment models of a closed economy. One of
the more recent theoretical avenues taken is based on the assumption
that MNCs are firms that possess some unique and often intangible
asset. Closely allied with this last group are those economists who
contend that the MNC is best studied using an internationalized version of industrial organization theory. Thus, the fourth school sees
FDI as an outcome of the failure of a market for some special asset.
The MNC, by internalizing the failure, ameliorates the departure
from perfect competition. The fifth group, on the other hand, views
FDI as a natural extension of the domestic rivalries of oligopolistic
industries in which several market imperfections are likely to be simultaneously present. The MNC merely widens the scope of rivalry
to the international arena and aids in solidifying latent noncompetitive
market structures. Thus, the two schools, while conceptually quite
close, occupy the opposite ends of a spectrum of likely outcomes running from the competitive to the monopoly model.*

----

*Imperfect competition is only one of many types of market fail-
ure. Markets may fail not only by their absence but also by generating
prices that do not reflect real scarcities. The standard causes of
market failures include: production and consumption interdependences
(externalities), economies of scale in production (the "natural monopoly"
case), high transactions costs, the existence of public goods, and in-
divisibilities in inputs or outputs. But in a capitalist economy, failure can occur by reason of structure as well, that is, because of
seller concentration, barriers to market entry or exit, product hetero-
geneity, or lack of perfect information.

Portfolio-Capital Analogies

As already alluded to above, the flows of portfolio capital were explained adequately by the principles of classical trade theory: Countries with an abundance of capital would experience declining interest rates and subsequently export their capital to other countries with relatively higher interest rates (Dunning 1970: 2). Equity capital is, by parallel reasoning, held to flow from capital-rich to capital-poor nations in response to profit rate differentials; the premium required is determined by the size of the expected risk involved (both nationalization and exchange risk) and by the costs of transferring the capital.

Several objections have been raised to this theory. First, it fails to explain the industrial pattern of FDI, that is, why FDI originates from only a few industries and flows to only the same few industries in the host economy and why, even in the LDCs, some industries remain free from MNC penetration. Second, the portfolio analogy theory implies a unidirectional movement of equity capital, and not the cross-investment pattern observed between the United States and the EC. Third, this approach ignores the inevitable accompaniment of other inputs when a foreign equity investment is made. Finally, the few statistical tests of this theory have been unsuccessful in establishing the expected results (Stevens 1974), possibly because observed profit rates often diverge from expected or target rates of return (Horst 1974a: 61).

While the simple profit-differential theory of FDI has not received much support in recent years, two near relatives have been propounded recently. A recent paper by Aliber (1970: 20) argues that "the key factor in explaining the pattern of foreign direct investment involves capital market relationships, exchange risk, and the market's preferences for holding assets denominated in selected currencies." Entrepreneurs from countries whose currencies are regarded as strongest have an advantage over local enterprise in countries with weak currencies. This theory does explain some of the geographic dispersion in FDI, particularly that from the United States to Europe and Canada in the 1960s, and it provides a motive for investments by merger. However, this theory is not so consistent with continued high rates of U.S. FDI in the 1970s (because of the known weakness of the U.S. dollar), finds the cross-hauling of FDI difficult to explain, and provides no solution for the industrial pattern of FDI. Moreover, if MNCs figure their return on foreign investments using the ratio of the present value of profits to assets, then the exchange risk factor cancels out because it affects both the numerator and the denominator of the ratio.*

A second related "portfolio theory" of FDI holds that the MNC chooses a bundle of investments so as to maximize a utility function positively related to the expected return and negatively related to risk (as measured by the variance of the return). This is an extension of the Markowitz-Tobin model (Markowitz 1959), a modified version of which has been shown to be consistent with the maximization of the market value of the firm (Lintner 1965). Two authors have tested this theory using aggregate U.S. FDI data. Prachowny (1972) found the crucial risk variables always insignificant, but Stevens (1969) found that manufacturing investments to Latin America were indeed significantly (negatively) related to the variance of past profits. A more recent test has been performed with a sample of 200 U.S. MNCs by Cohen (1975). He regressed his measure of firm risk (the standard deviation of the deviations from a 1961-69 fitted trend line of after-tax profits) against two indexes of the degree of foreign investment, controlling for product diversification, size, and three-digit industry. The results indicated that the level of involvement had the expected (highly significant) negative effect on firm profit instability (Cohen 1975: 44-51).[†]

It is well known that the GNPs of different countries can have quite low or negative correlations over time; the same is true of the international sales within given industries (see Cohen 1975: 51-54). The Markowitz-Tobin theory implies that a less than perfect correlation between home- and host-country risks can lower the total risk of a firm even though the foreign risk is higher and the expected return lower. Differences in interindustry stability in the investor countries might explain differences in FDI propensities. The incorporation of risk into investment functions is in its infancy even in domestic studies,

---

*Exchange rate "risk" can and has been largely eliminated by MNCs by borrowing heavily on host-country capital markets. If a host country devalues its currency (or it floats down freely), the loss in asset values and dividends can be canceled by reduced loan balances and interest payments. Furthermore, host-country devaluation often encourages MNC acquisitions. There was, for example, a surge in Japanese FDI in the United States after the mid-1971 dollar devaluation (Tsurumi 1976).

[†]In Cohen's experiment the effect on sales instability was not significant and results using the coefficient of variation in place of the standard deviation did not prove as strong. But in tests involving some 500 firms, sales (export, domestic, and both) stability was found to be positively associated with the extent of geographic diversification of sales (Hirsch and Lev 1971).

and empirical studies are generally limited to using past, observed variance as a proxy for future uncertainty. Yet the oft cited importance of risk in international operations and the initial empirical studies both point to an added richness in positive economic models of FDI.

Pure Trade Theory

Orthodox theories of the international trade in real goods are highly formal, rigorous general equilibrium models typically presented in terms of two goods produced using two factors and traded between two countries. Trade occurs because of the comparative cost advantages of one country over another. The currently most influential version is that associated with the names of Heckscher, Ohlin, and Samuelson (H-O-S). By assuming, inter alia, that (1) resources are fixed in each country (that is, labor and capital are immobile across frontiers), (2) production functions are exogenously determined in each country and describe a constant returns to scale technology, (3) production is perfectly competitive within and between countries, (4) markets are costlessly efficient, and (5) government is neutral, non-interventionist, and desires Pareto optimal efficiency, the simpler H-O-S model is able to establish the normative maxim that both countries gain from trade and that free trade is globally income-maximizing.* In addition to these welfare conclusions, there are a substantial number of positive economic predictions concerning the direction of trade, changes in rents and prices ratios, the types of goods traded, and so forth (see, for example, Heller 1973).

The appearance of the MNC has vitiated many of the assumptions of orthodox trade theory. With respect to the factor immobility assumption, Baldwin (1970) has argued forcefully that, in the light of the vast movements of (usually less skilled) labor in the nineteenth century and of various forms of capital in the twentieth, trade theorists ought to develop models of the international trade of inputs as well as outputs. Unless this is done, trade theory cannot handle such elementary economic decisions of MNCs as the choice between direct foreign investment and the licensing of production to other firms, because this involves making explicit the ratios of transfer costs to the values of goods or inputs.

---

*There are two major "first-best" policy exceptions to the free-trade argument. One is that countries with some monopoly or monopsony power may increase their national welfare by placing an "optimal tariff"; the other exception is the familiar "infant industry" subsidy argument.

In recent years, several trade theorists have attempted to modify the H-O-S model by relaxing the capital-immobility assumption (Kemp 1966, 1969; Jones 1967, 1970; Chipman 1971). Corden (1974) believes that these adaptations ought to be applicable to the transfer of technology and managerial know-how, which is so central to the purpose of the MNC because it is basically a transfer of human capital. But several other economists have criticized even the more recent models for explaining only the transfer of loan capital and not that of equity capital (Bos 1974; Vaitsos 1974; Cohen 1975). It may be a rather straightforward extension of these models to allow for economies of scale and for additional mobile factors of production, but at some loss in rigor (Corden 1974: 192). Corden (1967), for example, developed a nonmathematical model that allows for "sector-specific" capital mobility, externalities, monopoly elements, and some nonneutral taxes on domestic capital. More recently Corden (1974) sketched a trade-theory type of analysis that may be useful in studying the location decisions of MNCs (pp. 195-99) and in suggesting various optimal tax schemes to correct for the ability of MNCs to carry on intrafirm trade and transfer pricing (pp. 204-08).

However successful such revisions may be, the available H-O-S trade models remain totally inadequate to incorporate the many other essential features of FDI as practiced by the MNC.* The reasons for this lie in the forms and assumptions of orthodox trade models. Although the more recent revisions (Kemp 1969; Jones 1970; Chipman 1971) do allow for different production functions across countries that may be altered exogenously by technical progress, none has allowed for the interdependence of production relations between countries that follows from the MNC's ability to transfer knowledge among its operating units. Neither has orthodox trade theory been able to provide for the phenomenon of intrafirm trade. Perhaps the most devastating criticism, however, is the inability of formal trade theory to introduce any monopolistic or oligopolistic considerations into the analysis; this limitation follows from trade theorists' adherence to general equilibrium frameworks, while rigorous oligopoly theories have only been partial equilibrium efforts to date.[†] A final questionable orientation

---

*Tests presented in Chapter 5 for MNCs operating in Brazil and Mexico show that levels of subsidiary profitability are unrelated to the extent of import protection. Also Caves (1974b) found that tariff protection and relative labor costs, two measures of comparative advantage, were unrelated to the extent of foreign asset ownership in Canadian manufacturing.

[†]However, there have been some recent advances in developing oligopoly models within set theoretic frameworks (for example, Nikaido

of trade theory is the adoption of the Pareto welfare criterion; thus, the income distribution effects of FDI cannot be effectively analyzed.

A dynamic trade model that departs from the restrictive assumptions of the H-O-S tradition and has gotten wide acceptance among writers on the MNC is the "product cycle model." This model was first formulated by Raymond Vernon in a celebrated 1966 article (Vernon 1966). It has received modest empirical support in the U.S. case by Gruber (1967) and in several case studies. Other theorists have attempted to integrate elements of the model into their own, quite different views (for example, Hymer 1972; Vaitsos 1974; Caves 1971). Most recently, Klein (1973) has sought to extend and formalize the model by incorporating the Arrovian learning-by-doing concept as a form of dynamic comparative advantage; he successfully tested part of his model using time-series data on a small sample of U.S. pharmaceutical companies.

The product life cycle upon which the theory is based consists of four stages: introduction, spread, maturity, and senescence. During the first, introductory, phase oligopolies are formed on the basis of some new, technologically advanced product or the differentiation of an old one. The innovators and early imitators reap early high profits and face very inelastic demand for the product. At first only final goods are exported from the home country because of continuing development and refinement of the product, but as it becomes standardized the initial firms build their first plants abroad so as not to lose their lead to foreign imitators. At first plants are located in the markets with the highest demand, because neither production costs nor tastes are known in advance or they are changing rapidly; later the location of plants and their scale come to be based on more careful calculations of factor and transfer costs. High monopoly profits during the introductory phase are necessary both for continuing R&D and to compensate for the high risk and uncertainty connected with the first foreign investments.

Later, when innovational leads are eroded, the firms enter into a period of "mature" oligopoly. The home units of the firms switch from exporting final products to primary inputs or intermediate products if the technology permits it. Their overriding concern at this point becomes pricing stability and raising barriers to entry (Vernon 1974a). Some pursue a strategy of raw materials source diversity (for example, oil, copper, aluminum, and nickel). Base-point pricing and other coordinated pricing systems are adopted and location decisions become even more reactive or defensive than before. Rivalry

---

1975). Also I consider some attempts to incorporate imperfect competition into trade models at the end of this section.

by "hostage" and other game theoretic plays become more likely, thus
concentrating production in the main marketing areas of rivals to a
greater extent than under competitive conditions. Other strategies
like joint foreign production subsidiaries and long-term bulk buying
agreements can ensure competitive forbearance. At this stage Weber-
Löschian location theory is a poor predictive device; "the existence of
multinational enterprises in the mature industries tends to concentrate
economic activity on geographical lines to a degree that is greater than
if multinational enterprises did not exist" (Vernon 1974a: 104).

Finally, when the technology and tastes become widely known
and standardized, the senescent oligopolies begin to place much more
emphasis on classical cost considerations, though the sunk costs of
learning the technology and the influence of home country factor price
ratios may dampen the strength of local (host country) factor costs in
MNC location decisions and will influence MNCs to choose countries
with factor costs most nearly similar to their headquarters country.
If innovation, differentiation, or other barriers fall far enough, the
senescent oligopolies will evolve into competitive industries and FDI
may end because the transfer costs of FDI will be exceeded by the
costs of learning about potential overseas markets (Johnson 1970).

The product-life-cycle theory is consistent with most of the essential features connected with FDI and with many case studies. Because national expenditures on R&D are often held to be the "uncaused
cause" of a new product cycle (though some have suggested induced innovation as an alternative), the policy implications for other developed
countries are rather benign. But in the LDCs a lack of any potential
national technological advantage is apparent, and thus FDI is seen as
a tool for the introduction, spread, and maintenance of monopoly forces
(Vaitsos 1974: 12-14). If the model is predictively accurate, most
LDCs have only the options of dismantling nearly senescent oligopolies
or whittling away at noncompetitive business practices piecemeal.
The main difficulty with the product-cycle model, as with so many
dynamic or stages theories, is in discovering the determinants of the
transitions from one phase to the next, for it is clearly in the interests
of the host country to speed up the cycle once the investment is made.
Another difficulty the theory has encountered, as Vernon (1971) admits,
is in broadening the scope of the theory to cover products developed in
order to save materials or energy.

A third task that has been undertaken in the field of trade theory
is to try to introduce monopoly elements into formal trade theories.
Several economic theorists have advocated fusing trade and industrial
organization theories, but the actual products have generally been one
more than the other. Caves (1971), for example, has developed a
two-country, two-product, three-factor (skilled labor, equity capital,
unskilled labor) general equilibrium model to investigate the effects

and optimum levels of tariffs. The monopoly element in his model is
the assumption that the "capital" factor is permitted to move between
countries but not between industries. He proves that, with free trade
in goods or capital, the rates of return on capital are equalized between countries but not between industries within the same country.
Another recent example is a paper by Rodriguez (1975). In his model,
there is no transfer of physical or equity capital, but a costless transfer of a technology between countries is allowed (one of his products
is called "Coca-Cola"). He investigates the welfare effects (on the owning country, importing country, and globally) of various policies; in
the last section, the assumption of perfect competition is dropped, and
he shows that the home country policy of enforcing competition at home
while allowing maximum monopoly profits abroad through price discrimination maximizes the real income of the home country.

Both of these examples show that methods exist for formally incorporating monopoly elements into general equilibrium models, though
not the richness of detail that may eventually be required for testable
predictions. Yet there has been considerable progress since the first
formal welfare model of FDI by MacDougall (1960), a one-sector analysis that concluded that both national and wage incomes would rise with
an influx of foreign, real capital.* Also a welcomed shift in attention
has occurred among trade theorists interested in FDI, from a focus
on gross national welfare analysis to attempts to understand the decision making of MNCs.

Adaptations of the Theory of the Firm

Much of the earlier body of economic literature on the MNC was
basically macroeconomic (Dunning 1971b). Part of this was due to the
overriding concern with the balance-of-payments effects of FDI during the 1960s. That question has still not been settled and some writers
have thought that it was the macroeconomic framework that was at
fault. In this section, theories will be discussed that seek to explain
the behavior of MNCs by adapting basic theories of the firm.

The seminal article in this category is one by Horst (1971). His
is a fairly simple, neoclassical partial equilibrium model of a monop-
olist selling and producing in two different countries. (It faces two
distinct cost and demand functions.) The MNC is assumed to maximize
global profits subject to two different tax rates and two distinct ad

---

*For a criticism and reworking of the MacDougall model see
Cohen (1975: 32-43), who demonstrates that, if FDI is accompanied by
a change in technology, both wages and national income may fall.

valorem tariff rates. There are some interesting results from this
model. If the two income tax rates converge, the MNC maximizes its
profits by minimizing the transfer price of goods exported. Furthermore, if the MNC is able to segment the two markets for its product,
(1) under increasing costs of production in both countries, the optimal
strategy is to produce in both countries and export some of the product
to the higher-cost country, * but (2) under decreasing costs in both
countries, the MNC will produce in the largest country (not necessarily
the lower-cost country) and export to the other. He also considers
the case of a nonprice-discriminating MNC, but the main conclusions
concern the effectiveness of taxes: (1) high tariffs do not always ensure
the expansion of local production of MNCs and (2) high tariffs aid MNCs
to discriminate between markets while rendering income tax policies
impotent.

Many of Horst's conclusions contradict the common wisdom.
Robertson (1971), for instance, is convinced that trade barriers are
the raison d'être for the MNC and provide in themselves sufficient
cause for FDI. But the burden of proof would appear to be on Horst's
critics to produce a more convincing alternative.

In a later paper, Horst (1974a) explores the question of whether
the profit-maximizing assumption is the most appropriate for the MNC.
He attempts to provide an answer by comparing the behavioral outcomes of an MNC choosing between exporting and foreign subsidiary
production under alternative assumptions of the MNC-objective function. It has been suggested that firms, and MNCs in particular, are
sales-maximizing (by Baumol and Williamson), growth-maximizing
(by Penrose and Marris), or behavioral organisms in which decisions
are made as the result of coalitions of several interest groups (Simon
and Cyert and March). Horst's main conclusion is that there are so
few and such subtle differences in FDI behavior between the profit-
maximization model and the others that there is no reason to abandon
the traditional axiom because these differences could not be detected.
Sales maximization, for example, would lead to the same choice of
location and technology as profit maximization; the differences are
one of timing of FDI (earlier under sales maximization) and the size
of foreign sales. Thus, even though the managerial and behavioral
theories may be a priori more plausible, the profit-maximization
model predicts roughly the same behavior for MNCs.

A second group of theoretical approaches to the MNC may be
considered an extension of the neoclassical theory of the firm. These
models are referred to as "investment functions" because investigators

---

*This point has also been demonstrated by Schmitz and Helm-
berger (1970).

often seek to find the determinants of corporate spending on (or financing for) fixed plant and equipment. The ascendant version of this
theory, the neoclassical schools', assumes that the firm maximizes
its discounted sum of all future net cash flows and yields the desired
stock of capital as a function of factor prices, interest rates, tax
rates, and the depreciation rate (Jorgenson 1971). This formulation,
when applied to quarterly, aggregate, or other U.S. data, has generally outperformed the older "accelerator," liquidity-cash flow, and
stock price models. Short-run forecasts have improved over the last
decade, but predictions of secular changes or changes due to policy
changes have had a more spotty record. The main criticisms of the
neoclassical investment functions are the assumptions of perfect fore-
sight, perfect competition, and the omission of supply-of-funds considerations.

An admirable recent survey of the determinants of foreign investment in the MNC was written by Stevens (1974). He notes that the
study of domestic corporate investment decisions has progressed in
isolation from the internationalization of production, but finds as yet
no compelling reason to reject or revise the neoclassical investment
model on the basis of studies of FDI, especially those that posit other
than profit maximization as the firm's objective. Moreover, studies
of MNCs' subsidiaries have found no tendency for fixed investment expenditures to be constrained by the subsidiaries' own retained earnings, though the pattern may hold for very small affiliates. There is
evidence, however, that some types of general financial constraints
do affect firm or subsidiary expenditure levels. Thus, supply of funds
may be a factor determining the total level of investment by an MNC or
its subsidiaries.

Several studies have attempted to explain aggregate U.S.-owned
foreign plant and equipment expenditures but only a few at the micro
level (Stevens 1974). By far the strongest result has been the positive
impact of sales or output (contemporaneous or lagged) on investment
levels, as expected by the neoclassical model; however, some other
predicted variables did not explain the variation in expenditure levels.
(Interest rates, depreciation rates, and tax rates were used.) A few
tests have found lagged capital stock significantly negative, as predicted by the flexible accelerator model. No models have incorporated
potentially important variables representing tariffs, exchange rate
movements, exchange controls, "investment climate," or a host of
overseas quantities (tax rates, wages, rents, interest rates, and capital goods prices). A final important omission is the interactions between foreign investment and domestic profits, depreciation, cost of
capital, and so forth. Hence, the empirical tests of FDI to date have
been unsatisfactory in discriminating between the neoclassical and accelerator models and have probably omitted several significant explana-

tory variables. Moreover, virtually no progress has been made in designing investment functions to predict the direction or location of FDI. And, finally, other components of the balance of payments (various financial flows) have been untouched by empirical testing, though the state of the theory of the optimal financial firm structure is undoubtably partially to blame (Stevens 1974: 76).

Even if future tests introduce many of the omitted variables into investment functions and quarterly data become available,* the prospects for decent predictive models of this type are not bright, on several counts. First, the transfer of plant and equipment is only one of many components of the package of complementary inputs that constitutes the typical foreign investment. Second, neoclassical investment function estimation assumes perfectly competitive, frictionless product and factor markets. However, in LDCs in particular, many markets do not provide prices reflecting real scarcities. Moreover, MNCs may be price makers and not price takers; that is, industrial market structures ought not to be ignored. Finally, the price or cost of some types of capital or inputs may be indeterminate for some item that is completely unique to a given firm.[†]

Intangible Asset Theories

Rather than being considered only one of several possible advantages of MNCs, the possession of some intangible asset has come to be accepted as a central and necessary determinant of FDI by many economic theorists. The asset has been variously identified as a differentiated product[‡] (sometimes this is termed advanced marketing

---

*Stevens (1974: 81) notes that "most of the recent advances in the field of domestic advancement have been made using quarterly data. Domestic studies of plant and equipment spending have usually found that from 12 to 15 or more independent variables are required to explain the dependent variable satisfactorily."

[†]Another question is the determination of the opportunity cost of capital for MNCs spread across several capital markets and currency zones.

[‡]This differentiation partially derives from advertising "spill-overs" from the source country through the usual information media, tourism, or the presence of foreign residents. Some products identified as "foreign" may be considered intrinsically of higher quality, particularly by consumers in the less developed countries. But for the most part, host-country consumer loyalty is likely to be generated through the promulgation of culturally appropriate psychological appeals, designed in the same way as domestic messages are (see Miracle 1972).

skills), productive or commercially valuable knowledge (or the capacity to generate such knowledge), or superior management and organizational skills.* If this special advantage is held to be common to every firm in the industry, this school verges into the industrial organization explanation of the causes of FDI (reviewed in the next section). In some ways the intangible-asset explanation of FDI resembles a static version of the product-life-cycle theory.

An elegant exposition of this theory has been delivered by Johnson (1970). He begins his discussion by noting that the production of new knowledge poses a real dilemma for a private enterprise economy because its public good character implies that it should be financed by society. In practice, however, the public tolerates temporary monopoly profits (through patents, process, secrecy, and so forth) in order to provide private incentives for invention. This is held to be socially inefficient because the price is set above its marginal cost of production (restricting society's consumption suboptimally for a time) and because rival firms are often encouraged to carry on wasteful attempts at duplicating the successful discoveries of other firms.

Thus, for Johnson the essence of the MNC is its ability to transfer advanced technology and managerial know-how. Moreover, this advantage devolves more upon large firms and large economies than small ones because the size of the reward depends on the size of the market (total effective demand). Complaints about U.S. dominance via FDI are, in his view, explained mostly by the United States' comparative advantage in labor-saving, science-rich innovations; cries of exploitation are merely the result of rents superimposed on the normal returns to investment in material capital by a price-discriminating MNC.[†] The only benefit to host countries is in the (second best solution) taxation of the monopoly profits; indeed, FDI may turn the host country's terms of trade against it and at the same time redistribute income away from laborers to capitalists. However, Johnson's general conclusion is that "inward foreign direct investment cannot harm

------

*Empirical studies have not been able to demonstrate any association between skilled entrepreneurial resources and FDI propensity. Caves (1974b) tested this notion for the Canadian manufacturing sector and concluded that "the 'entrepreneurial resources' hypothesis suffers from weaker theoretical underpinning and gains weaker empirical support" (p. 292) once monopoly factors are taken into account.

[†] Even this effect is alleged to be ultimately sanguine because a price discriminator will charge higher rents in the developed countries (DCs) than in the LDCs, thus redistributing income in the LDSc' favor. However, there is little evidence of lower prices being charged in the LDCs; quite the contrary (see Cohen 1975; Vaitsos 1974).

a country and may confer substantial benefits upon it" (Johnson 1970: 47).

A similar advantage is claimed for MNCs that have been able to differentiate their products.* Like knowledge, an advertising slogan or other methods of generating consumer loyalty must be of the nature of a public good within the firm; that is, development costs are sunk and the marginal costs of internal transfer are negligible. The rents from this asset also must outweigh the information costs of being alien if production is to be located abroad (Caves 1971). Otherwise, the rents on the firm-specific asset would be collected via exporting or licensing. One way of reducing the extra costs associated with being a foreign firm in making a new investment is by developing the special management skills needed to operate in an unfamiliar environment and coordinate ongoing farflung operations (Negandhi 1975). But the mere transfer of management skills by MNCs is generally believed to be inadequate to explain foreign production and certainly does not explain the continuing dominance of MNCs in the markets of many host countries (Caves 1971).

Theories that focus on a single, firm-specific asset may well explain the strategies of some MNCs, particularly those at an early stage of international spread. Some MNCs have continued to follow a strategy of exploiting one fairly simple advantage, but in recent years "the very large and complex multinational enterprises do not rely on a single predominant strength" (Stopford and Wells 1972: 6). Rather, MNCs typically offer a package of inputs no one of which can itself explain the successful movement of a given MNC into the markets of several different countries, but when taken together they may constitute an infrangible foundation of commercial strength. Moreover, theories that concentrate on single sources of advantage will offer oversimplified policy prescriptions for restoring the social optimum.

The Industrial Organization Approach

The industrial organization (IO) model proposes to explain the flow and stock of FDI as symptomatic of an extension of oligopolistic rivalries in the investing countries to the world arena. The sources of MNC advantage (vis-a-vis other MNCs, potential MNCs, or domestic firms) lie in the structural elements of industries in which they operate. Thus, in this framework the superiority of MNCs arises not

---

*It may be noted that Johnson (1970: 37) specifically rejects the notion that MNCs can create demand; for even new products the demand is "latent in the utility functions of consumers."

so much from a special, firm-specific asset as from certain stable characteristics unique to an industry. Moreover, though the special strength of MNCs originates from the national aspects of their markets, as internationalization proceeds the international dimensions also become determining. In a sense, the industrial organization theory of the MNC is a generalization of the intangible asset theories: Where the latter identifies as the cause of FDI a single instance of market failure, the industrial organization model attributes it to a host of interrelated market imperfections. The one model sees the power of MNCs arising from special internal resources of the firm, the other from factors largely external (though manipulable in the longer run).

The origins of the industrial organization theory of the MNC lie in a doctoral dissertation by the late Stephen Hymer (1960). He subsequently revised and extended his original ideas, tending to place more emphasis on the political aspects of FDI and on the redistribution income and power resulting from the actions of the MNC. The industrial organization framework has come to be favored by Kindleberger (Hymer's mentor) and an impressive array of scholars who specialize in the international firm (for example, Dunning 1974b; Cohen 1975; Caves 1974a; Vaitsos 1974).

Kindleberger's (1969) version proceeds from the premise that FDI can occur only if the expected long-run rates of return are not only higher than the best alternative domestic opportunities but also higher than those of comparable host-country firms (including potential entrants). The return on FDI must be higher than these two rates because of the greater risk of foreign operations and the greater costs of information and transactions (communication, translation, time lags, and others). Otherwise all foreign area investment would be the portfolio type or would be undertaken by local firms. Thus, the existence of FDI is evidence that the MNC possesses some special, non-marketed, firm-specific advantage relative to local competitors. He places these advantages into four categories. First, there may be imperfect competition in the final goods markets; a new product or differentiation of an old one is the most likely source of the imperfection. Second, imperfections in the factor markets may arise from patents, process secrecy, the differential access to financial capital, or possibly the ownership of special management skills (but he considers this last category "very elusive"). Third, internal or external (that is, firm or industry) economies of scale can confer advantages to MNCs in production processes where vertical integration is economic. Finally, government regulations on output or firm entry can encourage foreign investors; tariffs in particular may prompt "defensive investments."

Despite his wholehearted espousal of the industrial organization explanation, Kindleberger's (1969) conclusions on the net effects of

FDI are relatively sanguine. "But while direct investment may gobble up competitors and exploit its monopolistic advantages, its main impact is in widening the area of competition" (p. 32). His argument is not elaborate. MNCs are presumed to be more efficient, so that even nonaggressive behavior will reduce prices and break the price discipline of the local producers. The infant industry argument aside, he would argue that the operations of the MNC are bound to lead to greater world efficiency.

The entry of MNCs into the industry of a particular host country often occurs in waves, a phenomenon called oligopolistic reaction. Knickerbocker (1973) has charted this behavioral feature for U.S. MNCs, and Tsurumi (1976) presents some intriguing examples of similar strategic behavior on the part of Japanese textile and electronic MNCs. However, while the initial result of MNC entry (particularly when it occurs en bloc) may be the disruption of domestic oligopolistic arrangements, the eventual dominance of the industry by MNCs allows them to reestablish their own pattern of competitive forbearance. Caves (1974c), for example, found that the profits of domestic Canadian firms were unrelated to the level of foreign entry into the industry; moreover, after allowing for the size of domestic firms, their profits are practically unrelated to the relative domination of foreign capital. Also, in Chapter 3, I show that market share shifting among MNC affiliates in Brazil and Mexico is notably absent in those industries with the greatest proportion of MNC ownership. Thus, the weight of the evidence is that massive FDI simply replaces one set of collusive actors with another.

Richard Caves has recently authored papers on the MNC that adhere fairly strictly to an industrial organization framework but integrate some aspects of the theory of pure trade as well (1971, 1974). He has argued that the essence of FDI is the transfer of an industry-specific package of equity and loan capital, entrepreneurship, and knowledge in several forms. The package of inputs is assumed to yield a positive return over direct costs (discovery costs having been sunk) where these direct costs include the presumably very low transfer costs within the firm and the extra costs associated with the penetration of a new, foreign market. (Local firms do not incur these second types of costs.) Up to this point Caves is in agreement with the special-asset school of FDI. But his original insight is that FDI tends to involve firm conduct that recognizes mutual market dependence beyond national boundaries. In particular, he makes the case that horizontal FDI is rooted in oligopoly with product differentiation and that vertical FDI is also typical of oligopoly, * but not necessarily differen-

---

*Empirical support for this notion comes from a recent work by Bergsten, Horst, and Moran (1977). They found a positive association

tiated so much as one with high entry barriers. The fact that trade
barriers provide an incentive for FDI he interprets as support for
the industrial organization model. In a perfectly competitive industry,
tariffs will provide only temporary windfall profits; where monopoly
rents are being earned, however, tariffs increase the rents on some
FDI while reducing the profitability of exporting.

The industrial organization approach is especially apt for explaining the entry advantages of MNCs' subsidiaries over entry by locally based firms, whether de novo or by diversification. Of course,
the market element of concentration would aid both types of firms
equally, so the differences lie in product differentiation capacities
or in overcoming capital barriers to entry. With respect to product
differentiation, the MNC's subsidiary often has the advantage of a
known, tested brand to draw upon; costs of developing advertising
techniques are already sunk and the costs of transfer slight; there may
even be some international brand identification spillovers from the
home country. Some scale economies may differentially affect MNC
and local entrants. For example, only some stages of fabrication may
enjoy substantial economies of scale, and the MNC's subsidiary has
the option of having that particular process undertaken by a sister affiliate abroad. The MNC's entrant may enjoy several absolute cost
advantages, for its parent organization may control one of a few sources
of some scarce input (raw material, patent, or advanced skill). Moreover, MNC affiliates can draw upon the retained earnings or lines of
credit of the parent.*

---

between domestic concentration (using profitability as a proxy) and
the degree of foreign direct investment in U.S. industry over the period 1965–71 (Chapter 8). See also Caves's (1974b) excellent econometric analysis of FDI in Canada's manufacturing sector. There he
shows the industrial variation in foreign-asset ownership to be causally
related to the outlays by U.S. firms on advertising and research and
development, as well as to the size of firms and incidence of multiplant production in U.S. industries.

*These notions have recently received a rigorous test using
Canadian data. Gorecki (1977), extending the work of Orr (1974), attempts to explain the gross entry of foreign versus domestic firms
into 62 manufacturing industries during 1963–67. For domestic firms,
entry was significantly discouraged by four different entry barriers:
high capital requirements, advertising intensity, R&D intensity, and
concentration of the industries. Neither the growth rate nor profits
acted as incentives to entry for domestic companies. But for foreign
firms (those with 50 percent or more of their assets owned by foreign
residents) none of the four barriers discouraged entry. However, un-

The conduct of MNCs's subsidiaries is also likely to differ from that of local entrants. Remittance and reinvestment rates will likely be more variable because of parental demands for funds. Moreover, because pricing practices may depend on the imposition of worldwide standards, MNCs's subsidiaries may make greater use of product design than local price collusion strategies. Finally, Caves hypothesizes that MNCs's affiliates may be particularly prone to predatory tactics because their much larger size makes countermoves much less credible and because they are likely to produce a less diversified product line than similarly sized local firms.* Except for allocative efficiency, Caves (1974a) concludes that the standard concepts of both performance and progressiveness are called into question because both dimensions are so dependent on decisions taken at the corporation's center.

A final example of the industrial organization model applied to the MNC is the Newfarmer-Mueller report (1975). This monograph extends the traditional domestic industrial organization framework so as to include both international and noneconomic features of market structure as determinants of the power of MNCs. Besides the three traditional elements of market in the product markets (seller concentration, product differentiation, and barriers to entry), these authors suggest two other recipient economy elements that may contribute to the special advantages of MNCs, namely, denationalization and multinational conglomeration. In addition, they propose that there are three dimensions of the international concentration of FDI (geographic, industrial, and aggregate) that may be regarded as sources of the success of MNCs.

Turning first to the two novel host country market structure elements, denationalization is defined as the degree to which a nation's industry is controlled by MNCs. Denationalization "implies the transfer of decision-making for industries to foreign centers" (Newfarmer and Mueller 1975: 22). The extent of denationalization in any given industry (or firm) is reflected by the institutional methods of control and by the extent of a subsidiary's integration into the corporate complex with respect to planned rates of growth, trade, finance, and technology. There are several macroeonomic consequences of such control, but it is also stated that the extent of subsidiary denationalization

---

like the domestic firms, high industry growth rates have a strong positive effect on the MNC's entry. Gorecki also shows that the ratio of foreign to domestic entry appears to be highest in the industries with high advertising intensities (p. 488).

*Many other industrial organization theorists believe that product diversity is, on the whole, an advantage for potential predators (see Scherer 1970: 273-78).

may have a significant effect on microeconomic performance as well, though the direction of influence is not predictable a priori. The testable hypothesis, however, is that both seller concentration and denationalization of an industry will have separate significant effects on either subsidiary of global performance of MNCs (both will be positive in the latter case).

The second host country market structure element introduced by Newfarmer and Mueller (1975) is multinational conglomeration, a many-faceted concept that includes absolute (and worldwide) multinational corporation size, product diversification, and "internal organization."* Absolute firm size of the whole corporation is an indication of the amounts of funds and credit potentially at its disposal; moreover, it is directly associated with the range of technologies available to the firm and the quality of skilled manpower needed to implement such technologies. Thus, size is an indicator of the ability of a firm to leap over absolute cost or scale barriers to entry. But more than that, it is related to the number of conduct options open to the firm. Product diversification is competitively benign to the extent that it reduces firm risk, but it may be a malignant force if it permits additional anticompetitive business practices. In particular, the multiproduct company may participate in cross-subsidization, predatory pricing, or competitive forbearance (Newfarmer and Mueller 1975: 27-28). Hence, both absolute size and diversification of the MNC are predicted to improve the firm's private performance record; by implication, these two additional structural elements may also be expected to affect subsidiary performance similarly.

Finally, Newfarmer and Mueller hypothesize that international market structures affect the nature of multinational competition. FDI is concentrated geographically in that it both originates in only a few countries and terminates in only a few nations; it is concentrated as to source and use in only a few industries as well; and FDI in any given host country or host industry is concentrated in an aggregate fashion, that is, among only a small number of firms. This state of affairs has important macro- and microeconomic implications because of the commonality of interests that are likely to emerge among the larger investing countries, industries, or firms. From the point of view of corporate performance, it is likely to enhance the market power of

---

*Internal organization includes the type and extent of centralized planning and intrafirm integration common in the areas of personnel deployment, growth targets, sourcing, trade, finance, and technology. But this really is the firm-level view of the denationalization concept already discussed above. To elaborate here would be repetitious.

firms from the few foreign direct investment source countries or
source industries; moreover, it may interact with concentration (in
the usual sense) to facilitate collusion by narrowing the range of acceptable forms of conduct among the favored MNCs. Thus, the testable hypothesis resulting from this aspect of the theory is that MNCs
(and their affiliates) from countries or industries with traditionally
large foreign investments will enjoy greater monopoly power than
others; the same is true for those characteristics on the recipient end
of the capital flows.*

CONCLUDING REMARKS

I believe that the industrial organization model of the causes of
FDI is the most comprehensive and consistent theory of the five somewhat distinct approaches surveyed herein. It is rather clearly consistent with the six "distinctive features" of foreign direct investment.
The industrial organization approach explains why FDI is corporate,
concentrated, mostly horizontal or backward vertical, oligopolistic,
cross-hauled, and available mainly as a bundle of complementary inputs. It also explains why MNCs tend to be large, diverse, oligopolistic firms with consequent reserves of market power.

Foreign horizontal direct investors generally offer a tied package
of coordinated factor inputs so as to make the offering unique to the
firm or industry. If only one of the components were for sale and
transfer internationally (that is, just financial capital, management
services, a certain product design, a trademark, an intermediate
input, or a component produced by an inimitable process), then a competitive market could develop for that single input with prices known
to both parties.† The market for portfolio capital or technology and

---

*For example, U.S. MNCs will be expected to have higher profits
than Norwegian MNCs; chemical MNCs, higher than textile; affiliates
in Mexico, higher than those located in Guyana; and affiliates among
the top ten investors in a given country, higher than those below. All
reasoning is ceteris paribus here.

†The production of new, commercially valuable knowledge sanc-
tioned as a monopoly by the state is an exception. Note also that oligopolies often arise or are fostered by explicit government policies.
A good example is the role of Japan's Ministry of International Trade
and Industry (MITI) in encouraging oligopoly (by rationing foreign licensing of technology and official loans) in Japan's shipbuilding, elec-
tronics, textile, and computer industries (Tsurumi 1976). The U.S.
government has also facilitated outward FDI by its MNCs through
various policies. (See Chapter 6.)

service contracts would under these circumstances come to replace direct investment between nations. Thus, the fact that at present most FDI takes place in the form of a differentiated bundle of factors of production is both the effect of preexisting oligopoly in the investor's economy and a cause of the transfer and maintenance of imperfect competition abroad. FDI is concentrated geographically and across certain industries because those countries have national programs of commercially applicable research, and industries within those countries have R&D or product differentiation expertise. Because within the developed countries this expertise is not distributed according to the same industrial pattern, some interpenetration of FDI takes place among the industrially advanced countries.*

Foreign vertical direct investments occur for somewhat different reasons. They too are intimately connected with oligopoly, but a form of oligopoly that rests primarily on barriers to entry. One cause may be concentration of ownership of the distribution stage in a vertically integrated industry; product or service differentiation may be quite important in maintaining concentration in these marketing channels. More common perhaps are substantial economies of scale of production or absolute cost barriers.[†] Restricting the free-market supply of some crucial raw materials, especially those of the highest quality, is a strategy followed in some industries to maintain high absolute cost barriers.

In the review above, the various deficiencies of the alternative models have been discussed.[‡] There are perhaps two areas in which the industrial organization approach needs some expansion or refine-

---

*It also explains why foreign direct investment interpenetration is nonexistent between the DCs and LDCs. If the theory of induced innovation has any substance, those LDCs with ample populations but few natural resources may in the future develop a comparative advantage in raw materials-saving technology in much the same way that the DCs developed a labor-saving one or Japan a land-saving one. However, another possible reason for investment interpenetration is the desire of MNCs to ensure competitive forbearance by establishing "hostage" subsidiaries in each other's main marketing zones.

[†]In the 1960s, oil and some electronic components were examples resting primarily on the first type of barrier, copper and aluminum on the second pair, according to Vernon (1971). The present situation in oil is rather fluid, but this was the historical pattern (Blair 1976).

[‡]As has been mentioned, the product-cycle theory of FDI appears to be a plausible, if somewhat descriptive, dynamic model that is almost fully consistent with an oligopolistic theory. Vaitsos (1974) has elaborated on this point.

ment. One such area is the risk-spreading motive of MNCs, particularly the very large and geographically diverse ones. The theories that draw a parallel between FDI across several countries and stock portfolios management do provide an intuitively and logically appealing explanation. Though the notion of multinational conglomeration introduced by Newfarmer and Mueller offers a suggestive route, the risk-spreading motive of FDI needs further elaboration and testing within an industrial organization framework. There is a second feature of FDI in which the trade-theory explanation has seemingly gone farther than the industrial organization version. Although the industrial organization model has something to say about the choice between horizontal direct investment and the licensing of technology, it sheds little light on the third alternative for a firm desiring to exploit its monopolistic advantage, namely, pure trade. What types of strategy induce the switch from exporting to local production, and what competitive factors determine the mix of local production plus exporting that is often observed? The leadership-followership syndrome (oligopolistic reaction) sheds more light on the followers than the leaders. Perhaps the leading firm investors are prompted by strategic considerations too manifold to systematize.*

In conclusion, it should be emphasized that the industrial organization approach to FDI is superior to all rival models in one crucial respect. The other models were designed from the point of view of the investing countries; they seek to explain the causes behind an initial foreign investment in terms of economic conditions in the donor economy. The industrial organization model, on the other hand, is not only uniquely capable of explaining the original impulse to invest but also goes deeply into the determinants of the continuing and deepening denationalization of receptor economies. It thus provides the beginnings of an organized body of knowledge about the behavior (that is, the conduct and performance) subsidiaries of MNCs vis-a-vis their national rivals and their own parent organizations, for "it is precisely in this area where existing theory has so little to offer and the need for new thinking is so pressing" (Dunning 1974c: 356).

---

*Chief among these, however, are (1) threats on the part of the host country's government to enter into direct production, (2) the standardization of the industry's technology to the point where a national firm poses a threat to export market shares of the MNC, (3) the chance to acquire a promising local producer, particularly one with a strong local trademark or distribution network that can be exploited.

2

**BRAZIL AND
MEXICO IN THE
WORLD ECONOMY:
ECONOMIC
GROWTH AND
INDUSTRIALIZATION**

This chapter is intended to provide a broad overview of the Brazilian and Mexican economies. In the first section, I describe the size and growth characteristics of the Latin American region and compare it with the other major world regions. My main purpose here is to show the large gap in development levels between the more developed areas (North America and Western Europe) and the less developed regions. Also, I want to demonstrate that there are some important differences among the less developed regions themselves that must be kept in mind by those who would generalize our findings on Latin America to the other regions. In particular, Latin America is in many ways the most developed and industrialized of all the less developed areas.

The second task of this chapter is to delineate in some detail the size, growth, sectoral composition, and international trade characteristics of Brazil and Mexico in the post-World War II era. This exercise is important for understanding differences in formulation and outcomes of the empirical tests described below. In addition to comparisons between Brazil and Mexico, comparable data are also provided for the United States. Not only does this permit contrasts based on differences in economic development levels but also it should allow most readers to get a good impression of the great differences in scale between the United States and the two Latin American nations.

Brazil and Mexico are apt subjects for case studies. Although both countries are still relatively poor, their rates of overall growth and industrialization have been especially impressive. In addition, they have come to be among the three largest recipients of foreign direct manufacturing investment among the less developed countries (India is the other). For U.S. corporate investors, Brazil and Mexico rank among the seven largest host countries in their stock of industrial investment (the other five countries, except Canada, are all in Western Europe). For these reasons, Brazil and Mexico have become leading examples for other less developed countries attempting to develop or industrialize rapidly. Like most other LDCs, Brazil and Mexico have been faced by many problems: high rates of population growth, highly unequal distribution of incomes, regional growth disparities, large agricultural sectors, chronic trade or payments deficits, dependence on raw materials exports, and growing import dependence in certain sectors. While rapid growth has not ameliorated all of these conditions (and may in fact have exacerbated them), most LDCs remain convinced that some growth is better than none.

Thus, Brazil and Mexico remain important test cases for countries opting for generally capitalistic development strategies. How these strategies were designed and implemented or encouraged is the subject of the third section of this chapter. The policies of Brazil and Mexico are traced historically, with emphasis given to those actions aiding industrialization generally. Considered here are government decisions on tariff protection or nontariff barriers to trade, exchange-rate policies, anti-inflation controls, official credit or tax incentives, centralized planning, and efforts at promoting exports. In the next chapter, policies relating more specifically to the control or inducement of foreign investments are outlined. Some of these discriminatory laws and rules relate to prohibitions of foreign ownership in certain industries, company registration requirements, technology contract review procedures, and controls over or taxes on foreign income or capital flows.

COMPARATIVE REGIONAL STATISTICS

Size and level of development are two crucial measures that allow comparisons among economic regions of the world. Size is ordinarily indicated by population and by various gross product and income figures. The most widely accepted indicator of the level of material development is gross product per capita.

In terms of population size and density, the New World ranks far below both Asia and Europe; Africa is more populous but less dense (Table 2.1). Although the northern and Latin sections of the Western Hemisphere are similar in their density and total populations, Latin America shares the characteristic of rapid population growth with the other less developed areas (roughly, Africa plus Asia).*

---

*Throughout, unless otherwise specified, "northern America" refers to the United States and Canada, Latin America" refers to the entire Western Hemisphere south of the United States, and "Europe" includes the entire Soviet Union.

TABLE 2.1

Population and Density by Region
(in millions)

	World	Africa	Northern America	Latin America	Asia	Europe	Oceania
1950	2,486	217	166	162	1,355	572	13
1960	2,982	270	199	213	1,645	639	16
1965	3,289	303	214	246	1,833	676	18
1970	3,632	344	228	283	2,056	705	19
Annual rate of population increase, 1963-70 (percent)	2.0	2.6	1.3	2.9	2.3	0.8	2.1
Density, 1970 (per square kilometer)	28	11	11	13	73	69	2

Source: United Nations, Statistical Yearbook 1974.

TABLE 2.2

Gross Domestic Product (GDP) in Purchasers' Values by Region, Market Economies
(in billions of dollars)

	World	Africa	Northern America	Latin America	Asia	Europe	Oceania
1960	1,128	35	547	69	135	324	21
1966	1,863	55	814	107	306	549	32
1970	2,470	75	1,077	151	478	760	44
1972	3,155p	92p	1,276	189p	513p	1,026	59

Note: p = preliminary.

Source: United Nations, Statistical Yearbook 1974.

As can be seen in Table 2.2, economic output is highly concentrated in Europe and northern America. In 1970 the roughly 700 million people residing in the "market economies" of Europe and northern America produced and consumed more than two-thirds of the world's output. By contrast, the approximately 1.7 billion living in the "market economies" of Africa, Latin America, and Asia (excluding Japan) must make do with less than 20 percent of the globe's goods. The more developed areas of the world produce roughly four times what the less developed regions are able to produce.

There is even more variation among regions in per capita production than in total production (Table 2.3). Latin America, by this measure, is considerably more developed than Asia or Africa, but much less developed than the other regions. The absolute gap in per capita incomes is very wide; in 1950 the gap between Latin America and the developed countries was slightly under $1,000, but by 1970 the difference had increased to more than $2,000 (both at 1960 prices). The overall growth of the less developed regions has tended to outstrip that in the more developed areas (Table 2.4). Development has been particularly rapid since 1960 and in western Asia and Latin America; however, growth in eastern and southern Asia (excluding Japan) has merely equaled the European rate. On the other hand, when the growth rates in gross domestic product (GDP) are adjusted for population increases (Table 2.5), the rates are more nearly equal. Asian growth (with or without Japan) is somewhat higher and African growth somewhat lower than the average. The two Americas have nearly identical patterns of growth. It should be noted that the data presented in Tables

TABLE 2.3

Per Capita GDP in Purchasers' Values by Region, Market
Economies
(in dollars)

	1960	1966	1970	1972
World	550	760	980	1,145^p
Africa	130	170	220	240^p
Northern America	2,750	3,750	4,760	5,530
Latin America	330	440	560	665^p
Asia	147	215	295	355^p
Europe	1,060	1,690	2,280	3,030^p
Oceania	1,320	1,770	2,290	2,950^p

Note: p = preliminary.

Source: United Nations, Statistical Yearbook 1974.

TABLE 2.4

Index Numbers of GDP by Region
(1963 = 100)

	1950	1960	1965	1970	1972
Africa	56	88	112	139	152
Northern America	64	88	112	134	146
Latin America	54	87	114	150	170
Asia	57	82	113	170	195
Europe	55	87	111	139	149
Oceania	61	87	110	142	151

Source: United Nations, Statistical Yearbook 1974.

2.2 and 2.3 are expressed in current dollars; world inflation was very modest during the 1960–67 period, but since then it has accelerated. World inflation during 1963–72 was between 25 and 30 percent, but at least half of that inflation took place during 1970–72. The data in Tables 2.4 and 2.5, however, are based on constant 1963 dollars.

Table 2.6 contains statistics on the industrial component of GDP. In 1963 northern America accounted for almost half of the world's industrial output and Europe for more than one-third. Asia is the most important of the remaining areas, but more than two-thirds of 1963 industrial activity in that region was due to Japan; similarly, more

TABLE 2.5

Index Numbers of per Capita GDP by Region
(1963 = 100)

	1950	1960	1965	1970	1972
Africa	74	95	107	116	120
Northern America	80	92	109	123	132
Latin America	77	95	108	123	132
Asia	74	89	108	144	157
Europe	63	90	109	132	139
Oceania	82	93	106	125	128

Source: United Nations, Statistical Yearbook 1974.

TABLE 2.6

Index Numbers of Industrial Activity by Region, Market Economies
(1963 = 100)

	1950	1960	1965	1970	1972	Weight
Africa	41	80	119	171	186	2.0
	(42)	(83)	(114)	(160)	(182)	(1.3)
Northern America	63	87	116	136	152	45.5
	(64)	(87)	(118)	(135)	(151)	(45.4)
Latin America	45	86	117	164	187	5.1
	(46)	(87)	(118)	(169)	(197)	(4.5)
Asia	39	74	120	217	250	10.3
	(40)	(74)	(119)	(222)	(257)	(9.8)
Europe	49	86	114	150	162	35.6
	(48)	(86)	(114)	(152)	(163)	(37.2)
Oceania	43	84	114	147	157	1.6
	(44)	(85)	(114)	(142)	(148)	(1.6)

Note: These data exclude the centrally planned economies.
"Industrial Activity" encompasses ISIC categories 1-4: mining, electricity, gas, water, and manufacturing. The first number designates
total industry; the numeral in parentheses is the manufacturing sub-
sector only. The "weight" is the 1963 percentage of world industrial
(manufacturing) output.

Source: United Nations, Statistical Yearbook 1974.

than one-third of Africa's industrial output is located in South Africa.
Thus, in 1963 only 11 percent of the world's industrial capacity was
located in the less developed countries, and almost half of that production was in Latin America. On a per capita basis these differences
are further magnified. By that measure Latin America is roughly
five times as industrialized as Africa and ten times as industrialized
as underdeveloped Asia.

An examination of the main subsectors of industry is revealing.
In 1963, the LDCs had only about 9 percent of the world's manufacturing activity; again, almost half was located in Latin America. Within
manufacturing, the LDCs tend to have a far greater proportion of that
activity concentrated in the food, tobacco, and textile industries than
is typical of the more industrialized countries. Conversely, a far
smaller percentage of manufacturing in LDCs is found in the paper,
printing, primary and fabricated metals, and machinery industries
than is characteristic of the most industrialized regions.

Industrial and manufacturing growth during 1960-72 has been roughly twice as great in Africa, Asia, and Latin America as in northern America. Industrial production has more than doubled in all three regions, even when Japan and South Africa are excluded. Starting from lower industrial bases, both less developed Asia and Africa have tended to outpace Latin American growth. In all the regions but Africa and western Asia, manufacturing growth has tended to exceed the growth of the extractive and energy subsectors.

Tables 2.7 and 2.8 summarize the absolute and relative amounts of external trade by the market economies in recent years. As in the cases of total or industrial activity, the developed regions also dominate international trade. In 1948 the presently developed market economies accounted for 70 percent of total world imports; by 1972 the proportion had risen to 83 percent. During that same quarter century, imports by LDCs rose by more than 280 percent and exports more than 370 percent, but the rates of increase in real trade have been even greater for northern America, Europe, and particularly Japan.

The ratio of imports to exports in a given year is an indicator of the current merchandise balance of trade. Since the end of World War II through about 1970, of the major regions only northern America and Oceania have had a trade surplus. At a slightly more disaggregated level, however, it can be inferred that the oil-producing states of western Asia and Latin America have also had surpluses since the late 1950s; in the late 1960s Japan's trading account also became positive. In the early 1970s, however, rising oil prices had intensified the deficits of the oil-importing countries and had reversed the trading balance for northern America.

COMPARATIVE COUNTRY STATISTICS

Brazil and Mexico are the two largest countries of Latin America. A comparison of Tables 2.1 and 2.9 shows that the two countries accounted for roughly half of Latin America's population in the 1960s. The United States is at present more populous than the other two combined, but by 1985 near equality should prevail. Latin America is the most rapidly growing region of the world, and Brazil and Mexico are at or above the Latin American average; moreover, their rates of population growth have tended to accelerate since the 1950s. The United States is growing much more slowly, and its rate of growth has tended to decline rapidly since the mid-1960s. Population density is above the Latin American average in Mexico and slighly below the average in Brazil. Unlike the U.S. population, the vast share of the two Latin countries' populations is highly concentrated around urban agglomerations, the Mexico City and the Rio-São Paulo areas, respectively.

TABLE 2.7

World Trade by Region (Imports c.i.f./Exports f.o.b.), Market Economies
(in billions of dollars)

	Africa	Northern America	Latin America	Asia	Europe	Oceania
1948	5.0/3.6	11.0/15.8	7.4/7.5	8.4/6.9	25.9/17.8	1.9/2.2
1958	7.6/5.7	20.2/23.0	10.5/9.6	14.3/13.5	45.9/41.8	3.0/2.5
1965	10.4/9.1	31.8/35.7	12.0/12.7	26.0/24.7	89.3/78.6	5.1/4.1
1970	14.6/14.8	56.7/59.5	18.9/17.3	45.6/44.8	150.4/137.0	7.0/6.1
1972	17.0/17.6	79.2/70.1	23.7/20.4	58.0/66.6	196.8/187.3	7.4/8.5

Note: The centrally planned economies of Eastern Europe form a largely self-contained trading bloc with imports and exports of about $40 billion in 1972. Imports and exports from the centrally planned economies of Asia comprised about $3.5 billion in 1972, but no data are available on intrabloc trade (that is, among China, Mongolia, North Korea, and North Vietnam). No countries of Africa or the Western Hemisphere are considered "centrally planned" by the United Nations.

Source: United Nations, Statistical Yearbook 1974.

TABLE 2.8

Index Numbers of the Quantity of World Trade of Market Economies by Region (Imports/Exports)
(1963 = 100)

	Africa	Northern America	Latin America	Asia	Europe	Oceania
1948	45/44	50/59	69/65	39/38	31/27	55/54
1960	99/89	88/89	89/94	90/83	83/88	89/94
1965	120/115	123/115	107/107	114/129	118/120	126/108
1970	151/165	191/163	153/132	210/260	186/193	153/170
1972	165/191	238/180	176/137	245/310	215/226	135/180

Source: United Nations, Statistical Yearbook 1974.

TABLE 2.9

Population and Density by Country
(in millions)

	Brazil	Mexico	United States
1958	65.7	32.9	174.9
1963	76.2	39.5	189.2
1970	93.3	48.4	204.9
1972	98.9	52.6	208.8
Projected 1985	142.6	84.4	236.1
Annual rate of increase (percent), 1963-72	2.9	3.5	1.1
Density 1972 (per square kilometer)	12	27	22

Sources: United Nations, Statistical Yearbook 1974; and Statistical Abstract of Latin America 1972.

Brazil and Mexico together account for almost half of Latin America's gross product (compare Tables 2.2 and 2.10), but even in the most recent years their combined products have been less than one-tenth that of the United States. Brazil's GDP is larger than Mexico's, but their ranks reverse when per capita GDP is considered. Mexican per capita incomes have been more than 50 percent higher

TABLE 2.10

Gross Domestic Product in Purchasers' Values by Country
(in billions of dollars)

	Brazil	Mexico	United States
1950	9.4	7.5	284.8
1960	14.5	12.0	509.0
1963	20.6	15.6	596.3
1970	37.3	33.5	983.2
1972	50.7	41.0	1,161.9

Sources: United Nations, Statistical Yearbook 1974, Statistical Abstract of Latin America 1972; and Statistical Abstract of the United States.

than those of Brazil, though this difference has generally narrowed over time (Table 2.11). Like population density, incomes are also distributed unequally within all three countries. Personal incomes in the Latin countries are typically at least twice as high in the major metropolitan areas as in the nations as a whole (Table 2.12). The distribution appears somewhat more equal within these cities than without.

In 1960, Mexico was very close to the average level of development in Latin America, but in recent years its per capita income has been more than one-third higher. Brazil was more than 40 percent under the Latin American mean in 1960 but has subsequently grown much closer to it (compare Tables 2.3 and 2.11).

TABLE 2.11

GDP per Capita in Purchasers' Values by Country
(in dollars)

	Brazil	Mexico	United States
1960	208	334	2,817
1963	269	404	3,151
1970	400	685	4,799
1972	513^p	782^p	5,561^p

Note: p = preliminary.

Source: United Nations, Statistical Yearbook 1974.

Total economic growth has been very rapid in both Brazil and Mexico, but much more erratic in the former. During the 1950s the change in GDP was very similar in both countries (5.5 to 6.0 percent per year), but it tended to accelerate in Brazil and slow down in Mexico (Table 2.13). The period 1960-65 was one of very slow growth for Brazil, especially the 1962-65 period, though recovery was very swift after the end of 1965 so that by the early 1970s real growth was in excess of 10 percent per year. Mexico, on the other hand, enjoyed one of its best periods of growth during the early 1960s, with the rate moderating only slightly in the latter part of that decade. Overall, GDP growth has been very impressive in both countries since 1950 and has generally exceeded those rates prevailing in other parts of the less developed world, and, except for Japan, in the developed areas as well (compare Tables 2.12 and 2.4). With respect to per capita

TABLE 2.12

Estimated Distribution of Average per Capita Personal Incomes by
Income Class, 1965
(in 1960 dollars)

	Brazil	Rio de Janeiro	São Paulo	Mexico	Federal District
Poorest 20 percent	45	200	225	85	280
30 percent below median	100	405	390	185	495
30 percent above median	200	780	675	415	935
Richest 15 percent	380	1,425	1,280	935	1,940
Richest 5 percent	2,055	3,880	4,340	2,755	5,460

Source: Statistical Abstract of Latin America 1972.

incomes, Brazil and Mexico, despite high rates of population growth,
have both managed to attain rates of increase greater than any of the
world's major regions (if Japan is again excluded—Table 2.14). Thus,
the relative, if not the absolute, income gaps between Mexico, Brazil,
and the developed countries have been closing throughout the postwar
period.

Overall increases in production have been accompanied by even
more rapid changes in industry and manufacturing (Tables 2.15 and
2.17). Except for Brazil in the early 1960s, per annum rates of growth
in manufacturing have generally exceeded the total growth rates by 2
or 3 percent. In the United States and other more industrialized econ-

TABLE 2.13

Index Numbers of GDP by Country
(1963 = 100)

	Brazil	Mexico	United States
1955	65	64	80
1960	85	84	89
1966	111	127	112
1970	152	167	132
1972	184[p]	194[p]	144[p]

Note: p = preliminary.
Source: United Nations, Statistical Yearbook 1974.

TABLE 2.14

Index Numbers of per Capita GDP by Country
(1963 = 100)

	Brazil	Mexico	United States
1955	82	84	91
1960	92	93	93
1965	102	115	109
1970	125	132	122
1972	142^p	137^p	131^p

Note: p = preliminary.

Source: United Nations, Statistical Yearbook 1974.

TABLE 2.15

Index Numbers of Industrial (Manufacturing) Activity by Country
(1963 = 100)

	Brazil	Mexico	United States
1948	28	38	56
	(28)	(36)	(55)
1958	68	71	76
	(67)	(70)	(75)
1966	114	135	128
	(112)	(138)	(130)
1970	167	186	139
	(164)	(189)	(139)
1972	210	210	150
	(207)^p	(212)^p	(150)

Note: p = preliminary.

Sources: United Nations, Statistical Yearbook 1974; and Statistical Abstract of Latin America 1972.

omies, however, general and manufacturing growth rates have been more nearly balanced. Even though Brazilian and Mexican growth rates of agriculture have been high (exceeding 4 percent) relative to those of most LDCs, the more rapid rates of industrialization would

imply radical structural changes (Table 2.16). When valued at domestic prices, as in Table 2.16, the shift from the agricultural to manufacturing sectors is readily apparent. However, because most LDCs
provide higher tariff protection for their industrial sectors than for
their agricultural sectors, the contribution of the individual sectors
to GDP is more appropriately measured if it is expressed in world
prices. Estimates for the years 1950 and 1967 using this method have
been prepared by Balassa (1971). For Brazil these calculations revealed that agriculture's share did not change and that industry's increased only slightly (24 to 27 percent). For Mexico, protection and
price distortions were less, so agriculture's share actually did decrease (from 18 to 13 percent) and industry's increased (28 to 31 percent). And Balassa's calculations indicate that growth rates also have
an upward bias in highly protectionist economies.

Other distortions in official statistics may be traced to the difficulties inherent in translating current figures to real or deflated
levels. In general, inflation was low in both the United States and
Mexico throughout the 1960s (Table 2.18). Indeed, since 1954 Mexico

TABLE 2.16

Sectoral Structures by Country
(in percent)

	1950	1960	1969
Brazil			
Agriculture	29	28	21
Industry	24	25	29
Manufacturing	22	28	27
Mexico			
Agriculture	23	19	13
Industry	27	30	37
Manufacturing	23	26	32
United States			
Agriculture	7	4	3
Industry	35	34	32
Manufacturing	32	30	28

Note: GDP is at domestic factor costs. See Table 2.6 for the
definition of "Industy"; "Manufacturing" is ISIC category 4.

Sources: United Nations, Statistical Yearbook 1974; and Statistical Abstract of Latin America 1972.

TABLE 2.17

Average Annual Rates of Growth of GDP (Manufacturing) at Constant
Prices
(in percent)

	Brazil	Mexico	United States
1950–60	5.7	6.0	5.3
	(9.0)	(6.2)	(3.5)
1960–65	3.4	7.3	5.2
	(2.5)	(10.5)	(6.8)
1965–70	7.6	7.1	3.4
	(10.3)	(8.9)	(3.0)
1960–70	5.5	7.2	4.3
	(6.4)	(9.7)	(4.9)
1971–72	11.0	8.5	7.0
	(12.7)[p]	(10.8)[p]	(8.0)[p]

Note: p = preliminary. Manufacturing rates of growth in parentheses. For the United States, GNP is used in place of GDP and is deflated by the wholesale price index.

Sources: United Nations, Statistical Yearbook 1974; and Statistical Abstract of Latin America 1972.

has "tied" its currency (the peso) directly to the U.S. dollar and even followed the United States in its devaluation in 1971. In both countries, however, inflation accelerated during the early 1970s. Brazil, on the other hand, has experienced chronic and irregular inflation. Rates of increase in the general price index (a composite of the wholesale, consumer, and construction indexes) have exceeded 10 percent in every year since 1949. The years 1957–64 saw a particularly severe acceleration in that index, which rose from about 10 percent to more than 90 percent per annum. But after 1964, the rates decreased rapidly; during 1967–69 the index lay in the 20 to 30 percent range; by 1970–72 it was in the 15 to 20 percent range (Conjunctura Economica, various issues).

The process of industrialization in Brazil and Mexico is intimately connected with international trade and with commercial policies in particular. One of the main theses of a major comparative study of industrialization and trade policies in several countries was that industrialization in the LDCs has been practically equivalent to import substitution (Little, Scitovsky, Scott 1970). Moreover, Morley and

TABLE 2.18

Wholesale (WPI) and Consumer (CPI) Price Indexes by Country
(1963 = 100)

	Brazil		Mexico		United States	
	WPI	CPI	WPI	CPI	WPI	CPI
1966	398	443	108	110	105	106
1970	902	1,047	122	126	117	127
1972	1,287	1,309p	131	136	125	137

Note: p = preliminary. Brazil's CPI is based on São Paulo and Mexico's on Mexico City.

Source: United Nations, Statistical Yearbook 1974.

Smith (1971) have argued that, in the case of Brazil at least, import-substitution policies have unnecessarily benefited foreign-owned firms over domestic ones. Trade policies are discussed in more detail below; here my purpose is to describe a few basic features of Mexico's and Brazil's foreign trade.

From Table 2.19 it is evident that, in absolute terms, international trade for Mexico and Brazil is quite limited; together the two countries accounted for only about 20 percent of Latin America's trade in the 1960s, but this proportion has increased in more recent years. Still, both countries remain considerably less "open," if one used the gross imports-to-GDP ratio as a measure of openness, than the average economy of an LDC (compare Table 2.7). After 1950 imports were generally less than 10 percent of GDP in both countries; this gross-imports ratio tended to decline throughout the period, except in Brazil after 1970, when a noticeable surge in trade took place. Both countries generally experienced commodity-trade deficits on their current accounts; these deficits were largely financed by inward foreign direct investment and, in Mexico especially, by government borrowing on international capital markets.

Although trade with other developing countries has increased in recent years, especially among members of the Latin American Free Trade Association (LAFTA), most trade is between the two countries and either Europe or northern America (Table 2.20). Brazil tends to trade proportionately more with Europe, and Mexico is more closely tied in trade with the United States.

Neither has the sectoral composition of commodity trade changed radically in recent years. The general pattern for both Brazil and

TABLE 2.19

World Trade by Country (Imports c.i.f./Exports f.o.b.)
(in billions of dollars)

	Brazil	Mexico	United States
1948	1.1/1.2	0.6/0.5	7.2/12.5
1958	1.4/1.2	1.1/0.7	13.3/17.8
1965	1.1/1.6	1.6/1.1	21.3/27.2
1970	2.8/2.7	2.5/1.4	39.8/42.6
1972	4.7/4.0	2.9/1.8	55.3/49.0

Source: United Nations, Statistical Yearbook 1974.

Mexico remains one of exporting primary products and importing
manufactures (Table 2.21). In 1953, 99 percent of Brazil's exports
consisted of primary commodities (roughly SITC 0 through 4); by 1967
that category had dropped to 90 percent (Balassa 1971); in 1970 exports
were 86 percent primary products. Mexico shows a steeper decline
in the primary exports-to-total exports ratio: 91 percent (1953), 79
percent (1967), and 60 percent (1970). Thus, the structural transformation of exports has gone faster and farther in Mexico than in Brazil.

TABLE 2.20

The Directions of Trade by Country, 1970
(Imports c.i.f./Exports f.o.b.)
(in millions of dollars)

	Brazil	Mexico
Africa	141/113	3/1
Northern America	988/717	1,617/859
Latin America	342/322	90/93
LAFTA	310/303	64/93
Developed Asia	181/151	87/70
Developing Asia	162/94	17/7
Europe	1,014/1,264	627/136
Oceania	5/3	13/3

Source: United Nations, Yearbook of International Trade Statistics 1972-73.

Both countries still depend on a small number of primary, major
products for the bulk of their exports (that is, products representing
more than 3 percent of the total exports). Brazil's major exports are
coffee, cotton, iron ore, sugar, lumber, and cocoa; these products
represented 71 percent of total exports during 1963-66. Mexico's
major exports, accounting for 36 percent during the same period,
were cotton, coffee, sugar, shellfish, corn, lead, copper, and fresh
fish. Thus, Mexico's exports are distinctly more diversified than
Brazil's.

The late 1960s and early 1970s witnessed greater export diversification in both countries. In addition to the traditional major exports
mentioned above, Brazil now exports "significant" amounts (more than
2 percent of total exports) of meat (frozen and canned), preserved
fruits, animal feeds, tobacco, soybeans, and soy oil. In addition, a
few nonprimary products had become significant by 1972: industrial
chemicals, leather, textile yarns, wrought iron and steel, nonelectrical machinery, motor vehicles, and footwear (United Nations, Yearbook of International Trade Statistics 1972-73). Mexico has also diversified its primary exports; meat, cattle, fresh and preserved fruits,
and fresh vegetables are now significant exports. But perhaps even
greater diversification has taken place among manufactured exports:
industrial chemicals, bulk medicinals, textiles, wrought iron and
steel, nonelectrical machineryparts, electrical machinery (mostly
switchgear and televisions), motor vehicles, and motor-vehicle parts
were all significant exports by 1972 (United Nations, Yearbook of International Trade Statistics 1972-73). Many of these latter exports
are due to its "border industry" program.

The composition of commodity imports has also changed in postwar Mexico and Brazil. Generally, the proportion of primary products and durable consumer goods imported has declined, while the
imports of chemicals and capital-goods machinery have increased.
In Brazil, the ratio of primary to total imports went from 47 percent
(1953) to 42 percent (1967) to 28 percent (1972), with most of the decrease occurring in the fuel, food, beverage, and tobacco categories.
Except for consumer goods, manufactures imports have generally increased proportionately; chemicals and machinery in 1972 accounted
for 15 and 40 percent of total imports, respectively—up from about
6 and 25 percent in the early 1950s. Mexico's primary imports have
likewise declined as a ratio of total imports, from 23 percent (1950)
to 16 percent (1967) to 18 percent (1972). Unlike the case of Brazil,
however, the importation of consumer durables has remained a fairly
constant share of the import bill, staying at the 11-12 percent level
(four times that of Brazil) throughout the period. Intermediate producer
goods were also quite steady, but the proportion of capital goods, especially industrial machinery, increased markedly, from 23 percent
(1950) to 36 percent (1967).

TABLE 2.21

The Structure of Trade by Country, 1970 (Imports/Exports)
(in millions of dollars)

SITC-Commodity		Brazil	Mexico
0.	Food	282/1,590	142/458
1.	Beverages, tobacco	0/34	5/16
2.	Crude materials	81/638	213/208
3.-4.	Fuels and oils	372/83	92/38
5.	Chemicals	473/39	302/98
6.	Basic manufactures	477/210	288/197
7.	Machinery	1,002/97	1,235/128
8.-9.	Miscellaneous manufactures	56/49	180/59
0.-9.	Total	2,743/2,740	2,447/1,202

Source: United Nations, Yearbook of International Trade Statistics 1972-72.

Like their overall GDP growth patterns, rates of change in world trade have been quite different in the two nations. Mexico's case is the simpler of the two. Throughout the 1950s and 1960s real rates of growth in imports tended to exceed the growth in GDP, while exports growth was considerably slower; imports grew at about 7 percent per annum and exports at only about 4 percent (compare Tables 2.13 and 2.22). In Brazil, on the other hand, growth has been unsteady. In real terms, imports roughly tripled in the decade after World War II, stagnated until 1967, and then doubled during the next five years. Brazilian exports have depended heavily on coffee prices, harvests, and international quota agreements. In real terms, gross exports grew not at all from the late 1940s to the mid-1960s, but since then there has been a real annual growth rate of about 6 percent. In the early years of the 1970s, trade has tended to grow faster than GDP in both Mexico and Brazil, though rapid worldwide inflation and the U.S. devaluation make an exact calculation risky.

To summarize, both Brazil and Mexico have experienced periods of rapid overall growth, especially in their industrial sectors. Both, moreover, have undergone some overall export diversification and import substitution. Much of the export diversification has been into manufactures, and most of the import substitution has been in manufactured consumer goods and producer durables. The rapid structural transformations due to industrialization have been causally connected to the adoption of protectionist trade policies, as I shall show in the next section.

INDUSTRIALIZATION AND TRADE POLICIES

The early stages of development by the presently industrialized market economies were not generally characterized by conscious or coordinated government intervention (Landes 1969). Of course, many of these countries pursued policies with respect to trade, colonization, finance, education, and infrastructure development that had important external benefits for the transformation of their economies into industrial powers. But the presently less developed countries have since the end of World War II implemented several policy changes that have as their aim the deliberate fostering of general economic development and of industrialization. Most LDCs have equated the goal of rapid development with the need for industrialization because of the presumed manifold obstacles to rapid agricultural growth.

Many policies have been adopted in the LDCs to promote rapid industrial growth. The early theories of economic development, associated with the names of Rostow, Nurske, and others, emphasized the need for capital accumulation. As a result, many governments made strong efforts to induce high rates of saving and investment. Reforms in taxation, public spending, and financial institutions were carried out to increase saving rates. Efforts were made by many countries to encourage increased reinvestment of domestic profits and flows of private and official foreign investment. Public investment was directed toward large-scale projects in water, energy, transportation, and communication that could be expected to bring important external economies for industry.

By the early 1960s, most LDCs had succeeded in raising their gross investment rates to well beyond the "critical" level of 15 percent of GNP, but with only mixed results for overall growth. Thus, present thinking on development theory has shifted somewhat away from

TABLE 2.22

Index Numbers of World Trade by Country (Imports/Exports)
(1963 = 100)

	Brazil	Mexico
1950	60/69	46/56
1960	109/80	96/80
1966	101/107	130/125
1970	170/137	199/146
1972	250/218	235/190

Source: United Nations, Statistical Yearbook 1974.

the emphasis on mere mobilization to the problems of the proper deployment of resources (Ward 1971). Today many experts advocate redressing the balance between industry and agriculture toward the latter, creating larger effective demand for smaller countries, promoting exports, inducing technological progress, and creating human capital. Customs unions, comprehensive planning, and trade protection have come under special scrutiny of late.

Most of these comments apply with equal force to Mexico and Brazil. The purpose of this section is to look closely at their industrialization and trade policies in the postwar period, in order to provide an institutional context for the statistical tests that follow.

Brazil

Postwar industrialization in Brazil has been characterized by an increasing number of deliberate policies of state intervention. While economic planning has played a role, the main instruments of public policy have been those related to import substitution and export promotion. The tools employed include, inter alia, import tariffs, quantitative restrictions, multiple exchange rates, tax exemptions, and direct and indirect subsidies.

Before World War II, tariff protection had been extended primarily to agriculture and a few other related industries such as textiles. Early in the first administration of Getulio Vargas (1930–47) most tariffs were levied on a specific rather than an ad valorem basis and inflation had quickly eroded their impact. Other than efforts to establish a steel industry, few positive steps were taken to encourage or protect Brazil's nascent industry. Until a 1947 balance-of-payments crisis developed, the exchange rate was generally overvalued in order to maximize coffee export earnings; to help control domestic inflation, the choice was made to impose selective import quotas rather than a general devaluation (Leff 1968a).

Thus, until 1947 most of Brazil's industrial development had followed from its static comparative advantage. Both the worldwide depression and the supply shortages of World War II had provided substantial stimulus to domestic industry (Baer 1965). During the war the first few of several state enterprises were established in iron, steel, and motor vehicles.

The policy of an overvalued exchange rate and strict import licensing was replaced with a multiple exchange rate system in 1953, and this in turn was supplanted by a comprehensive set of ad valorem tariffs in 1957 (Bergsman 1970). All three systems had essentially the same effect: the rapid replacement of finished consumer goods imports by domestic production and a rapid shift to imports of only raw industrial and capital goods. After 1957 even some capital goods industries were extended protection.

What had begun as a balance-of-payments measure had, during the second Vargas (1951-54) and Kubitschek (1956-60) regimes, become a deliberate policy of internal development through import substitution (desenvolvimentismo) (Baer 1965). Aided by high coffee prices up to 1954 and by huge deficit spending by the Kubitschek government, manufacturing growth rates averaged 9 to 10 percent during 1949-62. Moreover, imports as a proportion of total supply dropped precipitously, from 19 percent to 5 percent over the same period (Balassa 1971: 107). Morley and Smith (1971), using the measure of manufacturing imports to manufacturing value added for the extent of import substitution, calculated the 1949-62 movement to be from 33 percent to 15 percent. These authors also found that industry growth rates and import-substitution rates were significantly correlated; only six industries (electrical and nonelectrical machinery, transportation equipment, chemicals, plastics, and metals) accounted for 53 percent of the increase in manufacturing value added and 87 percent of the import substitution.

These protectionist policies were slowly supplemented by other measures intended to promote industrial growth. An old law (the "Law of Similars"), which prohibited importation of goods recognized by the government as being sufficiently available domestically, was more strictly enforced, especially after 1967 (Bergsman 1970). In a few instances import monopolies and price controls were used to protect domestic industries. Power and infrastructure planning was coordinated with industrial development, especially after the Metas program was initiated in 1957 (Ohara 1974). Finally, special tax, credit, and foreign-exchange advantages were provided to foreign firms and joint ventures (Newfarmer and Mueller 1975).

Extreme inflation, the 1962-64 recession, political instability, a slowing of foreign investment, and imminent default on foreign loans all led to the 1964 military coup (Baer 1965). Each military president has formulated and implemented his own three-year development plan. The essential strategy of high import tariff protection remains, though there was a major reduction in the rates in 1967 (Bergsman 1970). The administration of Castelo Branco had as its primary goal inflation control; reduced deficits and tax reforms went far toward accomplishing this aim, but the recession lingered on through 1965 and unemployment increased (Syvrud 1974). But the public foreign debt was repaid and foreign direct investment was actively encouraged. The development program of the Costa e Silva regime (1967-70) involved expanded money and credit supplies and also brought a new emphasis to export promotion; these and other reforms laid the foundation for a new period of rapid growth.

The economic theories that had provided some support for Brazil's import-substitution program were probably never meant to exclude the simultaneous pursuit of export-promotion efforts. Raul Prebisch and other economists of the U.S. Economic Commission for Latin America (ECLA) had shown a fairly constant concern for the establishment of low-cost industries, though their advocacy of industrial export expansion became more evident in the late 1960s (compare Prebisch 1959 and ECLA 1969). At any rate, import substitution remained almost the sole means of promoting industrialization in Brazil through the early 1960s (Balassa 1971: 115). But the 1967 Strategic Development Program, while retaining the emphasis on inflation control and government investment in infrastructure and the basic industries, coincided with a series of new policies meant to promote nontraditional industrial exports (Syvrud 1974). These policies were reinforced by the development plan of the Medici Administration for the years 1972-74. A flexible exchange-rate system, ravious tax incentives and export subsidies, new port and warehousing facilities, the creation of a new National Council of Foreign Trade (CONCEX) in 1966 and a new National Investment Fund for Export (FINEX) in 1967, and several schemes that allowed reduced import duties in return for increased exports—all encouraged rapid export expansion (Ohara 1974: 148-49; Tyler 1973). Manufactured exports as a percentage of total exports increased from about 11 percent over 1966-70 to 20 percent during 1971-72. In dollar terms, 1972 manufactured exports were four times the 1966-70 annual average. Also an important trend is a shift away from the more protected LAFTA market (56 percent of 1968-69 exports) to non-LAFTA areas (52 percent of 1970-71 exports).

Thus, while a few industries such as the machine tool industry remain internationally competitive in costs and prices (primarily because they were established before the imposition of high tariffs in the early 1950s), most industries in Brazil are not internationally competitive, because of high effective rates of protection. Estimates of the net effective protection afforded some Brazilian major industry groups (circa 1966) are provided by Bergsman (1970: 48). (See Appendix F.) Very high rates (averaging 240 percent) are found in many consumer nondurables industries (toiletries, clothing, tobacco, furniture, beverages, and so forth). But high rates (averaging about 100 percent) were also extended to other industries (electrical equipment, plastics, rubber products, transportation equipment, and paper); most of these industries also exhibited high rates of import substitution during the 1950-62 period. The metal, nonelectrical machinery, chemical, and drug industries received relatively little net effective protection (10 to 25 percent).

On the whole, postwar Brazilian import substitution can be said to have proceeded by way of "backward linkages," and it was not

grounded in the infant industry argument often used to justify tariff
protection in the LDCs (Balassa 1971). This protection has led to
both misallocations through price distortions and the survival of many
inefficient industries that could have been efficient had other policies
been followed. The social costs of protection have been high for Brazilian consumers; for 1966, Bergsman estimated these costs to consumers (supranormal profits and wages of industries that would not
survive under free trade or would be forced to become competitive
under free trade, decreases in consumer surplus, and other costs)
to amount to roughly 9 percent of GNP.*

    To summarize, postwar Brazilian industrialization, at first an
unintended outcome of balance-of-payments concerns, became after
the mid-1950s a deliberate objective of national commercial policy.
An overvalued exchange rate discouraged all exports and had the effect
of replacing imports with domestic manufacture. The industrial structure of protection favored the more rapid substitution of imported
finished consumer goods than of raw materials or capital goods. But
high demand, local content requirements, the structure of government
investment, and fiscal policies were also factors encouraging the local
production of all but a few raw materials and capital goods. In the
late 1960s, there was a shift away from complete reliance on import
substitution measures toward export promotion and more sectorally
balanced development policies as the possibilities of further substitution became limited and as means of promoting greater industrial efficiency.

    The post-1964 economic reforms have generally been praised for
their effectiveness in reducing inflation (or at least its ill effects) and
promoting industrial growth. But Fishlow (1973) and others have been
highly critical of some of their other effects. There is some evidence
that the austerity measures may have contributed to a worsening distribution of income. Little has been done to alleviate the disparities
in regional incomes and between urban and rural incomes, though the
Medici plan does recognize the problems to some extent. Employment
generation in industry has been disappointing, though unemployment
rates have declined slowly since 1964 (Morley 1974).

---

    *Some of these quantities, though costs to consumers, are not
costs to society. Specifically, supranormal profits and wages are societal transfers. Real costs to society would include excess advertising, efficiency losses due to suboptimal capacity, losses in allocative
efficiency due to price distortions, and income lost because of failure
to innovate.

Mexico

While overall industrial development and trade policies have
paralleled those of Brazil in many respects, one major difference in
Mexican policies is much lower levels of protection for industry (Appendix F). In the mid-1960s, average effective rates of manufacturing protection in Mexico were estimated to be only 27 percent (as
compared to 118 percent in Brazil and 162 percent in Argentina) (Little,
Scitovsky, and Scott 1970). As a result, the estimated costs of protection, though high (2 or 3 percent of GDP), are considerably lower than
those in Brazil (Balassa 1971: 82).

The earliest industrial development in Mexico occurred during
the rule of Porfirio Díaz (1876-1910) under conditions of almost free
trade. Considerable import substitution took place; by 1910 only 8
percent of GDP was being imported. Tariffs were first imposed in
the early 1930s; these and several peso devaluations were primarily
responsible for manufacturing growth rates of about 5 percent annually
during 1933-40, despite the large land reforms, oil company expro-
priations, and consequent foreign-capital flight during the Cárdenas
administration (1936-40). By 1940 about 17 percent of Mexico's GDP
was the result of manufacturing activity (King 1970).

But it was World War II that was responsible for Mexico's industrial "takeoff"; rates of manufacturing growth averaged 8 percent
annually during 1940-46, and real GDP grew by 6 percent. Tariff
protection was enlarged and new tax concessions given to manufacturing. Export demand was high for steel, paper, cement, and especially
textiles; production increases came about mainly from increased capacity utilization, because little industrial capital could be imported
(Vernon 1963).

The Aleman and Cortines administrations (1946-58) increased
the tariff protection of domestic industry. For the first time, import
bans were placed on several score "luxury items." Fiscal and monetary measures were taken to control inflation, with Mexico's last devaluation occurring in 1954. Foreign direct investment was again encouraged, and large government infrastructure expenditures were
made; since 1960 about 40 percent of all direct investment was by
public agencies (King 1970).

During the war, the primary purpose of tariffs was that of increasing tax revenues. In the decade following the war, however,
both the redress of the balance of payments and industrial protection
became added objectives. Since 1955 these three objectives have been
largely pursued by the more direct domestic monetary and fiscal
means and by large-scale government borrowing from foreign countries, especially from the United States (Balassa 1971).

Since 1955, trade policies have made increasing use of quantitative import controls (first applied in 1947). The controls take the

form of import licenses granted on the advice of industrial committees. Many criteria are employed, but if no domestic substitutes are available or if the domestic price exceeds the import price by 100 percent or more, the permit to import is normally granted. By the mid-1960s more than 3,000 such licenses were being approved weekly, covering more than two-thirds of all Mexican imports (King 1970). Naturally, such a system involves delays, a large bureaucracy, and tends to breed corruption (Hansen 1971). Yet there is apparently little pressure within Mexico for changes in the system. And as in Brazil, the system has been effective in rapidly shifting the composition of imports: during the 1950-67 period, the importation of capital goods increased (from 27 to 41 percent of total imports) and that of consumer goods decreased (Balassa 1971).

The system of import controls is not coordinated with the import tariff schedule. Tariffs are retained mainly for the small tax revenue they generate and for purposes of international trade negotiations (King 1970). During the Mateos and Ordaz presidencies (1958-70), the government supplemented the system of tariffs and quotas with other industrial policies. Government and quasi-government credit institutions were founded or expanded for domestic industrial investors. Local content requirements and other backward integration schemes were imposed on new investors, especially foreign firms. Lists of specific products suitable for import substitution have been promulgated (for example, Olizar 1972). Since 1962, private sector investment has been included in each president's development plan, but these tend to be merely indicative and striking changes in policies are the rule when a new administration takes office. Export licensing has become an important restriction. (Export taxes are imposed on a small and declining proportion of mineral exports.) Price controls are fairly widespread, especially on drugs, soaps, industrial chemicals, fuels, and motor vehicles. Finally, tax holidays of five to ten years can be granted to firms that wish to produce some "new," "necessary," or "basic" product. In return the firm may have to guarantee certain price and quality levels. In the late 1960s these became of declining importance and were never intended as alternatives to import relief (King 1970).

In the late 1960s, manufacturing export promotion objectives came to the fore in Mexico (as in Brazil). Export credits and rail transport subsidies were instituted. Direct export subsidies are given to only a few industries (for example, textiles). More recently, new concerns have arisen over industrial efficiency, geographic decentralization, and employment generation (Balassa 1971).

These policies, and other factors, have led to rapid, sustained, and highly even rates of industrial growth in Mexico. In 1967, the manufacturing value added per capita, measured at world market prices, was about $130; this is roughly double the Brazilian level, though in both countries this represents a doubling over the 1950-67 period in real terms. Since 1967, Brazil's manufacturing growth has generally outpaced that of Mexico. Partly because net effective manufacturing protection in Mexico is only one-fourth that of Brazil's, price distortions are likely lower in Mexico. For example, measured at domestic prices the share of the industrial sector in GDP in 1967 was nearly identical in both countries (about 28 percent); measured at world market prices, however, Brazil is far less industrialized (only 31 percent of GDP) than Mexico (43 percent) (Balassa 1971).*

Among the other factors accounting for Mexico's industrial growth, perhaps the most important is proximity to the United States (Rhodes 1970). This has permitted large export earnings from tourism and agricultural products. More important, it has, because of the likelihood of smuggling, prevented too high price differentials from developing and has constrained the government from imposing too high tariffs or too low quotes (King 1970). In addition, as in Brazil, the agricultural sector has been able to generate sufficient food surpluses to keep agricultural prices low. Political stability and ideological continuity certainly have played a role, particularly with respect to public and foreign direct investments (Vernon 1963). And finally, the Mexican government has, to a larger extent than those of most LDCs in recent decades, been able to borrow large amounts of foreign financial capital from both private and official sources and has also been more effective than most in mobilizing domestic savings.

---

*The estimates of net effective protection in Mexico were based on actual price differences between Mexican and world levels resulting from the quantitative restrictions, rather than being based on tariff schedules and input-output relationships, as in Brazil.

3

FOREIGN DIRECT
INVESTMENT AND
INDUSTRIAL
MARKET STRUCTURES

Foreign direct investment (FDI) has been a key element in the industrialization strategies of both Brazil and Mexico. From FDI was expected to flow a panoply of direct and indirect economic benefits. Initially, the foreign funds transferred from abroad would have an immediate, positive impact on the host country's deficit-prone balance of payments. Then, the financial flows would be accompanied by a parallel movement of managers and machinery, both scarce and advanced factors of production in LDCs, eventually to be harnessed to the country's superabundant supply of relatively unskilled labor. Superior management and engineering skills, as well as the technology embodied in the machines themselves, would raise the economy's productivity, increase incomes, provide a larger tax base, and replace formerly imported goods with locally made ones. Indirect benefits would devolve primarily in the form of training for workers, technicians, input suppliers, and distributors of the investor's products. But additional advantages might accrue if the entering firm helped break up preexisting local oligopolies or later used its good connections in the home country market to aid the host country in developing its industrial exports.

That was the usual scenario. Some of these benefits have been real and permanent, but others have been elusive and illusory, particularly in the longer run. Clearly, tremendous increases in industrial output have accompanied the influx of foreign capital into Brazil's and Mexico's manufacturing sectors. Doubtless, highly productive technologies, perhaps unobtainable other than via foreign direct investment, have been transferred internationally and many sectoral linkages have been forged, both within manufacturing and between it and the agriculture, construction, finance, and other service sectors. Employment generation and import replacement effects, on the other

hand, are definitely more disappointing. The development of manufactured exports has also been slow.

Granted that increases in foreign manufacturing investments
have been <u>concurrent with</u> increases in manufacturing activity of the
most modern types, this still does not allow one to conclude that a
heavy reliance on FDI was on balance beneficial. The reason is, of
course, that it is almost impossible to assess what the rapidity of industrial development would have been in the absence of foreign investment. In other words, the proper evaluation of the net social benefits
to Brazil and Mexico from FDI involves a comparison of the present
state of development with what Brazil and Mexico would have become
with only domestic sources of entrepreneurship and capital. These
sorts of comparisons are admittedly very difficult to make and are
fraught with numerous methodological pitfalls.

What have become more apparent of late are the large costs associated with foreign economic penetration and control. Many of
these costs have to do with losses of political sovereignty and societal
self-determination. Most of the disadvantages asserted by critics to
be causally related to foreign investment dwell, however, on more
purely economic aspects of independence. Chief among these accusations are the creation of new economic classes within the nation and
new, subtler forms of economic dependence internationally. That is,
MNCs are charged with exacerbating the maldistribution of incomes
and wealth, increasing financial and trade dependence between LDCs
and the stronger home countries, and introducing new goods and production processes that are inappropriate for poor countries.

The scope of this book is far too narrow to allow me to pass
judgement on all or even most of these crucial issues. Rather, I
shall focus in this chapter on an effect of foreign investment that has
not received much attention from researchers until quite recently:
the loss of national control over industrial decision making and the
construction of oligopolistic market structures strongly reminiscent
of the home country industries that follows the entry of MNCs.

The discussion opens with brief narratives of policies explicitly
directed at foreign investments by the Brazilian and Mexican governments. A common theme running through these discussions is the
remarkable similarity, approaching contagion, of policies meant to
control or promote FDI in the two countries. This conclusion is all
the more remarkable in the light of Mexico's generally nationalistic
pronouncements and Brazil's ostensibly laissez-faire image.

The second section attempts to quantify the role of foreign, especially U.S., corporations in the manufacturing sectors of Brazil and
Mexico. In particular, the topics to be covered include the amounts
and distribution of FDI in recent years, the extent of foreign ownership and other forms of denationalization, and the growth and conglom-

eration of manufacturing affiliates of MNCs. Some of these data were derived from public sources, but some were developed from a special questionnaire survey of the U.S. Senate Subcommittee on Multinational Corporations. (See Newfarmer and Mueller 1975.) The general picture that emerges from this discussion is of very high and generally increasing levels of denationalization in both Brazil and Mexico.

The special survey responses were also used to present and analyze data on several dimensions of the market structures of manufacturing industries in Brazil and Mexico. Data were developed to show the distribution of U.S. multinational market shares and the levels of concentration and product differentiation. Moreover, the market structures of the two Latin American countries are compared with each other and with those of comparable U.S. industries. These analyses throw considerable light on the competitive environments of U.S. MNCs abroad and suggest that MNCs themselves may be the institutional link among the observed structural associations. Put another way, MNCs apparently restructure the industries of recipient economies so as to create competitive environments hospitable to the growth of their corporate offspring—environments that are remarkably similar to those in which the parent corporations learned to thrive.

POLICIES TOWARD FDI

Many of the official actions taken with respect to domestic industrialization or international trade had or were intended to have impacts on domestic as well as foreign-owned firms. Many of these influences were essentially neutral, but some policies were discriminatory in intent or effect. It is the purpose of this section to review briefly those official rules, practices, or laws that were designed to facilitate, hinder, or otherwise control the flow of foreign direct investment into Brazil or Mexico since 1945. Of special interest are policies that prohibit or restrict FDI in certain sectors, foreign company or contract registration requirements, and direct taxes or subsidies on foreign capital or income flows.

Brazil

Brazil has over the last decade earned a reputation for being "wide open" to foreign investment. That is, from the point of view of MNCs, flows of business funds are relatively unhindered, those in power favor a generally capitalist road to development, and the risks of expropriation are viewed as low. The investment "climate" is regarded not only as more inviting than in most LDCs but also as less

subject to variability. Enforcement of the rules of the investment game
is often stricter in Brazil than elsewhere in Latin America, but there
is overall greater certainty on the part of investors on the rules
(Behrman 1974a).

Since 1945 Brazil's government has adopted a fairly comprehensive and interlocking set of policies toward FDI. A few sectors are
proscribed for foreign investment, but most of these sectors are
service activities (domestic airlines, newspapers, coastal shipping,
electric power generation, communication, and so forth). Petrobras
has a monopoly over the exploration, extraction, and refining of petroleum; foreign firms may still distribute petroleum products, however.
In some construction, mining, and petrochemical activities foreign
investments may be restricted in certain ways. But on the whole, there
are few limits as to the forms or amounts of foreign investment in the
manufacturing sector.

Prior registration of the ownership and capital structure of a
firm is required if profit remittances out of Brazil are to be allowed.
Prior submission of production plans is not required, but in order to
qualify for special investment incentives given to all firms, plans must
be submitted for approval to a kind of planning agency, the Industrial
Development Council (CDI). The CDI bases its decisions on the recom-
mendations of several sectoral study groups composed of businessmen
and civil servants who study the proposal's vertical integration potential. These groups are currently established for almost all the consumer products, metals, chemicals, nonmetallic minerals, and motor
vehicles industries. "Local content" requirements are frequently imposed for motor-vehicles production and are at present nearly 100 percent for automobiles. Some direct subsidies are given to specific
exporters; Volkswagen, for example, has been awarded a 40 percent
subsidy on the production of engines exported to the United States or
Europe (Behrman 1974a).

But not all Brazilian policies have led to increased constraints
on the operations of MNCs. Through 1955, monetary regulations and
the overvalued exchange rate hampered capital movements by foreign
investors (Baer 1965). From 1955 to 1962, the monetary authority
enforced its "Instruction 113," which allowed foreign firms to import
effectively capital equipment at tariff levels below those imposed on
domestic firms. During 1956-60 more than 80 percent of all FDI entering Brazil was in the form of machinery imports that qualified under the provisions of Instruction 113 (Bergsman 1970). Almost 90
percent of the exemptions were awarded in the metals, chemicals,
machinery, and automotive industries. No doubt these advantages, and
the "climate" created, had a strong positive influence on the surge in
FDI that took place (Gordon 1962). Like many other important decisions of the time, the original concern was to improve the balance-of-

payments situation in a period of rapidly declining coffee prices.
Later, however, the policy was defended as an integral part of the
new import-substitution objective and as necessary in order to obtain
the benefits of "high technology" industries (Leff 1968a).

The economic problems that arose during the Goulart presidency
(1961-64) were also accompanied by a shift in attitude toward foreign
capital, one that emphasized the growing "dependence" and consequent
dominance of Latin American countries by foreign interests (for example, Furtado 1970). About the same time, the outflows attributable
to FDI had begun to outweigh direct investment inflows. These
changes brought about the enactment in 1962 of a new profits remission
law establishing fairly severe limits on the outflow of earnings.

These restrictions on profits or other remissions were lifted
in 1964. Since that time, no upper limits have been placed on dividend
flows, but a 25 percent withholding tax is collected on all remittances
of up to 12 percent (three-year average) of registered capital plus
reinvested earnings. On dividend repatriations above 12 percent, the
withholding tax rate is progressive (rising from 40 to 60 percent), but
a firm would, under reasonable assumptions about the ratio of registered capital to stockholders' equity, need to earn (and sustain for
three years) more than 50 percent before-tax profits on equity to be
subject to these higher rates. Foreign exchange is freely available
for profit repatriation, but in times of balance-of-payments stress
foreign remittances can be restricted to only 10 percent of a firm's
registered capital (5 percent in "luxury" goods industries). This last
provision has never been used, however.

Two fairly tough additional restrictions on outward flows of funds
have been enacted. In most countries, even those with laws limiting
profit repatriations, the repayment of loans and interest is normally
free and unregulated (Robbins and Stobaugh 1973). Brazil's Central
Bank, however, has the authority to disallow interest payments on
foreign loans whose rates exceed those in the lending country.

The second set of laws relates to technology and licensing agreements. Like foreign loans, all technology contracts must be registered, the latter with the Department of Industrial Property. Approval
of the agreement is uncertain and often lengthy—up to five years on the
average, by one estimate (Behrman 1974a). Royalties are limited to
5 percent of gross sales for patents or "know-how" and to 1 percent
for trademarks. Licensing agreements must expire within ten years,
and fees paid for technical assistance must be justified on the basis of
actual services provided (that is, long-term or lump-sum payments
for technical assistance are ruled out). Moreover, royalty payments
made to a firm's parent organization are not tax-deductible; hence,
royalty payments are treated as ordinary distribution of profits and
are subject to the remittance withholding tax. Finally, a 1969 decree

has very strictly limited the use of patents in Brazil; in many industries (for example, foods or drugs) products or processes are simply not patentable, recourse to litigation is cumbersome, and unused patents are quickly forfeited.

Mexico

The present situation in Mexico is much the same: Some sectors have restrictions on foreign investment, and there have been some recent moves toward the control of technology tranfers, but on the whole policies on the access to foreign exchange and the repatriation of foreign investment income remain quite liberal. But, as in the case of the system of import licensing already discussed, enforcement is on a case-by-case basis and therefore is somewhat more changeable and arbitrary than in Brazil.

Government permission is required to begin business operations in Mexico. As in Brazil, petroleum is a government monopoly, including distribution of final products. In addition, the electricity, transportation, communications, basic petrochemicals, and some mining industries are closed to foreign investors. Neither country goes quite as far as the new Andean Group agreement, which prohibits foreign ownership in banking, insurance, advertising, and retailing as well. Since 1973, however, the laws governing "Mexicanization" of industry have been expanded.* New product expansion can only be carried out by minority-held foreign firms; in some industries (for example, secondary petrochemicals and motor vehicle parts) foreign ownership must be below 40 percent. The National Commission on Foreign Investment may make exceptions, of course. More than one observer of the Mexicanization program (which before 1973 used tax concessions as an incentive) considers it merely a form of "political tokenism" because there is no guarantee that a real transfer of power will occur simply because a stock transfer takes place (for example, King 1970: 64). Some exception must be made for those few cases where the government itself has purchased a majority share of a company.

In Mexico, foreign exchange has been freely available and no limits have been placed on profit repatriation. Neither have any restrictions been placed on local or foreign borrowing. A recent (1973) proclamation was made, however, on technology transfers. All agreements must be registered with the government, and as in the recent

---

*Before 1973, joint ventures were required only in a few industries, few of which have considered manufacturing.

Andean code, many "restrictive business practices" are forbidden.
These include export restrictions, exclusive grantbacks, tying clauses,
and excessive duration (about ten years). "Excessive compensation"
is also prohibited; currently, this being interpreted as rates above 3
percent of sales.

In summary, Brazil, in defiance of its reputation, in many ways
regulates foreign manufacturing firms and investments in greater detail than most Latin American countries. Mexico has also earned a
somewhat unjustified image for strongly nationalistic policies. Both
countries have generally created a favorable environment for foreign
investors in the postwar period while moving toward increasing their
public policy controls. This movement toward greater government
intervention in FDI and away from the classical prescriptions of free
trade is quite general in Latin America (Vaitsos 1973).

PATTERNS OF FDI IN BRAZIL AND MEXICO

It is the purpose of this section to review, compare, and contrast the extent and forms of FDI in Brazil and Mexico. The discussion covers the sources and amounts of FDI, the sectoral concentration, and the aggregate foreign ownership of these countries' manufacturing sectors. Then the topics of multinationals' growth patterns,
acquisition activity, and multinational conglomeration are examined.*

The Stock of FDI

In 1967 the total stock of foreign direct investment in Brazil
was about $3.7 billion; by 1972 it had risen to about $7 billion. About
70 percent of the stock of FDI was located in the manufacturing sector,
and roughly 75 percent was controlled by only four countries: the
United States (36 percent), Canada (17 percent), West Germany (14
percent), and France (7 percent). Although the amount of FDI in
Brazil seems large, even during the 1955-60 period (when the ratio
may have been highest), the inflow of FDI amounted to less than 3 percent of total Brazilian fixed capital investment (Leff 1968a). Most real
investment is in the form of buildings, roads, and agricultural improvements, particularly trees.

---

*This section borrows liberally from data originally presented
in the Newfarmer-Mueller report (1975), which was prepared for the
U.S. Senate Subcommittee on Multinational Corporations in conjunction
with Connor (1976).

Total FDI in Mexico has been smaller (only $2.8 billion in 1970), but as in Brazil most of it has gone into the manufacturing sector (74 percent in 1970). In both countries, the proportion being directed into manufacturing appears to be rising over time. Unlike Brazil, Mexican FDI originates mainly from only one country, the United States. In 1970, 79 percent of the stock of Mexican FDI was held by U.S. residents and 3 percent each by persons in the United Kingdom, Germany, or Switzerland.

The U.S. FDI in Brazil has been growing at an increasing rate since 1950 (Table 3.1). During the 1950-60 period, U.S. investment expanded at a rate of 4 percent annually; it then rose to 5 percent during 1960-66, even though during the years of political uncertainty and economic recession (1962-65) net investment was virtually zero; finally, FDI rose at an annual rate of about 12 percent over the years 1966-72. Most new U.S. direct investment since 1950 has been in manufacturing, though petroleum investments have also increased and in 1970 accounted for nearly 90 percent of that sector's foreign participation.

The U.S. FDI in Mexico has likewise increased since 1950, but its growth has been steadier than that in Brazil (Table 3.2). Although U.S. direct investments in mining have virtually stagnated, those in manufacturing grew about 11 percent per year throughout 1950-72. As a proportion of total U.S. investment, manufacturing has risen steadily from only 32 percent in 1950 to 69 percent in 1972.

In both Brazil and Mexico, U.S. manufacturing investments have been made in only a few major industry groups. In 1972 only four such industries accounted for 75 percent of all U.S. assets in Brazilian manufacturing: transportation equipment (24 percent), chemicals (25 percent), and electrical and nonelectrical machinery (26 percent) (Table 3.3). Food processing and rubber products accounted for an additional 6 percent each. In terms of sales, aggregate FDI concentration is just as high: These six industry groups were responsible for 86 percent of all 1972 sales of U.S. manufacturing firms. Moreover, fewer than 15 firms control the major part of U.S. manufacturing fixed assets or sales in Brazil. The sectoral concentration of U.S. manufacturing assets has increased slightly since 1966, when the same six industry groups accounted for only 85 percent of the total.

Most of the same industries have received the bulk of U.S. manufacturing FDI in Mexico (Table 3.4). In terms of total assets in 1972, only eight industry groups owned 86 percent of the total in U.S. manufacturing: chemical (30 percent), transportation equipment (12 percent), electrical and nonelectrical machinery (12 percent and 7 percent, respectively), primary and fabricated metals (10 percent), food manufacturing (8 percent), and rubber products (6 percent). These

TABLE 3.1

Brazil: Book Value of U.S. Foreign Direct Investment by Sector, Selected Years
(in millions of dollars)

Sector	1929		1946		1950		1960		1966		1972	
	Amount	Percent	Amount	Percent	Amount	Percent	Amount	Percent	Amount	Percent	Amount	Percent
Petroleum	23	12	45	14	112	17	76	8	69	6	169	7
Manufacturing	46	24	126	39	284	44	515	54	846	68	1,745	70
Mining	*	*	*	*	*	*	10	1	58	5	136	5
Trade	*	*	*	*	*	*	130	14	183	15	*	*
Public utilities	97	50	125	39	138	21	200	20	38	3	*	*
Other	28	14	27	8	110	17	23	3	53	4	440	18
Total	194	100	323	100	644	100	953	100	1,247	100	2,490	100

*Included in "Other" for the selected years.

Sources: Department of Commerce, U.S. Investments in the Latin American Economy, 1957 (Washington, D.C.: Government Printing Office, 1958) for years 1929, 1946, and 1950; Survey of Current Business, various issue for years 1960, 1962, and 1972.

TABLE 3.2

Mexico: Book Value of U.S. Foreign Direct Investment by Sector, Selected Years
(in millions of dollars)

Sector	1929		1946		1950		1960		1966		1972	
	Amount	Percent	Amount	Percent	Amount	Percent	Amount	Percent	Amount	Percent	Amount	Percent
Mining	230	34	111	35	121	29	130	16	103	9	124	6
Petroleum	206	30	7	2	13	3	32	4	42	3	32	2
Manufacturing	6	1	66	21	133	32	391	49	802	64	1,385	69
Public utilities	164	24	112	35	107	26	119	15	29	2	*	*
Agriculture	59	9	4	1	3	1	*	*	*	*	*	*
Other	18	3	16	5	38	9	124	16	266	29	451	23
Total	683	100	316	100	415	100	795	100	1,248	100	1,993	100

*Included in "Other" industries.

Sources: For years 1929, 1946, and 1950, U.S. Department of Commerce, U.S. Foreign Direct Investment in Latin America, 1957 (Washington D.C.: Government Printing Office, 1960), p. 180; Survey of Current Business, various issues for years 1960, 1966, and 1972.

TABLE 3.3

Brazil: Growth in Total Assets of Reporting U.S. Affiliates,
1960-72
(in thousands of dollars)

Industry	1960	1966	1972
Food	20,087	36,532	195,326
Textiles	*	*	*
Paper	14,274	30,827	106,800
Chemicals	105,857	189,259	785,702
Rubber	61,319	80,854	188,772
Stone, glass, and clay	23,127	51,811	97,392
Primary and fabricated metals	10,222	17,968	78,413
Nonelectrical machinery	62,280	118,677	440,021
Electrical machinery	39,389	169,530	364,405
Transportation	164,629	154,559	766,052
Instruments	4,897	10,401	49,527
Other	10,997	21,007	59,632
Total manufacturing	517,078	881,425	3,132,042
Petroleum and primary activities	664	4,114	4,864
Service and trade	171,092	208,587	654,693
All industries	688,834	1,094,126	3,791,599

*Included in "Other" to avoid disclosure.

Source: Special survey of the U.S. Senate Subcommittee on
Multinational Corporations.

same industries also were responsible for 89 percent of all 1972 sales
by U.S. manufacturing affiliates in Mexico. Thus, the level of industrial concentration of U.S. manufacturing FDI is somewhat lower than
Brazil's, but the pattern is quite similar. Transportation equipment
and machinery are relatively more important in Brazil, while chemicals and metals receive relatively more investment by U.S. MNCs in
Mexico. However, fewer than ten MNCs owned more than half the
assets of U.S. manufacturers in Mexico in 1972. Thus, by this measure, U.S. MNC asset concentration is higher in Mexican manufacturing than in Brazilian manufacturing.

The U.S. and other foreign firms have generally followed a
strategy of investing in the most capital-intensive and technology-in-

tensive industries in Brazil and Mexico. These same industries have
been the ones most favored by the earlier import substitution and more
recent export-promotion policies in the two countries. As a result,
MNCs have come to occupy a leading and often dominant position in
these manufacturing sectors.

Industrial Denationalization

Having examined the extent and distribution of U.S. FDI in Brazil and Mexico, it is important to analyze the cumulative effects of
that investment and relate U.S. operations to those of other MNCs.
In particular, the next few paragraphs discuss the extent and distribution of total foreign ownership and control (denationalization) of
Brazilian and Mexican industry in recent years.

TABLE 3.4

Mexico: Growth in Total Assets of Reporting U.S. Affiliates,
1960-72
(in thousands of dollars)

Industry	1960	1966	1972
Food	22,225	93,849	207,422
Textiles	0	21,794	35,161
Paper	16,821	37,083	103,541
Chemicals	166,457	372,720	763,249
Rubber	51,598	83,785	152,090
Stone, glass, and clay	5,336	32,866	74,022
Primary and fabricated metals	10,509	82,768	263,211
Nonelectrical machinery	27,531	82,012	184,913
Electrical machinery	35,762	117,613	315,026
Transportation	46,648	210,551	313,911
Instruments	1,866	3,792	46,769
Other	2,845	20,900	88,390
Total manufacturing	387,598	1,159,733	2,547,705
Petroleum and primary ac-tivities	2,944	31,924	25,034
Service and trade	41,809	100,867	201,119
All industries	432,351	1,292,524	2,773,858

Source: Special survey of the U.S. Senate Subcommittee on
Multinational Corporations.

Though usually small relative to their home-country operations, the affiliates of MNCs located in even semiindustrialized LDCs tend to be quite large by local standards. In Brazil in 1972, for example, of the largest 500 nonfinancial corporations, some 158 were foreign-owned (of which 59 were U.S.-owned), and another 92 were state-owned enterprises. But in the same year, there were 147 foreign-controlled (57 U.S.-controlled) firms among the 300 largest manufacturing firms (Table 3.5). Therefore, in 1972 half of the largest manufacturing firms were foreign-owned; this proportion has increased since 1966, when only 45 percent were foreign-owned. Moreover, in both years foreign-owned firms were larger in asset size than the Brazilian-owned firms among the top 300 manufacturers.

As was the case with U.S. MNCs, the total foreign ownership (denationalization) of manufacturing assets is quite widespread. Of 15 Brazilian major industry groups in 1972, 6 were at least 50 percent denationalized (Table 3.6). They were electrical machinery, nonelectrical machinery, transport equipment, rubber, chemicals, and "miscellaneous." The extent of aggregate manufacturing denationalization (about 50 percent) has remained virtually constant among the largest 300 firms during 1966-72, but the asset share of state-owned enterprises has nearly doubled over the period (from 8 to 15 percent), mainly in steel, petroleum refining, and industrial chemicals. Thus, the share of the privately owned manufacturing firms has markedly declined.

Although the share of all MNCs in manufacturing sales has remained fairly constant, the U.S. MNC share is increasing. From 1966 to 1972, U.S. MNCs' sales of manufactured products rose from 13 to 20 percent of Brazil's total. Increases were seen in chemicals, metals, machinery, and transport equipment.

Both the level and rate of denationalization in Mexico's industrial sector are somewhat higher than Brazil's, but the pattern is startlingly similar in many respects. Among the largest 500 nonfinancial firms in Mexico in 1970, there were 161 affiliates of MNCs, or 32 percent (the same proportion as in Brazil). But among the 300 largest manufacturing companies, exactly half were foreign-controlled (again, the same as in Brazil) (Table 3.7). Furthermore, foreign firms were larger in asset size than the national firms; thus, 52 percent of Mexico's 1972 manufacturing assets were MNC-owned among the largest 300 firms. State-owned firms controlled 16 percent of these assets, leaving only one-third in private, national hands.

If the extent of denationalization in Mexico is measured by the foreign share of value added in manufacturing GDP, then in 1970 MNCs contributed only 23 percent (of which U.S. MNCs were responsible for 70 percent). Unlike the case in Brazil, however, that share is apparently growing quite fast, for in 1962 the comparable figure was

TABLE 3.5

Brazil: Ownership of the Largest 300 Manufacturing Firms, [a] 1966 and 1972

| Size Class of Firm | Foreign | | | | | | Private | | Brazilian | | | |
| | United States | | Other Foreign | | Total Foreign | | | | State | | Total | |
	1966	1972	1966	1972	1966	1972	1966	1972	1966	1972	1966	1972
Top 100	27	19	31	40	58	59	35	32	7	9	42	41
101 to 200	23	20	25	28	48	48	51	50	1	2	52	52
201 to 300	16	18	12	22	28	40	70	57	2	3	72	60
Total	66	57	68	90[b]	134	147	156	139	10	14	166	153
Percent	22	19	23	30	45	49	52	46	3	5	55	51
Average size[c]	28	137	37	174	33	161	23	118	86	600	26	154

[a] Includes 13 firms in petroleum refining.

[b] A breakdown of these firms by country of ownership is as follows: Germany, 23; France, 16; Italy, 14; Britain, 11; Japan, 9; Canada, 7; Argentina, 1; other (most European), 9.

[c] 1966 in billions of cruzeiros; 1972 in billions of new cruzeiros.

Sources: This table was compiled from an analysis of the "Quem é Quem na Econômia Brasileira." Distribution of 500 largest firms for 1972 in Visão, August 1973 and for 1966 in Visão, September 1967. Those firms where foreign ownership was greater than 25 percent were classified as foreign, except when the state was the joint venture partner. Ownership was researched using: Geraldo Banas, ed., Brasil Industrial (São Paulo: Editora Banas, various years); Jean Bernet, Interinvest Guide 1972 (Rio de Janeiro: Editora Interinvest, 1973); Brazil, Ministerio da Industria e do Comércio, Levantamento das Sociedades Nacionais com Participacão de Capital Estrangeiro (Rio de Janeiro: Departamento Nacional do Comércio, 1968); Brazil, Ministerio da Industria e da Comércio, Cadastro Nacional (Rio de Janeiro: Divisão de Autorizãcoes e Cadastro, 1969); Brazil Report 1972 (Rio de Janeiro: Visão Editora, 1973); Department of Commerce, Trade Lists for Brazil 1972 (Washington, D.C.: U.S. Government Printing Office, 1973); Moody's Industrial Manual (New York: various years); Securities Exchange Commission, 10K, Annual Public Reports; Visão (Rio de Janeiro: Visão Editora, various years); Who Owns Whom? (Oxford: Staples, 1972-73).

TABLE 3.6

Brazil: Share of the Largest 300 Manufacturing Firms by Industry, 1972
(percent of assets)

Industry	Total in Sample	Foreign			Brazilian		
		United States	Other Foreign	Total	Private	State	Total
Nonmetallic ores	29	11	11	22	78	0	78
Metal fabrication	47	4	21	25	25	51	76
Iron and steel	18	0	15	15	16	70	86
Nonferrous metals	8	21	40	61	39	0	39
Other	21	9	36	45	55	0	55
Machinery	14	34	40	74	26	0	26
Motors and industrial equipment	12	29	40	69	31	0	31
Electrical machinery	16	22	56	78	22	0	22
Transport equipment	28	37	47	84	12	4	16
Motor vehicles	8	42	58	100	0	0	0
Vehicle parts	8	53	8	61	40	0	40
Wood, paper, furniture	17	10	19	29	71	0	71
Rubber	3	100	0	100	0	0	0
Chemicals	51	34	35	69	19	12	31
Chemicals and petroleum	31	35	30	65	16	18	34
Plastics	8	41	30	71	29	0	29
Pharmaceutical and others	7	35	65	100	0	0	0
Textiles	27	6	38	44	56	0	56
Food and beverages	41	2	30	32	67	0	67
Other*	14	3	49	52	48	0	48
Petroleum refining	13	8	4	12	6	82	83
Total including petroleum	300	14	28	42	28	30	58
Total manufacturing only	287	16	34	50	35	15	50

*Includes leather, tobacco, printing and publishing, and "other."

Sources: This table was compiled from an analysis of the "Quem é Quem na Econômia Brasileira." Distribution of 500 largest firms for 1972 in Visão, August 1973 and for 1966 in Visão, September 1967. Those firms where foreign ownership was greater than 25 percent were classified as foreign, except when the state was the joint venture partner. Ownership was researched using: Geraldo Banas, ed., Brasil Industrial (São Paulo: Editora Banas, various years); Jean Bernet, Interinvest Guide 1972 (Rio de Janeiro: Editora Interinvest, 1972); Brazil, Ministério da Indústria e do Comércio, Levantamento das Sociedades Nacionals com Participacão de Capital Estrangeiro (Rio de Janeiro: Departamento Nacional do Comércio, 1968); Brazil, Ministério da Indústria e da Comércio, Cadastro Nacional (Rio de Janeiro: Divasão de Autorizãcoes e Cadastro, 1969); Brazil Report 1972 (Rio de Janeiro: Visão Editora, 1973); Department of Commerce, Trade Lists for Brazil 1972 (Washington, D.C.: U.S. Government Printing Office, 1973); Moody's Industrial Manual (New York: various years); Securities Exchange Commission, 10K, Annual Public Reports; Visão Editora, various years); Who Owns Whom? (Oxford: Staples, 1972-73).

TABLE 3.7

Mexico: Ownership Distribution of 300 Largest Manufacturers,[a] 1972

(number and percent)

Size Class	Foreign			Mexican		
	United States	Other Foreign	Total	Private	State	Total
Top 100	39	22	61	27	12	39
101 to 200	31	15	46	43	11	54
201 to 300	27	16	43	54	3	57
Total	97	53	150	124	26	150
Percent	32	18	50	41	9	50
Average size[b]	142.3	115.2	132.8	98.9	235.4	122.6

[a]Includes 20 mining firms.
[b]Millions of pesos.

Sources: The original list was taken from J. M. Christman, ed., "500 Largest Companies in Mexico," Business Trends, 1973. Firms were identified by percent of foreign ownership and country of investor. Those firms where foreign ownership was greater than 25 percent were classified as foreign, except where the joint venture partner was the state. Within the foreign sector, residence was accorded to the country with the highest percentage. Research for each company on the 500 list was done using: J. Bernet, ed., Guía Interinvest 1972 (Rio de Janeiro: Editora Interinvest, 1973); Business Trends, December 1973; Comité Bilateral de Hombres de Negocios, Inversiones extranjeras privadas directas en México (Mexico: Confederación Patronal, 1971); A. Sepúlveda and A. Chumacero, La inversión extranjera en México (Mexico: Fondo de Cultura, 1973); U.S. Department of Commerce, Trade Lists Mexico (Washington, D.C.: Government Printing Office, 1971); Who Owns Whom? (London: Roskill & Company, 1973).

TABLE 3.8

Mexico: Largest 300 MNCs and Mexican Manufacturing Firms in 1972 and Percent Assets Held by Largest Firms in Each Industry
(percent of assets)

Industry	Total	Foreign			Mexican		
		United States	Other	Total	Private	State	Total
Mining	20	38	6	44	17	39	56
Food	50	20	6	26	67	7	74
Tobacco	5	34	66	100	0	0	0
Textiles	18	0	5	5	73	22	95
Lumber	2	39	61	100	0	0	0
Paper	15	22	29	51	39	10	49
Printing	3	38	0	38	30	32	62
Chemicals	48	54	14	68	12	20	32
Rubber	3	100	0	100	0	0	0
Leather	1	0	0	0	100	0	100
Stone, glass, and clay	26	9	23	32	66	2	68
Primary metals	27	31	10	41	35	24	59
Fabricated metals	17	48	8	56	33	11	44
Nonelectrical machinery	14	36	58	95	5	0	5
Electrical machinery	25	35	25	60	24	16	40
Transportation	18	70	9	79	8	13	21
Instruments	7	65	35	100	0	0	0
Other	1	100	0	100	0	0	0
Total manufacturing	300	36	16	52	32	16	48

Sources: The original list was taken from J. M. Christman, ed., "500 Largest Companies in Mexico," Business Trends, 1973. Firms were identified by percent of foreign ownership and country of investor. Those firms where foreign ownership was greater than 25 percent were classified as foreign, except where the joint venture partner was the state. Within the foreign sector, residence was accorded to the country with the highest percentage. Research for each company on the 500 list was done using: J. Bernet, ed., Guía Interinvest 1972 (Rio de Janeiro: Editora Interinvest, 1973); Business Trends, December 1973; Comité Bilateral de Hombres de Negocios, Inversiones extranjeras privadas directas en México (Mexico: Confederación Patronal, 1971); A. Sepúlveda and A. Chumacero, La inversión extranjera en México (Mexico: Fondo de Cultura, 1973); U.S. Department of Commerce, Trade Lists Mexico (Washington, D.C.: Government Printing Office, 1971); Who Owns Whom? (London: Roskill & Company, 1973).

only 18 percent (Table 3.8). If one eliminates the sales of manufacturing firms with fewer than ten employees, the sales figures of MNCs
were 38 percent (1962) and 45 percent (1970). Although strictly comparable data are not available, most of the same industry groups have
been effectively denationalized in both Brazil and Mexico. Among
the largest 300 manufacturing firms in Mexico, 11 of 18 Mexican major
industry groups had 50 percent or more of their assets foreign-owned
in 1972. As in Brazil, these industries included electrical machinery,
nonelectrical machinery, transportation equipment, rubber, chemicals,
and "miscellaneous," but in addition the list covers lumber, paper,
tobacco, fabricated metals, and precision instruments. Hence, the
industrial pattern of denationalization in Mexico is similar, but more
inclusive, than Brazil's.

Growth and Conglomeration of MNCs

Data collected on about 230 subsidiaries of U.S. MNCs in Brazil
show that rates of sales growth were both high (8 percent per year in
1960-66) and accelerating (23 percent annually in 1966-72). These expansion rates paralleled but exceeded the general sales' rates of
growth in Brazilian industry. But not all growth was purely internal
in these affiliates; at least 25 percent was due to acquisition activity
by MNCs. Up to 1972, roughly 30 percent of all these subsidiaries
had been acquired rather than newly established, but the acquisition
rate (the ratio of U.S.-acquired firms to all new firms) is increasing:
Before 1960 the rate was less than 30 percent, but after 1965 the rate
was over 50 percent (Table 3.9). Since 1972, more than 20 takeovers
by U.S. firms have occurred each year.* Throughout the period,
more than 60 percent of these firms have been acquired from private
Brazilian parties. Few of these mergers occurred because the Brazilian companies were failing. On the contrary, in the year prior to
being taken over, three-fourths of the acquired firms were making
profits and two-thirds were highly profitable (earning more than 9 percent after-tax profits on their assets).
      Because of the steady growth path of the Mexican economy gen-
erally, the 370 U.S. subsidiaries expanded somewhat faster on average during 1960-72 (17 percent annually) than those in Brazil (only 15
percent annually). In almost every industry U.S. affiliates grew
faster than the total industry. As in Brazil, the Mexican subsidiaries'

------

*For a particularly good study of the effects of merger activity
of MNCs on denationalization in the Brazilian electrical equipment industry, see Newfarmer (1977).

TABLE 3.9

Brazil: Percent of New U.S. Manufacturing Affiliates Established
by Acquisition

Time Period	Percent of New Affiliates Established by Acquisition	Total Number of Newly Established Affiliates
Prior to 1945	0	28
1946–50	9	11
1951–55	22	22
1956–60	33	36
1961–65	38	16
1966–70	52	46
1971–73	61	18
Total, all periods	33	177

Source: Special survey of the U.S. Senate Subcommittee on
Multinational Corporations.

growth was partially (at least 20 percent) attributable to takeovers of
mainly privately held Mexican firms (more than 80 percent). After
1961, more than 60 percent of all new subsidiaries of U.S. MNCs were
acquired rather than formed (Table 3.10). In the year prior to acquisition roughly half of the Mexican firms were highly profitable (making
at least 9 percent profit on assets) while only one-fourth did not make
profits. Based on a new series of foreign acquisitions by U.S. firms
reported by the Federal Trade Commission (FTC) since 1972, the trend
is toward greater merger-induced denationalization in Brazil. The
U.S. MNCs acquired 11 firms in Brazil in 1972 but made 50 more acquisitions during 1973–74. In Mexico, on the other hand, the acquisition rate has declined sharply since 1972. The U.S. MNCs acquired
only 7 Mexican firms during 1973–74.

The aspects of multinational conglomeration described here are
evidence relating to the centralization of multinational control and the
extent of intrafirm trade integration. One overt sign of central headquarters control is the high proportion of voting stock retained by the
parent organization in the face of host country (especially Mexican)
pressures to adopt joint venture partners. On the other hand, the
lack of highly developed stock markets (particularly in Mexico) may
have contributed to the high proportion of majority-owned U.S. affiliates:
more than 85 percent in Brazil and more than 80 percent in Mexico in

1972. Within manufacturing, however, there is a trend toward lower levels of equity ownership among the more newly established subsidiaries.

In addition to voting rights, the ownership of the stock of long-term debt of foreign affiliates provides another lever of control for the parent organization. Among the Brazilian affiliates, U.S. interests owned about 85 percent of the long-term debt; the parent corporations directly or indirectly controlled nearly half. In Mexico the respective ratios were 79 percent and 41 percent in 1972. It should be noted that while almost all U.S. affiliates are corporations and are therefore required to issue voting stock, not all affiliates have long-term debt. In 1972 only about 25 percent of all Brazilian and 20 percent of all Mexican manufacturing subsidiaries included some long-term debt among their liabilities. On average all these firms' 1972 long-term debt constituted less than 20 percent of their total liabilities, but among those affiliates with some long-term debt the proportion was much greater, about 60 to 75 percent. Therefore, for those U.S. affiliates that obtained at least some long-term loans, the parent corporation had discretion in determining repayment rates and interest payments on an amount that represented about 18 to 20 percent of their affiliate's total assets. There is some evidence from our sample that this form of affiliate control is used more frequently with newly established subsidiaries than with older ones; in both countries,

TABLE 3.10

Mexico: Percent of New U.S. Manufacturing Affiliates Established
by Acquisition

Time Period	Percent of New Affiliates Established by Acquisition	Total Number of Newly Established Affiliates
Prior to 1945	9	35
1946–50	6	18
1951–55	11	18
1956–60	39	54
1961–65	43	60
1966–70	64	77
1971–72	75	32
Total, all periods	43	294

Source: Special survey of the U.S. Senate Subcommittee on Multinational Corporations.

the year of formation of the MNC's affiliate was negatively correlated with both (1) the proportion of firms having at least some long-term debt owned by the parent and (2) the size of that debt expressed as a percentage of the affiliate's total assets.

One of the more tangible measures of the degree of intrafirm planning and integration among the many divisions of the modern MNC is the extent of intrafirm pure trade. In Brazil and Mexico the export propensities of firms, though increasing, are generally quite low. Exports comprised less than 1 percent of total sales of U.S. manufacturing affiliates in both countries in 1960; by 1972 export intensity had risen to 3 percent in Brazil and to 5 percent in Mexico (Tables 3.11 and 3.12). But what is remarkable is the very large proportion of those exports being sold within the parent organization: more than 70 percent in Brazil and more than 80 percent in Mexico in 1972. Moreover, both these ratios have increased since 1960.

The situation with respect to the importation of production inputs is in many ways the obverse. While only a minority of U.S. affiliates in Brazil and Mexico export any of their production, the majority import. Further, the manufacturing subsidiaries of U.S. corporations have displayed a tendency to import a nonincreasing share of their total material production inputs (Tables 3.13 and 3.14). In Brazil, where import substitution at the producer intermediate and capital goods levels had begun in the 1950s, these subsidiaries imported about one-fourth of their inputs during the 1966-72 period; in Mexico the import ratio declined from nearly one-half to less than one-third over the same time span. And finally, in both countries the proportion of imported material inputs obtained from within these affiliates' own multinational complex has not increased over time. In Brazil the parent organization supplied 50 percent of all imported inputs in 1972, down from 65 percent in 1966; in Mexico the same ratio was 60 percent in both years. Therefore, international intrafirm import integration is somewhat less encompassing in Brazil than in Mexico and shows some signs of declining in the former country.

However, it should be recognized that great scope for transfer pricing still remains: Not only is the intrafirm export share tending to rise over time, but also the absolute and real value of both intrafirm exports and imports is increasing for manufacturing affiliates of U.S. MNCs. Thus, the host country subsidiaries of MNCs can satisfy both the government objectives of increasing the "local content" of their operations and the export propensity of their domestic industries and simultaneously satisfy their headquarters' goal of increasing the real value of intra-MNC trade.

TABLE 3.11

Brazil: U.S. Affiliate Manufactured Exports and Intrafirm International Trade
(in thousands of dollars)

Industry	1960 Total Exports	1960 To Parent Organization	1966 Total Exports	1966 To Parent Organization	1972 Total Exports	1972 To Parent Organization	Percent 1960 Intra-Firm Trade	Percent 1972 Intra-Firm Trade
Food	0	0	873	0	2,350	391	0	17
Textiles	*	*	*	*	*	*	*	*
Paper	0	0	1,260	14	2,947	85	0	3
Chemicals	382	382	484	474	6,204	3,894	100	63
Rubber	0	0	80	20	1,191	557	0	47
Stone, glass, and clay	0	0	0	0	2,663	0	0	0
Primary and fabricated metals	5	0	346	60	2,151	218	0	10
Nonelectrical machinery	543	25	5,829	4,181	31,455	24,431	5	78
Electrical machinery	684	684	1,823	1,416	17,533	13,959	100	80
Transportation	0	0	990	990	27,508	24,247	0	89
Instruments	22	22	295	295	1,211	1,211	100	100
Other	0	0	0	0	3,711	3,644	0	98
Total manufacturing	1,636	1,113	11,980	7,450	98,924	72,637	68	73

*Included in "Other" to avoid disclosure.

Source: Special survey of the U.S. Senate Subcommittee on Multinational Corporations.

TABLE 3.12

Mexico: U.S. Affiliate Manufactured Exports and Intrafirm International Trade
(in millions of dollars)

Industry	1960 Total Exports	1960 To Parent Organization	1966 Total Exports	1966 To Parent Organization	1972 Total Exports	1972 To Parent Organization	1960 Percent Intrafirm Trade	1972 Percent Intrafirm Trade
Food	35	0	2,601	2,320	7,093	5,446	0	77
Textiles	0	0	0	0	0	0	0	0
Paper	0	0	0	0	0	0	0	0
Chemicals	5,102	2,752	12,472	8,222	32,941	18,466	54	56
Rubber	0	0	107	94	520	394	0	76
Stone, glass, and clay	0	0	628	0	1,616	154	0	10
Primary and fabricated metals	0	0	35	0	2,361	1,310	0	55
Nonelectrical machinery	43	17	488	444	7,320	5,093	39	70
Electrical machinery	56	0	599	293	28,529	25,498	0	89
Transportation	0	0	4,379	4,379	40,514	46,480	0	100
Instruments	185	185	875	875	8,989	8,949	100	100
Other	0	0	0	0	1,188	934	0	79
Total manufacturing	5,421	2,954	22,184	16,627	137,071	112,724	54	82

Source: Special survey of the U.S. Senate Subcommittee on Multinational Corporations.

TABLE 3.13

Brazil: Sources of Material Inputs of U.S. Affiliates
(in thousands of dollars)

Value of Material Inputs and Their Sources	Total	Food	Textiles	Paper	Chemicals	Rubber	Stone, Glass, and Clay	Metals	Nonelectrical Machinery	Electrical Machinery	Transportation	Instruments	Other
1972													
Total material costs	1,173,884	53,842	*	32,881	217,553	114,648	15,955	27,894	115,159	108,292	482,668	457	4,535
Of which:													
Parent supplied	138,512	840	*	578	52,262	4,649	906	2,027	55,318	12,407	8,981	256	288
Other imports	138,171	4,823	*	2,264	68,089	3,667	2,020	2,490	17,874	30,902	4,999	150	893
Percent from parent	12	2	*	2	24	4	6	7	48	12	2	56	6
Percent imported	12	9	*	7	31	3	13	9	16	29	1	33	20
1966													
Total material costs	330,469	8,635	*	5,965	87,782	67,633	7,765	9,598	24,729	43,052	94,633	102	575
Of which:													
Parent supplied	48,060	0	*	64	16,470	1,985	179	387	10,986	2,170	15,810	9	0
Other imports	27,507	20	*	481	15,923	1,606	362	733	3,778	3,417	1,121	9	57
Percent from parent	15	0	*	1	24	3	2	4	44	5	17	11	0
Percent imported	8	0	*	8	23	2	5	8	15	8	1	11	10

*Included in "Other" to avoid disclosure.

Source: Special survey of the U.S. Senate Subcommittee on Multinational Corporations.

TABLE 3.14

Mexico: Sources of Material Inputs of U.S. Affiliates
(in thousands of dollars)

Value of Material Inputs and Their Sources	Total	Food	Tex-tiles	Paper	Chemi-cals	Rubber	Stone, Glass, and Clay	Metals	Nonelec-trical Ma-chinery	Electri-cal Ma-chinery	Trans-porta-tion	In-stru-ments	Other
1972													
Total material costs	1,145,081	144,987	14,104	46,418	254,124	46,301	19,000	41,377	35,853	89,406	418,238	4,284	30,989
Of which:													
Supplied by parent	207,708	1,473	76	356	38,904	2,835	3,341	1,181	11,384	15,013	130,963	1,757	425
Other imports	152,492	3,175	750	2,667	76,054	2,480	2,980	2,609	8,079	19,285	33,489	613	313
Percent from parent	18	1	1	1	15	6	18	3	32	17	31	41	1
Percent imported	13	2	5	6	30	5	16	6	23	22	8	14	1
1966													
Total material costs	489,338	52,823	4,193	12,595	120,431	22,225	6,104	10,045	13,198	31,316	213,054	355	2,999
Of which:													
Parent supplied	142,717	290	41	172	39,362	2,442	464	234	4,120	2,709	92,846	27	10
Other imports	95,557	195	454	733	43,362	3,974	2,044	1,046	3,853	8,869	30,889	138	
Percent from parent	29	1	1	1	33	11	8	2	31	9	44	8	0
Percent imported	20	0	11	6	36	18	33	10	29	28	15	39	0

Source: Special survey of the U.S. Senate Subcommittee on Multinational Corporations.

Concluding Remarks

In summary, the process of industrial denationalization by foreign multinational corporations (unwittingly perhaps), instigated by
official policies designed for other purposes, continues and deepens
by means of a variety of mechanisms. The relatively permissive climate and regulations governing the movement of foreign capital into
the manufacturing sectors of Brazil and Mexico in recent decades,
coupled with policies designed to encourage import substitution, export promotion, and the formation of strong domestic linkages, have
facilitated the transfer of productive assets into foreign hands in many
of the most dynamic industries. Entry by MNCs has increasingly occurred by means of merger rather than new formation. Once established, the affiliates of MNCs are manipulated by the parent corporation through a wide variety of levers. In this chapter I documented
only three measurable means of integration and control: management
and financial control via direct ownership of voting rights, the ownership of long-term debt instruments, and intrafirm trade. Many other
mechanisms for global integration of MNCs exist, but these are probably the main economic ones.

Although the facts assembled here throw a more penetrating
light on the extent of denationalization in Brazil and Mexico, the general outlines of the phenomenon have been readily apparent to scholars
and national policy makers for some time. In general, the success of
MNCs vis-a-vis locally owned firms has been attributed to some unique
and superior features of MNCs stemming from their specifically multinational characteristics. Superior management practices, possession
of advanced technology, and privileged access to international financial markets are often cited in this context. The discussion in the next
section, however, suggests that the problem of entrenchment of MNCs
is more deeply rooted. Continuing denationalization appears to be intimately connected to the relatively inflexible structures of the local
markets and in particular to massive competitive imperfections in
those markets.

THE MARKET STRUCTURES OF BRAZIL, MEXICO,
AND THE UNITED STATES

In the preceding section we examined the methods of entry,
forms of multinational conglomeration, and positions of dominance of
MNCs in the economies of Brazil and Mexico. Some of those topics
bear on the nature of competition in those countries, particularly the
facts presented on acquisitions by MNCs and the many potential levers
of centralized control poised over MNC subsidiaries. We also found

that U.S. MNCs tend to cluster in only a few major industry groups. In this section, I present and analyze some original and richly detailed statistics on the market structures of Brazil's and Mexico's manufacturing sectors. In addition, I compare the market structures of these two countries with each other and with the structures of comparable U.S. industries. These data throw considerable light on the market environments in which U.S. MNCs operate abroad. Moreover, the analysis suggests that the MNCs may be the causal link in the observed similarities in industrial structures.* That these aspects of multinational involvement have not received more attention in the past can be largely ascribed to the informational vacuum existing in the LDCs on the structures of their markets.

Sources of Data

Data deficiencies are commonplace in nearly all fields of specialization. Indeed, the near impossibility of performing controlled experiments in the social sciences implies that measurement and testing must proceed using historical data often collected for purposes unrelated to the particular objectives of the research at hand. The information on the ownership of the 500 largest Brazilian and Mexican corporations presented above, for example, was painstakingly garnered from manuals and directories aimed primarily at aiding businessmen operating in those countries. Clearly, data limitations constraining economists examining the multinational corporation are especially acute relative to those working on problems of U.S. industrial organization or international trade and finance.

The data employed in this and the remaining chapters were derived primarily from an unprecedented special survey of 197 U.S. MNCs and more than 600 of their subsidiaries sponsored by the U.S. Senate Subcommittee on Multinational Corporations.[†] There are two

---

*Most of the remainder of this chapter first appeared in 1977 as Staff Paper No. 120, "The Shaping of Market Structures by Multinationals," by John M. Connor and Willard F. Mueller (Madison, Wis.: Department of Agricultural Economics, University of Wisconsin).

[†]The subcommittee, chaired by Senator Frank Church, possessed but did not finally exercise subpoena powers. Response to the questionnaire was nonetheless unusually high. In both Mexico and Brazil the special-survey coverage exceeded 80 percent of the 1972 manufacturing operations of U.S. MNCs, whether measured by net book value or by sales. For a detailed discussion of sampling methods, response rates, and coverage, see Appendix A.

types of data: One deals with U.S.-owned affiliates' market shares,
advertising expenditures, and research and development; the other is
based on their "products," both principal and secondary, as defined
by the Standard Industrial Classification (SIC) system.*

Although the quality of the data is quite high, several caveats
are in order. First, the response rate to the questionnaire varied across industries. Based on a comparison of the 1972 sales of majority-
owned affiliates in the special survey with those affiliates in the Department of Commerce's annual survey of U.S. companies' overseas
investments, the response rate averaged 80 percent in Brazil and 86
percent in Mexico in the manufacturing sector. Coverage was below
average among affiliates of MNCs in the food-processing and metals
industries but was high in rubber products and transportation equipment in both countries.[†] Second, coverage is uneven across the Latin
American countries' industries because U.S. MNCs are quite selective in the industrial distribution of their direct investments. In general, the data are most complete for industries in which MNCs are
most prominent. These usually are industries that are relatively
capital- and technology-intensive or are producing goods appealing to
affluent consumers. Thus, fairly comprehensive information is available for many of the food, rubber, chemicals, electrical equipment,
and machinery industries. But for many of the other industries still
largely in local hands, coverage is relatively incomplete; examples
here include textiles, clothing, wood, furniture, printing, leather,
and nonmetallic minerals. Third, the responding U.S. MNCs generally
were larger than the nonrespondents, though all survey companies
were among the top 500 U.S. industrials in 1972. Furthermore, MNCs
with larger holdings in Brazil and Mexico tended to reply with somewhat greater frequency than those with relatively small foreign affiliates. Despite the above data characteristics, they provide the most
comprehensive and accurate description available to date of the industrial market structures of any LDC.[‡]

---

*The coding system used throughout this book is the new 1972
basis as found in the Numerical List of Manufactured Products (MC72-
1.2) prepared by the U.S. Department of Commerce (Washington,
D.C.: Government Printing Office, 1973).

[†]For details on the response at the major industry group level,
see Newfarmer and Mueller (1975: 194-96).

[‡]White's (1974b) study of Pakistan provides concentration and
profit data for several manufacturing industries. The Fajnzylber
(1970, 1975) estimates of four plant-concentration ratios in Brazil
(1968) and Mexico (1970) are valuable additions to the literature.
Somewhat less comprehensive efforts are available for Kenya and

U.S. MNC Market Shares

Most subsidiaries of U.S. MNCs control very substantial shares of the markets in which they operate. Among the Brazilian manufacturing affiliates in 1972, nearly one-fourth reported market shares for their principal products of 50 percentage points or more and one-half of the firms reported principal product market shares of at least 25 percent.* These are considerably larger individual product market shares than are held by firms in the United States. In a study of 60 of the 100 largest U.S. manufacturing companies in 1967, Shepherd (1972) estimated that only 27 percent of the firms had market shares for their primary products of at least 25 percentage points. Because only a proportion (30 percent) of the responding U.S. parents of the Latin American subsidiaries were among the 100 largest corporations in 1972 and because principal product market shares generally decline with lower sales position, it is apparent that the sample U.S. MNCs held considerably more entrenched market positions in Brazil than they did in their U.S. markets.[†]

The distribution of market share levels of products sold by affiliates of U.S. MNCs tends to vary considerably across manufacturing industries. Table 3.15 shows the average 1972 market shares of over 900 products sold by U.S. manufacturing subsidiaries located in Brazil or Mexico.[‡] About two-thirds of the foreign affiliates queried in

---

Korea, by House (1973) and Nam (1975), respectively. A useful contrast is provided by the case of Chile (Zeitlin 1974).

*Respondents were asked to provide their subsidiaries' market-share data for each of their five-digit products in three years: 1960, 1966, and 1972. In addition, for 1972 only, they were asked to identify by name their principal rivals in each of their markets.

By "principal product" I mean the single five-digit SIC product accounting for the largest amount of dollar sales in 1972. The entire sample of 625 subsidiaries averaged slightly more than two such five-digit SIC products each.

[†]Only 28 percent of the 269 MNCs, respondents plus nonrespondents, with Mexican or Brazilian affiliates were in the top 100 of the Fortune 500 in 1972.

[‡]Consistent with Department of Commerce practice in reporting data on MNCs, I normally follow the convention of omitting petroleum (major industry group 29) from the manufacturing sector because in Brazil and Mexico foreign companies are not permitted to refine petroleum. In Brazil, the state-owned firm Petrobras has a monopoly in petroleum refining but holds only 20 percent or less of the market for finished petroleum products. In Mexico, the state-owned enter-

the special survey supplied product market share estimates directly.*
By comparing the sales and market share data of firms producing
the same products in the same country, it was a straightforward matter to infer many additional market share figures for firms that did
not respond directly. In total, Brazilian affiliate market share estimates are available for 80 percent of all responding U.S. affiliate
sales in 1972; in Mexico this coverage is 74 percent.

In Brazil the industries with exceptionally high average market
shares are the same industries that are most heavily occupied by
MNCs: food processing, chemicals (except drugs and soaps), rubber
products, nonelectrical machinery, electrical equipment, transportation equipment, and precision instruments. The nonmetallic minerals
and fabricated metals industry groups, though not dominated by MNCs,
also exhibit relatively high average market shares. The low level of
involvement of U.S. MNCs in several major industry groups (for example, textiles, apparel, wood, printing, and leather) does not per-

---

prise Pemex has a monopoly on both the refining and distribution stages
for petroleum, but a few U.S. affiliates in Mexico are permitted to
manufacture petroleum-based products that are considered chemicals
under the Mexican industrial coding system. Therefore, where the
petroleum industry data can be separated from the rest, as in Table
3.15, I include the petroleum subsidiaries' responses because they
may be of interest to other researchers.

Also in Table 3.15 but in no subsequent tables, separate plants
of MNCs producing the same products in the same country that happened to be distinct corporations were consolidated and treated as
though a single entity. The industry groups affected were 32 in Brazil
and 204, 208, 26, 281, 289, and 32 in Mexico. This procedure raised
reported average shares by an average of 4.6 percent in the seven
groups.

*These data were often derived from relatively sophisticated mar-
ket surveys available to headquarters or local personnel. However,
many large, diversified companies initially reported their shares at
the three- or four-digit levels, and many could not give the shares of
their minor products. (These were then coded with a 1 percent share
if sales were quite small.) On the other hand, a few smaller and
more specialized companies reported their shares on a finer basis
(for example, seven-digit SIC). In many cases, further contact with
the reporters resulted in more accurate estimates. But on the whole
I believe that only a small minority of the market share figures are
biased and that the biases remaining are generally downward. Comparable market share data for the parent corporations are not available.

TABLE 3.15

Average Market Shares of Affiliates of U.S. MNCs in the Brazilian and Mexican Manufacturing Sectors, 1972

		Brazil				Mexico			
SIC	Industry	Number of Five-Digit Products	Average Five-Digit Market Share[a] (percent)	Distribution of Sales[b] ($ millions)	Percentage Sales[c]	Number of Five-Digit Products	Average Five-Digit Market Share[a] (percent)	Distribution of Sales[b] ($ millions)	Percentage Sales
20	Grain products (204)	3	51	50	2.1	12	26	126	5.5
	Beverages (208)	6	36	68	2.9	4	18	44	1.9
	Other food	11[d]	32[d]	47[d]	2.0[d]	46	25	143	6.3
21	Tobacco					3	9	49	2.2
22	Textiles	6	20	23	1.0	4	11	19	0.8
23	Apparel	0	–	–	–	3	14	1	0.0
24, 25	Wood and furniture	d	d	d	d	7	23	8	0.4
26	Paper	13[d]	19[d]	78[d]	3.3[d]	31	23	96	4.2
27	Printing	d	d	d	d	6	33	11	0.5
28	Industrial inorganic chemicals (281)	10	31	32	1.4	25	44	53	2.3
	Plastics and synthetics (282)	13	20	67	2.8	20	38	134	5.9
	Drugs (283)	79	8	156	6.6	85	11	137	6.0
	Soaps and cosmetics (284)	20	11	31	1.3	37	18	160	7.0
	Other chemicals	42	28	180	7.6	61	33	123	5.4
29	Petroleum	24	20	1,187	–	5	28	21	–

Industry								
30 Tires (301)	13	24	209	8.9	18	21	138	6.1
31 Other rubber and plastic	6	39	31	1.3	10	46	20	0.8
Leather	d	d	d	d	d	d	d	d
32 Stone, clay, and glass	9	31	58	2.5	19	38	44	1.9
33 Primary metals	11	17	34	1.4	16	35	31	1.4
34 Fabricated metals	15	32	29	1.2	26	41	70	3.1
35 Industrial machinery (355, 356)	12	38	22	0.9	22	30	23	1.0
Office and computer (357)	10	24	137	5.8	20	25	63	2.8
Other machinery	22	32	97	4.1	14	31	27	1.2
36 Appliances (363)	8	39	69	2.9	7	8	31	1.4
Radio and television (367)	4	39	7	0.3	3	62	4	0.2
Other electrical	25	24	171	7.3	27	27	169	7.4
37 Transportation equipment	15	38	689	29.2	13	35	487	21.4
38 Precision instruments	12	31	34	1.4	13	50	28	1.2
39 Miscellaneous manufacturing	4	6	40	1.7	5	59	22	1.0
Total	394	23	3,544	100.0	562	28	2,299	100.0

[a] The averages shown are the simple arithmetic means of the five-digit SIC product market shares. In one industry group in Brazil (32) and six in Mexico (204, 208, 26, 281, 289, and 32), subsidiaries of the same U.S. firm producing the same goods were consolidated, thus aggregating their individual market shares. On average, this procedure increased the average market share in those by 4.6 percentage points.

[b] These are not the total sales of all producers in these industries. Rather, they are the sales of all the five-digit SIC products for which we have data on the market shares of affiliates of U.S. MNCs.

[c] Excluding petroleum

[d] Included in "Miscellaneous" industry category below to avoid disclosure.

Source: Special survey of the U.S. Senate Subcommittee on Multinational Corporations.

mit inferences about the entrenchment of foreign firms in those areas, except that it is very probably slight. In other instances (for example, paper and primary metals), average market shares are low because the leading firms are nationally owned or non-U.S. MNCs.*

In Mexico, generally the same pattern is evident. Market shares are decidedly higher in Mexico than in Brazil, but again above-average market shares are characteristic of the most heavily MNC-dominated industries: chemicals, rubber, machinery, electrical equipment, transportation equipment, and instruments. The exceptions to the rule include food manufacturing and household appliances, industries from which several leading U.S. MNCs failed to respond. As before, in industries in Mexico that have substantial local participation, U.S. MNCs have low average market shares.

Table 3.16 shows the number and total sales of manufactured products sold by U.S. MNCs distributed according to the size of the market share for those products, both the principal and minor products of reporting affiliates. In Brazil and Mexico, about 61 percent and 49 percent, respectively, of all sales are made in markets where a single U.S. subsidiary's market share exceeds 20 percent. About 15 percent of all sales are made by dominant affiliates of MNCs (that is, firms accounting for more than half of all sales in a particular market). Comparable data for U.S. companies are not available.

The Position of All MNCs in Selected Industries in Brazil and Mexico

Although firm market share data are not available for non-U.S. MNCs, except by inference, the special survey did permit identifying other leading competitors of U.S. affiliates and their rankings in their industries. With these data it is possible to determine the positions of both U.S. and non-U.S. MNCs in the industries where they operated and accounted for large shares of total industry sales.

The transportation equipment industries in both countries consist of two quite distinct product groups: one of finished vehicles, the other of vehicle parts and accessories. The 1972 sales of new assembled motor vehicles in Brazil and Mexico were about $1.500 billion and $900 million, respectively.* The average market share of the

---

*For example, the leading Mexican tobacco company in 1972 was British-American Tobacco, and the leading automobile producer in Brazil in 1972 was Volkswagen. Primary metals is an industry group with several nationally owned leading firms in both Brazil and Mexico.

†The sales data mentioned in this section of the text are estimated total local sales, not the "sales" shown in Table 3.15, which are for reporting affiliates of MNCs only.

TABLE 3.16

Distribution of Product Market Shares of Affiliates of U.S. MNCs in the Brazilian and Mexican Manufacturing Industries, 1972

Affiliate Market Share (percentage range)	Brazil				Mexico			
	Number of Products[a]	Average Five-Digit Market Share[b] (percent)	Distribution of Sales[c] ($ millions)	Percentage of Sales	Number of Products[a]	Average Five-Digit Market Share[b] (percent)	Distribution of Sales[c] ($ millions)	Percentage of Sales
0–10	161	4.1	411.7	17.5	202	4.5	354.7	15.6
11–20	55	15.5	516.2	21.9	94	16.0	801.0	35.2
21–30	55	26.2	759.8	32.2	84	26.4	444.7	19.5
31–40	32	35.9	207.7	8.8	56	36.3	229.5	10.1
41–50	15	47.9	78.6	3.3	35	47.5	107.8	4.7
51–60	12	56.4	75.3	3.2	20	56.7	108.0	4.7
61–70	17	65.9	93.1	3.9	21	67.9	84.9	3.7
71–80	13	77.3	138.9	5.9	11	77.8	14.6	0.6
81–90	5	85.2	56.0	2.4	9	87.0	11.4	0.5
91–100	5	99.0	21.5	0.9	24	99.2	120.5	5.3
Total	370	23.1	2,357.8	100.0	557	26.8	2,277.1	100.0

[a]Number of five-digit SIC product classes with market shares reported in this range in 1972, petroleum excluded. In Brazil, most of the 1972 sales of affiliates of U.S. petroleum MNCs fell into three market-share ranges: 0–10 (14 percent), 11–20 (31 percent), and 21–30 (49 percent).

[b]Averages shown are the simple arithmetic means of the reported market shares.

[c]Sales of all products sold for which market share data were reported.

Source: Special survey of the U.S. Senate Subcommittee on Multinational Corporations.

three U.S. MNCs for assembled motor vehicles (Ford, General
Motors, Chrysler) is lower than those for components: 15 percent in
Brazil and 16 percent in Mexico in 1972, the latter averages having
declined since 1966. In 1972 Volkswagen was the market leader in
both countries, with a Mexican market share of almost 25 percent and
a Brazilian share of about 50 percent (Jenkins 1976). The total sales
of motor vehicle parts are much smaller, but the average shares of
those U.S. companies tend to be considerably larger than for the auto
makers, roughly 31 percent in Brazil and 22 percent in Mexico.

The pattern of chemical affiliates' market shares is quite similar in both countries (Table 3.15). Generally, the three industry
groups producing primarily intermediate goods (industrial chemicals,
plastics, synthetic fibers, and "other") have considerably higher average shares than do the consumer goods chemical industries (drugs,
soaps, and cosmetics).* In the latter cases the existence of many
nonsubstitutable products within a single five-digit product class makes
them appear less concentrated than they are. Pharmaceutical (SIC
283) sales of $300 million to $400 million in Mexico in 1972 were divided among at least 20 U.S. parents and five European MNCs; the
tenth-ranked drug MNC in Mexico had sales of only $10 million, and
practically all of the top ten firms had sales of under $20 million.
In Brazil in the early 1970s, the situation was much the same. Pharmaceutical sales of $550 million to $600 million were shared by about
30 large international drug companies; the largest ones had sales of
about $25 million, and the tenth-ranking MNC had sales of about $12
million-$14 million (including three or four large European firms).
However, specialization among these firms in certain product classes
(in analgesics or vitamins, for example) means that the leading firms
typically have market shares of 25 to 30 percent for their principal
products, when properly defined.

The soaps and cosmetics industries (SIC 284) is another area
with substantial participation by MNCs, especially in Mexico. The
household soaps and detergents market in Mexico totaled about $200
million in 1972 and was dominated by four firms including one British
and two U.S. multinationals. The top three firms in both household
cleaner markets each held shares of about 25 percent. The toiletries
and cosmetics market (the other main part of SIC 284) in both Brazil
and Mexico was about a $100 million business in 1972. Many small
affiliates of MNCs produce these products, and a fair number of lo-

---

*The consumer-producer distinction in goods is not clear-cut at
the three-digit SIC level. "Other" chemicals may include a few final
goods: salt and paint, for example; also, some drugs and soaps may
be producer goods, particularly bulk medicinals, veterinary drugs,
and some specialty cleaners and polishes.

cally owned companies as well, but the two largest firms in these industries in both countries are foreign-owned MNCs with average market shares exceeding 25 percent each. Thus, again the market share
averages in Table 3.15 tend to mask some fairly strong market positions of U.S. and other foreign affiliates of MNCs.

Transportation equipment and chemicals account for the lion's
share of multinational participation in the Brazilian and Mexican manufacturing sectors, but there are four other industry groups of a second order of importance: food processing, rubber products, nonelectrical machinery, and electrical equipment. The last three of these
industry groups all display generally higher than average market
shares and are industries where MNCs are especially important. In
Brazil's food processing industries, U.S. MNCs hold very high individual market shares (more than 50 percentage points) in ice cream,
soup mixes, breakfast cereals, animal feeds, chewing gum, distilled
liquors, and beverage syrups. In Mexico, U.S. food processing affiliates are far more diversified and face much more local competition
for many of their products but also have very high market shares in
canned milk, baby foods, canned soups, canned fruit juices, breakfast
cereals, and corn milling products, but high market shares (over 25
percent) are also reported in the product markets for canned meats,
cream and butter, catsup and tomato sauces, dried soup mixes, pet
foods, animal feeds, chocolate candies, margarine, powdered coffee,
and ready-to-mix desserts. There are, however, many U.S. affiliates
with low market shares in such industries as vegetable canning, milling, baking, fluid milk, and some types of candies. Multinational
corporations simply have not entered production of fresh meat or fish,
sugar, many grains, beer, or other widely consumed foods.

Almost all of the sales of affiliates of U.S. MNC in rubber products are of motor vehicle tires. In Brazil, the affiliates of only three
foreign MNCs (one Italian and two U.S.) shared almost 95 percent of
the $310 million tire and tube market. In Mexico, virtually 100 per-
cent of this same product was sold by the five leading U.S. tire manufacturers, with the three largest sharing 81 percent of that $160 mil-
lion market. The remainder of the rubber products industry group
is composed of subsidiaries producing such varied products as rubber
hoses, medical and infant sundries, plastic packaging materials, and
plastic dinnerware, with high average market shares the rule.

The nonelectrical machinery industry is also characterized by
generally high market shares. In Brazil sales of MNCs' affiliates
are highly concentrated in construction machinery and office and computing machines. For some particular types of road-building equipment, the top three sellers are all U.S. subsidiaries, and these three
firms often control 85 percent or more of the market. The U.S. MNCs
are also prominent in the production of elevators, industrial conveyors,
pumps, and air conditioners.

In both Brazil and Mexico, <u>office and computing equipment</u> is one of the most important of the "nonelectrical" machinery industries. With items like typewriters and adding machines, there are one or two U.S. affiliates among the leading firms with market shares usually above 25 percent, the remaining leaders being European. But in rental of electronic calculating equipment, U.S. MNCs are completely dominant. Sales of computers have grown tenfold in Brazil during 1966-72, from about $10 million to $100 million; in Mexico, sales have increased from about $15 million to $40 million during the same period. Average firm market shares are deceptive in this case because, just as in the United States, the industry leader has had well over 50 percent of the market during the entire 1966-72 period, while the second-ranking affiliate has typically held only 10 to 15 percent of the market. Rental shares appear to be even more skewed.

In Mexico, U.S. nonelectrical machinery affiliates have had only a relatively small proportion of their sales outside of office and computing equipment. Industries with U.S. MNCs that have quite high market shares include diesel engines, farm tractors, elevators, power hand tools, pumps, and commercial refrigeration equipment.

<u>Electrical equipment</u> is the final of the six major industry groups with a substantial presence of U.S. MNCs combined with strong market positions. In Brazil these firms have been drawn to the household appliance, television and phonograph, telecommunications equipment, and batteries industries. The U.S. affiliates sell most kinds of household appliances in Brazil but are in rivalry with several affiliates of European MNCs and have dominant shares only in washer-dryers and sewing machines. Three of the top five television receiver producers in Brazil are U.S. companies. Several national firms produce radios, however. The three leading Brazilian phonograph record sellers are MNCs, with average market shares of 19 percent; two of the three are U.S.-owned. The Brazilian telephone equipment market is composed almost entirely of only six sellers, two U.S. and four other foreign MNCs; the top two or three companies have average market shares of 30 percent in each of the telephone equipment product classes. One affiliate of a U.S. MNC in Brazil is the dominant firm in dry cell battery production. The television, telephone equipment, and dry cell battery markets were quite large in Brazil in 1972, with sales of about $150 million, $175 million, and $75 million, respectively.

In Mexico's electrical equipment industries, U.S. MNCs have affiliates with strong market positions in many of the same product markets: some household appliances, televisions and phonograph records, telecommunications equipment, and batteries. Four of the top six large household appliance manufacturers are U.S. MNCs in Mexico, but apparently two locally owned firms are among the leading sellers in these markets. The major part of the $70 million Mexican television market is controlled by only three subsidiaries of U.S. MNCs; the manufacture of many television components is even more securely in the hands of U.S. MNCs. The Mexican phonograph record business is largely controlled by four companies, two national and two U.S.-owned. Finally, the $70 million-plus Mexican dry cell battery market is dominated by the three leading U.S. manufacturers of this product.

In addition to the six major industry groups covered above, there are pockets of multinational presence in the paper, nonmetallic minerals, metals, and instruments industries. The U.S. MNCs are important producers of book and writing paper, paperboard, bags, and boxes; some U.S.-owned affiliates have quite high market shares in these markets, but a comprehensive picture of these industries is difficult to infer from our data. The U.S. MNCs are also among the leading firms in the production of scientific glass in Mexico, cement in Brazil, and abrasives in both countries. In the primary metals industries, U.S. subsidiaries are prominent in the production of sheet steel, magnesium, and aluminum wire in Brazil and of aluminum plate and foil and nonferrous wire in Mexico; in most cases these affiliates have more than 25 percent of the market. In both Brazil and Mexico ferrous metal products markets have fairly high levels of local-firm participation, but in the nonferrous metals most of the markets are shared among U.S., European, and Canadian firms for the most part. In the fabricated metals industries of Brazil, U.S. MNCs are involved in only a few product markets: culverts, small arms, ammunition, and valves. In Mexico, on the other hand, they stand out in the production of a wider range of fabricated metals products: steel cans, some tools, heating furnaces, ammunition pipe fittings, and metal strapping. Finally, in the precision instruments industries, subsidiaries of U.S. MNCs hold large portions of several important markets: temperature and control instruments, surgical and dental equipment, and photographic and photocopying equipment. In all of these industries a U.S. affiliate is the leading and often dominant producer; moreover, except for photographic film, the majority of the leading firm's rivals are affiliates of other U.S. MNCs.

Changes in Market Shares of U.S. MNCs in Brazil and Mexico

The above review provided a picture of the kinds of products manufactured and market shares held by affiliates of U.S. and other foreign MNCs in Brazil and Mexico. A related relevant question is: What is happening to MNCs' shares over time? Because no information was available on the ranking of competitors before 1972, all comparisons are restricted to U.S. MNCs.

TABLE 3.17

Average Market Shares in 1966 and 1972 of Affiliates of U.S. MNCs Operating in 1972

SIC	Industry	Brazil				Mexico			
		Number of Five-Digit Products in 1972	Average Market Shares[a] (five-digit SIC products)			Number of Five-Digit Products in 1972	Average Market Shares[a] (five-digit SIC products)		
			1966 (percent)	1972 (percent)	Change[b] (percent)		1966 (percent)	1972 (percent)	Change[b] (percent)
20	Grain products (204)	3	43	51	+8	12	12	20	+8
	Beverages (208)	6	22	36	+14	4	7	13	+6
	Other food	11[c]	34[c]	32[c]	-2[c]	46	17	25	+7
21	Tobacco	[c]	[c]	[c]	[c]	3	0	9	+9
22	Textiles	6	1	20	+19	4	1	11	+10
23	Apparel	0	—	—	—	3	3	14	+11
24 25	Wood and furniture	[c]	[c]	[c]	[c]	7	13	23	+11
26	Paper	13[c]	14[c]	19[c]	+5[c]	31	6	20	+14
27	Printing	[c]	[c]	[c]	[c]	6	20	33	+13
28	Industrial inorganic chemicals (281)	10	12	31	+19	25	29	42	+14
	Plastics and synthetics (282)	13	13	20	+7	20	26	38	+12
	Drugs (283)	79	6	8	+2	85	10	11	+1
	Soaps and cosmetics (284)	20	5	11	+5	37	10	18	+8
	Other chemicals	42	15	28	+13	61	19	32	+13

SIC	Industry								
29	Petroleum	24	15	20	+5	5	6	28	+22
30	Tires (301)	13	26	24	-2	18	23	21	-2
	Other rubber and plastics	6	13	39	+26	10	19	46	+27
31	Leather	c	c	c	c	c	c	c	c
32	Stone, clay, and glass	9	31	26	-4	19	10	30	+20
33	Primary metals	11	5	17	+13	16	18	34	+16
34	Fabricated metals	15	15	32	+17	26	23	41	+18
35	Industrial machinery (355, 356)	12	25	38	+13	22	18	30	+12
	Office and computer (357)	10	16	24	+9	20	18	25	+7
	Other machinery	22	12	32	+20	14	21	31	+10
36	Appliances (363)	8	37	39	+2	7	10	8	-2
	Radio and television (367)	4	29	39	+8	3	0	62	+62
	Other electrical	25	20	23	+3	27	18	28	+10
37	Transportation equipment	15	14	38	+24	13	32	35	+3
38	Precision instruments	12	12	31	+18	13	20	50	+30
39	Miscellaneous manufacturing	5	3	7	+4	5	28	59	+31
	Total	394	14	23	+9	562	16	27	+11

[a] The averages shown are the simple arithmetic means of the five-digit SIC product market shares.

[b] Due to rounding, the "change" shown may not exactly correspond to the difference in the average market shares in the table. Weighted by 1972 sales, the total change was +12.7 percent in Brazil and +8.6 percent in Mexico, petroleum excluded.

[c] Included in "miscellaneous" industry category below to avoid disclosure.

Source: Special survey of the U.S. Senate Subcommittee on Multinational Corporations.

TABLE 3.18

Average Market Shares of Affiliates of U.S. MNCs Operating in Both 1966 and 1972

SIC	Industry	Brazil				Mexico			
		Number of Five-Digit Products[a]	Average Market Shares[b] (five-digit SIC products)			Number of Five-Digit Products[a]	Average Market Shares[b] (five-digit SIC products)		
			1966 (percent)	1972 (percent)	Change (percent)		1966 (percent)	1972 (percent)	Change (percent)
20	Grain products (204)	e	e	e	e	3[e]	29[e]	28[e]	0[e]
	Beverages (208)	3	36	27	-9	28	28	29	+1
	Other food	6	65	64	-1	0	—	—	—
21	Tobacco	0	—	—	—	d	d	d	d
22	Textiles	d	d	d	d	d	d	d	d
23	Apparel	0	—	—	—				
24	Wood and furniture	0	—	—	—	5	18	16	-2
25	Paper	6	25	27	+3	9	20	29	+9
26	Printing	0	—	—	—	d	d	d	d
28	Industrial inorganic chemicals (281)	e	e	e	e	20	37	35	-2
	Plastics and synthetics (282)	6	25	24	-1	14	35	33	12
	Drugs (283)	51	8	8	0	59	12	11	-1
	Soap and cosmetics (284)	8	11	11	0	27	13	16	+3
	Other chemicals	23	25	27	+2	39	26	26	+1
29	Petroleum	16	20	17	-3	3	8	6	-2

SIC	Industry								
30	Tires (301)	12	28	26	-2	18	23	21	-2
	Other rubber and plastic	3	26	29	+3	6	31	35	+4
31	Leather	d	d	d	d	d	d	d	d
32	Stone, clay, and glass	7	36	30	-6	6	27	33	+7
33	Primary metals	3	15	23	+9	7	28	46	+18
34	Fabricated metals	7	28	32	+3	13	35	39	+3
35	Industrial machinery (355, 356)	8	34	37	+3	11	31	36	+5
	Office and computer (357)	8	20	23	+3	14	22	21	-1
	Other machinery	7	28	28	0	8	27	28	+1
36	Appliances (363)	6	43	50	+7	6	12	9	-3
	Radio and television (367)	3	38	36	-2	e	e	e	e
	Other electrical	12	34	28	-6	15	24	28	+4
37	Transportation equipment	4	35	38	+4	8	36	30	-6
38	Precision instruments	6	25	29	+4	6	37	51	+14
39	Miscellaneous manufacturing	2	3	5	+2	6	37	38	+1
	Total	209	23	24	+0.4	331	24	25	+1.3

aNumber of five-digit SIC products in industry for firms reporting their market shares in both 1966 and 1972.

bThe averages shown are the simple arithmetic means of the five-digit SIC product market shares.

cDue to rounding the "change" shown may not exactly correspond to the difference in the average market shares in the table. Weighted by 1972 sales, the total change was +1.04 percent in Brazil, and -0.84 percent in Mexico, petroleum excluded.

dIncluded in "miscellaneous" industry category below to avoid disclosure.

eIncluded in "other" industry category below to avoid disclosure.

Source: Special survey of the U.S. Senate Subcommittee on Multinational Corporations.

Tables 3.17 and 3.18 present data on changes in the average market shares of U.S. MNCs' manufacturing sales in both Brazil and Mexico over the 1966–72 period.* Table 3.17 includes all products being sold by firms active in 1972, including those that initiated production during the 1966–72 period. Table 3.18, on the other hand, includes only those products being sold in both years. The market share changes calculated in Table 3.18 should always be equal to or lower than those in Table 3.17, the difference being accounted for by the entry of new subsidiaries of U.S. MNCs into the market or by diversification of an existing affiliate into a new product line.

Looking first at the firm market share changes in Table 3.17 for Brazil, we note that shares increased an average of 9 percentage points during the six-year period 1966–72. When weighted by 1972 sales, the increase in Brazil is even more striking: 12.7 percentage points. Average changes were positive in every industry group save nonmetallic minerals, tires, and "other" food processing. Most of the increase in the weighted market share was due to the transportation equipment industries.[†] This increase can be attributed both to increased shares by two of the three large U.S. motor vehicle manufacturers and to entry by a large number of automobile parts makers (and one vehicle assembler as well). Next in importance were the chemicals industries, especially the producer chemicals; drugs, soaps, and cosmetics accounted for relatively little of the weighted market share increase. A close third in rank would be the nonelectrical machinery industries. Finally, four industry groups were only slightly responsible for the increase: food processing (especially beverages), other rubber and plastic products, electrical equipment, and precision instruments. Other industries contributed only negligibly to the increase in market shares of affiliates of U.S. MNCs.

Most of the increased shares of U.S. companies in Brazil during 1966–72 were due to new entry or diversification into new products. As can be seen from Table 3.18, the market shares of U.S. affiliates in production throughout the 1966–72 period exhibit far greater stability. On average, product market shares in Brazil increased only 0.4 percent (or 1.04 percent when weighted by 1972 sales levels), and the pattern across industries is quite mixed. By far the largest component

*In a few industries average 1972 market shares may appear to be slightly lower in Tables 3.17 and 3.18 than in Table 3.15. This occurs because similar but separately incorporated plants of MNCs in the same country were not consolidated.

[†]The "importance" of the influence on the total market share change was measured by multiplying the industry's average market share change by its 1972 sales.

of the weighted share increase is due to the four transportation equipment products. Other significant positive increases were in home
appliances, office and computing equipment, "other" chemicals, metals,
and paper. Fairly substantial losses were recorded in grain products,
beverages, petroleum, tires, nonmetallic minerals, and "other" electrical.

The pattern of weighted affiliate market share gains and losses
is quite similar in Mexico, with one major exception: Large market
share losses were reported in the transportation equipment industries.* During 1966-72, U.S. motor vehicle manufacturers as a group
suffered a decline in their market positions as a result of incursions
by both Nissan and Volkswagen (their shares increased from 16 to 34
percent of the market over the same period) (Jenkins 1976). Except
for transportation equipment, household appliances, tires, and some
of the chemical industries, U.S. MNCs generally experienced gains
in market shares during 1966-72. These increases were substantial
in "other" food processing, paper, soaps and cosmetics, "other" rubber and plastic products, metals, "other" electrical equipment, and
instruments. The slight drop in office and computer equipment noted
in Table 3.18 is due entirely to the office equipment component. With
five or six exceptions market shares were remarkably stable in Mexico
during the 1966-72 period for firms in production throughout.

Table 3.18 documents that U.S. MNCs as a group have increased
significantly their shares of the Brazilian and Mexican manufacturing
markets over the six-year interval. But Table 3.18 indicates that
with a few exceptions (paper, metals, other rubber and plastic products, and instruments), their increased shares have come primarily
because additional U.S. MNCs entered these industries, not because
existing firms expanded their shares. Some new entry has taken the
form of the establishment of new subsidiaries or new plant capacity
by established affiliates in product markets formerly served entirely
by imports, but this phenomenon was much more common before 1966
than after. The major part of the new entry involved shifts in market
shares from locally owned companies to U.S. MNCs. During 1966-72,
about 60 percent of subsidiary formations involved MNC takeovers of
domestic firms. Generally, it appears that in product markets with
several U.S. MNCs well established as rivals throughout the period
(such as in drugs, soaps, tires, computers, and autos), market shares
have been relatively stable, whereas they have tended to increase in
markets where U.S. affiliates faced locally owned rivals.

---

*It is for this reason that the weighted market share change
dropped by 0.8 percentage points while the unweighted average change
was a positive 1.3 percentage points.

Market Concentration

Many studies have been made of industrial concentration in the more developed economies because of its presumed crucial relationship to market power. (See Chapter 4.) Studies of market concentration in the LDCs are at a relatively rudimentary stage.*

There are several indexes of seller concentration, but most U.S. studies have used four-firm or eight-firm concentration ratios, that is, the ratio of the sales of the top four or eight companies in an industry to the sales of products in that industry. Measuring concentration always requires the proper delineation of the "market." If the SIC definitions are adopted, adjustments often need to be made to allow for industries that are too broadly or narrowly defined. Imports and exports also affect the accuracy of concentration ratios in some industries.

Official data on market concentration in Brazil and Mexico are not publicly available. However, I was able to develop minimum esti-

---

*Only a few investigations have been made of international differences in industrial concentration. The first was by Bain (1966). In his sample of 38 comparable industries in 8 countries, he estimated that 20 plant-concentration ratios in the 1950s were generally quite high relative to U.S. national data; in three countries (India, Canada, and Sweden), the average of the 38 ratios was roughly twice as high. In the remaining four cases (Japan, Britain, France, and Italy), the average was only 10 to 30 percent higher. These results suggest that it is not so much the level of development as the large size of the market for manufactures that allows for lower industrial concentration.

A paper by Pryor (1972) looked at aggregate and major industry concentration in 20-odd developed nations during the early 1960s. He found that weighted four-firm aggregate manufacturing concentration was significantly and negatively correlated with GNP, but not with per capita GNP. Therefore, it is again confirmed that the primary determinant of industry concentration is not so much the level of development (as measured by per capita GNP) as the size of the market. One can expect industrial concentration to more nearly resemble that of the United States in India, South Africa, or Brazil than in Pakistan, Kenya, or Chile, for example, if Pryor's results may be extrapolated to such narrow markets.

Three further studies provide concentration comparisons for three semi-industrialized LDCs. White (1974b) found that for the late 1960s in 51 comparable industries four-firm sales concentration was 66 percent in Pakistan but only 49 percent in the United States. For all 82 of his sample industries, the simple average four-firm concentration ratio was 70 percent. Fajnzylber (1970 and 1975) has provided four-plant concentration estimates for Brazil (circa 1968) and Mexico (circa 1970).

mates of four-firm sales-concentration ratios for many five-digit SIC
product markets.

Appendix B contains the minimum estimates of four-firm concentration ratios (CR4s) for Brazil and Mexico for the year 1972.*
The average CR4s given are not for the three-digit SIC industry groups
listed but for the mean CR4s of the various five-digit "product classes"
falling within each three-digit "industry group." The CR4 estimates
tend to cluster fairly closely together in any given industry group.

Market concentration is slightly lower in Brazil than in Mexico,
but not significantly so. Industries with high CR4s in Brazil also
tended to be high in Mexico. Concentration in both countries is relatively high in many of the industries dominated by MNCs: many in
food processing, some in chemicals (except drugs where the five-
digit SIC level definition is inappropriately broad), rubber products,
fabricated metals, nonelectrical machinery, electrical equipment,
and transportation equipment. Concentration may also appear unexpectedly high in a few other industries: textiles, paper, tobacco, and
nonmetallic minerals. This phenomenon is partially explained by the
ability of MNCs to locate in "niches" within even the relatively na-
tional-controlled industries in which they can produce some high income (for example, snack foods, synthetics weaving, or mild cigarettes) or relatively high-technology products (frozen-juice containers
and abrasives). Conversely, MNCs do not appear to be attracted to
invest in manufacturing industries with lower proportions of foreign
participation and lower levels of concentration: textiles, clothing,
wood products, printing, leather, and primary metals.

Table 3.19 gives the aggregate distribution of the minimum four-
firm sales concentration ratios for the manufacturing sectors of Brazil and Mexico in which U.S. MNCs operate. The products included
in the table cover 70 percent of the sales of all reporting manufacturing affiliates of U.S. MNCs in Brazil and 76 percent in Mexico. The
sales distribution of the concentration ratios is highly skewed in both
Latin American countries, with the Brazilian estimates even more
skewed than the Mexican. In Brazil two-thirds of all sales of manufactured goods by MNC affiliates are in markets with four-firm concentration in excess of 80 percent. In Mexico, on the other hand, two-
thirds of all those goods are sold in markets with concentration exceeding 70 percent. The most striking difference is in the over 90 percent
category of concentration; by these estimates almost three-fifths of
sales by U.S. MNCs in Brazil fall in this highest level of concentration,
whereas only about one-fifth of sales by U.S. MNCs in Mexico are in

---

*Estimates for 1966 could not be made because, even where 1966
market share data were available, the ranking of rivals was not.

TABLE 3.19

Distribution of the Minimum, Four-Firm, Five-Digit SIC Product Concentration Ratios in Brazilian, Mexican, and U.S. Manufacturing Industries, 1972

CR4 Percentage Range	Brazil				Mexico				United States			
	Number of Products[a]	Mean CR4 (percent)	Sales[c] ($millions)	Percentage of Sales	Number of Products[a]	Mean CR4 (percent)	Sales[c] ($millions)	Percentage of Sales	Number of Products[b]	Mean CR4 (percent)	Sales[d] ($millions)	Percentage of Sales
0–20	24	19	56	2	35	17	81	4	9	16	16,558	9.0
20.1–30	59	26	121	5	18	28	21	1	22	26	27,499	15.0
30.1–40	24	36	87	4	61	35	99	4	18	35	20,440	11.2
40.1–50	37	46	159	7	57	46	140	6	23	46	20,823	11.4
50.1–60	28	56	159	7	33	55	160	7	15	54	9,756	5.3
60.1–70	26	65	115	5	58	66	257	11	13	65	26,158	14.3
70.1–80	15	75	114	5	41	75	643	29	15	77	12,142	6.6
80.1–90	31	86	198	8	79	86	369	16	7	85	7,493	4.1
90.1–100	127	99	1,404	58	169	99	486	21	4	94	42,354	23.1
Total	371	65	2,414	100	551	69	2,256	100	126	49	183,173	100.0

aThese are five-digit SIC product classes. Major group 29, petroleum, is excluded.
bThese are five-digit SIC product classes common to both Brazil and Mexico.
cSales of affiliates of U.S. MNCs only.
dValue of shipments of entire industry in 1972 census.

Sources: Special survey of the U.S. Senate Subcommittee on Multinational Corporations; and 1972 Census of Manufactures, Concentration Ratios in Manufacturing.

such markets. By contrast, the levels of concentration in comparable
U.S. product markets display no marked skewness. For the 126 comparable product markets that MNCs have entered in both Brazil and
Mexico, roughly half of all U.S. shipments (by value) originated in
highly concentrated industries (four-firm concentration exceeding 50
percent).

The statistics in Table 3.20 show the extent to which market
concentration configurations are similar in Brazil and Mexico. The
122 five-digit product classes for which CR4s are available in both
countries were significantly correlated: The simple correlation coefficient of 0.53 is statistically significant at the 1 percent level. On
the other hand, the relative levels of concentration among industries
in Brazil and Mexico were less closely correlated with concentration
in the United States. Comparable Brazilian and U.S. industries had
a simple correlation coefficient of 0.30; comparable Mexican and
U.S. industries had a simple correlation coefficient of 0.26. Thus,
not only was the average level of concentration higher in Brazil and
Mexico than in the United States, but the relative levels of concentration of these two LDCs were more closely correlated with one another
than with that of the United States. This suggests that somewhat different economic forces are responsible for forging the structure of
industry in these two LDCs than in the United States. Perhaps most
important are differences in the size of LDC and U.S. markets, and
the greater impact that multinational corporations have in shaping the
structure of some industries in LDCs than in the United States.

In summary, the relative concentration patterns among industries generally are similar in all three countries. Furthermore, the
most concentrated major industry groups are the same industries in
which MNCs are most prominent. In both national markets more than
four-fifths of the sales of manufactured goods by affiliates of U.S.
MNCs occur in the very highly concentrated industries (those with
four-firm, five-digit SIC-level concentration ratios exceeding 50 percent). Finally, overall concentration appears to be lowest in the
United States, slightly lower in Brazil than in Mexico, but most highly
skewed in Brazil.

Product Differentiation

Product differentiation is possible when a product has attributes
that allow it to be distinguished from near substitutes in the minds of
buyers. That is, some products can be designed, packaged, or otherwise "differentiated" so that consumers view them as in some way
unique compared to products with the same general physical character-

TABLE 3.20

Matrix of Correlations between Product-Class Four-Firm
Concentration Ratios in Brazil, Mexico,
and the United States, 1972

Brazil CR4	Mexico CR4	United States CR4	
r = 1.0	n = 122, r = 0.526*	n = 184, r = 0.297*	Brazil CR4
	r = 1.0	n = 252, r = 0.263*	Mexico CR4
		r = 1.0	United States CR4

*Indicates significance at the 1 percent confidence level, as calculated in Fisher (1948: 209).

Note: Correlation coefficients, r, were calculated only for the n product classes (five-digit SIC level) for which estimates were available in both countries. Eight of the "other" or "n.e.c." classes were omitted (for example, 20999, 26495, 28199, 28995, and so forth).

Sources: Four-firm CR4s for the United States were taken from the U.S. Department of Commerce, Bureau of the Census, 1972 Census of Manufactures, Concentration Ratios in Manufacturing (MC72 [SR]-2). Four-firm CR4s for Brazil and Mexico were derived from the special survey of the U.S. Senate Subcommittee on Multinational Corporations.

istics.* Other products, such as graded lumber or steel, are so inherently homogeneous that no such differences can exist between dif-

---

*Comanor and Wilson present an elaborate, formal model of consumer choice among brands that is based on ignorance, search costs, and risk aversion by consumers. They also show, by means of a sophisticated consumer expenditures model for the United States, that expenditure levels between industries are strongly determined by industry advertising levels, more strongly than the prices of the products themselves (Comanor and Wilson 1974).

ferent producers. Moreover, it is usually more difficult to differentiate goods sold to other producers; if such producer goods are differentiated, it is frequently by means of ancillary services rather than
image advertising.

When a seller is able to differentiate his product from those of
competitors, he is able to charge a higher price for it. If such higher
prices enable the seller to enjoy supranormal profits, there is an incentive for new firms to produce similar products. In order to retain
its advantage and discourage competition, the first firm (or group of
firms) in the market must create consumer loyalty to the brand itself
once the product comes to be accepted. Various means may be used
to create or maintain a felicitous brand image that may or may not be
related to the product's physical characteristics. Although this end
may be achieved in various ways (such as additional services or an
effective distribution network), advertising often is the most successful marketing strategy to achieve and maintain product differentiation.*
Thus, whereas advertising is used initially to create product differentiation, its longer-term effect may be to create barriers to entry.

Estimates of the industry distribution of advertising intensities,
derived from the special subcommittee survey, are presented in Appendix C. These were calculated by taking the total advertising expenditures of affiliates of U.S. MNCs in the industry and dividing by their
total sales in the same year. The 426 affiliates are generally assigned
to the industry of their principal product line.

These advertising intensity estimates hold few surprises for
those familiar with like data for U.S. markets. Generally, high advertising ratios are found in the consumer goods industries while relatively low ratios are observed in the producer goods industries. Very
high advertising intensities (exceeding 4 percent) exist in the fruit and

---

*Direct evidence of the efficacy of product differentiation through
advertising in the LDCs is difficult to come by. Scattered material,
mainly referring to Latin America, can be found in Barnet and Müller
(1974: 143-46 and 172-78) and in Ledogar (1975). But their few facts
indicate that many MNCs carry on extensive advertising campaigns in
the LDCs and that these are having definite consumption impacts on
all strata of the populations. Much advertising is done outside the
United States for U.S. MNCs by non-U.S. advertising agencies. However, data on the billings of the 707 largest U.S. advertising agencies
in 1975 clearly show the vast importance of advertising outside the
United States. In 1975, gross billings amounted to $14.6 billion;
among the ten largest agencies alone, their gross billings accounted
for $6.037 billion, and of that amount 49 percent was foreign (Adver-
tising Age, March 14, 1977).

vegetable canning, breakfast cereals and baking, candy, liquor and
soft drinks, cigarettes, pharmaceutical, soaps, toiletries, and fabricated plastics industries. Fairly high advertising ratios are also
reported for several other industry groups: writing paper, radio and
television, batteries, medical instruments, photographic and photocopying equipment, and some other miscellaneous manufactures.
Furthermore, some consumer items with modest advertising-to-sales
ratios have high per-unit prices and hence high <u>absolute</u> advertising
outlays: tires, tractors, household appliances, and motor vehicles.
Generally, low levels of product differentiation are characteristic
of intermediate paper products, animal feeds, industrial chemicals,
primary metals, industrial machinery, electronic components, and
control instruments.

The observed advertising ratios are lower in Brazil than in
Mexico, but relative levels are closely associated. A correlation coefficient was calculated for 57 five-digit SIC product classes for which
we have data from both Brazil and Mexico; the coefficient, 0.82, is
large and highly significant statistically.* This close association reflects the fact that many of the MNCs in the sample market identical
products through similar subsidiaries in both countries.

The structure of product differentiation is not only parallel between the two Latin American nations but also between them and the
United States. A crude test of this proposition was made by correlating
our data on Brazil and Mexico with that found in a recent study of advertising in the United States by Comanor and Wilson (1974: 134–35).
I correlated the advertising intensities for 21 comparable consumer
goods industries. The U.S. data are based on Internal Revenue Service returns averaged over 1954–57 and the data on MNCs' affiliates
are based on the average of Brazilian and Mexican product-class ratios
for 1972. The correlation coefficient of 0.84 is quite high and statistically very significant.

A more ambitious and detailed test of this proposition was made
using the four- and five-digit SIC data on 1972 advertising intensities
in Brazil and Mexico. These data were correlated with advertising
outlays-to-sales ratios in comparable U.S. industries for 1967.[†] Despite the fact that we are relating the average intensities of a few

---

*Not all of these 57 common product classes could be shown in
Appendix C, because of disclosure concerns. However, the results
of correlating the 38 pairs of industry groups appearing in that table
are only slightly weaker; the correlation coefficient is 0.51 and is also
significant at better than 1 percent.

[†]The U.S. data were taken from the <u>U.S. Input-Output Tables</u>,
Vol. 2 (DOC 1974).

firms with a census of manufacturing plants and using nonoverlapping industry definitions in some cases, the correlations are quite impressive. For 75 comparable industries, the Mexican-U.S. correlation was 0.68; for 49 comparable industries, the correlation between Brazilian and U.S. advertising ratios was 0.85. Both coefficients are statistically significant at a confidence level better than 99 percent.

This evidence indicates that U.S. MNCs' product-differentiation patterns in Brazil and Mexico are similar to those in the United States. This "exportation" of product differentiation patterns probably results because MNCs tend to implement modes of rivalry they are most familiar with and have found most successful in the industries of their "home" country, the United States in this case.

In addition to examining correspondences among industry advertising intensities, I examined closely firm-level advertising practices. Publicly available data were collected on advertising expenditures by the parent MNCs in 1972, and these data were regressed against the advertising-to-sales ratios of their subsidiaries in Brazil and Mexico that produced roughly the same products.* As expected, the correlation coefficients were both positive and highly significant (0.72 and 0.73 for Mexico and Brazil, respectively). These results clearly imply that the marketing techniques of U.S. MNCs are being transferred to, and employed by, their foreign subsidiaries, even in countries with distinctly different cultures, income levels, and mass media systems. As shown in Connor and Mueller (1977), heavy advertising is one method used by MNCs' subsidiaries for maintaining high profit rates.

In addition to advertising, it is possible that research and development (R&D) expenditures may, particularly among consumer goods industries, provide another index of product differentiation.[†] Even in

---

*The data on the parent corporations were taken from the well known COMPUSTAT tape compiled by Moody's. Both advertising and sales figures usually represent consolidated, worldwide operations. For the Latin American subsidiaries, all affiliates in the same country were treated as one company. All together, 92 pairs of U.S.-Mexican companies were available and 63 U.S.-Brazilian pairs for 1972.

[†]As in the case of advertising, the full effect of R&D activity may be delayed for a few years; that is, sales or profits may exhibit only lagged responses to current R&D outlays. On the other hand, the establishment of a commercial research office is likely to be the beginning of a permanent activity in this area. Hence, current R&D outlays are likely to correlate highly with past R&D expenditures (Branch 1974). The term R&D covers much more than research proper; it may also include market surveys, testing, quality control, legal fees for

highly industrialized countries R&D is carried on both to generate new products and to redesign old ones; this latter objective, minor product adaptation, is conceptually very close to other product-differentiation activities (Imel and Helmberger 1971). * There is a growing body of evidence supporting the idea that most R&D activities by MNCs are located in their "home" areas (Mansfield 1974). Moreover, what little R&D is done by MNC affiliates in the less developed host countries is mainly of the product adaptation type (Duerr 1970; National Academy of Sciences 1973).

Data on R&D-to-sales ratios by MNCs in Brazil and Mexico appear to confirm these statements partially (Appendix D). It is clear that overall R&D expenditures are modest, averaging 0.5 percent of sales in Brazil and 0.3 percent of sales in Mexico. These are considerably less than in the United States. [†] Indeed, they are only one-fifth or less on average than the R&D expenditures of the parent corporations themselves. In Brazil the only producer-good industry spending more than 1 percent of sales on R&D is nonmetallic minerals (1.6 percent). The highest expenditure ratio reported for any product was in the "miscellaneous" category (2.3 percent). Transportation equipment, which also is mainly a consumer good, had R&D expenditures of 1.6 percent in Brazil and 1.0 percent in Mexico. No industries in Mexico averaged more than 1 percent in R&D-to-sales ratio.

Listed in Appendix D are several industries that one would expect, extrapolating from the U.S. situation, to have fairly high R&D intensities but in fact have relatively low outlays: chemicals, rubber, machinery, electrical equipment, and instruments. To test this notion a bit further, I regressed the R&D-to-sales ratios of the Brazilian and Mexican operations on their parents' R&D intensities, using 1972 data in both cases. [‡] The correlation coefficients were calculated to

---

patents on new products, and even the expenses of "detail men" or salesmen used for market surveys.

*A weak test of this hypothesis was performed. For the food and tobacco processing subsidiaries in Mexico, the correlation of R&D-to-sales ratios on parental advertising-to-sales ratios was stronger (+.23) than the correlation of their respective R&D intensities (+.12), but neither was significant.

[†] In 1972, the average R&D expenditures of large U.S. manufacturing corporations (those with more than 10,000 employees) was 4.1 percent of sales (National Science Foundation, Research and Development in Industry 1972, NSF 74-312, p. 59). Most of the MNCs represented in Appendix Table D.1 were in this size class.

[‡] As was the case with the advertising-to-sales regressions reported immediately above, public data were used for the MNCs, and

be +.03 and +.30 for Brazil and Mexico, respectively. Thus, there
appears to be little tendency for more R&D-prone U.S. multinationals
to spawn equally R&D-prone subsidiaries in these less developed countries. Nor was there any significant relationship when the experiment
was repeated for only those subsidiaries with some R&D expenditures;*
that is, high R&D in the U.S. firm is not associated with high R&D expenditures in its Latin American subsidiaries. The MNCs most capable of transferring the expertise needed to operate local R&D facilities
do not display any tendency actually to set up such units in the semi-
industrialized countries in which they have invested.

Thus, the evidence from Brazil and Mexico is mixed. Some
R&D is being carried out in a few producer goods industries and may
be similar to R&D in the advanced countries. Much R&D, however,
occurs in some consumer goods industries, and probably involves
product differentiation by means of product redesign. In absolute
terms, 1972 R&D expenditures were highly concentrated in only a few
industries. In Brazil, 88 percent of all reported R&D costs among affiliates of U.S. MNCs were in only five industries: transportation
equipment (52 percent), "other" electrical (16 percent), plastics and
synthetics (11 percent), drugs (6 percent), and soaps and cosmetics
(3 percent). In Mexico five industries also account for 88 percent of
the Special Survey firms' R&D: transportation equipment (37 percent),
"other food" (25 percent), drugs (16 percent), soaps and cosmetics
(7 percent), and "other" electrical (4 percent).

Both indexes of product differentiation also have highly skewed
distributions across firms. Looking first at the advertising intensities,
we see that roughly half of the MNCs' subsidiaries (by number) have
no advertising (Table 3.21).[†] However, the affiliates with no advertising account for one-fifth or less of sales in both countries. Roughly
half of MNCs' sales in both Latin American countries are made by af-

---

all the subsidiaries of a U.S. company in one country were consolidated
for these tests. This procedure yielded data for 114 parent-subsidiary
pairs for Mexico and 84 for Brazil.

*Only 36 Brazilian and 45 Mexican consolidated multinational op-
erations were available for this test. The correlation coefficients
were -.21 and +.25, respectively. Tests made for two likely industry groups—drugs and cosmetics and machinery and instruments—also
failed to turn up any significant correlations.

[†] The sample used in this table is not directly comparable to Table
3.20, because 93 manufacturing subsidiaries are included, most of
which have no advertising or R&D expenses. The major exceptions
are the nine petroleum affiliates in Brazil; these had $2.6 million in
advertising for $1.162 million in sales in 1972.

TABLE 3.21

Distribution of Firm Advertising-to-Sales Ratios of U.S. MNCs and Their Active Affiliates in Brazil and Mexico, 1972

Advertising Intensity Percentage Range	Brazil				Mexico				United States			
	Number of Firms	Mean Advertising Intensity[a] (percent)	Sales[b] ($ millions)	Percentage of Sales	Number of Firms	Mean Advertising Intensity[a] (percent)	Sales[b] ($ millions)	Percentage of Sales	Number of Firms	Mean Advertising Intensity[a] (percent)	Sales[b] ($ millions)	Percentage of Sales
0	106	0.0	519	12	183	0.0	645	20	12	0.0	10,031	6
0.01–0.50	38	0.2	1,745	39	63	0.2	1,057	33	11	0.3	10,607	6
0.51–1.00	22	0.7	523	12	24	0.7	387	12	12	0.8	14,645	8
1.01–2.00	20	1.4	958	21	26	1.4	248	8	33	1.4	77,221	44
2.01–3.00	16	2.4	347	8	21	2.5	208	7	17	2.4	22,793	13
3.01–4.00	9	3.6	135	3	9	3.5	100	3	14	3.5	12,131	7
4.01–5.00	2	4.3	59	1	11	4.4	127	4	7	4.4	7,800	5
5.01–10.00	7	7.3	94	2	14	6.8	185	6	9	7.4	13,246	8
10.01–20.00	7	12.8	47	1	14	14.1	112	4	7	13.9	5,114	3
20.01–50.00	4	24.7	30	1	3	27.5	92	3	1	21.3	721	[d]
50.01–100.00	2	74.0	3[c]	[d]	0	–	–	0	0	–	–	0
Total	233	2.2	4,457	100	368	1.6	3,162	100	123	3.0	174,309	100

[a]Mean advertising intensity is the sum of each firm's advertising intensity divided by the number of firms. Both manufacturing and marketing firms are included.

[b]Sales in Brazil and Mexico are local sales, but sales under "United States" are global MNC sales.

[c]Less than $500,000 in 1972 sales.

[d]Less than 0.5 percent of total 1972 sales.

Sources: Special survey of the U.S. Senate Subcommittee on Multinational Corporations and Moody's COMPUSTAT tape. Data were unavailable for 74 U.S. MNCs, mainly in major groups 29, 35, 36, and 37; most of these companies probably have advertising intensities in the .01 to 2.00 percent range.

filiates with low advertising intensities (less than 1 percent). Mexico has a greater proportion of sales by firms with high advertising propensities than does Brazil: 20 percent of Mexican sales are by firms with advertising ratios exceeding 3 percent, but less than 10 percent of MNCs' sales in Brazil fall into this group. Advertising expenditures of the parent corporations are decidedly higher, relative to sales, than those of their LDC subsidiaries: More than half of all their sales are by companies with advertising intensities of from 1 to 3 percent.* The fact that only about one-fifth of all MNCs' sales originate from low-advertising-intensity corporations may imply that affiliate advertising rates can be expected to rise over time, especially in Brazil.

The R&D ratios are even more skewed across firms (Table 3.22). Fully 80 percent of the active Brazilian subsidiaries of U.S. MNCs had no R&D outlays in 1972; in Mexico the proportion was 82 percent of all firms. Measured as a proportion of sales, however, R&D effort was more widespread. In Brazil, at least 34 percent of all output came from MNCs' subsidiaries with some R&D activity;[†] in Mexico 66 percent of all sales originated in firms with some R&D outlays in 1972. In Brazil those 24 subsidiaries of U.S. MNCs that might be considered relatively R&D-"intensive" (a ratio exceeding 1 percent) had average 1972 sales 2.2 times as large as those of the remaining firms;[‡] in Mexico the 29 relatively R&D-intensive firms were 2.5 times as large as the other affiliates. Among the U.S. parent corporations, the same strong relationship of R&D intensity to size remains. But what is most striking about the size distribution of R&D-to-sales ratios of these companies is the large proportion (as measured by sales) with quite high R&D levels: Nearly half had R&D expenditures exceeding 3 percent of sales. Moreover, unlike their Latin American subsidiaries, virtually none had no R&D activity.

An important policy question for countries that are hosts to large amounts of direct investment in manufacturing is whether to allow unrestricted payments for royalties and other intangibles by MNCs' subsidiaries to their parent corporations as Mexico does, or whether to treat such payments generally as profit remittances and, hence, as

---

*Even with a more complete sample, this statement is likely to stand. From data on other years or companies in the same industries, it appears that, excluding petroleum companies, most of the missing observations lie in the 1 to 2 percent advertising-intensity range.

[†]If the nine petroleum affiliates are omitted, the proportion of Brazilian sales from R&D-prone firms rises to 46 percent.

[‡]Excluding the nine Brazilian petroleum affiliates, the R&D-intensive firms' sales were 3.9 times larger than those of the remaining 200 affiliates.

TABLE 3.22

Distribution of Firm R&D-to-Sales Ratios of U.S. MNCs and Their Active Affiliates in Brazil and Mexico, 1972

R&D-Intensity Percentage Range	Brazil				Mexico				United States			
	Number of Firms	Mean R&D Intensity[a] (percent)	Sales[b] ($ millions)	Percentage of Sales	Number of Firms	Mean R&D Intensity[a] (percent)	Sales[b] ($ millions)	Percentage of Sales	Number of Firms	Mean R&D Intensity[a] (percent)	Sales[b] ($ millions)	Percentage of Sales
0	186	0.0	2,948	66	301	0.0	1,717	54	3	0.0	2,854	1
0.01-0.50	11	0.3	282	6	27	0.2	747	24	16	0.3	17,603	7
0.51-1.00	12	0.8	172	4	12	0.7	136	4	24	0.8	21,900	9
1.01-2.00	13	0.5	923	21	16	1.3	493	16	35	1.5	47,519	19
2.01-3.00	1	2.8	4	c	8	2.6	40	1	24	2.4	44,255	18
3.01-4.00	2	3.4	8	c	2	3.6	4	c	15	3.4	67,204	27
4.01-5.00	3	4.7	49	1	1	4.3	15	c	16	4.4	17,162	7
5.01-10.00	3	7.8	59	1	0	0	0	0	16	7.1	29,615	12
10.01-20.00	1	13.6	1	c	1	15.9	1	c	1	13.2	272	c
20.01-50.00	1	34.8	10	c	1	34.1	9	c	0	—	—	0
50.01-100.00	0	0	0	0	0	0	0	0	0	—	—	0
Total	233	0.5	4,457	100	369	0.3	3,162	100	150	2.6	248,384	100

[a]R&D intensity is the sum of each firm's R&D intensity divided by the number of firms. Both manufacturing and marketing firms are included, except those in major group 129, petroleum, most of which would fall into the 0.51 to 1.00 percent range.
[b]Sales in Brazil and Mexico are local sales, but sales under "U.S." are global MNC sales.
[c]Less than 0.5 percent of total 1972 sales.

Sources: Special survey of the U.S. Senate Subcommittee on Multinational Corporations and Moody's COMPUSTAT tape. Data were unavailable for 38 U.S. MNCs in 1972.

114

subject to taxation, as Brazil does. The argument most often made
by MNCs' spokesmen is that technology payments by their subsidiaries
are necessary to defray the costs of centralized R&D activity by the
company. To examine this defense in greater detail, I calculated the
correlation between technology payments (as a percentage of sales)
of MNCs' subsidiaries and the intensity of parental R&D.* This test
did, indeed, provide support for the argument in the Mexican case.
That is, high rates of technology payments were found to be somewhat
correlated with high rates of corporate R&D activity. However, these
payments are often extraordinarily high: In 104 Mexican cases examined where technology payments were positive in 1972, their payments
ratio exceeded the parent company R&D ratio in 45 instances. (In 32
cases the technology payments ratio exceeded the parent corporations'
R&D ratio by more than one percentage point.) Therefore, there is
some substance to the charge that MNCs' subsidiaries are often "over-
charged" for the services provided by corporate headquarters.

Concluding Remarks

There are many more similarities than differences in the industrial market structures of Brazil, Mexico, and the United States.
Not only are most markets quite highly concentrated in both LDCs,
but the levels of concentration are similar in many industries. Many
similarities also exist with respect to other structural dimensions:
market shares, advertising, and R&D. These observed structural
parallelisms in the Brazilian and Mexican manufacturing sectors suggest that both result from similar underlying economic forces.
In most respects the market structures of Brazil and Mexico
are small-scale replicas of the American markets from which the
U.S. MNCs originate. This is particularly true in consumer goods
industries where MNCs pursue product differentiation practices that
have served them well in the United States. It is likely that MNCs
generally follow other familiar and time-tested strategies characteristic of their home markets, at least in host countries where there is
much foreign investment. Nor is the market environment likely to
change their marketing strategies, because MNCs' affiliates tend to

---

*There were 133 observations for Mexico and 84 for Brazil; the
correlation coefficients were +.36 in Mexico (but only +.23 when only
positive payments were used) and +.04 in Brazil. Given the Brazilian
policy of disallowing most royalty remittances within companies, the
low correlation coefficient merely indicates the effectiveness of that
policy; only 35 Brazilian subsidiaries had positive technology payments,
most of them quite low.

be located in industries where most of their rivals are other MNCs' subsidiaries.* Traditional modes of oligopolistic conduct, positively reinforced by supranormal profits (see Chapter 5), in turn lead to the restructuring of denationalized host country industries to fit home country molds.

The findings also lend support to the theory that private-international-investment flows originate in and reflect the oligopolistic industries of the investing country. Thus, to fully understand many features of foreign direct investment in LDCs requires an examination of the roots of such investments in the industrial structures of the MNCs' homelands.

---

*Newfarmer and Mueller (1975) show that in Brazil and Mexico well over half of the leading competitors of MNCs' affiliates are other MNCs.

4

THE THEORY AND STATISTICAL STUDY OF INDUSTRIAL MARKET POWER

This chapter has several objectives: (1) to review the purposes of, and interpretations given to, statistical market structure—profit performance studies of industrial organization, (2) to determine the theoretical justification given for the inclusion of various dependent and independent variables in such studies, (3) to establish a priori expectations concerning the strength and direction of the influence of the causal variables upon performance, (4) to examine how the statistical models have been operationalized (that is, what data sources, period, levels, and proxies were used), and (5) to review and assess the overall results of such tests. All of the above objectives will be pursued from the point of view of applying such tests to data from a semi-industrialized less developed country.

The exposition is organized into four main sections. In the first part, there is a general description of statistical, cross-sectional, market structure-performance studies, their place in industrial organization (IO), and a critique of their limitations. The second part, in seven subsections, discusses many of the variables employed in such tests. This is followed by a short commentary on some likely special problems arising from the implementation of these studies in newly industrializing countries. Finally, the concluding remarks deal with some recent and proposed improvements in the studies under review.

STRUCTURE-PERFORMANCE STUDIES IN GENERAL

Statistical, and especially cross-industry, industrial organization analyses are of a relatively recent origin. Individual industry studies were the main vehicle through which the Masonian paradigm (structure→conduct→performance) was applied during the first two

decades of industrial organization studies (Mason 1973). But beginning with the early 1950s econometric techniques were being increasingly applied to cross-industry data, partly because of the availability
of trustworthy data and partly because of the dissatisfaction of economists with the case study approach (which, because of its essentially
historical character, tended to emphasize the particularities of the
case, hence making generalizations and comparisons difficult).

The basic model of IO posits a causal chain running generally
from the elements of market structure to the forms of firm or market
conduct to various measures of performance to such ultimate norms
of economic welfare as the levels, growth, and distribution of income
and wealth. Market structure refers to those aspects of a firm's or
industry's environment that are relatively unalterable in the shorter
run. Conduct is the term used to encompass the dominant pattern of
decision-making characteristics of the firms in a market and refers
especially to reactions to structural influences and to pricing or
product design strategies, adopted vis-a-vis other rivals in their market. Performance is measured in several ways, but the levels of
supranormal profits, supracompetitive prices, macro stability, and
rates of technological progressiveness are the most common criteria.

It is the inclusion of the conduct dimension that distinguishes IO
from other branches of production economies, for in the latter cases
the markets are assumed to be perfectly competitive and the conduct
of firms completely deterministic. Thus, firm conduct is only of interest in the context of imperfectly competitive markets. Because IO
has been by custom and by data availability largely restricted to the
manufacturing sector, it might well be characterized as the study of
imperfect industrial competition. *

The hypothesizing of this linear chain of causality would appear
to lend itself to the application of two-stage or stepwise ordinary least-
squares models. One equation would express the quality of performance as a function of conduct variables that would, in turn, be expressed as a function of the relevant market structure characteristics.
But instead, cross-industry and cross-firm testing has largely omitted
the conduct aspect; performance has been linked directly to structural
conditions and has subsumed some intervening modes of conduct.
This omission is hardly surprising in view of the difficulty of operationalizing such concepts as the degree of cooperation (as opposed to
the degree of rivalry) or collusion, the effectivensss of market shar-

---

*More recently, however, industrial organization economists
have been branching out to examine competitiveness statistically in
other, nonindustrial sectors, such as banking (Heggestad and Rhoades
1976) and food retailing (Marion et al. 1977).

ing agreements, the proximity of a cartel to a joint profit-maximization arrangement, or the level of product design and other (nonprice)
competition—even if such conduct were readily observable. Thus,
the study of firm conduct has been related to market structure almost
entirely at the theoretical level via the generation of a plethora of
oligopoly models (see McKie 1970: 9-20) relevant to the study of modern industrial organizations each based on special behavioral assumptions. Practically no statistical studies have been done on the relationship of conduct to performance. *

The class of empirical structure-performance studies has not
been without its detractors, or at least critics. Mason himself advocated a more inductive approach, that is, inferences based on generalization from a large number of in-depth studies of particular firms or
industries (Bain 1970a: 169). Often the choice of subject was determined by public access to sufficiently detailed data, and this usually
meant that some major antitrust case had to precede the study. George
Stigler was only the most prominent of several economists who expressed grave reservations over early large-scale cross-industry
statistical studies. Earlier statistical work tended to confirm his belief, for his 1963 monograph was the first study (and has remained
one of the few studies) that failed to find a statistically significant relationship between profit rates and an element of market structure.
Subsequently, however, he was able to establish such a relationship
(Stigler 1964).

Another view, which implies that statistical structure-performance
experiments only "prove" a sufficient connection and not a necessary
one, is a version of Gibrat's law of proportionate growth. This law
explains how stochastic growth processes generate a skewed size distribution of firms. A recent statement of this position is by Mancke
(1974), who essentially argues that "lucky" (or successful) firms will
have both high market shares and high profits and that this is the underlying mechanism explaining the resulting log normal distribution of
firms. While this may provide a sufficient explanation for observed
concentration in a few industries, it flies in the face of the long-run
stability of market structures. Moreover, many industries remain
atomistically structured despite the concentrating tendency of stochastic growth processes. Clearly, chance plays a strong role in industrial restructuring, and that is precisely why stochastic disturbance
terms are specified in econometric studies of performance.

---

*A very interesting exception is a study that suggests that the in-
cidence of discovered overt collusion is causally related to declines
in industry profitability (Asch and Seneca 1976).

Other criticisms have been more specific and ex post rather than ex ante. One set of objections centers on the functional forms of the basic models and their underlying behavioral assumptions. Comanor (1971), for example, notes that the absence of any generally agreed upon oligopoly model implies that the functional forms adopted have no claim to being fully specified. "On the contrary, investigators appear content to study one aspect of the total picture, to investigate the impact of one variable upon another" (p. 406). Related to this point is the concern that some variables specified as exogenous may, in fact, be endogenously determined. That is, the technique of regression analysis by its very construction is asymmetrical and requires that the direction of causality run from the "independent" to the "dependent" variables. Some variables typically specified as market structure elements, advertising or R&D expenditures, for example, may in reality be simultaneously (or lagged) determined by the firm's or industry's performance, because they are often "noncontractual costs." This is Bain's term for highly discretionary expenditures that depend on a firm's gross margin and are often accounting transfers within the firm. This somewhat technical point is merely a special example of a more general reservation held by many industrial organization economists of the field's linear structure-behavior-performance approach. Phillips (1976), for one, considers this a naive, Cournot-like approach that ignores various potentially significant "feedbacks" stemming from the adaptive responses of firms. He would include under this rubric not only product differentiation and sales promotion intensities (already mentioned) but also limit pricing, technological innovation, wages, and even industrial regulation. An assessment of these charges is made in the last section of this chapter, and criticisms regarding model and variable specification appear in the following sections.

One final set of criticisms appears to center on the purposes of such studies. What objective is being pursued? What problem has been selected? To answer these questions, it is convenient to consider the goals under three successive headings: verification, prescription, and parameter estimation.

The primary and for a while the only objective of statistical structure-performance analyses was the testing of hypotheses derived from the corpus of oligopoly theories as a means of verifying the theoretical foundations of industrial organization, and the tripartite Masonian hypothesis in particular. Precisely which of the many alternative oligopoly theories was being verified by the data was seldom made explicit. This is an important issue, however, because if the different oligopoly models yield different predictions and if different models best represent different industries, it is legitimate to apply statistical tests only to intraindustry data (or to groups of industries

known to fall into the same oligopoly category); that is, if it is true
that oligopoly theories are industry-specific, general interindustry
empirical hypothesis testing lacks a theoretical foundation (Demsetz
1974: 166). Another, related objection concerns the static nature of
most oligopoly models. Most of these models are explanations of
supracompetitive pricing or profits with a given level of industry concentration or other market characteristics. Most early oligopoly
models provided no explanation of the structure of the industry (Cour-
not's may be an exception) or how supranormal returns are maintained.
For empirical tests, the second of these objections implies that the
confirmation of such models ought to be restricted to a time period
sufficiently short to preclude any significant changes in the underlying
industry structure, especially in the number of sellers.

It is also possible to resolve these objections to statistical interindustry tests of theoretical verification along several other lines.
One tack is to examine the various oligopoly models for uniformity of
predictions despite the diversity of behavioral assumptions. Weiss,
having done just that, concludes that "of the theories covered, most
predict a positive effect of concentration on profits" (Weiss 1974: 192).
Only the "kinked demand curve" theory does not predict higher than
competitive prices in the long run, but this theory is largely discredited
today (Bain 1960; Scherer 1970: 148). A second survey of oligopoly
theories likewise concludes that under conditions of high market concentration and the recognition of interdependence, "we should expect
oligopolistic industries to exhibit a tendency toward the maximization
of collective profits, approximating the pricing behavior associated
with pure monopoly" (Scherer 1970: 157). Of course, many factors
can either strengthen or weaken this basic tendency (Scherer: 1970:
158-212).

Thus, while the consensus is that concentration at least has a
predictable influence on performance across industries, it remains
to consider the other hypothesized causal factors. Many of these
posited influences (product differentiation, absolute costs of capital
investment, and economies of large scale) can be considered barriers
to entry). The theory of barriers to entry, an important addition to
the understanding of industrial organization, was first formulated by
Bain (1951). Although often developed within a comparative-static
framework (for example, Bain 1958: 252-69), the theory is basically
a dynamic explanation of how firms are able to establish and maintain
supracompetitive prices over long periods of time. The three main
types of barriers thus act as sufficient determinants of too high long-
run profits in concentrated industries so long as firms attempt to
maximize their value. Clearly, Bain intended the theory to apply across all manufacturing industries not subject to regulation (and some
other forms of blocked entry—although these may be considered within
his theory as extreme cases of an infinite, immediate condition of entry).

Taken as a whole, the body of still valid economic theories of oligopoly, together with the theory of barriers to entry, provides a sufficient theoretical foundation for empirical tests of the influence of the elements of market structure upon industrial performance. It must be admitted, however, that these two complementary theories have not been presented as yet in a cohesive formal model. Nor do the independent variables listed exhaust the possible long- and short-run influences on performance. In a recent brief industrial organization survey, for example, McKie lists about 20 structural characteristics likely to bear on performance (1970: 9-10). In addition to the level of seller concentration and the height of barriers to entry, he includes the conditions of demand, product design characteristics, cost and factor market conditions, the type of technology used, government regulations, and buyer concentration; if the researcher is primarily interested in the effects of seller concentration and barriers to entry, the other factors may be considered "control" variables that allow for interindustry differences and thus hold them constant for the purpose of analysis of the "pure" effects of the other variables. Many of the more recent tests have had as their primary purpose the introduction of novel causal variables.

A slightly different tack may be taken to justify the statistical testing of industrial organization hypotheses. One can admit that all the various available measures of seller concentration are only rough substitutes for the effectiveness of collusion, which is at any rate one conduct-related characteristic that may over time alter market structure. Moreover, one can view concentration in a market as the outcome of several other truly independent elements of market structure. This view of concentration (or changes in concentration) has some empirical support (Mueller and Hamm 1974; Comanor and Wilson 1974) and suggests at least two possible empirical approaches to deal with it. One method would be to estimate concentration as a function of the appropriate market structure dimensions and then estimate a second function where the performance index is related to the predicted concentration level and other conduct variables. Two-stage least-squares regression may be the appropriate tool to use in this case. A second method, which also recognizes that concentration is an intermediate variable, is simply to present alternate results: one that includes concentration but excludes its determinants, and vice versa.

In addition to verifying the predictions of the oligoply and barriers-to-competition theories, another structure-performance thesis (logically distinct from the others) is that relating to the dominant firm. Assuming that the dominant firm has no scale advantages over its (possibly many) smaller rivals, the theory predicts a gradual loss of market share for the large firm. This result could be delayed, however, by several tactics reminiscent of oligopoly conduct: limit pricing,

collusion with fringe firms, or the erection of barriers to establishment of new plant capacity. A convincing test of this theory would
require market share data and a performance index at the firm level,
as well as market level data on the other above-mentioned factors.
Only one, rather exploratory test of the dominant-firm hypothesis
has been performed, but its results confirmed the persistence of the
phenomenon (Weiss 1974: 184-87).

The second major purpose of statistical market structure-performance analyses is to aid public policy formation. Most of the policies under consideration were "antitrust"-oriented and at the national
level. In particular, many of these studies have had something to recommend on the issues of horizontal and conglomerate mergers and industrial deconcentration policies (for example, FTC 1969; Weiss 1974),
even though this may not have been the primary objective of the author.
(Indeed, such conclusions may have been drawn and publicized by other
people long after the original publication date.*) A few studies have
addressed other policy issues: the efficient functioning of capital and
labor markets (Shepherd 1964); the question of excessive advertising
(Comanor and Wilson 1974); the efficacy of price controls or other
tools of macrostabilization (Weiss 1966); the effects of patents, taxation rules, regulation, and other forms of government or legal intervention (though many of these have been industry, rather than cross-
industry, studies); and the effects of trade policy (especially as a form
of foreign firm market entry). There have been a few public economic
issues as yet relatively untouched by these studies: public ownership
of manufacturing enterprises, the effects of "moral suasion," and
most of the aspects of oligopolistic conduct, such as price fixing,
price discrimination, vertical integration, and restrictive practices.

The third main objective to be distinguished is that of parametric
estimation. Unlike the case of demand equations or production functions, there has been little interest in structural estimation per se in
IO. The lack of agreement on the general forms of the basic market
structure-performance models has led to an almost total reliance on
uncomplicated, additive, linear models, and interest has centered
on the significance and direction of the influence of the explanatory
variables. Until fairly recently, with the exception of the debates on
the "critical level" and "marginal" concentration, the absolute size
of a parameter has generally been left undiscussed (Comanor 1971).

---

*Some analyses have explicitly introduced merger-activity varia-
bles with a view to guiding public policy making. Marion et al. (1977),
for example, found that food chains' performance was adversely affected by both merger activity and de novo entry by other large food
chains.

Two examples of studies in this category are Siegfried and Weiss (1974) and Comanor and Wilson (1974). In the first study, the authors estimate a market structure-profits function for the purpose of providing conservative numerical estimates of the degree of misreporting of profits due to the current treatment of advertising outlays as a current expense under the tax rules. The Comanor and Wilson book is an extensive test of the hypothesis that advertising is a source of market power, and it includes a generous discussion of public policies toward advertising; part of their analysis includes fairly sophisticated estimates of the aggregate losses to consumers or society as a whole due to excessive advertising, allocative and "X" inefficiencies, and monopoly transfers. The provision of such estimates, particularly when large and expressed in terms relating to GNP or personal income, can help persuade the public and policy makers alike of the necessity of some particular industrial policy change.

The application of structure-performance tests to data from LDCs presents several special problems as well as opportunities. With respect to the basic structure-conduct-performance paradigm of IO, if the results of such tests are to be applied to policies in the LDCs, they must be especially strong and convincing because of the widespread antipathy displayed toward orthodox economies by intellectuals in LDCs. Because these intellectuals often view their countries as in a relationship of economic dependency or inferiority with the more industrialized economies, they may deny that their industrial structures resemble those of the more advanced areas. Moreover, the presence of considerable foreign ownership in many industries may introduce new behavioral modes not heretofore considered in models based on the experience of the developed economies. With respect to policy questions, any economist employing such data must recognize that the overriding goal of LDCs today is that of development, and any research findings must if possible relate to that goal. Studies of industry in LDCs should also recognize the great sensitivity that exists with respect to the power of multinational corporations (in those economies that are not centrally planned); moreover, the issue of mergers by MNCs is an important one with many international ramifications.

The issue of the acceptability of orthodox economics does not necessarily revolve strictly around basic values. It may partially be resolved by a comparison of the predictive quality of the competing thought systems. Whether IO is sufficiently neutral to encampass different national industrial structures and divergent cultures is also an empirical question.* Recent investigations have shown that the in-

---

*A fine example of the application of the industrial organization model to a non-Western nation is the comprehensive study of Japanese

dustrial structures of some LDCs are similar enough to warrant more
formal analyses (Newfarmer and Mueller 1975; Fajnzylber 1970;
Fajnzylber and Tarrago 1975). Special macroeconomic features,
such as openness to foreign trade, can presumably be adequately han-
dled through the introduction of additional variables. The issue of special behavioral characteristics of national or multinational firms operating in the LDCs is clearly a serious one, as recent testimony before
the Senate Subcommittee on Multinational Corporations has revealed,
especially the apparent tampering with the traditional categories of
firm accounts. Specifically, many large MNCs have admitted to entering bribery expenses under their "product development" or "research
and development" categories (Wall Street Journal, May 9, 1975).*
To the extent that special features of international business practices,
such as the bribery factor, are unmeasurable, estimated structure-
performance relationships are likely to be systematically dampened.

Perhaps the most candid position to take in this controversy is
to admit that the empirical work of the last two decades has been exploratory and inductive to a large extent; that is, the received theory
has been a solid but rather general guide to model specification. Thus,
it is only natural to adopt an experimental approach in respect to the
inclusion of certain variables and the adoption of specific functional
forms. The interpretation of results has from the beginning required
some post hoc theorizing, but this has often had the advantage of per-
mitting future testing to attain a higher degree of refinement.

STRUCTURE AND PERFORMANCE VARIABLES

In this section the theoretical justification, a priori expectations,
and actual operationalizing of the variables used in empirical, cross-
sectional tests of the relation of market structure elements to industrial performance will be discussed. It is convenient to organize this
exposition into seven main parts, each corresponding to a group of
variables: profit performance, concentration and market positions,
product differentiation and barriers to entry, technological and cost

---

industrial organization by Caves and Uekusa (1976). In their study
special care was taken to adjust for the presence of the remnants of
those financial-industrial agglomerations called zaibatsu.

*A total of $400 million in improper payments made during 1970-
76 has been divulged by more than 300 U.S. corporations (Wall Street
Journal, February 28, 1977). Such practices are clearly widespread
and even customary in many countries and are not limited to U.S.
corporations.

variables, managerial and organizational variables, and miscellaneous variables. The final paragraphs of this section will consider the implications for testing in the context of LDCs.

Profit Performance

Profit rates are only one measure of performance. Other indexes include macrostability, selling costs, rates of technological progressiveness, and wealth or income distribution. A few experiments have been conducted on all of these other criteria (compare Weiss 1974: 382-97), but by far the largest number of such tests have been applied to profits or excess profits.

Perfectly competitive markets imply zero profits for all firms in the long run. Conversely, high profit rates (measurement problems aside), if persistent and inexplicable in terms of legal-institutional interventions into the market, have come to be accepted as an indirect measure of monopoly power; that is, high profits rates are a sufficient (but not necessary) condition of market power. Monopoly or market power is, strictly speaking, the ability of a firm to hold the price of a given product above the level predicted by the model of a perfectly competitive market, assuming cost and demand conditions hold constant across firms in that market. In the case of the pure monopoly model and most of the oligopoly models, supracompetitive prices translate directly into supranormal profits (that is, profits in excess of the opportunity cost of management services and venture capital), so long as the Marshallian "law of demand" holds and seller entry is restricted or effectively impeded. It can also be shown as a corollary that the existence of market power implies price distortions that lead to allocative inefficiency and losses in social welfare. Therefore, persistent supranormal profits are an indicator of poor economic performance, even where cost minimization is pursued by firms.

All this is well accepted in the case of pure monopoly, but in the contemporarily developed market economies this is often an empirically empty box. The oligopoly theories require the introduction of the idea that firms recognize that their individual profit rates are dependent on the moves made by rivals; that is, the possibility of "oligopolistic reaction" must be admitted. One form of reaction is that of collusion or accommodation with rivals. If there is successful overt or tacit collusion on prices or production levels in a given market with no excess capacity, the "small numbers" case of Chamberlin predicts a movement toward the attainment of maximum joint profits, which will always be above the sum of maximum individual firm profits. If one or more of the necessary conditions is not fulfilled (instantaneous response to rival moves, insensitivity of market share to rival price cuts, and

identical cost functions), the outcome could be any price yielding profits between those of the joint monopoly and competitive limits. This
model may well have been Chamberlin's great contribution to industrial
organization theory, certainly surpassing his doubtful monopolistic-
competition theory (Bain 1968). Both models predict supracompetitive
prices, but only the first points to high long-run prices relative to
marginal costs as well.

Although this theory explains why high profits are indicative of
poor performance, it provides no guidance on which rate is the most
appropriate, other than one that comes closest to measuring pure
economic profit. Bain himself, in the first cross-industry statistical
investigation (1951), considered profits expressed as a proportion of
sales, assets, or net worth (stockholders' equity) to be "effectively
interchangeable." He did, however, point out that, in addition to
"contractual costs," imputed interest charges should be netted from
revenues in the case of the ratio to sales but not subtracted when the
ratio is to equity. The imputed interest rate is often taken to be the
equilibrium market or "prime" rate of interest on borrowed capital,
though in a few studies actual interest payments have been used (for
example, FTC 1969). All authors agree that because of interindustry
variation in effective taxation rates, profits should be expressed after
taxes.

The third measure, the rate of return to total assets, has generated more discussion concerning its proper specification. Because
assets include both equity and long-term debt, interfirm profit rates
can be expected to vary according to the variability in degrees of firm
leverage. Highly leveraged firms, those with high long-term debt-
to-equity ratios, have lower true profits than those firms of the same
asset size that have financed investment through internal sources of
funds. Hence, researchers have attempted to correct for this distor-
tion by adding interest payments (the return to debt) to net profits
(the return to equity) when expressing it as a ratio of total assets.
Alternatively, when interest payments have not been available, a
leverage term has been introduced to control for the effect (for example, Hall and Weiss 1967). Not all researchers agree with this analysis, however. Miller, Modigliani, and others take the position that
there are great variations in the degree of interindustry risk. It is
known, for example, that the rates of return on total assets are considerably lower in banking and public utilities than in durable goods
manufacturing but that the rates of return on equity are roughly the
same for all three of those sectors. Firms in high-external-risk
industries may, therefore, find their ability to borrow diminished.
This line of reasoning implies that firms in high-risk industries must
earn a "risk premium" on their profits in order to attract additional
capital. Conversely, high leverage ratios may be regarded as evi-

dence of a "vote of confidence" by the capital market in a firm's growth or profit potential. I return to this below.

A fourth measure of profits has sometimes been employed, especially by researchers using plant level data. The "price-cost margin" is approximated by the value of shipments net of labor and materials costs expressed as a proportion of the value of shipments. Collins and Preston (1969) consider this measure conceptually superior to, though closely correlated with, the other three rates. If advertising and other central-office expenses could be subtracted also, Weiss (1974: 199) would agree, if the test could also control for interindustry differences in fixed capital-output ratios.

A fifth index of firm performance, and one that is compatible with the "managerial and behavioral" theories of the firm, is the "valuation ratio," the ratio of the stock market value of a firm to its book value. It is argued that after ensuring the firm has enough profits to satisfy the stockholders at least minimally, managers attempt to implement business strategies that attract buyers to their stock. This goal makes raising capital easier, prevents takeovers, and provides personal satisfaction for both the firm's managers and its stockholders.

The preference for one index over another does not appear to be rooted in theory. Indeed, Helmberger (1976) has shown that from the point of view of predicting misallocation of resources, none of the ratios has any intrinsic advantage over the others. Rather, preferences for refined price-cost margins appear to be based on two measurement considerations. Most profit data have heretofore been taken from annual reports or tax returns; these sources suffer from well-known biases because of standard accounting practices pertaining to the valuation of physical assets, managerial prerequisites, and the treatment of intangibles (Weiss 1974: 196-97). Second, indexes based on plant shipments are largely free from the problems engendered by product diversity. On the other hand, many researchers have argued that the correct choice of the profit rate turns on the question of the locus of firm decision making. If managers of corporations take their decisions solely on the basis of stockholders' interests, the net profit-to-equity or valuation ratio measures are the most appropriate. If corporate managers are sales maximizers or empire builders, the rates based on sales or assets levels may be preferred. Few would argue that plant managers have authority to decide production levels. There is another argument in favor of accounting rates; when working with a set of undiversified firms or with firm data supplemented with product-level sales figures, it is possible to use a weighting procedure for the available market structure variables (for example, FTC 1969: 3-5). In the end, however, the choice of measures is likely to depend on data access. Those studies with access to highly detailed sources generally report their results with multiple specifications of the dependent variable when they are able, and the results are generally quite similar. Net accounting profits as a proportion of net worth have remained the most frequently used, but it is probably true, as John Blair states, that for the United States at least, "as the methods of analysis have become more complex and sophisticated . . . the underlying financial data on which they are based have become less and less usable for the purpose" (Blair 1972: 535).

A few minor points remain to be discussed. One problem is the period of time covered by the analysis. To test the market structure-profits hypothesis, theory suggests that equilibrium long-run profits ought to be used. Gambeles's (1969) study has shown that some of the dimensions of market structure are highly sensitive to swings in the business cycle. Thus, ideally profits ought to be averaged over a period of years. Even tests that have relied on short-run profits have sometimes provided significant results; however, when corrections are made for conditions likely to give rise to "windfall" profits, such as prior sales growth (see, for example, Collins and Preston 1969; Rhoades 1973; Khalilzadeh 1974). Yet, as Bain (1970b) warns, the period of analysis should not be so long as to abrogate the stability of the underlying market structure; he suggests that an upper limit may be about ten years. Another problem, first pointed out by Stigler, is that "entrepreneurial withdrawals" are likely to be inversely related to firm size; hence, small, and especially privately held, firms should be dropped from the sample if no estimates of these withdrawals are available.

One final point concerns the level of analysis. Many of the earliest studies assigned some leading firms to their industries, averaged their profit rates, and then used the industries as the units of observation; Bain (1951) pioneered this method. Some later studies used the profits of all firms in a given two-, three-, or four-digit industry. In addition to the diversification problem, it is generally conceded that higher levels of aggregation imply better statistical "fits" because the averaging of profits (or other variables) tends to dampen the extreme values associated with individual firms (FTC 1969). Thus, while the use of plant- or firm-level data is generally preferable, weak results must be expected unless several variables are introduced to control for likely differences in capacity utilization, managerial techniques, product characteristics, historical performance, multiplant or firm economies of scale, location, debt structure, or other characteristics.

Additional complications would result if the data base were controlled subsidiaries or if the affiliates were located overseas. Studies of the management styles of multinational corporations tend to conclude that the locus of decision making tends to swing away from the foreign affiliate to the central headquarters as the corporation gains more experience in the foreign area or as foreign sales become a larger part of total sales (Brooke and Remmers 1970). As the firm develops a more global view, the profits of individual affiliates tend to become secondary to the goal of global, firm-wide profit maximization. Moreover, the international aspects of the situation may imply additional distortions in accounting profits. Accounting practices across countries are even less standardized than those within the same country; the treatment of inventories and the translation of currencies is crucial in view of currency exchange risks and differing rates of international inflation. The existence of joint-venture partners may alter profit reporting. Perhaps most important is the opportunity for shifting profits by means of transfer pricing in interaffiliate trade (see Robbins and Stobaugh 1973). While every attempt should be made to adjust for such practices, the availability of even the most detailed company accounts is unlikely to offer much scope for adjustment of the more clandestine distortions. On the other hand, microdata analyses that manage to explain even half of the variance in profit rates ought to be considered especially impressive and credible.

Concentration and Market Position

The relation of market concentration to profits has been traditionally the primary focus of cross-industry statistical analyses. Weiss (1974) includes 55 separate studies of this type in his survey, and more have appeared since early 1974. No other causal variable has been so universally included in empirical studies of industrial organization, and, along with entry barriers, its theoretical underpinnings seem to be best developed. Interest in aggregate concentration in the industrial sector goes back a long way (relative to the life of IO as a separate field), partly as a result of seemingly endless popular and official concern with the power of "big business" (Scherer 1970: 11). The first systematic study of concentration appeared in an article by Gardiner Means (1931), and the first sectoral data four years later. Finally, more empirical work has been done on the determinants of concentration (for example, Mueller and Hamm 1974; Bain 1970a; Shepherd 1972; Porter 1974) than on any other aspect of market structure, save perhaps advertising (Comanor and Wilgon 1974; Greer 1971) or R&D intensities (for example, Mansfield 1968; Scherer 1965; Comanor 1967; Grabowski 1968).

The theory, which posits a positive association between concentration and monopoly profits, is based on a presumption of oligopolistic interdependence: The benefit of collusion is a movement toward maximum joint profits, but the costs of collusion are like market-transac-

tion or information costs. In Stigler's version of the approach oligopolists who wish to set a monopoly price are limited by the difficulty
of detecting clandestine price cuts or other noncooperative maneuvers
by individual firms (Stigler 1968: 39-63). Both the costs of policing
effective agreements and the probability of not detecting such strategic
moves tend to rise with the number of participants (or potential participants) in a given market. The main mechanism of discovery of
"competitive" behavior is through shifts in individual-firm market
shares, and the punishment of mavericks would typically take the form
of price wars or setting prices near enough to competitive levels to
lower the inducement to cheat. In either case, however, market concentration, if a measure of the likelihood of effective collusion, is
directly related to the attainment of joint monopoly profits.

Like Chamberlin's, Stigler's oligopoly theory represents a significant improvement over classical models because, other than the
general presumption of a desire for oligopolistic coordination, behavioral models are deduced from the hypothesis of profit maximization and not simply assumed. Unlike some previous theories, his
model implies a specific concentration measure, the Herfindahl index.
The entropy index and others have also been suggested, but most researchers have used four-or eight-firm sales concentration ratios,
entered either as a continuous variable or in a qualitative form. The
Herfindahl index enjoys many advantages over the concentration ratio;
it handles mergers in an unambiguous way* and allows for inequality
among the leading firms. On the other hand, the Herfindahl index
tends to give great weight to the largest two or three firms in a market
and yields very low values in moderately concentrated industries.
Perhaps for this reason some studies have found stronger profit relationships using concentration ratios than Herfindahl indexes (for
example, Marion et al. 1977).

The use of national concentration ratios has been largely dictated
by availability, though studies in the United States have shown a close
correlation between the simple and Herfindahl indexes. More serious
is the problem of the proper delineation of the market. To correspond more closely to the economic concept, adjustments ought to be

---

*A merger of, say, the sixth- and tenth-ranked firms in a given
industry may or may not be registered by a four-firm concentration
ratio; this depends on the position of the new, postmerger, firm. If
the new firm ends up in the fifth position, the eight-firm ratio will be
affected but not the four-firm. If the new firm ranks fourth, both indexes will reflect the merger. Any intraindustry merger, is, however, automatically reflected by an increase in the Herfindahl index.

made for the existence of regional submarkets, noncompeting subproducts (both of which tend to lead to understated concentration figures), interindustry competition or imports (which bias the ratio upward). The existence of exports can bias the ratio in either direction,
depending on whether it is the industry leaders or the fringe firms that
export more intensively. The use of data at the product level (five-
or seven-digit census) will partially adjust for the problem of noncompeting subproducts; additionally some studies have introduced a "local
market" variable to correct for the submarket problem (for example,
Collins and Preston 1969; Rhoades 1973). Another, related defect of
using unadjusted concentration indexes of a firm's main product can
arise from profit distortions due to firm diversification biases; the
best procedure requires weighting by individual product sales (see
Dalton and Penn 1971), but even this method requires the assumption
of a linear relationship between concentration and profits (Weiss 1974:
195-96). On the whole, these various adjustments and weightings are
probably preferable to an arbitrary exclusion of certain observations.

As was mentioned above, the theory of the price leadership rep-
Another conceptually different concentration measure is the
"marginal concentration ratio," that is, the additional sales by the firm
or group of firms. Miller (1967) used the increased sales concentration accounted for by the fifth- through eight-ranked firms. If the effect on industry profits is negative (as Miller found), the strong policy
conclusion is to aid these "second tier" firms. But later studies using superior data apparently reverse his finding (FTC 1969: 34-35;
Weiss 1974: 373). Moreover, this marginal index is suspect because
of the unusual constraint to which it is subject.

As was mentioned above, the theory of the price leadership represents a model of oligopolistic interdependence conceptually distinct
from that of collusion, though some may regard it as a special form
of tacit collusion. The theory of the dominant firm was first developed
almost 70 years ago. In its present form and variations (dominant,
collusive, and barometric) price leadership provides a plausible mechanism for communicating and coordinating pricing decisions in at least
somewhat concentrated markets. The price leader (the firm that
first announces price changes and, by custom, is followed by other
firms in the industry) is not always the firm with the largest share.
Occasionally, smaller competitors with lower production costs or with
large shares in some subproducts may exercise leadership, but in
general the U.S. experience has demonstrated a historical association
between dominance (in the sense of having the largest market share)
and price leadership (Scherer 1970: 164-73). Effective price leadership will lead to profits above the competitive level for all firms in
the industry, especially if fringe firms can slightly differentiate their
products.

There are several possible variables that might be introduced
into a structure-profit function in order to capture the profit effects

of market leadership. One possible crude index of potential price leadership would be the rank of the firm in its industry, but simple rank is unlikely to reflect this potential unless accompanied by a large market share. Even a large market share (unless more than 50 percent) may be ineffective, however, if several competitors have similarly high shares. Thus, there appear to be two likely candidates for measuring the profit benefits of firm leadership. One of these is the firm's share, either by itself or combined with "high" rank (say, first or second in its market). Of course, market share, if it is intended to measure a form of market power of a firm, ought to be introduced along with an estimate of concentration, because some economists believe that market share and high returns may both reflect simply a superior product, better management, patent protection, luck, or the like (Demsetz 1974). The more important question is whether firm market share and industry concentration have independent influences on returns. Shepherd (1972) is one investigator to have included firm market share as a market-structure variable, but his data are from secondary sources, judgmental, and of doubtful accuracy. Moreover, his market share variable is based on a firm's primary product only, whereas the correct procedure for a diversified firm would involve weighting by sales of its individual products. For a highly diversified firm this would tend to lower the index because most firms have their largest share in their primary products. This method was followed by Dalton and Penn (1971) with highly significant and satisfactory results, even though the weighted firm market shares were highly correlated with the weighted four-firm concentration ratio ($r = 0.53$).

It should be noted that many studies have included a variable for firm size, and though the authors have not given this interpretation to it, the size variable may have captured some of the leadership effect (for example, Hall and Weiss 1968; Telser 1972; Gale 1972). The paper by Gale (1972) provides the most complete analysis of the expected effect of firm market share on firm profitability. Share, he argues, in part is merely a proxy for the historical possession of rent-yielding intangible assets. But also large market shares may be expected to exercise direct causal influences on profitability for several reasons: (1) because risk averse consumers may favor large share firms, (2) because a relatively large share will increase a firm's bargaining power within an oligopoly, and (3) because the firm may be able to take advantage of potential economies of scale. Gale also gives a cogent argument for expecting firm size and industry concentration to interact positively with share, while share and industry growth may interact negatively on profits. His own empirical results are somewhat unconvincing, however.

A second possible measure of firm entrenchment is called the "relative market share," the ratio of an individual firm's market share to a market-concentration ratio. This index is superior to mere share because it adjusts for the degree of concentration; thus, a firm with a 20 percent share would register high by this measure if all the other firms were fringe firms but would not, for example, be as "dominant" if four-firm concentration exceeded 80 percent. The 1969 FTC study first employed the relative market-share variable as a substitute for the cross elasticity of demand for the products of established firms with respect to the products of potential market entrants; that is, it was interpreted as a proxy for the intraindustry barriers to competition due to product differentiation in consumer-goods industries (p. 10). While its authors make a persuasive case for this interpretation in the case of consumer goods (and especially nondurable consumer goods where "repeat" buying is important), the historical accumulation of consumer loyalty is less likely in the case of consumer durables and producer goods (Comanor and Wilson 1974). Furthermore, except in the case of newly introduced products, very high values of relative market share may be best interpreted as dominance even when applied to consumer products. Imel and Helmberger (1971) too have indicated some uneasiness over the FTC interpretation, but both studies found that the variable had a strong, positive effect on profit rates among food industry firms. A resolution of these differences in interpretation would involve the simultaneous inclusion of both cross elasticities of demand and the relative market share in a regression test.

Product Differentiation and Barriers to Entry

The theory of barriers to entry as an element of market structure was initially developed by Bain in a series of important papers (1951, 1954) but is most fully developed in his 1956 monograph Barriers to New Competition. He was also the first to test the concept that the higher the barriers to new entry by firms, the higher are the profit rates of already established firms. The condition of entry is "the extent to which, in the long run, established firms can elevate their selling prices above the minimal average costs of production and distribution . . . without inducing potential entrants to enter the industry" (Bain 1968: 252). Thus, the overall, "immediate" condition of entry is measured by the percentage by which the maximum entry-forestalling price exceeds the minimum attainable average costs of established firms.

In practice, such price data are rarely available, and for cross-industry studies have never been available in sufficient numbers for statistical testing. The "prices" involved are not actual price-cost margins, but must be derived from other, separate analyses. However, Bain distinguished three sources or types of barriers to entry,

and it is these individual barriers that have been operationalized in
empirical structure-profits investigations. At the same time, Bain
recognized that any two of them may interact with each other, raising
the overall condition of entry in a multiplicative way; in particular,
the combination of important product differentiation disadvantaged
with significant economies of scale may result in exceptionally high
barriers to entry (Bain 1968). Also, subsequent researchers have
introduced new types of barriers to entry, as described below.

The first Bainian barrier to entry (and independent element of
market structure) is product differentiation, and its inclusion in empirical studies has been especially well argued for by Comanor and
Wilson (1974). Products are highly differentiated when consumer
loyalty is high and when the ability of rivals to imitate the product is
low; thus, the most direct measure of product differentiation is low
cross elasticities of demand and supply between products or producers,
but such data are not normally available for a wide array of products.
Consumer loyalty can be created and maintained through product design, service facilities, distribution methods (especially forward vertical integration), and advertising, but the last is widely asserted to
be the most effective, especially in consumer goods industries. Advertising outlays are both a source and a symptom of product differentiation. Past outlays have a cumulative effect on current consumer
habits, and present outlays are partly a result of advertising by rivals.
Comanor and Wilson present an elaborate formal model of consumer
choice among brands that is based on ignorance, search costs, and
risk aversion by consumers. *

Thus, advertising, as well as other forms of sales promotion,
has effects on both intraindustry (that is, brand) and interindustry
demand, but there is also a third effect, that of the creation or raising
of barriers to entry by potential rivals. Product differentiation via
advertising can raise entry barriers in four main ways:

1. Because it often requires less advertising per dollar of
sales to influence "repeat buying" by consumers than to induce brand
switching, there may be an absolute cost barrier created for new market entrants, above that originally faced by existing firms. This advantage for the established firms is similar to the temporary rents
earned from innovation, but these rewards will persist.
2. There may be a range over which there is increasing effectiveness in demand per advertising message; this is akin to the concept of technological economies of scale.

----

*They also show, by means of a sophisticated consumer expendi-
ture model for the United States, that consumer expenditure levels
among industries are strongly determined by industry advertising levels, more strongly than the prices of the products themselves.

3. For some kinds of national advertising, there is evidence of substantial declines in costs per message because of volume discounts; this situation is similar to pecuniary economies of scale.

4. Finally, entry may be more costly for new firms than for existing firms because of imperfections in the capital markets. In particular, the goodwill capital that may be created by future advertising is considered poor collateral by lending institutions.

Many tests of the advertising-as-a-barrier-to-entry hypothesis have been carried out since the first by Comanor and Wilson in 1967. Most have used the industry advertising-to-sales ratio as their index of advertising intensity; this should be most closely related to the economies-of-scale effects of advertising. Dalton and Penn (1971) obtained strong results using a weighted ratio for each firm. The absolute level of outlays may be more closely related to the absolute cost barrier aspects of advertising. Almost all of the tests have resulted in a strong positive relationship, at least in the consumer goods industries.*

Another index used is the short-run and long-run elasticities of demand with respect to price; they have been shown to have a strong positive effect on profits even when included along with the advertising-to-sales ratio (Comanor and Wilson 1974). Strangely, the advertising-to-sales ratios of individual firms have rarely been included in studies thus far, perhaps because of data limitations (an exception is Bloch 1971); a natural extension of the theory presented above would view such a variable as evidence of intraindustry rivalry via product differentiation.

It is reasonable to apply a similar interpretation to firm data on R&D intensities, as have Imel and Helmberger (1971).[†] Branch (1974)

---

*For a negative critique of these tests, see Brozen (1974). The experiments mentioned in this paragraph did not distinguish between the direct, static effect of product differentiation in the industry on profits (that resulting from the steepening of the demand curve) and the indirect, delayed effect on profits from entry discouraged by product differentiation. That is why the later Comanor and Wilson work is so important.

[†]Most researchers have treated normalized R&D activity as a measure of firm or industry progressiveness. Some others see R&D as a mode of behavior contributing to product design rivalry. Considering R&D as an element of market structure implies that in some industries it is so widespread as to force virtually all firms to carry on some minimally acceptable level of "new" product development. In this view, R&D inputs (expenditures or employees) are closely related

shows via a distributed lag analysis that R&D output (an introduction
of an innovation to practice) as a proportion of firm assets has a significant positive influence on profit rates, with the effect peaking after
about two years and decaying rapidly to near nil in about six years.
Moreover, he demonstrates that R&D activity is in turn affected by
current profits in most industries. A similar simultaneous equation
model has been tested for advertising intensity by Comanor and Wilson (1974: 153-63). They too show that the advertising budget and a
firm's cash flow are simultaneously determined. One corollary of
these studies is that ordinary least-squares methods of estimating
structure-profit relations are quite robust, that is, produce estimates
of coefficients whose significance levels are biased downward relative
to simultaneous equation techniques. Another conclusion is that under
conditions of growing advertising and sales current accounting profits
tend to be overstated relative to true profits because of the practice
of expensing rather than amortizing advertising and R&D expenditures
(Siegfried and Weiss 1974).

The second barrier to entry suggested by Bain is the absolute
cost advantages in production. (The possibility of absolute cost advantages in sales promotion has already been discussed.) These advantages may rest with the established firms because of (1) the control of lower cost production processes by patents, secrecy, or other
means, (2) the control of superior resources or inputs (including management services, labor, equipment, and raw materials) and the inability of potential entrants to acquire these inputs, or (3) the rationing or higher cost of liquid funds for the establishment of new plant
capacity. Absolute capital requirements barriers have usually been
measured by the outlay required for one efficient-sized plant.* Bain's
pioneering study (1954) of 19 U.S. manufacturing industries found that
in 13 this barrier was "substantial"—that is, it exceeded $10 million
(circa 1951)—and positively related to profits. In 7 of the 19 industries,
the barrier was "serious"—exceeding $100 million. Comanor and
Wilson (1974) used a similar measure, the product of estimated plant
minimum efficient scale times the ratio of total assets to total sales,
with significant and positive results.

Further refinements are needed for this concept; the "start-up"
costs of a new plant may be substantial and additional credit for inven-

---

to the marketing strategies of companies while other measures (for
example, R&D outputs or productivity changes) more accurately capture firm progressiveness.

*Plant efficiency here is understood to encompass both direct
production costs and costs related to physical distribution.

tories and working capital should be included. Moreover, methods
of calculating the minimum efficient plant scale have been quite crude
in most studies. In addition, few if any attempts have been made to
estimate the cost of developing alternatives to existing patents, of
penetrating rival secrecy (industrial espionage), of "raiding" a rival's
top management or technical staff, or of other absolute cost barriers.

The third barrier distinguished by Bain is economies of large-
scale firms, both plant and multiplant economies. Assuming that the
established firms do not all reduce their output in order to accommodate a new entrant (the "optimistic assumption" of Sylos-Labini), the
entrant must either produce at a suboptional scale or, by entering at
the minimum optional scale, force the pre-entry price down. In
either case, the established firms have an advantage over potential
entrants, and they can enhance this advantage by limit pricing.* Barriers due to economies of scale have been entered in structure-profit
functions by estimating the minimum efficient plant scale (MES) as
an average of a class of current plant outputs expressed as the percentage market share that output represents.

In Bain's 20-industry study, at least 5 or 6 had a minimum efficient scale exceeding 7.5 percent of U.S. GNP in 1951, but he also
found that in at least half of the cases, substantial increases in costs
occurred at suboptimal scales (Bain 1954). Multiplant economies of
scale were absent in most industries and were less than 5 percent in
the remainder. Bain's results have been essentially upheld by subsequent studies; minimum optional scales in the United States and internationally have had a median national market share of 2 to 3 percent.
Moreover, though small multiplant economies of scale do exist, they
arise only if noncompetitive input markets exist (Scherer 1974). Although the usefulness of statistical and engineering studies of cost
relationships has been challenged by some (McGee 1974), the consensus remains that firm economies of scale, especially those at the
plant level, can effectively raise barriers to entry. As is the case
with many elements of market structure, those barriers may interact
with each other or with concentration to raise profits in the long run
(Weiss 1974: 376).

Bain's is one of few studies to employ direct engineering estimates of MES in a statistical analysis of market power. Subsequent
studies have attempted to derive various proxies from public data on
plant sizes. One popular procedure, initiated by Comanor and Wilson

---

*Limit pricing is a strategy open to a dominant firm that involves
reducing prices below the level that will maximize short-run profits
but will, by limiting entry, lead to great long-run profits.

(1967), is to use the average industry share of the largest plants accounting for at least 50 percent of industry shipments as a proxy for
the MES barrier. In addition to problems associated with the definition of a single plant in the data, this measure is highly correlated
with seller concentration and is based on many assumptions, as Caves,
Khalilzadeh-Shirazi, and Porter (1975) point out. Moreover, it provides only one point on the (presumably L-shaped) long-run average
cost curve and indicates nothing about the curve's steepness (the dis-
economy of small scale). Caves suggests a variation on the MES index
that removes some of the collinearity problem and also puts forward
a new variable (the ratio of value added per worker in the smallest
plants in an industry to labor productivity in the largest plants), which
he interprets as being inversely related to the diseconomies of small
scale. * These two variables can be expected to interact to raise entry
barriers; that is, MES ought to exert a stronger effect in the presence
of substantial diseconomies of scale than if the long-run average cost
curve is nearly flat. When tested by Caves (1975), the new interaction variables for scale economies perform quite well, increasing the
fit and the significance of concentration over what obtained in two former studies (Khalilzadeh-Shirazi 1974; Comanor and Wilson 1967).

Clearly, some measure of the diseconomies of small scale
should be included where computable in future studies, for reasons
other than the reduction in multicollinearity likely to result. But the
current MES index also leaves much to be desired. A less arbitrary
index, were such data available, might be the size of the single "new-
est" (relative to the time period under study) plant built by a single-
plant firm that had recently entered the industry or had just replaced
an older facility. The only assumptions made by such a "marginal"
MES measure are careful engineering- and transportation-costs estimates by the plant's designers. Moreover, variables that could capture some of the effect of multiplant economies of scale have yet to
be designed and tested. One possible avenue that may be explored is
through the legal structure of the firm—the amount of intrafirm sales
integration among the firm's various subsidiaries, for instance.

A few other factors have been suggested to operate as entry barriers. Rhoades (1973, 1974), for example, has hypothesized that industry diversification raises barriers to entry into the industry. Diversification, he asserts, enhances the ability of firms to sustain
losses in some product lines and thus makes predatory pricing a
ble mode of conduct in their industries, though the incentive to employ

---

*Conceptually, this variable is appealing, but, in spite of the em-
pirical improvements noted below, the productivity measures for the
smallest plants are thought by many to be quite unreliable in the United
States.

this tactic is likely to be greatest in the concentrated industries. Furthermore, diversification implies a loss of public information about the existence of excess profits in any one industry that might have induced new entry into that industry. His measures of industry specialization partly incorporate the concept of industry vertical integration; one of his indexes is significant and of the expected sign, but the other apparently reflects the ease of entry. Given the theoretical justification provided, an argument could be made that the calculation of such indexes at the firm level might be the more valid procedure, together with a more precise vertical integration variable. This method was followed in the FTC (1969) study; here diversification was not interpreted a priori as a type of barrier so much as an index of the potential to exercise conglomerate power: the ability to practice cross-subsidization, reciprocity, and other special forms of conduct that can alter market structures. Profits may be enhanced for reasons unrelated to market power, for example, through a fuller utilization of the firm's resources, but because conglomeration may also lower risk (as a trade-off for higher average profits) and increase the likelihood of management diseconomies of scale, the net effect on profits is uncertain. In fact, this study found diversification significantly negative in its effect on profits, especially when defined at the product level. But Dalton and Penn (1971), using the same sample as the FTC study and a slightly different measure of diversification, find only nonsignificant negative coefficients in their structure-performance analysis. Telser (1972) also finds diversification negatively related to profits, but significantly so only in the least concentrated industries. Thus, the hypothesis concerning diversification seems to lead to unpredictable results and appears to be sensitive to the particular measure adopted in the experiment.

    Another variable related to entry conditions has been introduced by Esposito and Esposito (1971). They argue that the extent of market penetration via exports by foreign firms is an index of the ease of entry. Although transportation and tariff charges raise barriers for foreign producers, the net height of barriers may be lower for them than for potential domestic entrants for several reasons: lower factor costs, smaller minimum optimum scales, easier product differentiation where imported goods carry snob appeal, and shorter time lags when faced by entry-inducing price changes. Their variable, the ratio of imports to domestic value of shipments, is significantly inversely related to profit rates in their test.

    As can be seen from the above short review, the complete specification of entry barriers in market structure-profits analyses is a complex task. Until the day the overall condition of entry is available as a single index, the researcher is likely to resort to an additive for-

mulation of several potential barriers.* Moreover, the proper formulation of interactions among barriers is till largely uncharted territory.

Technological and Cost Variables

From the beginning of statistical testing of market power it was
recognized that it was desirable to control for interindustry differences
in the nature of production. Bain (1951), for example, apparently
tested for an association between profit rates and several variables
other than concentration: the capital-to-assets ratio, overhead-to-
total costs ratio, the consumer-producer good distinction, and product
durability. Partly because he apparently sought for significant simple
correlations and did not employ a multivariate technique, no significant relationships were discovered. Soon afterward, various authors
provided rationales for including other cost and technological factors
in multivariate regressions on profit. Sato (1961) proposed the insertion of the fixed assets-to-sales ratio and proxies for rates of technological change and excess capacity due to business cycle movements.
Fuchs (1972) and Sato both included indexes of market fragmentation,
partly to correct any understatement in national concentration levels
and partly to reflect differences in shipping costs across products.
Bain (1951) simply excluded fragmented industries from his experiment. Other technical controls used are the total assets-to-sales
ratio (Collins and Preston 1969), R&D intensity (Imel and Helmberger
(1971), the stock of human capital, and even dummy variables for each
major industry group (Telser 1972). Finally, many factors relating
to the long-run average cost of production have been considered above
as barriers to entry.

Variables of the types listed in the paragraph above and in the
sections that follow have been specified in structure-profit functions
for a number of reasons. One prime purpose is to "correct" the variation in the dependent variable; when regressing profits over sales,
for example, some index of interindustry variation in capital intensities

---

*An example of how an overall index (I0 of the condition of entry
might be constructed for various industries is given by Orr (1974) and
Gorecki (1977) for Canada. First, one regresses the gross rate of
entry onto several plausible barriers to entry, such as capital requirements (K), advertising intensity (A), R&D intensity (R), concentration
(C), and the minimum optimum scale of production (M). The regression coefficients, b_i, then become the weights for the composite barriers index. Thus, $I = b_1K + b_2A + b_3R + b_4C + b_5M$.

should be introduced to allow for normal returns on invested capital
and hence permit the market structure variables to reflect their effects on monopoly profits. Other variables introduced in order to reflect conditions likely to induce "windfall" or temporary profits also
lie in this category. A second and related purpose is to "correct"
the effects of the independent variables in the equation. The "regional
market" qualitative variable is often specified to adjust for market
definitions that are too wide in a geographic sense and thus clarify the
influence of concentration on profits. The incorporation of various
control variables also helps to avoid the problem of spurious correlations in the data and introduces greater certainty in the estimates of
the parameters of interest.

     Though of less interest from the point of view of industrial or-
ganization theory and policy, the expected direction and strength of
influence of some of the controls will be briefly reviewed here.

     One of the most widely used technological controls is that of
capital intensity (capital-to-sales, assets-to-sales, net book value-
to-shipments, and other ratios). A familiar theorem of classical
economics states that in long-run, competitive equilibrium, firm profit
rates on sales will be roughly proportional to optimal capital-to-output
ratios. Sato (1961), indeed, finds that these ratios have a very strong
positive influence on net profits as a percentage of sales. Collins
and Preston (1969), using different data and profit rates, also discovered a significant, positive effect of capital intensities on profits,
especially in industries with nonincreasing concentration. Virtually
all succeeding studies have obtained the same result (Rhoades 1973;
Caves, Khalilazdeh-Shirazi, and Porter 1975; Telser 1972; Khalilzadeh-Shirazi 1974), but they have also all used sales or shipments to
express the profit rates. Weiss (1974) suggests that the rate of return on equity also should be corrected for the capital-to-sales ratio
and that the rate of return to sales could alternatively be adjusted using the equity-to-sales ratio instead (pp. 198-99).

     If a variable for firm capital intensity were included in an equa-
tion in which differences in fixed costs were accounted for in some
other way, the interpretation given to the capital-to-output ratio might
be different; then it might be argued that it is a proxy for excess capacity and would be expected to be negatively related to profits. The
inclusion of variables that reflect capital or labor productivity across
firms is an indirect way of testing Leibenstein's "X" efficiency thesis.
A more direct procedure would specify an index of total factor productivity in the function to be estimated, perhaps in interaction with concentration. By itself, high productivity would be expected to generate
higher returns to management that are unrelated to the existence of
market power, but Leibenstein (1966) proposes that concentration and
"X" efficiency may be inversely related. In either case, correction

for success at cost minimization is a further refinement of the profits concept, and one that may be especially important in the less developed areas.

A second popular "technological" control is a qualitative variable for the existence of local or subnational markets. Sato (1961) was apparently the first to employ this variable, and his regressions demonstrated that it had the expected positive effect on profits, for the reasons mentioned above. Collins and Preston (1969) and Rhoades (1973) have successfully tested continuous indexes of market fragmentation or dispersion, thus validating the usefulness of such a variable when the experiment uses national data from a territorially large market like the United States.

Some related controls intended to correct for under- or overstatement in national concentration ratios are the export and import ratios. In a study of U.S. manufacturing-industry groups, Gambeles (1969) found that the ratio of export sales to total sales had a generally positive effect on profit rates and the import ratio had the opposite effect, but his results were not strong. Some of the significance of the import ratio that was the focus of Esposito and Esposito (1971) may contain this effect. Khalilzadeh-Shirazi (1974) found results similar to, but stronger than, Gambeles's for a structure-profits investigation of some U.K. manufacturing industries, but he interpreted the positive coefficient of the export-to-sales ratio as a return to increased risk for intrepid firms. Other researchers have attempted to correct the concentration ratio itself in a direct fashion (for example, Hall and Weiss 1967). These trade ratios may not merely reflect market structures; export-prone industries are generally those with favorable cost structures and some international comparative advantage. So far, only national import and export ratios have been calculated; an interesting extension would be the specification of firm-level export propensity, as measured by the total exports-to-sales ratio, in order to provide a more precise test of the Khalilzadeh risk hypothesis.

Very few statistical studies have included qualitative variables for the consumer-versus-producer goods and durable-versus-nondurable goods dichotomies as Bain suggested 25 years ago. Rhoades (1973) includes a consumer goods industry dummy variable in his regressions, but, as he notes (p. 154), the relation is positively biased because advertising expenditures are incorporated in the dependent variable, the "price-cost margin." One possible reason for excluding such a variable is that an advertising-to-sales variable is likely to capture almost the entire effect of the consumer-to-producer distinction, *

------

*However, Leonard Weiss, in a personal communication, reports that the introduction of both advertising-to-sales and consumer demand-

especially when specified as a qualitative variable (for example, Khalilzadeh 1974). Moreover, unless the test is carried out at the individual product level, there is likely to be little precision in assigning industries to a wholly consumer or producer good category.

The durability of a producer good helps distinguish between capital goods and intermediate products such as components and raw materials, but admittedly it is difficult to predict the direction of any systematic influence on firm profits. One can argue, however, that capital goods, because orders for them are likely to be lumpy with respect to size and time, do not lend themselves to facile tacit seller collusion (Scherer 1970: 206-8). If the complexity of the goods were also associated with their durability, this would provide an additional reason to expect durability to affect adversely the potential for price collusion among capital goods producers.

In the consumer goods industries, nondurability is held to enhance the potential for product differentiation in certain respects. To the extent that durability is associated with higher unit prices, consumers will benefit from information searches to determine actual quality differences and the ability of sellers to charge a premium or create consumer loyalty will be diminished. Moreover, nondurable goods are often characterized by frequent "repeat" buying; thus, advertising may be more effective for nondurable goods because it lowers the risks associated with changes in quality between purchases (Comanor and Wilson 1974). On the other hand, product durability may be associated with complexity, and this tends to diminish the value of personal inspection (a substitute for brand advertising). In these cases, it is likely that the "quality" image of the manufacturer itself or the retail outlet will sway consumers more effectively than the specific features of a particular model of a durable product (Porter 1974). Unlike advertising intensity, therefore, product durability is an ex ante aspect of consumer product differentiation and has an ambiguous a priori influence on seller profits.

Managerial and Organizational Variables

In this section, variables relating to differences in firm management or organization are considered. Some of these differences often derive from the nature of the product and may thus be characteristic of the industry as well. Moreover, much of the variation between

---

to-total demand variables (derived from an input-output table) into a market structure-profits equation reveals quite distinct effects on profits.

firms in managerial techniques either borders on conduct-related features (for example, R&D intensities) or may be captured by variables
already discussed in the preceding categories. The decision of a
firm to diversify, to innovate, or to export, for example, may be
partly conditioned by factors in the firm's environment, but it also
would be partly due to the level of risk aversion adopted by the firm's
management. So, too, some may consider the relative market share
of a firm or a firm's capital extensity to reflect the quality of the
firm's managers or the effectiveness of its organization. But some
aspects of firm or industry structure seem more particularly manage-
ment-related than those above. In particular, factors associated with
risk, debt structure, and the degree of management control will be
discussed.

There appears to be considerable controversy over inter- and
intraindustry risk and leverage in statistical market structure-profit
analyses. It seems helpful to distinguish between the risk associated
with the markets in which a firm operates (business risk) and the risk
to stockholders associated with the amount of debt relative to capital
(financial risk). "Leverage" is commonly measured by the ratio of
common equity to total assets. Thus, between industries business risk
is said to be represented by a high equity-to-assets ratio, but within
an industry financial risk is measured by a low ratio (Gale 1972).
Conventional financial theory posits that because of the risk aversion
of lenders, stockholders will require a higher rate of return, a "risk
premium," the higher the ratio of debts to assets: "Leverage" and
rates of return should be inversely related for the same levels of business risk. Hall and Weiss (1967) expected this inverse relationship
with rates of return on equity and using firm level data but expected
a positive relationship when using the rate of return on assets (especially where interest payments have not been subtracted from net
profits). Caves (1971) concurs with the Hall and Weiss position with
respect to profits as a proportion of equity. In their regressions on
profits-to-equity, both Gale and Hall and Weiss found "leverage"
positively and significantly related to profits (though the Hall-Weiss
results were sensitive to the specification of concentration); hence, increasing financial risk, after controlling for size, growth rate, and
concentration is negatively related to profits in these studies.

Not all investigators agree with the above approach. Shepherd
(1972) uses a different measure for "risk," the standard error of a
ten-year trend line fitted to each firm's profits. He unexpectedly
found that this risk measure was negatively related to profits, though
at a confidence level slightly below the conventional 10 percent standard.
A more recent paper by Hurdle (1974) calls into question the use of
debt structure as a proxy for risk. Leverage may have an independent
effect on profits and it may not be a good measure of business risk,

that is, industry-level risk. Moreover, she argues, there is no a priori predictability of the relationship between business risk and profitability or between the debts-to-assets ratio and profitability. Using the absolute annual deviation in firm profits as the index of business risk, a regression shows leverage to be statistically unrelated to risk. But the results of her empirical test of the structure-profits relationship are highly significant; here risk has both a positive and a negative effect on profits, depending on whether two-stage or ordinary least-squares procedures are followed; the leverage term is similarly ambiguous in sign, but significant, even when included with the standard deviation of profits. Hurdle's results point to the necessity of extreme care in interpreting the effects of risk on profits and the specification of a proxy for business risk. While it is still valid to interpret the debt ratio (nearly the inverse of equity-to-assets) as a good proxy for financial risk, a negative influence of this risk on profits may be evidence of the ascendance of managerial over stockholder risk aversion.

The degree of ownership control also arises in the context of high degrees of foreign ownership in industry or where the units of observation include some affiliates of foreign firms only partially owned by the parent firms (Stopford and Wells 1972). Wholly owned subsidiaries may systematically report profits in a biased way because of international differences in taxation structure (of which wholly resident-owned firms will not be able to take advantage). Generally, one would expect underreporting of net revenues in countries with relatively high effective rates of corporate income taxes. Moreover, the wholly owned affiliates of foreign companies have greater opportunities to transfer funds internationally than do nationally controlled firms (Robbins and Stobaugh 1973). Foreign joint ventures are more likely to have host-country nationals in top management or on boards of directors. Moreover, private host-country partners are likely to have lower time horizons than a large MNC. Thus, they may both press for higher short-run dividend declarations and frustrate nondividend transfers of profits out of the country. On the other hand, access to some centralized facilities of the parent complex may impart economies to the subsidiaries that will raise true profits. Therefore, the net effect of foreign ownership on reported accounting profits is highly uncertain. Khalilzadeh-Shirazi (1974) found a positive but insignificant impact of foreign ownership on profits, but his criterion was very crude (a 10 percent dummy variable), and his data were at the industry level. More precise data on the degree of parental control at the subsidiary level may prove more revealing.

Miscellaneous Variables

Some variables included as controls in statistical market structure-profits analyses fall into none of the main categories above. One set of miscellaneous controls refers to demand of conditions and a second set relates to the sheer size or conglomeratedness of firms in the market.

One of the most common of all control variables to be inserted in structure-profit functions is the rate of growth in output or shipments during or immediately preceding the period under study. Sato (1961) may have been the first to argue for this procedure. His main concern was to try to distinguish the secular from the cyclical components in manufacturing profit margins, for it is only upon the former component that the elements of market structure are assumed to act; that is, unexpected increases in demand or decreases in cost may yield profits even in competitive industries. In his test the trend rates of growth in industry output are included along with estimates of a cyclical excess capacity primarily to correct for chronic excess capacity in industries with low or negative rates of growth; in others of his equations the average rates of growth in industry assets are specified. His results indicate that growth by either measure has a strong positive influence directly on profits and does not necessarily act through the creation of excess capacity.

Most subsequent research has included industry sales growth as a proxy for long-run shifts in consumer demand.* Other authors have mentioned that industry growth may also partially reflect cost-decreasing changes in production techniques over the period (for example, FTC 1969: 12), but most have emphasized the demand side. It is possible that rapid increases in consumer demand could cause profit rates to decline in some circumstances. For example, plants could be forced to operate so close to maximum capacity that increasing unit costs of production are encountered; or entry could be encouraged; or rapid growth could have an external effect on prices in certain input markets. But most arguments in favor of a direct relationship center on anticipations: Unexpected increases in demand and lags in the provision of new capacity allow an industry to raise prices temporarily. Evidently this effect has triumphed in practice, because most experiments have discovered a strong positive effect of

---

*The proper measure is the rate or extent of change in lateral movement of the demand curve only. Growth, on the other hand, captures lateral shifts in the demand-supply equilibrium point. Thus, this substitute measure is accurate only if the price elasticity of demand is unity or if prices were stable over the period.

growth on profits (for example, Hall and Weiss 1967; Shepherd 1972; Esposito and Esposito 1971; Gambeles 1969), though a few have found nonsignificant relationships (FTC 1969; Weiss 1974). Many tests have discovered that a logarithmic term is most appropriate for growth.

The growth variable has typically been specified in an additive fashion, but Gale (1972) gives reasons to expect growth and market share to interact inversely. First, seller coordination in oligopolies is easiest under conditions of moderate growth. Rapid growth often finds firms sacrificing current profits in an effort to secure larger shares. Declining growth affects price discipline when firms have high fixed costs to cover. Second, small firms are generally more flexible and adaptable to changing market conditions, because they are often unhampered by bureaucratic decision-making methods. Gale's choice of variable is the difference between firm growth and industry sales growth, which will also reflect a firm's "aggressiveness, growth orientation, and acquisitiveness" (p. 417). Both growth-control variables result in highly significant, positive coefficients, and his moderated growth-share interaction hypothesis is also sustained. Thus, firm growth is similar to market share in its effect on profits, and the two may have common determinants. Porter (1974) has suggested that industry growth and concentration may also interact. First, true concentration may be overstated in high-growth industries if the concentration data are taken from other than the end of the period. Second, rapid growth is widely held to disrupt the maintenance of collusive agreements in highly concentrated industries, partly because market-sharing agreements must be augmented by growth-sharing arrangements (Shepherd 1964). In his empirical results, Porter's predicted negative relationship is sustained; moreover, the previously negative coefficient on the simple concentration variable was significantly reversed.

A second aspect of demand receiving less attention until recently is conditions in the buyers' markets. Oligopoly theory suggests that for a given level of seller concentration, the probability of successful collusion by sellers is directly related to the extent of buyer concentration. Buyer concentration is apt to be especially high in producer-goods industries or where special, restricted marketing channels exist (for example, in automobile tires). A loose test of this hypothesis was reported by Stigler (1968: 146); for 19 highly concentrated national industries, none with the highest level of 1953-55 rates of return dealt with only a few buyers.

Porter's (1974) study is among the more recent statistical works to appear on this topic. * He hypothesizes that the effects of market

---

*Other recent statistical studies dealing with this subject include Clevenger and Campbell (1977) and Lustgarten (1975).

structure on profit performance are likely to be stronger in the "convenience goods" consumer industries than in the "nonconvenience goods" industries. Convenience goods are those sold with relatively low unit prices, generally through outlets that provide little sales assistance and that are locationally dense. Thus, products typically sold in supermarkets and drugstores are distinguished from those in large, well-staffed department stores, furniture stores, and the like. It is argued that convenience goods are inherently differentiable, while nonconvenience products have many of the characteristics of producer goods; that is, there is greater market power among the buyers (the retail outlets themselves) of nonconvenience goods and a greater incentive for these retailers to search for objective quality and price information than is the case among convenience outlets. The regression estimates presented tend to support the distinction; a much better fit is obtained for the convenience goods subsample, and the effect of advertising intensity is found to be stronger; the same model proves nearly useless in explaining nonconvenience goods producers' profits. Porter also shows that a proxy for the existence of retailer bargaining power has the expected negative effect on seller profits.

The second miscellaneous factor to consider is a topic that has concerned economists for a long time: the relationship of a firm's size to its performance. Corwin Edwards (1951) and others have taken the position that there are direct links between size, market power, and performance. Baumol (1959) proposed that the links may reside in imperfect capital markets and the consequent absolute capital barrier to entry. More recent experience has prompted theorizing over the connections between size and the many special forms of conduct open to conglomerate enterprises (Mueller 1974).

The first test of the thesis was by Hall and Weiss (1967). Using firm-level data and controlling for industry concentration, leverage, and firm growth, they discivered that total asset size and profit margins were strongly and positively related. However, the results of this first experiment may have been partially due to the recession years of the period of observation or to the lack of control for firm market share. The FTC (1969) test, also using the inverse natural logarithm specification, found somewhat weaker confirmation of the effect. Indeed, the significance of the size term was strongly dependent upon the specification of the "firm diversification" variable (that is, whether at the three-, four-, or five-digit SIC level). Shepherd (1972), however, finds a significant negative relationship, though he employed somewhat different controls and omitted many conglomerate firms from his sample. On the other hand, Telser (1972) uses gross book value and Gale (1972) simple sales size and both find positive effects on profits. In addition, as noted above, many investigations have found that a capital-requirements variable, a proxy for size, is

also a positive determinant of profits. Therefore, the weight of the
evidence points to a direct correlation between size and profits, when
sufficient adjustments are made for differences in growth, debt structure, seller concentration, and other factors.

STRUCTURE-PERFORMANCE STUDIES
IN THE LDCs

The application of multivariate regression techniques to industrial data on market structures and performance indexes is fraught
with novel difficulties and challenges to the researcher. The major
obstacle to research is likely to be access to the data itself. The first
cross-industry studies done in the United States made use of diverse
government and private statistical series, but these series have not
yet been developed in many semi-industrialized countries, and when
available, they are often released in a form so aggregated as to provide too few observations for meaningful statistical testing purposes.
White's (1974) book on Pakistan illustrates the paucity of data even
where full government cooperation is extended. As a result of that
cooperation, his study is one of the very few structure-profit relationship estimates accomplished in a LDC.

An additional difficulty is the widespread presence in the industrial sectors of most developing countries of multinational corporations.
This phenomenon introduces complications of several sorts. Under
the laws of some countries (for example, Canada), a wholly owned
subsidiary of an MNC is a "private company," one not subject to all
of the same regulations as a publicly held company. Data on a given
branch or incorporated affiliate in an LDC may be kept in the "home"
office of the firm, beyond the reach of host-country law or questionnaire. One obvious route is to sample the parent organization itself,
but even here difficulties may arise because of financial account con-
solidation procedures, other variations in accounting practices, and
exchange-rate problems. (See Robbins and Stobaugh 1973.) Data
collected by the "home" country government, that of the United States
for example, are rarely available on an establishment basis and are
always in value terms. For these reasons, Horst (1974) concluded
that with respect to the development of dependable predictive models
of behavior by MNCs, "the major roadblocks will be empirical—in the
realm of data availability" (p. 79).

The dominance of MNCs' affiliates in many industries in LDCs
introduces further problems unrelated to data availability. The question arises of the locus of decision making. If such affiliates are
tightly controlled by the company headquarters, then the firm may not
have as its goal the maximization of affiliate profits; rather, the af-

filiate may be directed to make frequent shifts in its stream of dividend
payments or other flows of funds to the parent. The timing of such
directives may move the multinational complex closer to global profit
maximization (by reducing exchange rate losses or effective corporate
taxation rates, for example), but individual units of the company will
at times be forced to delay or abandon profitable local reinvestment
opportunities. Moreover, certain items that appear as costs on the
subsidiary's books are revenues for the parent. In particular, subsidiary payments for research and development, technical assistance,
or licensing rights often have very low marginal costs associated
with them for the parent; such rents are not clearly distinguishable
from economic profits, except perhaps for tax purposes. Furthermore,
international trade transactions between affiliated units open up the
possibility of profit transfers by means of accounting prices manipu-
lation. Thus, accepting the general objective of global profit maximization by an MNC does not translate into simple, independent net-
revenue maximization by every profit center within it. Clearly the
choice of the proper index of performance for foreign affiliates of
MNCs is not an easy one, and the issues of "technology payments"
and the "transfer pricing" or profits cannot be ignored.

The remaining paragraphs of this section discuss the validity
and applicability of the numerous sources of market power that have
been modeled in statistical studies of market power in highly industrialized economies to parallel studies in the LDCs.

Only a few investigations have been made of international differences in industrial concentration. The first international comparative
study of industrial concentration was authored by Bain (1966). In
his sample of 38 comparable industries in 8 countries, he estimated
that 20 plant concentration ratios in the 1950s were generally quite
high relative to national U.S. data. In 3 countries (India, Canada, and
Sweden), the average of the 38 ratios was roughly twice as high. In
the remaining 4 cases (Japan, Britain, France, and Italy), the average was only 10 to 30 percent higher. These results suggest that it is
not so much the level of development as the large size of the market
for manufactures that allows for lower industrial concentration.

A recent paper by Pryor (1972) looks at aggregate and major
industry concentration across 20-odd developed nations during the
early 1960s. He finds that weighted four-firm aggregate manufacturing
concentration was significantly and negatively correlated with GNP in
his sample, though he suspects that the true relationship may be nonlinear. Pryor also discovered that concentration within (roughly
two-digit SIC) industries was highly and directly correlated across
nations. Per capita GNP was not related to concentration; therefore,
it is again confirmed that the primary determinant of industry concentration is not so much the level of development (as measured by per

capita GNP) as the size of the market. One can expect industrial
concentration to more nearly resemble that of the United States in India, South Africa, or Brazil than in Pakistan, Kenya, or Chile, for
example, if Pryor's results can be extrapolated to such narrow markets. *

Three further studies provide concentration comparisons for
three semi-industrialized LDCs. White (1974) finds that in the late
1960s in 51 comparable industries four-firm sales concentration was
66 percent in Pakistan but only 49 percent in the United States. For
all 82 of his sample industries, the simple average four-firm concentration ratio was 70 percent. Fajnzylber (1970) and Fajnzylber and
Tarrago (1975) provide four-plant concentration estimates for Brazil
(circa 1968) and Mexico (circa 1970); compared with that in the United
States, aggregate manufacturing concentration is 105 percent in Brazil
and 112 percent in Mexico.

There are reasons to believe that concentration indexes may have
somewhat statistically weaker effects on measured profits in LDC-
based investigations. For one, cultural differences between the managers of domestic and the officers of multinational firms may make
oligopolistic collusion more difficult. Moreover, generally higher
transportation costs are likely to lead to especially severe distortions
in national concentration indexes in the territorially extensive LDCs.
Third, even in moderately developing LDCs, the rate of growth and
structural change in the industrial sector have been typically extremely
sharp in recent decades. This point is merely a generalization of
Gale's thesis: Rapid change interacts negatively with concentration.
Finally, most LDCs have economies relatively "open" to international
trade, in the sense that a large proportion of their primary production
is often exported, while a large percentage of their manufactures is
imported. As was pointed out above, export propensities and foreign
competition can both weaken the impact of simple domestic concentration measures. However, the facts that most exports by LDCs are
in the primary products sectors and that many LDCs pursue highly
protectionist trade policies for manufactures suggest that this last
caveat may not in reality be too important. Besides, the absence of
an antitrust tradition like that of Canada, the United States, or some
European countries may facilitate collusion.

---

*The concentration estimates tabulated in this study (see Chapter
3 and Appendix B) are consistent with Pryor's findings. Brazil, though
it has a lower per capita income, is roughly the same economic size
as Mexico, but both are about one-twentieth the economic size of the
United States. The two Latin countries have roughly equal levels of
industrial concentration, but both are higher than the level in the
United States.

   In summary, carefully calculated concentration ratios are likely
to have the predicted positive influence on firm or industry profits in
LDC-based studies. Correct if somewhat weak results have already
been obtained by White (1974) for Pakistan and by House (1973) for
Kenya. But the introduction of trade and "regional market" variables
should be considered. With respect to the market share and relative
share variables, the advantages of firm dominance would appear to
need little alteration for application to the environment of an LDC, unless the firm is frustrated by price controls or rigid planning.
   Direct evidence of product differentiation through advertising
in the LDCs is difficult to come by. Scattered material, mainly referring to Latin America, can be found in Barnet and Müller (1974:
143-46, 172-78) and in Ledagar (1975), but their few facts indicate
that many MNCs carry on extensive advertising campaigns in the
LDCs and that these are having definite consumption impacts on all
strata of the populations. The executives of advertising agencies
serving MNCs clearly believe in the efficacy of culturally adapted advertising campaigns abroad. (See Miracle 1972.) Moreover, the consumer theory basis for advertising effectiveness may be especially
pertinent in developing areas: Search costs and consumer unfamiliar-
ity may be particularly high. But it is difficult to predict the relative
efficacy of other forms of sales promotion. One activity of MNCs' affiliates that may be interpreted as a form of sales promotion is research and development. The reasons are that virtually all inventive
R&D is carried on in the headquarters country (Mansfield 1974) and
that overseas R&D, except in other OECD countries, is primarily performed to make slight product design alterations that reflect cultural
differences in taste (Duerr 1970; National Academy of Sciences 1973).
   The absolute cost to establish a minimum efficient size plant may
not be as large in the LDCs as in the more developed countries. Again,
Bain (1966) has done the pioneering study of this topic. His basic
result is that in 36 out of 38 internationally comparable industries in
8 countries, the average number of employees for the 20 largest
plants is smaller than in the United States. Except in the United Kingdom, these plants averaged only one-third or less the size of their
U.S. counterparts. These disparities in average plant size may be
partly explained by a tendency of the largest U.S. plants to be built
at scales well above the minimum optimal level and by generally higher
transportation and distribution costs outside the United States. Pryor
(1974) presents data that indicate that both firm and plant sizes are
strongly positively related to country GNP and to country export propensity in manufactures. Both factor price differences and basic
technical endowments may cause shifts in production-possibilities
frontiers across nations. But it may not be the absolute size of the
minimum efficient scale barrier that is the relevant measure so much

as the MES relative to the size of the capital market, for it is well
known that both domestic and multinational firms obtain most of their
investment capital from the local markets, and it is widely believed
that capital markets in LDCs are even more imperfect than those in
the developed countries.* However, expressing the MES as a percentage of the market may be a good proxy for the implied ratio.

The Esposito-and-Esposito thesis that the extent of foreign market penetration is an index of the ease of entry must be regarded as
of doubtful validity in the LDCs. One reason is the aforementioned
high trade barriers, but another is the fact that entry is often by acquisition of local firms rather than the formation of new subsidiaries
(Vernon 1971; Newfarmer and Mueller 1974). Nor is the extent of
foreign ownership in an industry likely to affect the extent of entry,
if the results of a recent empirical investigation of Canada hold true
for the LDCs (Orr 1974).

But the forms and extent of foreign ownership may be quite important as controls in a firm-level study of market power in LDCs.
The extent of interaffiliate sales may be an indication of multiplant
and multifirm economies of scale. If the intrafirm trade is international, however, it may simply reflect the potential an MNC has for
"transfer pricing"; hence, the degree of intrafirm international trade
may well be systematically related to reported subsidiary profits in
certain countries. For many of the same reasons, the degree of control by the parent may also be inversely related to reported profits;
in other words, joint venture partners, like public ownership, may
discourage various "entrepreneurial withdrawals" of the parent organization.

The extent of firm diversification may have a generally negative
influence on profits in the LDCs also, but not for the same reason.
Diversification in LDCs is at least partially necessitated by the lack
of adequate components and increasing local content requirements of
host governments. Thus, both diversification and vertical integration
are related to failures in input markets and are likely to affect profits
adversely.

None of the critique given above concerning controls for market
growth, firm size, or capital intensity has to be altered for an LDC.
The problem of debt management and business or financial risk, however, is a particularly knotty question in the context of MNCs' affiliates
operating abroad. Loans obtained from disinterested parties in an
arm's length manner operate in much the same way as already described, but loan capital obtained from the parent organization (or from

---

*For an elaborate study in support of this statement, see Gold-
smith (1969).

financial institutions linked with the parent) is quite another matter.
Here the return-on-investment criterion may not be paramount. As
I suggested above, debt is another form of centralized control and
debt retirement can easily become an indirect means of remitting
dividends. Thus, it is entirely possible that affiliate debt incurred
from the two sources will have opposite effects on profits.

CONCLUDING REMARKS

Rather than provide a summary of this lengthy survey, I
shall confine my concluding remarks to two fairly narrow questions.
First, to what extent has progress in statistical structure-performance studies overcome the negative criticisms mentioned
above? Second, what are the legitimate purposes and likely prospects of geographic extensions of these tests to the semi-industrialized areas of the world?
One criticism above was the lack of explicit cross-industry
treatment of the forms of conduct, and it must be admitted that little
progress has been made in the direction of a unified model encompassing the three parts of the industrial organization paradigm. The steady
improvement in statistical closeness of fit as more independent variables are added to the functions does suggest that some of those variables may be capturing at least some of the modal forms of rivalry.
Should the data ever be plentiful enough, an instructive test would involve using a sample of firms all within the same fairly narrow industry (for example, drugs) where it might be assumed that the types of
conduct are fairly uniform. Some recent investigations along these
lines have been carried out for food retailing (FTC 1966; Marion 1977)
and the fluid-milk industry (Manchester 1974; Mueller, Hamm, and
Cook 1976).
More progress can be observed in the development of simultaneous
causation models. Perhaps the most comforting result is the apparent
robustness of ordinary least-squares techniques; only Hurdle's (1974)
paper has indicated coefficient estimates highly sensitive to the choice
of technique. Meanwhile, experimentation and refinement continue
with respect to forms, variables, and data sources. The objectives
of such tests have not substantially broadened of late, however. Hypothesis testing remains the primary goal of most investigations,
though one may discern a slight tendency to append at least a few
paragraphs on policy implications. Parametric estimation still lies
mainly in the background, but it is alarming to note that increasingly
accurate estimates of the social welfare losses due to market power
show no decreases over time; Scherer (1970) estimates that the 1966
U.S. losses were about 6.2 percent of current GNP, while Comanor
and Wilson (1974) find that consumer losses were 5.5-6.0 percent of

manufacturing value added in the 1950s. These estimates far exceed those made using the conventional, Hotelling-type, deadweight loss method.

The provision of welfare loss estimates like those above seems a long way off for LDC-based studies, but the mere verification of the existence of allocative distortions in manufacturing could have important development policy implications. In the last decade or more, many empirical studies have demonstrated that the agricultural sectors of most developing economies are highly efficient in resource allocation. If it is found that industry in LDCs is generally inefficient and distributionally regressive, there is a strong case for a shift in the balance of public investment between sectors.

More important perhaps are the implications for antitrust policies. Deconcentration and antimerger programs can provide additional social controls over industrial development in those LDCs already at moderate levels of industrialization, many of which have often had to rely solely on the blunt instruments available in tax or trade parameters —or on selective and perhaps arbitrary nationalization. Furthermore, evidence that the problems of market power are global can assist in the solution of such international problems of antitrust enforcement as that of "extraterritoriality." To the extent that trade barriers can be shown to encourage imperfect competition, these may be important suggestions for trade policies of LDCs. The United Nations and other regional bodies have repeatedly recommended multinational cooperation in the area of "restrictive business practices" by MNCs and the international enforcement of patents; industrial organization studies of the type outlined above can, doubtelessly, aid in designing effective policy.

The review above is intended to suggest that there are no theoretical or technical obstacles to cross-industry research into LDC market structure-performance causal relationships, albeit data limitations may prove formidable. The openness of these economies, the prominence of multinational corporations, and some novel modes of firm conduct due to cultural differences simply imply the necessity of additional control variables. However, all of the empirical evidence presented in Chapter 3 is consistent with the same conclusion: Industrial market structures and the sources of market power are remarkably homomorphic across nations.

5

PROFIT-MARKET
STRUCTURE
RELATIONSHIPS

The competitive performance of an industry in a market economy is measured in many ways (Bain 1968). The measure most often used is relative profitability. Economic theory and industrial experience support the proposition that as the market power of sellers increases, their profit rates also increase. Many studies have tested this hypothesis in the United States and other advanced, capitalistic market economies. Although these studies generally support the expected hypothesis, it is not clear that the market power-profit relationship holds in less developed countries. Conceivably, special institutional and cultural conditions may negate such relationships. The MNCs may pursue different profit goals in LDCs than in the United States. Transfer pricing, the timing of international flows of funds, and differing accounting procedures may introduce distortions in company accounts that make interfirm comparisons of profitability meaningless. This chapter, therefore, examines the profitability of U.S. MNCs in Brazil and Mexico and attempts to identify various factors, especially those measuring market power, that may determine the level of such profits. *

PROFIT RATES OF U.S. MNCs, 1972

After-tax profit as a percentage of equity capital averaged 16.1 percent for 176 Brazilian affiliates and 12.7 percent for 308 Mexican affiliates of U.S. MNCs (Table 5.1). The apparent difference in aver-

---

*Much of this chapter appeared previously as Chapter 3 of Connor and Mueller (1977).

TABLE 5.1

Average After-Tax Profit Rates of Affiliates of U.S. MNCs in Various Brazilian and Mexican
Manufacturing Industries, 1972
(weighted profit rates[d] in percent)

SIC	Industry	Brazil			Mexico		
		Number of Affiliates[c]	Profits over Equity (percent)	Broad Profits over Equity (percent)	Number of Affiliates[c]	Profits over Equity (percent)	Broad Profits over Equity (percent)
20	Grain products (204)	3	33.7	34.3	10	16.7	27.4
	Beverages (208)	5	9.4	9.4	4	19.0	48.4
	Other food	4	9.0	9.0	18	11.3	14.8
21	Tobacco	a	a	a	3	-15.8	-12.1
22	Textiles	a	a	a	4	6.3	8.3
23	Apparel	0	—	—	a	a	a
24	Wood and						
25	furniture	a	a	a	a	a	a
26	Paper	6	22.5	23.6	12	11.7	12.2
27	Printing	a	a	a	4	18.0	20.3
28	Industrial chemicals (281)	7	13.1	13.4	22	11.9	16.1
	Plastics and synthetics (282)	7	0.1	0.6	13	12.1	14.5
	Drugs (283)	18	21.9	24.9	23	15.0	23.8
	Soap and cosmetics (284)	6	26.0	33.3	14	24.2	34.9
	Other chemicals	17	0.1	0.4	29	15.1	18.4
29	Petroleum	9	20.4	20.4	a	a	a
30	Tires (301)	b	b	b	5	12.6	16.3
	Other rubber	5	27.7	27.7	7	9.4	11.5
31	Leather	a	a	a	0	—	—
32	Stone, clay, and glass	9	13.4	14.8	15	10.4	12.6
33	Primary metals	5	11.3	11.3	6	9.6	10.1
34	Fabricated metals	8	29.1	29.6	15	2.5	3.4
35	Industrial machinery (355, 356)	9	23.3	23.4	12	5.0	7.6
	Office and computer (357)	4	10.5	10.5	7	12.7	23.7
	Other machinery	11	24.6	25.9	20	10.3	14.1
36	Appliances (363)	3	22.8	22.8	6	11.0	14.2
	Radio and television (367)	b	b	b	10	13.7	14.9
	Other electrical	10	19.9	21.4	15	18.7	23.5
37	Transportation equipment	16	19.1	19.7	15	10.1	12.5
38	Precision instruments	8	27.9	27.9	11	11.0	20.3
39	Miscellaneous manufacturing	6	-16.5	-16.4	8	17.8	19.5
	Total	176	16.1	16.8	308	12.7	16.9

[a]Included in "miscellaneous" category, because based on fewer than three observations.
[b]Included in "other" industry category, because based on fewer than three observations.
[c]All active subsidiaries with positive net worth.
[d]Reported rates are total industry profits after taxes as a percentage of total industry net worth. "Broad Profits" includes technology payments.

Source: Special survey of the U.S. Senate Subcommittee on Multinational Corporations.

age profit rates in the two countries virtually disappears when "broad earnings" (net income plus technology payments) are used: 16.8 percent and 16.9 percent, respectively. The difference between the two earnings figures reflects different public policies toward technology payments in Brazil and Mexico in 1972. Broad profits, the more meaningful measure of profitability, was considerably higher in both nations in 1972 than the net profits of large U.S. manufacturing corporations on their total operations, domestic and foreign.*

Profit rates varied considerably across industries in Brazil and Mexico. In Table 5.1 profits are measured in two ways: after-tax net income as a percentage of equity and "broad" earnings (profits plus payments to the parent organization for the use of technology or other intangibles) after taxes as a percentage of equity.[†] The table includes all active manufacturing affiliates that reported their 1972 net income and had positive net worth. Affiliates of U.S. MNCs are classified by industry according to their principal product, and the industry profit rates shown are weighted by the total sales of the affiliates in that industry.

By either measure of profitability, it appears that many U.S. MNCs earn very high profits in Brazil.[‡] In most cases the highest profits occurred in the industries where MNCs were most prominent: chemicals (especially the "consumer" chemical industries: drugs and soaps and cosmetics), rubber, machinery, electrical equipment, and transportation equipment. These are also, as shown above, the same industry groups with higher levels of concentration, average firm market shares, and advertising intensities. Profits are also high in the paper, fabricated metals, and precision instruments industries, but there are some industry groups with unexpectedly low profit rates: beverages, some of the chemicals industries, and office and computer equipment.

---

*FTC, Quarterly Financial Reports on Corporate Manufacturing Profits, fourth quarter, 1972, reported average after-tax profits of 10.5 percent of equity for manufacturing corporations with assets exceeding $100 million.

[†] The definition of "broad profits" used herein conforms to the U.S. Department of Commerce concept of "balance of payments income" from foreign direct investment employed prior to 1974, except for dividends and interest payments. Since 1974, this term has been rechristened "direct investor's ownership benefits."

[‡] Discussion of petroleum distribution affiliates of U.S. MNCs is generally omitted from the text. In both Brazil and Mexico, however, these subsidiaries have average profits close to the mean for all profitable affiliates (that is, those shown in Table 5.2).

TABLE 5.2

Average After-Tax Profit Rates of Affiliates of U.S. MNCs in Various Brazilian and Mexican
Manufacturing Industries, Profitable Affiliates Only, 1972
(weighted profit rates[d] in percent)

SIC	Industry	Brazil			Mexico		
		Number of Affiliates[c]	Profits over Equity (percent)	Broad Profits over Equity (percent)	Number of Affiliates[c]	Profits over Equity (percent)	Broad Profits over Equity (percent)
20	Grain products (204)	b	b	b	9	19.4	30.3
	Beverages (208)	4	12.8	12.8	4	19.0	48.4
	Other food	5	24.7	24.9	15	15.9	20.0
21	Tobacco	0	—	—	a		
22	Textiles	0	—	—	4	6.3	8.3
23	Apparel	0	—	—	a		
24, 25	Wood and furniture	a	a	a	a		
26	Paper	5	23.1	24.3	7	13.3	13.8
27	Printing	0	—	—	4	18.0	20.3
28	Industrial chemicals (281)	5	18.2	18.7	18	14.3	15.5
	Plastics and synthetics (282)	6	17.5	18.7	12	12.1	14.5
	Drugs (283)	17	22.2	25.1	19	17.0	25.8
	Soap and cosmetics (284)	5	26.0	33.3	10	26.1	36.9
	Other chemicals	11	20.9	21.7	22	18.5	22.1
29	Petroleum	9	20.4	20.4	b	b	b
30	Tires (301)	b	b	b	5	12.6	16.3
	Other rubber	5	27.7	27.7	7	9.4	11.5
31	Leather	a	a	a	0	—	—
32	Stone, clay, and glass	8	14.1	15.5	14	13.5	16.0
33	Primary metals	a	a	a	5	9.8	10.4
34	Fabricated metals	6	35.5	36.1	11	14.3	16.6
35	Industrial machinery (355, 356)	9	23.3	23.4	11	5.6	8.2
	Office and computer (357)	3	11.2	11.2	5	13.6	24.8
	Other machinery	8	32.3	32.5	15	16.1	21.0
36	Appliances (363)	3	22.8	22.8	5	11.3	14.5
	Radio and television (367)	b	b	b	7	18.3	19.5
	Other electrical	8	22.4	24.0	13	19.3	24.2
37	Transportation equipment	13	21.0	21.7	13	10.3	12.8
38	Precision instruments	7	28.6	28.6	9	21.0	29.8
39	Miscellaneous manufacturing	5	21.1	21.1	9	15.3	16.8
	Total	142	21.4	22.2	253	14.3	18.4

[a]Included in "miscellaneous" category, because based on fewer than three observations.
[b]Included in "other" industry category, because based on fewer than three observations.
[c]All active with positive net worth and positive after-tax net income.
[d]Reported rates are total industry profits after taxes as a percentage of total industry net worth. "Broad Profits" includes technology payments.

Source: Special survey of the U.S. Senate Subcommittee on Multinational Corporations.

Many firms with large start-up costs or other transient conditions distort the true profit picture for established subsidiaries. Table 5.2, therefore, omits the losing firms. The effect on average profits is most important in Brazil, where it causes average profits to rise appreciably in several industries: food manufacturing, the three non-consumer chemical industry groups, fabricated metals, "other" machinery, "other" electrical equipment, and the miscellaneous manufacturing category.* Overall, weighted 1972 profits on equity rises fully 5 percentage points by eliminating the 34 losing affiliates.

The interindustry distribution of profit rates in Mexico is very similar to Brazil's in most respects. With the exception of transportation equipment,[†] the most denationalized industry groups tend to exhibit supranormal profit configurations. Noncompetitive profit performance is suggested in the food processing, the more consumer-oriented chemical, the nonindustrial machinery, the electrical equipment, and the precision instrument industries. The addition of technology payments to simple after-tax net income often makes an enormous difference in profit rates.[‡] Particularly striking in this regard are the beverage, drugs, soaps and cosmetics, tire, computer, "other" electrical, and instruments groups. Unlike Brazil, in 1972 Mexico permitted the payment of fees and royalties to parent corporations on a tax-free basis; the cost of this tax treatment is reflected in the differences between simple and "broad" earnings rates in Table 5.1 (or 5.2).

Table 5.3 shows the distribution of active affiliates of MNCs by the size of their profit rates. In both countries most affiliates (measured by sales) had net profits of 10 to 50 percent of equity capital; fewer than half of the affiliates (by number) lie in this range, however, that indicates that the larger affiliates in both countries have higher profits. Brazil has a far higher proportion of firms in the extremes of the profit ranges than Mexico: 13.3 percent of Brazilian affiliates (measured by their sales) had losses, compared to 6.3 percent in Mexi-

---

*This involves a loss of only 13 percent of all the manufacturing subsidiaries by sales; no Brazilian petroleum subsidiaries incurred losses in 1972 (see Table 5.2).

[†] The three major U.S. auto makers were losing ground to Volkswagen and Nissan in Mexico in the years prior to 1972. In the Mexican context, long-run profits in the 10 to 13 percent range may appropriately be viewed as essentially competitive.

[‡] There is not much difference between Tables 5.1 and 5.2 for the Mexican data, because only 6 percent of all the affiliates in Mexico (measured by sales) had negative net incomes in 1972 (see Table 5.3).

TABLE 5.3

Distribution of Net Profits as Percentage of Stockholders' Equity of Affiliates of U.S. MNCs in the Brazilian and Mexican Manufacturing Sectors, 1972

Profit Rate Percentage Range	Brazil				Mexico			
	Number of Affiliates[a]	Mean[b] Profit (percent)	Sales ($ millions)	Percentage of Sales	Number of Affiliates[a]	Mean[b] Profit (percent)	Sales ($ millions)	Percentage of Sales
Less than -10.00	18	-73.1	247.6	7.9	26	-103.9	78.8	2.6
-9.99- -5.00	5	-7.2	66.7	2.1	12	-7.7	30.1	1.0
-4.99- 0.00	11	-1.1	104.5	3.3	17	-1.6	82.8	2.7
0.01- 5.00	11	3.3	45.8	1.5	36	3.0	466.4	15.3
5.01- 10.00	12	8.0	259.7	8.3	46	7.5	376.0	12.4
10.01- 15.00	16	12.2	201.7	6.4	53	12.6	685.9	22.5
15.01- 20.00	19	17.6	673.7	21.5	40	17.2	558.2	18.3
20.01- 30.00	30	24.0	860.0	27.5	42	23.1	539.5	17.7
30.01- 50.00	27	35.8	550.7	17.6	22	37.5	184.9	6.1
50.01-100.00	12	68.0	86.6	2.8	11	57.4	40.3	1.3
More than 100.00	6	237.8	35.4	1.1	1	195.0	0.4	0.0
Total (weighted)	167	16.1	3,132.5	100.0	306	12.7	3,043.4	100.0

[a]All active subsidiaries with positive net worth, petroleum excluded.
[b]The means for the various profit-rate ranges are unweighted averages. The means for total affiliates are weighted averages.

Source: Special survey of the U.S. Senate Subcommittee on Multinational Corporations.

co. In both countries, however, companies generally fall in the extreme positive categories because they have very low net worth figures rather than large losses or profits.

In conclusion, it appears that Brazilian and Mexican affiliates' profit performance records, like their market structures, are more remarkable for their parallelisms than their differences. There are intracountry differences in the profit performances of individual industries. Case studies may identify causes for these differences. However, I did identify one potentially significant source of these differences, large variations in their growth rates. (See Connor and Mueller 1977: Appendix E.) And it is likely that further differences exist with respect to some aspects of business strategies, measures of performance other than profits or technology payments, and some elements of true economic profits that do not appear in the accounting records of firms.

Nonetheless, the overall impression one is left with is of the closely parallel market structures and performance levels of manufacturers in Brazil and Mexico. The question remains, however, whether the underlying causal factors are also similar. To establish the nature of these associations when many causal factors are potentially involved requires the application of somewhat complicated statistical methods.

EMPIRICAL FINDINGS

The theory of industrial organization predicts that the relative profit performance of firms is determined in large part by several dimensions of the structures of their national and international markets. Therefore, in what follows, I specify equations that have a profit rate as the dependent variable and several indexes of market structure or other control factors as the independent variables. Then least-squares regression techniques are applied in order to estimate the value of the equation's coefficients and their statistical significance.* For

---

*In interpreting the statistical results reported in this study it should be kept in mind that industrial organization theory is concerned primarily with explaining differences in the behavior among industries; thus, these studies typically use average data for all or most firms in the industry. Because there usually is considerable variance in the profit performance among the individual firms composing an industry, the theory loses explanatory power when explaining the performance of individual firms, but because each observation in this study is of an individual firm rather than the average of a group of firms, the

the Brazilian tests, the data base consists of 70 manufacturing affiliates of U.S. MNCs and for the Mexican tests 125 affiliates.* Almost half of the manufacturing subsidiaries reporting in the special survey had to be omitted because they were inactive in 1972, had negative net worth, did not report some crucial information, or for some other reason explained in detail in Appendix A of Connor and Mueller (1977).

The remainder of this chapter consists of six main parts. In the first section, the main variables used in the regressions below are defined and discussed. The second, third, and fourth parts present the statistical results of some linear, "nonlinear," and "weighted" models, respectively. The fifth section describes the outcomes of several "special" experiments performed. The final part of the chapter presents regressions that pool the data from both countries.

---

study undertakes the more difficult task of explaining profit rates of individual firms. As a result, insofar as this analysis uncovers statistically significant relationships based on firm data, the level of statistical significance of the structural variables in the analysis very probably would have been greater had grouped (industry) data been used.

This point has been illustrated by comparing the results when using grouped firm data in a study by Stigler (1964). He correlated average profit rates of the leading firms in 17 industries with the level of four-firm concentration of these industries. This explained 28 percent of the variance in industry profit rates. However, when each of the firms used to compute his average profit rates is treated as a separate observation, only 4 percent of the explained variance in profits can be explained by differences in market concentration (FTC 1969: 5-6).

Another characteristic of the data used in the analysis that tends to result in lower levels of statistical significance is that most affiliates of U.S. MNCs operating in Brazil and Mexico are quite small. In both countries the average-size firm had assets of about $6 million, with 46 percent of the firms having assets of less than $5 million. Because there generally is more variation in the profit rates of small firms than in those of large ones, statistical analyses using small firms generally have lower levels of explained variance than those using large firms.

*When the two subsets are combined for some later regressions, the resulting "pooled" data set comprises these 195 affiliates plus 11 others admitted into the analysis because fewer variables were used in these equations.

DEFINITIONS OF VARIABLES

Indexes of Performance

In the tests reported below, four different but closely related profit rates are employed. All four ratios are meant to capture the "return on investment" criterion commonly used by business managers of large corporations to judge the value of a particular business investment or line of activity. A survey by the National Industrial Conference Board of senior international executives of U.S. MNCs confirms that return on investment ratios were indeed the most widespread method of measuring the return on various foreign investments (Basche 1970).*

---

*As is true also of domestic investments, the Conference Board study found that there are several indexes of performance being used concurrently by different multinational companies. Some measure the return as a proportion of their "invested capital"; others use "total capital" or "net capital employed"; many use total depreciated or "gross" assets. The first of these concepts of investment, invested capital, most closely corresponds to the accounting category of net worth, or stockholders' equity in the case of an incorporated subsidiary. The second definition of "investment" is roughly equivalent to stockholders' equity plus long-term debt. Only very few MNCs were reported as using returns over sales, and none claimed to employ the original cost of their overseas investments to judge their affiliates' returns on investment.

The numerator term of the ratio, "return," is also variously defined. In general, there is less unanimity on its choice than on the definition of "investment." The following items were included as components of return by one or more of the firms samples: after-tax foreign affiliate profits, dividends paid out, royalties, fees, rentals, commissions, and export profits on inputs sold to affiliates. Only a few firms with foreign affiliates indicated that net profits was the only component of returns considered. Much more typical in the survey responses was the practice of including such payments as royalties for the use of patents, technical and management service fees, and rental or license fees for the use of certain technical materials, machinery, or production processes abroad. These payments for intangibles will be referred to as "technology payments" (Basche 1970: 9).

The treatment of interest payments on internal loans and of intrafirm export profits was not uniform, but from the survey responses reported it appears that most firms were content to allow export prof-

Managerial studies of MNCs (for example, Brooke and Remmers 1970) find that in most firms uniform operating-budget statements are required of all domestic and foreign subsidiaries, that these financial reports are examined and approved at the highest levels of company management, and that these budgets are the prime and often sole method of evaluating foreign affiliate performance in the larger MNCs. However, some of these budgets are often so distorted for foreign operating units that similarities to domestic unit reports are only superficial. And though some MNCs may employ global financial evaluation systems, the weight of the evidence from the managerial literature on MNCs is that, up through at least the late 1960s, individual subsidiary profit maximization was the rule followed by most overseas managers. Hence, in the present report, profit rates derived from traditional accounting budgets were adopted as the most appropriate criterion of foreign affiliate performance.

In the empirical tests below, four rates of return on investment are employed. All use the foreign affiliate's net income measured in current dollars and taken after the removal of local (that is, Brazilian or Mexican) corporate income taxes but before the application of U.S. income taxes. The latitude necessarily given to the special survey respondents in converting the local currencies to dollars introduces an element of experimental disturbance not usually encountered in single-country studies. Some firms convert their accounts monthly, but others convert only quarterly or yearly. Moreover, some affiliates reported their accounts on a calendar year basis but others chose to report on a fiscal year standard. In Brazil, inflation and frequent, sometimes monthly, devaluations are likely to affect comparability among firms, though by 1972 several years of experience in "indexing" of most prices may have reduced the problem of comparability.

The first profitability rate employed in the analyses below is the ratio of after-tax net income to equity capital (EQUITYPROF). The second measure of profit performance, broad earnings (BROADEQUITY), is very similar to the first except that "Payments on Royalties, Patents, License Fees, Management Contracts and Other Payments for Use of Intangibles" was added to net income. In the sample used for 1972,

----

its to be made by the exporting affiliate even though it was recognized that such exports might not have occurred had not the importing affiliate been controlled by the same parent corporation. The location of international trade profits is, of course, highly sensitive to the form of intrafirm trade pricing adopted by the MNC. Other studies have shown that some companies allow bargaining between affiliated subsidiaries while others have universal company price schedules (Robbins and Stobaugh 1973).

consisting of 70 Brazilian manufacturing affiliates of U.S. MNCs, EQUITYPROF averaged 17.9 percent; the respective BROADEQUITY mean was 19.3 percent in Brazil and 20.0 percent among 125 Mexican subsidiaries.* But the closeness of the averages in both countries is not matched by a close clustering of values within the countries, for there is great variation in profit rates among firms (Table 5.4). For example, the range of values in Brazil for BROADEQUITY is -12.9 to +82.6 percent. This large range would have been even larger had it not been for the selection procedures followed. (See Connor and Mueller 1977: Appendix A.)

The third profit ratio employed is after-tax income expressed as a proportion of total assets (ASSETPROF). As discussed above, the ratio of net income plus interest expenses to "total capital" is conceptually superior, but given the unavailability of interest charges in the special survey data, an independent variable was included in most regression models to control for the leverage position of the firm. The fourth profit measure employed is BROADASSET, the ratio of broad earnings (after-tax net income plus technology payments) to total assets.

Market Structure Variables

Four aspects of market structure were introduced into most of the regressions. The first is market concentration. In Appendix B the methods of derivation are discussed. The particular measure employed here is a weighted, minimum, four-firm concentration ratio, CR4. A weighting procedure was adopted in order to overcome partially the problem of firm diversification into several different product markets. The weights used were the five-digit SIC-level sales data.[†] For example, an affiliate selling $10 million worth of computers in Brazil in 1972 (market CR4 = 96) and $2 million worth of calculators (market CR4= 63) would have a weighted firm CR4 of 90.5 percent. Because high concentration is held to facilitate the coordination of moves among oligopolists who recognize their mutual interdependence,

---

*Note that the means discussed here are for a smaller number of observations than are used in the regression below. However, average profits for these subsets lie quite close to the fuller body of data employed in Tables 5.1 and 5.2.

[†]Only local (that is, domestic Brazilian or Mexican) sales were used in this procedure. The market-share and concentration concepts cannot meaningfully be extended to either foreign or intrafirm sales.

TABLE 5.4

Basic Descriptive Statistics of Selected Variables Used in the Profit Performance–Market Structure Regressions

Variable	Symbol*	Brazil (n = 70) Mean	Standard Deviation	Mexico (n = 125) Mean	Standard Deviation	Expected Impact on Profit Rates
Four-firm, minimum concentration ratio, weighted by product sales, percent	CR4	63.8	26.8	64.2	26.4	Positive
Firm relative market share, weighted	FRMS	0.387	0.257	0.428	0.288	Positive
Advertising intensity of the "market," percent	AD	1.94	2.84	2.02	3.39	Positive
Advertising intensity of the firm, percent	AD/S	2.21	4.14	2.81	5.19	Positive
Research-and-development intensity, percent	R&D	0.55	1.31	1.06	3.40	Positive
"Leverage," the equity-to-assets ratio	LEVER	0.513	0.192	0.556	0.202	Uncertain
Capital-intensiveness, the fixed assets-to-sales ratio	K/S	0.326	0.344	0.271	0.232	Negative
Total asset size (dollars × 10³), natural log units	SIZE	9.05	1.55	8.48	1.26	Positive
Sales growth per year of the firm's major industry group, 1966–70 or 1962–70, percent	GRO	7.68	2.81	13.3	3.57	Positive
Percentage voting stock owned by parent firm (reporter)	OWN	90.9	17.5	84.6	22.8	Uncertain
Export-intensity (exports-to-sales ratio)	EXP	0.028	0.068	0.032	0.100	Positive
Import-intensity (imports-to-sales ratio)	IMP	0.079	0.125	0.068	0.129	Uncertain
Intrafirm exports-to-total-exports ratio	AFFEXP	0.261	0.411	0.216	0.381	Uncertain
	DAFFEXP	0.314	0.464	0.184	0.387	Uncertain
Intrafirm imports-to-total material inputs ratio	AFFIMP	0.189	0.280	0.149	0.240	Uncertain
	DAFFIMP	0.671	0.470	0.568	0.495	Uncertain
Net income-to-stockholders' equity ratio, percent	EQUITY PROF	17.89	16.27	14.22	12.74	n.a.
Net income-to-total assets ratio, percent	ASSETPROF	9.05	8.20	7.86	7.16	n.a.
Net income plus technology payments-to-equity ratio, percent	BROADEQUITY	19.31	17.88	20.00	16.27	n.a.
Net income plus technology payments-to-assets ratio, percent	BROADASSET	9.92	9.61	10.96	9.10	n.a.

*"Dummy" or qualitative variables begin with the letter "D."

Note: n.a. means not applicable.

Source: Special survey of the U.S. Senate Subcommittee on Multinational Corporations.

the CR4 term in my regressions is expected to have a significantly positive effect on profits. These concentration data are given in Appendix B.

A second measure of the structure of markets is the firm's relative market share (FRMS). This statistic is simply the ratio of the firm's weighted market share to the four-firm concentration ratio in that market (like CR4, FRMS is weighted by product sales for diversified subsidiaries). This variable is conceptually quite close to the weighted market share of a firm (FMS), but FRMS measures the sales of a single affiliate relative to the sales of the four largest firms in its markets rather than the total sales of its markets. The firm under consideration may itself, of course, be one of the four industry leaders, and the special survey has shown this to be typically the case for subsidiaries of U.S. MNCs in Brazil and Mexico. Thus, FRMS may be taken to be an index of the potential capacity of a firm to exercise dominance or leadership in its industry relative to the other firms in the industry. For consumer goods products, FRMS reflects the firm's success in building up consumer loyalty to its brands—that is, its success in differentiating its products relative to the success of its competitors. Finally, when there are substantial economies of scale in production or distribution, FRMS may serve as a proxy of a firm's cost advantage relative to its competitors. (See FTC 1969: 10.) Under any of these interpretations, FRMS should exert a positive influence on firm profits. In both the Brazilian and Mexican samples, the typical affiliate of a U.S. MNC controls an average of about 40 percent of the markets served by its top three or four competitors (Table 5.4). This average is likely to be a little higher than the true value because the denominator, CR4, is a minimum estimate in many industries.

The third dimension of market structure included in most tests below is the market advertising intensity (AD) for the firm's principal product. This statistic, summarized in Appendix C, is the weighted average advertising-to-sales ratios of affiliates of U.S. MNCs, with a few adjustments made. These data are good proxies for the actual industry advertising only to the extent that competing MNCs or nationally owned firms (not included in the special survey) have the same advertising-to-sales ratios for their principal products as do the reporting affiliates. Because AD is expected to represent both consumer insensitivity to price changes and the height of barriers to entry into the consumer goods industries, the effect on profits should also be positive.

The fourth structural variable used in many of the regressions is the research-and-development intensity (R&D) of a firm. As I point out in Chapter 3, I believe there is little evidence of basic research by affiliates of U.S. MNCs in the LDCs; rather, much R&D

effort is at best mere superficial design or brand adaptation. As such, it is another form of product differentiation. Thus, we expect R&D expenditures, like AD expenditures, to be positively associated with profits of MNCs' affiliates.

Among the affiliates used in the regressions below, 1972 firm advertising-to-sales ratios (AD) averaged about 2.2 percent in Brazil and about 2.8 percent in Mexico. Because 20 percent of all firms did no advertising whatever, among firms with some advertising outlays the advertising-to-sales ratios averaged 2.7 percent in Brazil and 3.8 percent in Mexico, but the average for the weighted market advertising intensity AD is only about 2 percent in both countries (Table 5.4); hence, smaller firms tend to have considerably higher firm intensities in both countries, especially in Mexico. The upper range for AD extends to about 18 percent.

Even larger proportions of firms have no R&D expenditures, roughly 60 percent in the Brazil and Mexico samples. Hence, mean R&D intensity is somewhat understated in Table 5.4, being almost 1 percent in Brazil among firms with at least some R&D outlays and almost 2 percent among similar Mexican subsidiaries.

Control Variables

Several control variables were also introduced into the analyses. Although not themselves the focus of attention in an analysis, control variables serve to clarify or isolate the precise influence of the structural variables that are of primary interest to the study. They are essentially, but not entirely, unrelated to the structures of markets. Some of these factors capture differences in technology or cost conditions among industries or firms. Other deal with differences among firms that arise from their internal organization or management practices. Still others reflect the special characteristics of MNCs that may give rise to advantages over strictly national firms. Newfarmer and Mueller (1975) have termed this source of MNC power "multinational conglomeration." It includes such factors as international flows of financial resources or products among various branches of the complex, the ability to plan and direct the dispersed units of the firm centrally, and the sheer size of the worldwide organization.

Interindustry variability in capital-intensiveness was measured using the ratio of the affiliates' net fixed assets to sales, K/S. It is assumed that the K/S of the firm is closely related to the capital-intensiveness of the industry by reason of a common technology.

1. In particular, a high K/S value will be more characteristic of producer goods than of consumer goods.* Because differentiated consumer goods firms tend to have higher profits than producer goods firms, the coefficient of K/S may be negative insofar as AD does not fully capture the effect.

2. Because the accounting category of net fixed assets includes capital spending on plant and equipment not yet productive, a high K/S may also be interpreted as a proxy for excess or unused plant capacity, or for "X" inefficiency (Leibenstein 1966). A similar interpretation for industry capital-to-output ratios is given by Sato (1961). This second interpretation would imply that K/S should have a negative impact on profit rates over equity or assets.

3. It is a common practice for MNCs first to establish their own wholesale and distribution facilities in a given foreign country and later to convert these facilities to assembly and manufacturing operations.[†] Marketing subsidiaries generally exhibit relatively high levels of sales for a small amount of fixed plant and equipment (though assets in the form of inventories may be large). Thus, a low K/S ratio may indicate that the sales function of such an affiliate is an important part of its total activity. A negative coefficient in this instance simply implies that the presumably better-established marketing operation is more profitable than the manufacturing segment of the subsidiary.

For all of the above reasons, one can expect K/S to exert a negative influence on profits.

A second often used control variable is the financial "leverage" of the affiliate, the equity-to-assets ratio, LEVER. The more usual measure of leverage is the debt-to-equity ratio, so LEVER is roughly the inverse of that concept. A highly leveraged firm is one with a low LEVER value. A highly leveraged company, because it has relatively large debts for its size, can be expected to make large interest payments. Thus, when regressing against profits on total assets uncorrected for interest payments, the variable LEVER should have a consistently positive coefficient (Hall and Weiss 1967).[‡] However, espe-

---

*The consumer-producer goods dichotomy, as well as the durable-nondurable distinction, was made and tried in some regressions. Their definitions are found in Appendix C of Connor and Mueller (1977).

[†]Note that when MNCs' affiliates described their activity as mixed sales and manufacture, they were classified as manufacturing operations. See Appendix A.

[‡]If P = reported net profits, I = interest payments, E = equity, D = debt, and A = total assets, then $(P + I)/A$ is closer to the true economic profit rate than P/A. Because $A = E + D$ approximately, then

cially if we use profits on equity as the dependent variable, other outcomes are possible for the leverage variable. In particular, LEVER has often been taken as a proxy for the degree of financial risk associated with an investment in a firm; within the same industry lenders may insist on higher earnings ratios, a so-called risk premium, the higher the debt-to-assets ratio.* If there are, however, not enough controls for interindustry differences, it may be argued that highly leveraged industries are in that position because they are appraised by lenders as having exceptionally good growth or profits prospects (Gale 1972). Therefore, a priori, the impact of the variable LEVER on affiliate profits over equity is uncertain.

One of the more commonly employed controls in statistical studies of profits and market structure is industry growth. Rates of long-term sales growth (GRO) were computed from public sources for the major industry groups of the MNCs' affiliates in the study (for Brazil 1966-70, for Mexico 1962-70).[†] Most researchers argue that in rapidly growing industries producers have generally anticipated smaller increases; unexpected shifts in consumer demand, combined with lags in the provision of new productive capacity, lead to temporary price rises and subsequently to "windfall" profits. Alternatively, high growth rates can also be the result of cost-decreasing changes in production techniques. In either case, the reasoning leads to an expectation of higher profit rates. But contrary arguments have also been advanced. High growth rates may also tend to reduce entry barriers, or rapid growth could strain input markets and cause input prices to rise. These two possibilities imply lower profits. Hence, the overall expectation of the effect of growth on profits is ambiguous.

E/A is high when D/A is low. If D/A is low, then I/A is low and P/A converges to (P + I)/A. If, on the other hand, D/A is high, then P/A understates true profitability ([P + I]/A). To correct for understatement, LEVER = E/A will have a positive effect on P/A.

*Presumably this applies to both stockholders and long-term lenders. An interesting question concerns the distinction between lending by the parent corporation and lending by overtly unrelated parties. If parental lending increases profits of recipient subsidiaries significantly while lending by unaffiliated interests has the opposite effect, this would give indirect support to the "multinational conglomeration" thesis. Results of such a test are reported below.

†In Brazil the data were extracted from two publications of the Brazilian Institute of Geography and Statistics (IBGE), Produçao Industial 1966 and Anuario Estadístico 1972; these data also appear in Newfarmer and Mueller (1975: 113). For Mexico the data on growth are from the Bank of Mexico and are reproduced in Fajnzylber and Tarrago (1975: 438).

In experiments using firm-level data, <u>firm size</u> has sometimes been introduced. Rather than a control variable, the asset size of firms, SIZE, may well represent a source of market power (Edwards 1951). However, the power inherent in an MNC's size is appropriately measured by its global size and conglomeration, not by the size of its individual affiliates. Affiliate size is most appropriately considered a proxy for the absolute cost requirements of scale. Thus, this variable should be positively associated with profits.

Several other control variables were specified to attempt to model various aspects of multinational conglomeration. As a proxy for the intention to provide centralized control or direction of affiliates, the percentage of stock <u>ownership</u> by the parent organization (OWN) was added to some equations. A previous study has found foreign ownership to be positively related to profits (Khalilzadeh-Shirazi 1974), but the use of firm-level data may lead to contrary results. In particular, wholly owned subsidiaries may report profits in a manner distinctly different from joint ventures. Local partners, especially if individuals, may insist on higher dividend payout ratios, thereby lowering subsequent profits.

Intrafirm trade and payments are more tangible evidence of interaffiliate connectedness. Some measures of trade proclivities are included in most of the tests below. The two simplest are simply <u>total exports</u> (EXP) and <u>total imports</u> (IMP) expressed as proportions of subsidiary sales size. These simple trade intensities may bear not only on integration of the MNC but also on cost conditions of the affiliate. Exports in particular may signal the presence of a highly efficient operation or the existence of government promotional subsidies, both of which will increase profits. Government pressures to export or switch to local inputs may, however, have the opposite effect.

Two variables were designed more specifically to capture the performance effects of <u>intrafirm trade</u> relations: AFFEXP, the ratio of intra-MNC exports to total exports, and AFFIMP, the ratio of intra-MNC imports to total material inputs. These two variables were usually included along with EXP and IMP so as to control for any differences among firms resulting from mere trade propensities, even though EXP and AFFEXP are highly correlated, as are IMP and AFFIMP.

In the regression sample of affiliates, imports were generally more than twice the size of exports; exports accounted for about 3 percent of sales on average (Table 5.4). But as with some other variables, many affiliates had no exports and a few firms had very high ratios.* Of the approximately 3 percent export intensity in Brazil and

_____

*The EXP ranged up to 40 percent in Brazil and up to 73 percent in Mexico. The IMP went as high as 55 percent in Brazil and 85 per-

Mexico, less than one-third was destined for unrelated firms. Of the
7 to 8 percent import ratios calculated for these subsidiaries of MNCs
in 1972, on average, less than 0.5 percent originated from unrelated
companies. Therefore, roughly two-thirds of all exports and more
than 90 percent of all imports were intra-MNC; on average, intra-
MNC imports satisfied 26 to 28 percent of all material production inputs required, among those affiliates who imported at all.

THE LINEAR MODELS

The regression models estimated in this subsection are of the
form:

$$\pi = b_0 + b_1 S_1 + \ldots + b_n S_n + b_{n+1} C_1 + \ldots + b_{n+m} C_m + U \tag{5.1}$$

where

π = one of four profit rates of the firm
b_0 = the constant term
S_i = one of several market structure variables, i = 1, . . . , n
C_j = one of several control variables, j = 1, . . . , m
U = a normally distributed, spherical disturbance term

The structural variables included in this subsection are

S_1 = CR4, the minimum, four-firm concentration ratio
S_2 = FRMS, the relative market share of the firm
S_3 = AD, the market advertising intensity
S_4 = R&D, the firm's research-and-development intensity

The control variable selected for inclusion in the simple, linear
models below are

C_1 = LEVER, the equity-to-assets ratio
C_2 = K/S, the capital-intensiveness of the firm
C_3 = GRO, the rate of major industry growth

---

cent in Mexico. Only about 20 percent of all the affiliates in the sample do any exporting, thus exporting manufacturers average about 15
percent of their sales being shipped abroad. About 55 percent of all
affiliates import at least some of their material production inputs.

C_4 = SIZE, the natural logarithm of total assets
C_5 = EXP, the export-intensiveness of the firm
C_6 = IMP, the import-intensiveness of the firm

Brazil Results

The coefficients of the estimated least-squares regression function (5.1) are displayed in Tables 5.5 through 5.8.* Table 5.5 uses EQUITYPROF for the profit rate, Table 5.6 uses BROADEQUITY, Table 5.7 uses ASSETPROF, and Table 5.8 uses BROADASSET. Thus, Tables 5.5 and 5.7 have the same numerator, and so do Tables 5.6 and 5.8. On the other hand, Tables 5.5 and 5.6 have the same denominator (equity), as do 5.7 and 5.8 (assets).

In Table 5.5, the coefficient of CR4 is positive and significant,[†] as predicted. The variable FRMS exhibits positive, highly significant coefficients in Equations 5.5.2 through 5.5.5. Moreover, the introduction of FRMS has a strong impact on increasing the overall fit of the model and also improves the confidence level of the coefficients of the CR4 variable.

The market advertising intensity, AD, has a positive influence on profit performance throughout, but it is statistically significant in only one of five equations. The FRMS also has a clarifying effect on AD. However, R&D does not have the expected positive sign, nor is

---

*Besides the estimated regression coefficients, Tables 5.5–5.8 also show each coefficient's "t" statistic. Additionally, an "F" statistic is included, which tests the hypothesis that $b_1 = b_2 = \ldots = b_{n+m} = 0$, and the superscripts on the F statistics indicate the maximum level at which the alternative hypothesis could be chance be accepted. Finally, R^2 and $\overline{R}^2$ statistics are given. The coefficient of multiple determination, R^2, indicates the percentage of profit variation "explained" by the independent variables. The corrected coefficient of determination, $\overline{R}^2$, is more appropriate for comparing the goodness of fit among models with different degrees of freedom.

Tables 5.5–5.8 contain five numbered equations each. Equations 5.5.1, 5.6.1, 5.7.1, and 5.8.1 are the simplest of the linear models in these tables. Equations of increasing numbers of independent variables always show higher levels of R^2, but the $\overline{R}^2$ statistic is the more meaningful standard of comparison.

[†] Herein I shall use the term "significant" for a confidence level of 10 percent or better; "very" or "highly" significant implies a level of 5 percent or higher, using a one-tailed test.

TABLE 5.5

Results of Regressions of Profit Rates[a] on Market Structure Variables, 70 Brazilian Manufacturing Affiliates of U.S. MNCs, 1972

Equation	Constant	CR4	FRMS	AD	R&D	LEVER	K/S	GRO	SIZE	EXP	IMP	F	R^2	$\bar{R}^2$
5.5.1	17.07[d] (1.33)	0.114[d] (1.39)		0.409 (0.54)			-20.14[b] (-3.52)	-0.471 (-0.67)	0.400 (0.32)			3.22[c]	0.20	0.14
5.52	8.92 (0.72)	0.120[d] (1.55)	21.81[b] (3.08)	0.988[d] (1.33)			-22.22[b] (-4.10)	-0.550 (-0.83)	0.357 (0.31)			4.62[b]	0.31	0.24
5.5.3	8.24 (0.66)	0.119[d] (1.52)	20.99[b] (2.92)	0.922 (1.23)	-1.06 (-0.77)		-22.78[b] (-4.15)	-0.571 (-0.86)	0.594 (0.49)			4.02[b]	0.31	0.23
5.5.4	6.70 (0.47)	0.119[d] (1.52)	20.93[b] (2.89)	0.926 (1.23)	-1.04 (-0.74)	2.14 (0.22)	-23.00[b] (-4.09)	-0.538 (-0.79)	0.619 (0.51)			3.47[b]	0.31	0.22
5.5.5	9.01 (0.61)	0.124[d] (1.56)	20.55[b] (2.80)	0.907 (1.18)	-1.24 (-0.87)	0.76 (0.18)	-23.09[b] (-4.04)	-0.67 (-0.96)	-.509 (0.41)	21.49 (0.78)	-8.62 (-0.60)	2.84[b]	0.32	0.21

[a]Net income after taxes divided by firm's net worth (EQUITYPROF).
[b]Statistical significance level of 1 percent for "t" and F statistics.
[c]Statistical significance level of 5 percent for "t" and F statistics.
[d]Statistical significance level of 10 percent for "t" and F statistics.

Note: "t" values are in parentheses.

Source: Special survey of the U.S. Senate Subcommittee on Multinational Corporations.

TABLE 5.6

Results of Regressions of Profit Rates[a] on Market Structure Variables, 70 Brazilian Manufacturing Affiliates of U.S. MNCs, 1972

Equation	Constant	CR4	FRMS	AD	R&D	LEVER	K/S	GRO	SIZE	EXP	IMP	F	R^2	$\bar{R}^2$
5.6.1	17.48 (1.24)	0.143[d] (1.58)		0.763 (0.91)			-21.12[b] (-3.36)	-0.759 (-0.99)	0.515 (0.38)			3.24[c]	0.20	0.14
5.6.2	9.26 (0.67)	0.149[c] (1.73)	22.00[b] (2.79)	1.35[d] (1.63)			-23.21[b] (-3.85)	-0.839 (-1.15)	0.471 (0.366)			4.29[c]	0.29	0.22
5.6.3	8.47 (0.61)	0.147[c] (1.70)	21.06[b] (2.64)	1.27[d] (1.53)	-1.23 (-0.80)		-23.85[b] (-3.92)	-1.863 (-1.17)	0.745 (0.557)			3.74[c]	0.30	0.22
5.6.4	4.14 (0.26)	0.150[c] (1.72)	20.89[b] (2.60)	1.28[d] (1.53)	-1.15 (-0.74)	6.01 (0.57)	-24.49[b] (-3.93)	-0.772 (-1.02)	0.816 (0.60)			3.28[c]	0.30	0.21
5.6.5	6.88 (0.42)	0.154[c] (1.74)	20.51[b] (2.52)	1.25[d] (1.46)	-1.36 (-0.87)	5.43 (0.50)	-24.51[b] (-3.87)	-0.914 (-1.17)	0.694 (0.51)	21.94 (0.72)	-10.52 (-0.66)	2.69[c]	0.31	0.20

[a] After-tax income plus technology payments divided by net worth (BROADEQUITY).
[b] Statistical significance level of 1 percent for "t" and F statistics.
[c] Statistical significance level of 5 percent for "t" and F statistics.
[d] Statistical significance level of 10 percent for "t" and F statistics.

Note: "t" values are in parentheses.

Source: Special survey of the U.S. Senate Subcommittee on Multinational Corporations.

TABLE 5.7

Results of Regressions of Profit Rates[a] on Market Structure Variables, 70 Brazilian Manufacturing Affiliates of U.S. MNCs, 1972

Equation	Constant	CR4	FRMS	AD	R&D	LEVER	K/S	GRO	SIZE	EXP	IMP	F	R^2	$\bar{R}^2$
5.7.1	6.43 (1.01)	0.070[c] (1.71)		0.442 (1.17)			-10.47[b] (-3.71)	-0.341 (-0.99)	0.412 (0.68)			3.96[b]	0.24	0.18
5.7.2	2.52 (0.41)	0.072[c] (1.88)	10.45[b] (2.98)	0.719[c] (1.96)			-11.46[b] (-4.27)	-0.379 (-1.16)	0.391 (0.68)			5.18[b]	0.33	0.27
5.7.3	2.26 (0.37)	0.072[c] (1.86)	10.13[b] (2.84)	0.694[c] (1.87)	-0.411 (-0.60)		-11.68[b] (-4.29)	-0.387 (-1.18)	0.483 (0.81)			4.45[b]	0.33	0.26
5.7.4	-7.36 (-1.11)	0.077[c] (2.11)	9.75[b] (2.91)	0.717[c] (2.05)	-0.242 (-0.37)	13.36[b] (3.02)	-13.09[b] (-5.03)	-0.186 (-0.59)	0.640 (1.14)			5.54[b]	0.42	0.35
5.7.5	-6.13 (-0.90)	0.077[c] (2.09)	9.67[b] (2.85)	0.693[c] (1.94)	-0.310 (-0.47)	12.93[b] (2.84)	-13.00[b] (-4.91)	-0.227 (-0.70)	0.596 (1.04)	5.82 (0.46)	-5.08 (-0.76)	4.43[b]	0.43	0.33

[a]After-tax income divided by total assets (ASSETPROF).
[b]Statistical significance level of 1 percent for "t" and F statistics.
[c]Statistical significance level of 5 percent for "t" and F statistics.

Note: "t" values are in parentheses.

Source: Special survey of the U.S. Senate Subcommittee on Multinational Corporations.

TABLE 5.8

Results of Regressions of Profit Rates[a] on Market Structure Variables, 70 Brazilian Manufacturing Affiliates of U.S. MNCs, 1972

Equation	Constant	CR4	FRMS	AD	R&D	LEVER	K/S	GRO	SIZE	EXP	IMP	F	R^2	$\bar{R}^2$
5.8.1	6.67 (0.89)	0.087[c] (1.82)		0.657[d] (1.48)				-0.515 (-1.26)	0.483 (0.67)			3.66[b]	0.22	0.16
5.8.2	2.71 (0.37)	0.090[c] (0.95)	10.57[b] (2.50)	0.937[c] (2.12)			-12.13[b] (-3.76)	-0.554[d] (-1.41)	0.462 (0.67)			4.35[b]	0.29	0.22
5.8.3	2.39 (0.32)	0.090[c] (1.93)	10.19[c] (2.37)	0.906[c] (2.03)	-0.502 (-0.61)		-12.39[b] (-3.79)	-0.564[d] (-1.43)	0.574 (0.80)			3.75[b]	0.30	0.22
5.8.4	-9.19 (-1.15)	0.096[c] (2.19)	9.73[b] (2.41)	0.934[c] (2.22)	-0.299 (-0.39)	16.08[b] (3.02)	-14.09[b] (-4.50)	-0.321 (-0.85)	0.764 (1.13)			4.85[b]	0.39	0.30
5.8.5	-7.69 (-0.93)	0.096[b] (2.15)	9.64[b] (2.36)	0.903[c] (2.10)	-0.337 (-0.48)	15.53[b] (2.83)	-13.97[b] (-4.38)	-0.369 (-0.94)	0.711 (1.04)	6.46 (0.42)	-6.25 (-0.78)	3.89[b]	0.40	0.30

[a]The profit rate used was after-tax earnings plus technology payments divided by total assets (BROADASSET).

[b]Statistical significance level of 1 percent for "t" and F statistics.

[c]Statistical significance level of 5 percent for "t" and F statistics.

[d]Statistical significance level of 10 percent for "t" and F statistics.

Note: "t" values are in parentheses.

Source: Special survey of the U.S. Senate Subcommittee on Multinational Corporations.

it statistically significant. Its introduction also has the effect of reducing slightly the statistical significance of the other structural variables.*

Therefore, except for R&D, all of the structural variables have
the expected positive impacts on profits, and all of them are sometimes significant. These initial results provide support for the hypothesis that market structure has a significant, positive impact on
profit rates of affiliates of U.S. MNCs in Brazil.

Looking at the control variables in Table 5.5, only K/S has a
significant negative influence on profits, as predicted. The GRO is
consistently negative, and LEVER and SIZE are always positive, but
none is significant. The addition of the two simple trade intensities
does appear to strengthen the influence of CR4 on profits while weakening that of FRMS and AD, but by themselves EXP and IMP are insignificant. The different signs on the two trade ratios are interesting
and may lend credence to the view that export-promotion and import-
substitution policies are having the desired consequences in Brazil.

The F test for the whole regression is highly significant, that
is (in four out of five cases) there is less than a 1 percent chance that
all the coefficients could be equal to zero. The best-fitting of the
equations in Table 5.5 explain nearly one-third of the variation in
profit rates among the 1972 sample firms. On the basis of parsimony,
Equation 5.5.2 would be chosen as the "best" equation of the lot.

The results of the linear-model regressions against BROADEQUITY
can be found in Table 5.6. These results closely parallel those in
Table 5.5. All of the first three structural variables (CR4, FRMS,
AD) are positive as before, but the coefficients themselves and their
levels of significance are distinctly higher for CR4 and AD. The data
in Table 5.6 confirm the expectation that BROADEQUITY would be
superior to EQUITYPROF because it more closely approximates the
"return on invested capital" criterion applied by MNCs to their foreign investments.

As was the case above, R&D explains little and carries a negative sign. Unlike FRMS, R&D is also unhelpful in strengthening the
influence of other structural variables or improving the fit. The comments made on the nonstructural variables in Table 5.5 apply equally
here. The overall goodness of fit is essentially the same. Equation
5.6.2. is perhaps the best of the equations in Table 5.6.

Table 5.7 displays the estimates resulting from linear regressions on ASSETPROF, the ratio of net income to total assets. Three
structural variables, CR4, FRMS, and AD, are repeatedly positive,

---

*Ceteris paribus reasoning is employed henceforth in illustra-
tions of this kind, unless otherwise noted.

and when all three are simultaneously included, their coefficients are
very significant. The comments made on R&D and the control variables in Tables 5.5 and 5.6 apply equally to Table 5.7 with one exception. Unlike the situation with equity rates, the use of profit rates on
assets radically changes the significance of the LEVER control. The
variable LEVER is not only highly significant itself, but its addition
to the model (compare equations 5.7.3. and 5.7.4) also improves the
significance of the three structural variables. Thus, the correction
on profits for interest payments provided by a leverage measure is
shown to be highly beneficial.

The results indicated in Table 5.8 for the dependent variable
BROADASSET are parallel to those in Table 5.7 for ASSETPROF.
The overall fit is not quite as close for BROADASSET as for
ASSETPROF, but both the asset ratios are superior on this basis to
their equity-ratio counterparts.

To summarize the results for the four tables, these fairly simple and entirely linear equations provide convincing evidence that these
tested dimensions of Brazilian market structure do, indeed, affect
the profit performance of U.S. manufacturing affiliates in the predicted fashion (except for R&D intensity). In all 20 equations, CR4
is shown to have a positive effect on profits, and this association has
only a small chance of being due to random variations. Moreover,
the variable designed to measure leadership and entrenchment, FRMS,
is highly significant and positive in all the equations. Even though
CR4 and FRMS are positively correlated, their simultaneous inclusion
only strengthens the effect of concentration on profits. Finally, the
variable representing the height of the product-differentiation barrier
to entry, AD, always has a positive effect on profits. Its significance
varies somewhat, however, with the choice of dependent variable.
With profits rates on assets (Tables 5.7 and 5.8), so long as FRMS
is also included, AD is highly significant. With profits taken as a
proportion of net worth (Tables 5.5 and 5.6), AD is significant at only
the 10 percent level or slightly below (as in equations 5.5.3 to 5.5.5).
It may be that the addition of R&D weakens the effect of AD, even
though they are uncorrelated. On the other hand, the influence of
AD is noticeably stronger when broad earnings are used as the dependent variable (Tables 5.6 and 5.8).

Of the control variables, only K/S has a consistently negative,
highly significant effect on profits in all equations. The growth control
is always negative and in some equations barely significant. SIZE,
on the other hand, is uniformly positive, but never quite significant.
The control for the firm's debt ratio, LEVER, is always positive but
is significant only when regressed against profit rates on assets (equations 5.7.4, 5.7.5, 5.8.4, 5.8.5). Because its introduction improves
the significance levels of the three primary structural variables,

LEVER is interpreted to correct primarily for interest payments by the firm rather than for risk factors; that is, the greater the firm's debt relative to its assets, the greater its interest payments, and the less its true profits. The two trade intensivenesses, EXP and IMP, are always opposite in signs, but are never close to significance and never appreciably improve the effects of the structural variables.

On the whole, the two performance rates using total assets (Table 5.7 and 5.8) "explain" a distinctly higher percentage of variation (about 40 percent in equations 5.7.4 and 5.8.4) than do the ratios over equity (about 30 percent in equations 5.5.2 and 5.6.2). Previous studies using both rates have not usually found such large differences, but this may be attributed to the very large range in equity ratios observed; in Brazil LEVER varies from 0.09 to 0.96. The total assets of the sample affiliates may not be as volatile or as subject to managerial discretion as the net-worth component. The use of broad earnings did not generally produce better fits than the narrow profit ratios, but the structural variables did appear to be stronger.

Mexico Results

This section presents the estimates of parameters of market structure-performance equations using data from the 1972 sample of 125 Mexican manufacturing affiliates of U.S. MNCs. The numerical results of some linear-model regressions appear in Tables 5.9 through 5.12 below. The tables exactly parallel Tables 5.5 through 5.8 for Brazil.

Tables 5.9-5.12 contain the estimated regression coefficients, their "t" statistics, the equation's coefficient of determination, and the overall F test for each model. As above, there are four parallel tables, each of which uses the same sets of independent variables but uses different dependent variables (EQUITYPROF, BROADEQUITY, ASSETPROF, and BROADASSET, respectively). The 20 regression functions fitted to the 125 firms' data are numbers, with 5 in each table.

Looking first at Table 5.9, it can be observed that the four structural variables (CR4, FRMS, AD, and R&D) all have the predicted positive sign. The CR4 is solidly significant in all five models, though the absolute size of the coefficient is nearly half that in the comparable Brazilian regressions. In Mexico, R&D has a highly significant impact on profits, but the other measure of product differentiation, advertising, has an insignificant effect. This unexpected weakness of AD seems partially due to specification error. The appropriate forms for both AD and R&D are explored more fully in the nonlinear regressions of the following subsection. In Table 5.9, the coefficient of

TABLE 5.9

Results of Regressions of Profit Rates[a] on Market Structure Variables, 125 Mexican Manufacturing Affiliates of U.S. MNCs, 1972

Equation	Constant	CR4	FRMS	AD	R&D	LEVER	K/S	GRO	SIZE	EXP	IMP	F	R^2	$\bar{R}^2$
5.9.1	11.47[d] (1.34)	0.074[c] (1.78)		0.094 (0.27)			-16.84[b] (-3.48)	-0.638[c] (-1.94)	1.28[d] (1.41)			3.67[b]	0.13	0.10
5.9.2	11.40[d] (1.33)	0.066[d] (1.53)	2.99 (0.77)	0.130 (0.38)			-18.06[b] (-3.51)	-0.648[c] (-1.96)	1.24[d] (1.37)			3.13	0.14	0.09
5.9.3	10.50 (1.24)	0.066[d] (1.54)	3.93 (0.95)	0.143 (0.42)	0.692[c] (2.16)		-17.78[b] (-3.51)	-0.582[c] (-1.78)	1.10 (1.23)			3.43[b]	0.17	0.11
5.9.4	13.86[d] (1.41)	0.060[d] (1.40)	4.27 (1.02)	0.141 (0.41)	0.674[c] (2.09)	-3.80 (-0.67)	-18.50[b] (-3.57)	-0.631[c] (-1.88)	1.08 (1.20)			3.05[b]	0.17	0.12
5.9.5	14.18[d] (1.44)	0.075[d] (1.65)	4.41 (1.06)	0.207 (0.605)	0.630[c] (1.95)	-4.48 (-0.80)	-19.35[b] (-3.74)	-0.720[c] (-2.12)	0.977 (1.09)	16.90[d] (1.46)	10.31 (1.19)	2.81[b]	0.20	0.13

[a]Net income after taxes divided by firm's net worth (EQUITYPROF).
[b]Statistical significance level of 1 percent for "t" and F statistics.
[c]Statistical significance level of 5 percent for "t" and F statistics.
[d]Statistical significance level of 10 percent for "t" and F statistics.

Note: "t" values are in parentheses.

Source: Special survey of the U.S. Senate Subcommittee on Multinational Corporations.

TABLE 5.10

Results of Regressions of Profit Rates[a] on Market Structure Variables, 125 Mexican Manufacturing Affiliates of U.S. MNCs, 1972

Equation	Constant	CR4	FRMS	AD	R&D	LEVER	K/S	GRO	SIZE	EXP	IMP	F	R^2	$\bar{R}^2$
5.10.1	12.63 (1.20)	0.061 (1.19)		1.00^b (2.38)			-23.12^b (-3.88)	-0.681^c (-1.68)	0.97^c (1.77)			5.72^b	0.19	0.16
5.10.2	12.53 (1.19)	0.050 (0.94)	4.23 (0.82)	1.05^b (2.47)			-24.83^b (-3.92)	-0.695^c (-1.71)	1.92^c (1.72)			4.86^b	0.20	0.16
5.10.3	11.79 (1.12)	0.049 (0.94)	5.01 (0.97)	1.06^b (2.51)	0.574^d (1.44)		-24.61^b (-3.91)	-0.640^d (-1.58)	1.81^d (1.62)			4.50^b	0.21	0.16
5.10.4	19.61^d (1.61)	0.037 (0.70)	5.79 (1.12)	1.06^b (2.50)	0.532^d (1.33)	-8.83 (-1.27)	-26.27^b (-4.09)	-0.754^d (-1.82)	1.75^d (1.57)			4.16^b	0.22	0.17
5.10.5	21.04^c (1.73)	0.043 (0.75)	6.02 (1.17)	1.15^b (2.73)	0.513 (1.29)	-9.83^d (-1.42)	-27.30^b (-4.27)	-0.903^c (-2.15)	1.64 (1.48)	13.19 (0.92)	18.57^c (1.73)	3.76^b	0.25	0.18

[a]After-tax income plus technology payments divided by net worth (BROADEQUITY).
[b]Statistical significance level of 1 percent for "t" and F statistics.
[c]Statistical significance level of 5 percent for "t" and F statistics.
[d]Statistical significance level of 10 percent for "t" and F statistics.

Note: "t" values are in parentheses.

Source: Special survey of the U.S. Senate Subcommittee on Multinational Corporations.

TABLE 5.11

Results of Regressions of Profit Rates[a] on Market Structure Variables, 125 Mexican Manufacturing Affiliates of U.S. MNCs, 1972

Equation	Constant	CR4	FRMS	AD	R&D	LEVER	K/S	GRO	SIZE	EXP	IMP	F	R^2	$\bar{R}^2$
5.11.1	10.07[c] (2.08)	0.007 (0.31)		-0.062 (-0.32)			-10.13[b] (-3.71)	-0.454[b] (-2.45)	0.736[d] (1.44)			3.54[b]	0.13	0.09
5.11.2	10.00[c] (2.08)	-0.0006 (-0.02)	2.97 (1.27)	-0.026 (-0.13)			-11.33[b] (-3.93)	-0.464[b] (-2.51)	0.699[d] (1.37)			3.24[b]	0.14	0.10
5.11.3	9.93[c] (2.05)	-0.0006 (-0.03)	3.04 (1.29)	-0.025 (-0.13)	0.049 (0.27)		-11.31[b] (-3.91)	-0.459[b] (-2.46)	0.689[d] (1.34)			2.76[c]	0.14	0.09
5.11.4	-3.96 (-0.79)	0.021 (0.94)	1.66 (0.78)	-0.015 (-0.08)	0.124 (0.75)	15.69[b] (5.45)	-8.36[b] (-3.16)	-0.259[d] (-1.51)	0.786[c] (1.71)			6.72[b]	0.32	0.27
5.11.5	-4.23 (-0.84)	0.033[d] (1.41)	1.70 (0.80)	0.011 (0.06)	0.090 (0.55)	15.44[b] (5.38)	-8.76[b] (-3.32)	-0.284[d] (-1.64)	0.730[d] (1.59)	10.80[c] (1.83)	2.41 (0.54)	5.81[b]	0.34	0.28

[a]After-tax income divided by total assets (ASSETPROF).
[b]Statistical significance level of 1 percent for "t" and F statistics.
[c]Statistical significance level of 5 percent for "t" and F statistics.
[d]Statistical significance level of 10 percent for "t" and F statistics.

Note: "t" values are in parentheses.

Source: Special survey of the U.S. Senate Subcommittee on Multinational Corporations.

TABLE 5.12

Results of Regressions of Profit Rates[a] on Market Structure Variables, 125 Mexican Manufacturing Affiliates of U.S. MNCs, 1972

Equation	Constant	CR4	FRMS	AD	R&D	LEVER	K/S	GRO	SIZE	EXP	IMP	F	R^2	$\bar{R}^2$
5.12.1	12.44[c] (2.10)	-0.007 (-0.26)		0.325[d] (1.38)			-14.21[b] (-4.25)	-0.579[b] (-2.55)	1.17[c] (1.86)			5.64[b]	0.19	0.16
5.12.2	12.34[c] (2.09)	-0.018 (-0.61)	4.01[d] (1.40)	0.374[d] (1.57)			-15.84[b] (-4.49)	-0.592[b] (-2.61)	1.12[c] (1.79)			5.06[b]	0.20	0.16
5.12.3	12.31[c] (2.08)	-0.018 (-0.61)	4.03[d] (1.39)	0.374[d] (1.57)	0.020 (0.09)		-15.83[b] (-4.47)	-0.590[b] (-2.58)	1.11[c] (1.77)			4.30[b]	0.20	0.16
5.12.4	-3.14 (-0.50)	0.006 (0.21)	2.49 (0.93)	0.386[c] (1.77)	0.103 (0.50)	17.46[b] (4.85)	-12.55[b] (-3.79)	-0.366[c] (-1.71)	1.22[c] (2.12)			7.43[b]	0.34	0.29
5.12.5	-2.95 (-0.47)	0.013 (0.46)	2.57 (0.96)	0.421[c] (1.92)	0.081 (0.39)	17.08[b] (4.74)	-13.01[b] (-3.92)	-0.415[c] (-1.90)	1.17[c] (2.02)	8.97 (1.21)	5.68 (1.01)	6.21[b]	0.35	0.30

[a]The profit rate used was broad earnings divided by total assets (BROADASSET).

[b]Statistical significance level of 1 percent for "t" and F statistics.

[c]Statistical significance level of 5 percent for "t" and F statistics.

[d]Statistical significance level of 10 percent for "t" and F statistics.

<u>Note:</u> "t" values are in parentheses.

<u>Source:</u> Special survey of the U.S. Senate Subcommittee on Multinational Corporations.

FRMS is also unexpectedly insignificant; moreover, adding FRMS to equation 5.9.2. lowers the significance level of CR4 instead of raising it (as happened in the Brazilian regressions). In sum, the structural variables all have the correct signs, but only two of the four are statistically significant.

The estimated coefficients of the control variables in Table 5.9 generally exhibit the expected signs. Capital intensity is strongly negative in all the equations. Firm size is nearly or weakly significant and positive. Major industry growth is very significantly negative in all models. These three results closely parallel those found for Brazil (compare Table 5.5). The control for debt structure, LEVER, is negative, but very weak. Finally, the two simple trade intensivenesses, EXP and IMP, both carry positive coefficients that are at the margin of the 10 percent confidence threshold. The signs for LEVER and IMP in these regressions are the reverse of those found for Brazil.

Although the regressions are highly significant in all cases, the proportion of variation explained is quite low; some equations (for example, 5.9.2), explain less than half the variation, as did the parallel equations for Brazil (for example, 5.5.2).

The results reported in Table 5.10 are somewhat better in some respects. The overall goodness of fit rises, and except for GRO and EXP, the significance level of the control variables also rises. As in Table 5.9 the signs of the four structural variables are all positive. The main difference between the EQUITYPROF and BROADEQUITY tables is that in the latter the size and significance of the AD coefficient increase markedly while those of CR4 and R&D fall. The influence of AD on profits is highly significant in all five equations (5.10.1 through 5.10.5), but CR4 drops below the 10 percent level.

The numerical outcomes reported in Tables 5.11 and 5.12 also reveal a great deal of instability for the coefficients of the structural variables. Examining only those equations including LEVER as a control (numbers 5.11.4, 5.11.5, 5.12.4, and 5.12.5), it is again true that generally all four are positive but that one at most is significant in any given equation. In equation 5.11.5, CR4 is significant, but no other structural variable is even close to significance. In equation 5.12.5, AD is highly significant, but CR4 and the other market structure elements are very weak explanatory variables.

Except for the change in sign and significance of LEVER, the control variables perform in a highly similar fashion in the profits on assets models and in the profits on equity models. Capital intensity and industry growth have consistently negative impacts on profits, while size and trade intensity have decisively opposite effects. In the models containing LEVER, the overall fit is remarkably improved relative to the results in Tables 5.9 and 5.10, though the fit is not quite as close as that for the same functions using the Brazilian data.

These linear models in Tables 5.9-5.12 do not provide as strong and clear support for the market power hypothesis of industrial organization theory as the regression results for Brazil. This is somewhat unexpected in view of the fact that the sample size in Mexico is larger and that the coverage of all MNCs in Mexico is consequently considerably more comprehensive. By implication, as discussed above, the estimates of certain market structure variables ought to have been less inaccurate. Part of the explanation may lie in omitted variables, and an attempt is made to remedy this situation in the following section. Another possible explanation is that the Mexican sample contains a larger proportion of smaller firms than the Brazilian sample, thereby increasing the variance in some of the dimensions of market structure and profit performance. (The Mexican firms in the sample average only about half of the asset size of the Brazilian firms.) If this creates a problem, a weighted regression procedure may partially correct for it. A final possible explanation of the relatively stronger Brazilian results may lie in the markedly higher levels of import protection offered by Brazil's tariff structure. Apparently, when Mexican prices on domestic manufactures rise too high above world levels, it is government policy to grant sufficient import permits to cause prices to decline (King 1970). Brazil, on the other hand, sanctions the operation of business-planning committees in numerous industries that may facilitate oligopolistic coordination of pricing or product design.

NONLINEAR* MODELS

The equations specified in the previous section were all "linear"; that is, the functions, if drawn, would be straight lines (or their equivalent in n-dimensional space). In this and the next section, terms are introduced that permit a relaxation of this constraint. Additional terms, or certain mathematical transformations of single terms, allow us to fit the observed data points to curves instead of lines.[†] Of-

---

*I do not use this term to mean "intrinsically nonlinear in the parameters." The models in this section are still "linear" in the sense that they can still be transformed into linear equations.

[†]In addition to first-degree terms, the models in this subsection contain groups of independent variables of the form $b_1 X + b_2 X^2 + b_3 X^3$, where either b_2 or b_3 may be zero. The justification for including second-degree, third-degree, logarithmic, or other nonlinear terms is that when the true relation is nonlinear, the estimation of only an additive, linear function leads to a loss of information. In particular,

ten the shape of the data does not justify the use of curvilinear formulations, and in such a case the original, single linear term is retained.

Equation 5.13.1 below (Table 5.13) is the least-squares regression estimate explaining the variation in EQUITYPROF rates for the
70 Brazilian manufacturing subsidiaries in the 1972 sample. Equation
5.13.2 uses ASSETPROF, and equation 5.13.3 uses BROADEQUITY.
In addition to the variable symbols and their coefficients, the appropriate "t" or "F" statistic is given in parentheses below the variables
to which they refer.*

---

specification error due to omitted variables leads to biased estimates
of the regression coefficients and to downward-biased estimates of
their "t" values (Kmenta 1971: 392-95). When all three polynomial
terms are estimated by least squares, the assumed relationship is a
curve with two critical points, a maxima and a minima. When the
form adopted conformed to $b_1X + b_2X^2$ or to $b_1X + b_3X^3$, the curve
being described was a parabola, which has only one critical point.
The only difference between the two formulations is that $b_1X + b_2X^2$
is restricted to a curve that is symmetric about its axis while $b_1X + b_3X^3$ may be assymetric.

An empirical procedure was adopted to identify the appropriate
form. Graphs of the residuals plotted against the independent variables were examined for certain characteristic patterns that signal the
presence of nonlinearities (Draper and Smith 1966: 86-92). For several variables—CR4, FRMS, R&D, LEVER, K/S, SIZE, and GRO—
there was some evidence of curvilinearity. In each case, the significance of adding additional terms was checked by introducing X^2, X^3,
and $X^2 + X^3$ in separate regressions and calculating a "partial" F
statistic (Johnston 1963: 124). The comparisons were made against
linear models similar to those in Tables 5.5-5.8. In some cases,
the significance of adding higher-indexed terms was at unacceptably
low levels; this was true of K/S. In other cases, such as SIZE, a
logarithmic term was found to fit as well as some polynomial combina-
tion. If the F test yielded higher levels of significance for the $b_1X + b_3X^3$ combination than for the more commonly used $b_1X + b_2X^2$ group,
the former was used. No term above the third degree was tested.

*Student's "t" statistic is used to test whether a given coefficient
could, by chance, be equal to zero. If there is a strong possibility
that the coefficient in question is zero, that is tantamout to a lack of
a cause-and-effect relationship between the coefficient's variable and
the dependent variable. The higher the absolute value of the "t" statistic, the lower the probability that the coefficient could be zero, and
the higher the level of statistical "significance" or confidence.

It should be noted that when polynomial expressions are used in
ordinary least-squares regressions, the appropriate test of signifi-

TABLE 5.13

Results of Basic "Nonlinear" Regressions of Profit Rates on Market Structure Variables, 70 Brazilian Manufacturing Affiliates of U.S. MNCs, 1972

$$\begin{aligned}
\text{EQUITYPROF} = \ & -34.78 + 34.32 \text{ WCR4} + 44.51 \text{ FRMS} - 30.18 \text{ FRMS}^3 + 1.97 \text{ AD} \\
& (-1.63)^c \quad (3.11)^a \qquad (5.31)^a \qquad\qquad (2.49)^a \\[4pt]
& + 3.00 \text{ R\&D} - 0.73 \text{ R\&D}^2 + 47.20 \text{ LEVER} - 46.28 \text{ LEVER}^3 - 13.72 \text{ K/S} \\
& \quad (2.68)^c \qquad\qquad\qquad (3.36)^b \qquad\qquad\qquad (-2.17)^b \\[4pt]
& - 30.80 \text{ EXP} - 2.27 \text{ IMP} + 18.55 \text{ DAFFEXP} - 2.09 \text{ DAFFIMP} \\
& \quad (-1.04) \quad (-0.16) \qquad (3.46)^a \qquad\qquad (-0.48) \\[4pt]
& - 3.71 \text{ SIZE} + 4.96 \text{ GRO} - 0.02 \text{ GRO}^3 + U_i. \qquad R^2 = 0.52 \qquad F = 3.60^a \\
& \quad (-2.51)^a \qquad (2.15)
\end{aligned}$$

(5.13.1)

$$\begin{aligned}
\text{ASSETPROF} = \ & -35.96 + 18.13 \text{ WCR4} + 17.16 \text{ FRMS} - 11.54 \text{ FRMS}^3 + 1.05 \text{ AD} \\
& (-3.90)^a \quad (3.79)^a \qquad (1.50) \qquad\qquad (3.07)^a \\[4pt]
& + 2.09 \text{ R\&D} - 0.42 \text{ R\&D}^2 + 42.64 \text{ LEVER} - 32.54 \text{ LEVER}^3 - 8.26 \text{ K/S} \\
& \quad (0.98) \qquad\qquad\qquad (4.71)^a \qquad\qquad\qquad (-3.01)^a \\[4pt]
& - 16.09 \text{ EXP} - 1.29 \text{ IMP} + 8.46 \text{ DAFFEXP} - 0.78 \text{ DAFFIMP} \\
& \quad (-1.25) \quad (-0.21) \qquad (3.64)^a \qquad\qquad (-0.41) \\[4pt]
& - 1.72 \text{ SIZE} + 4.38 \text{ GRO} - 0.02 \text{ GRO}^3 + U_i. \qquad R^2 = 0.65 \qquad F = 6.03^a \\
& \quad (-2.35)^a \qquad (1.56)
\end{aligned}$$

(5.13.2)

$$\text{BROADEQUITY} = \underset{(-1.76)^b}{-41.78} + \underset{(3.22)^a}{39.58\ \text{WCR4}} + \underset{(2.15)}{46.94\ \text{FRMS}} - 33.84\ \text{FRMS}^3 + \underset{(2.79)^a}{2.45\ \text{AD}}$$

$$+ \underset{(1.27)}{2.95\ \text{R\&D}} - 0.75\ \text{R\&D}^2 + \underset{(1.95)}{58.42\ \text{LEVER}} - 55.29\ \text{LEVER}^3 - \underset{(-2.04)^b}{14.36\ \text{K/S}}$$

$$- \underset{(-1.01)}{33.27\ \text{EXP}} - \underset{(-0.11)}{1.64\ \text{IMP}} + \underset{(3.36)^a}{20.07\ \text{DAFFEXP}} - \underset{(-0.75)}{3.65\ \text{DAFFIMP}}$$

$$- \underset{(-2.02)^b}{3.77\ \text{SIZE}} + \underset{(1.05)}{5.00\ \text{GRO}} - 0.02\ \text{GRO}^3 + U_i. \qquad R^2 = 0.51 \qquad F = 3.43$$

$$(5.13.3)$$

Note: The variable WCR4 is the Weibull function transformation of the four-firm concentration ratio CR4. The Weibull function is of the form $1 - \exp[-(\frac{\text{CR4}}{30})^2]$ and describes an S-shaped curve similar to the cumulative normal distribution function, a shape suggested by industrial organization theory (Figure 5.1). The parameters of the function (30 and 2 in the case of equation 5.13.1) were chosen by an empirical method that minimizes the standard error, and the estimated regression coefficient (28.14 here) represents the vertical height of the upper horizontal asymptote; it is the percentage impact on profits over equity as CR4 rises to, and beyond, 100 percent from zero. (See Hastings and Peacock 1975: 124-29.) The term symbolized by U_i is a random disturbance term with the usual spherical distribution properties. The a, b, and c superscripts indicate that the regression coefficient is significantly different from zero at the 1, 5, and 10 percent confidence levels, respectively, using a one-tailed "t" test or an F test. For this sample the mean value of WCR4 if 0.8916.

Source: Compiled by the author.

191

Equations 5.13.1-5.13.3 are similar to the fullest of the linear models above (5.5.5, 5.6.5, 5.7.5, 5.8.5) except that (1) a second-degree term is added for R&D, (2) cubic terms are added for FRMS, LEVER, and GRO, (3) the linear CR4 term is replaced by the Weibull transformation of CR4, and (4) the two variables DAFFEXP and DAFFIMP are newly included. Counting polynomial expressions of the same variable as a single unit, there are 12 independent variables in equations 5.13.1-5.12.3.

The estimates for Brazil in equations 5.13.1-5.13.3 generally reinforce the results of the linear experiments.* Concentration, as expected, produces a highly significant and positive effect on profits (Figure 5.1). Irrespective of the measure of performance used, levels of concentration at about the average (CR4 = 70 percent) lead to affiliate profit levels about three times as high as those of firms in the most competitive industries (CR4 = 20).† Like concentration, the firm's relative market share is also highly significant in equation 5.13.1. But the shape of the influence of FRMS, like that of all the polynomial pairs of independent variables, is like that of an upward-bending parabola; that is, as FRMS increases, the effect on profit rates also increases up to some point and then declines beyond that point. In the case of FRMS, its maximum impact occurs at about 0.85.

The market advertising intensity, AD, a proxy measure of the extent of product differentiation in Brazilian markets, is also positive

_____

cance is not the usual "t" test on each b_i. Rather, because the expressions $b_1 X$, $b_1 X + b_2 X^2$, and $b_2 X^2 + b_3 X^3$ are simply three different representations of the same concept, the appropriate test of significance for quadratic or cubic combinations is the "group" F test. Thus, for some groups of variables in the nonlinear models below, the F statistic is substituted for the "t" statistic in the parentheses under the independent variable. The procedure was not always followed in previous statistical studies of market power (that is, FTC 1969). Unfortunately, the significance level of the "t" statistics calculated for polynomial groups often exceeds the calculated significance level of the group F statistic, thus failing to reject relationships that are not statistically different from zero.

*Experiments employing BROADASSET as the measures of profit performance yield highly similar results to its respective narrow profits counterpart. The main difference is that the effect of AD on profits is heightened and that of FRMS slightly weakened.

†Numerical illustrations of this kind always assume that the other independent variables are being held constant at their mean values. For further examples, see Tables 5.15 through 5.18, below.

FIGURE 5.1

Predicted Relationship of Profits to Four–Firm Concentration in
Brazilian Manufacturing, 1972

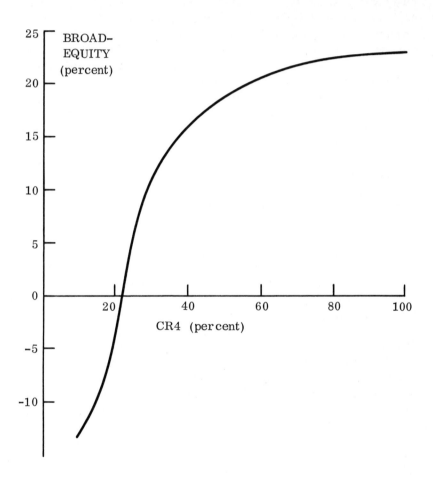

Note: Based on equation 5.13.3 of Table 5.13.

Source: Special survey of the U.S. Senate Subcommittee on
Multinational Corporations.

and highly significant in all of the nonlinear models shown. Holding all else constant, firms in industries that differ by only one percentage point in their average advertising ratios also differ by more than two percentage points in their profits on equity (or by more than one percentage point in assets). Net income is raised by more than five percentage points on net worth for affiliates in industries with average advertising rates relative to those with no advertising. Therefore, with respect to these three market structure variables, the nonlinear model results reinforce the conclusions of the linear models discussed above. Concentration, relative market share, and product differentiation all have statistically strong, positive effects on profit performance. The existence of market power and the predictions of industrial organization theory are strongly verified in the case of U.S. MNCs' manufacturing affiliates operating in Brazil in 1972.

The results for some of the other causal variables differ somewhat between the linear and the nonlinear models. Research-and-development intensity is a case in point. Though only weakly significant, R&D was consistently negative in its impact on performance in the linear models of Tables 5.5–5.8, but in the nonlinear equations 5.13.1–5.13.3 a quadratic specification of R&D indicates that it has a net positive effect over the relevant range (say 0.1 to 2.0 percent). For R&D intensities exceeding about 2.5 percent (there are only five or six such observations), the net effect on profits is negative. Therefore, for the greatest part of the Brazilian sample, R&D has the expected positive influence on profits; had prior, rather than current, R&D expenditures been available, this relationship might have been more powerful.

Absolute asset size is another independent variable whose sign is reversed in the more complex models. Although previously never significant but always positive, SIZE proves to be very significant and negative in its impact upon all four profit measures. More complex (that is, higher-ordered) polynomial expressions did not exhibit greater explanatory power than the simple logarithmic formulation employed. Thus, in Brazil in 1972, there appears to be some evidence of diseconomies of firm size. The coefficient of K/S remains highly significantly negative (though its absolute size is considerably lower in the nonlinear results), supporting my hypotheses regarding capacity underutilization and the contribution of distribution activities to profits.

The debt position of the sample firms is shown to be somewhat stronger in its parabolic formulation than it was in its linear form. In equations 5.13.1–5.13.3, the net effect of LEVER is positive over the entire range of observation (0.09 to 0.96), but its effect on profits reaches a maximum at an intermediate point. Profits reach their maximum when the equity-to-assets ratio is about 0.60 for the equity rates of profit and about 0.65 for the asset rates. Thus, the "optimal"

debt for these Brazilian subsidiaries is predicted to be about one-third
(or slightly more) of total assets. As was true in the linear models
above, LEVER is the one variable whose significance level is drasti-
cally different for one pair of dependent variables (the asset ratios)
than for the other pair (the equity ratios). The group F tests for the
LEVER expression are extremely high in parts in equation 5.13.2 but
are borderline (that is, about 10 percent) in the other equations.

The interpretation to be given to major industry growth effects
is quite similar to that for LEVER. The calculated coefficients indicate that the effect of GRO is positive over the entire range (4.1 to
13.2 percent growth per year), but the highest profit rate is achieved
when growth is between 9.0 and 9.5 percent per year for both profit
measures; this is slightly above the average of 7.7 percent for all 70
observations. Thus, rates below or above this level adversely affected
the profit performance of firms at least with respect to their impact
on profits in 1972.

The final set of causal variables to consider is the four variables
representing the international trade involvement of the affiliate. Two
variables, EXP and IMP, are simple intensities (that is, ratios over
sales). Two other variables designate intrafirm trade relative to the
total trade: DAFFEXP and DAFFIMP.* Both trade intensities display negative coefficients in all equations, but neither is significant.
The DAFFIMP intensity is also negative, but its significance level is
very low.

The only consistently strong trade variable is DAFFEXP; it is
highly significant and positive throughout the nonlinear models tested
for Brazil. Because it is entered into the equations as a "zero-one"
variable, the coefficient implies that the 22 firms exporting to sister
affiliates enjoyed on average 18 to 19 percentage points higher profits
on equity than did the 48 other Brazilian firms, all other things held
constant. However, it should be noted that among the things being
held constant are the other trade variables. Among the firms that
participate to any degree in such activities, the average EXP was
about 0.05 and the average IMP 0.10. Adjusting for the overall trade
levels yields a net "trade effect" on profits of about 15 percentage
points on equity. Hence, the profit advantages apparently accruing
to these subsidiaries as a result of exports within MNCs are not
quite as large as the coefficient of DAFFEXP may at first indicate,
but these benefits are nevertheless substantial.

The overall fit of the nonlinear models (Table 5.13) is quite impressive, relative to previous studies using firm-level data from only

---

*Recall that variables beginning with a "D" are zero-one varia-
bles, not continuous ones.

one year (except for GRO, of course). Well over half of the variation
in profit rates is explained by both models, and nearly two-thirds is
explained by the ASSETPROF equation. The F test of significance for
the whole equation reveals that there is a far less than 1 percent chance
that all of the coefficients could equal zero. Considering the crudeness
of the estimation procedures used for some of the independent variables (that is, CR4, AD, and GRO), these results are remarkably
strong and stable.

The remainder of this section discusses the regression estimates
of similar nonlinear models using data on 125 manufacturing affiliates
of U.S. MNCs located in Mexico. As will be seen, most of the hypotheses verified for Brazil are also sustained in the Mexican case.

Equations 5.14.1-5.14.3 are the three nonlinear equations fitted
to the 1972 Mexican data (Table 5.14). They closely parallel the Brazilian equations 5.13.1-5.13.3.

The nonlinear equations for Mexico (5.14.1-5.14.3) are similar to the ones for Brazil above except that (1) R&D is omitted, (2)
FRMS is entered in a linear fashion, (3) continuous rather than dichoto-
mous variables are used for the two affiliate trade ratios, and (4) an
additional variable, SUPPLY, is included.* The reasons for including
SUPPLY and dropping R&D are given below.

The three nonlinear models in Table 5.14 represent a considerable improvement over the fullest of the linear models in Tables 5.9-
5.12. For a rather small loss in degrees of freedom, the proportion
of the variation in "explained" profit rates increases considerably,
but perhaps the main improvement is increased stability in the estimated coefficients of the three structural variables.[†] In all equations,
CR4, FRMS, and AD are always positive, as predicted, but the strength
of the influence is less (Figure 5.2). Both concentration and advertising are significant in equation 5.14.1, but both are only on the borderline of significance in equation 5.14.2.[‡] The FRMS term is quite

---

*The definitions and descriptive statistics for most of these vari-
ables can be found in Table 5.4 above. The SUPPLY variable is the
ratio of local sales to sister affiliates of the same MNC to total local
sales. This variable is designed to capture the special profits effects
of domestic sales within MNCs, just as AFFEXP and AFFIMP do for
international sales within MNCs.

[†]That is, the estimated coefficients are closer in absolute values
when compared across models than was the case with the linear models.

[‡]However, when regressed against the two broad profits ratios,
AD was much stronger. The "t" values for AD were 3.55[a] and 2.73[a]
when regressed against BROADEQUITY and BROADASSET, respectively. For each 1 percent increase in AD, a 1.5 percent increase in

TABLE 5.14

Results of Basic "Nonlinear" Regressions of Profit Rates on Market Structure Variables, 125 Mexican Manufacturing Affiliates of U.S. MNCs, 1972

$$
\begin{aligned}
\text{EQUITYPROF} =\ & 23.52 + \underset{(2.10)^b}{24.95}\ \text{WCR4} + \underset{(0.66)}{2.50}\ \text{FRMS} + \underset{(1.63)^c}{0.52}\ \text{AD} \\
& \underset{(1.27)}{} \\
& - \underset{(7.01)^a}{257.67}\ \text{LEVER} + 405.72\ \text{LEVER}^2 - 194.88\ \text{LEVER}^3 - \underset{(-4.16)^a}{19.90}\ \text{K/S} \\
& + \underset{(2.91)^b}{2.50}\ \text{SIZE} + \underset{(3.89)^a}{0.37}\ \text{SUPPLY} + 0.71\ \text{GRO} - \underset{(3.69)^b}{0.002}\ \text{GRO}^2 + \underset{(2.35)^a}{27.70}\ \text{EXP} \\
& + \underset{(0.71)}{5.87}\ \text{IMP} - \underset{(-2.26)}{7.18}\ \text{AFFEXP} + \underset{(1.49)^c}{6.89}\ \text{AFFIMP} + U_i.
\end{aligned}
\tag{5.14.1}
$$

$$R^2 = 0.40 \qquad F = 4.79^a$$

$$
\begin{aligned}
\text{ASSETPROF} =\ & -\underset{(-1.44)^c}{14.31} + \underset{(1.23)}{7.80}\ \text{WCR4} + \underset{(0.91)}{1.83}\ \text{FRMS} + \underset{(1.15)}{0.20}\ \text{AD} \\
& - \underset{(11.80)^a}{36.81}\ \text{LEVER} + 71.74\ \text{LEVER}^2 - 27.58\ \text{LEVER}^3 - \underset{(-3.90)^a}{9.96}\ \text{K/S} \\
& + \underset{(3.00)^a}{1.38}\ \text{SIZE} + \underset{(3.48)^a}{0.18}\ \text{SUPPLY} + 1.02\ \text{GRO} - \underset{(3.46)^b}{0.002}\ \text{GRO}^2 + \underset{(2.26)^b}{14.24}\ \text{EXP} \\
& + \underset{(0.19)}{0.86}\ \text{IMP} - \underset{(-2.19)^b}{3.73}\ \text{AFFEXP} + \underset{(1.40)^c}{3.46}\ \text{AFFIMP} + U_i.
\end{aligned}
\tag{5.14.2}
$$

$$R^2 = 0.45 \qquad F = 6.05^a$$

197

$$\begin{aligned}
\text{BROADEQUITY} = \quad & 27.59 + 19.18 \text{ WCR4} + 4.51 \text{ FRMS} + 1.47 \text{ AD} \\
& (1.14) \quad (1.16) \qquad\quad (0.92) \qquad\qquad (3.55)^a \\[6pt]
& - 209.0 \text{ LEVER} + 326.9 \text{ LEVER}^2 - 161.1 \text{ LEVER}^3 - 27.49 \text{ K/S} + 3.16 \text{ SIZE} \\
& \underline{\qquad\qquad (3.04)^c \qquad\qquad\qquad\qquad (1.88)} \qquad\qquad\qquad (-4.42)^a \quad (2.83)^a \\[6pt]
& + 0.43 \text{ SUPPLY} - 0.22 \text{ GRO} - 0.001 \text{ GRO}^3 + 19.45 \text{ EXP} + 12.21 \text{ IMP} \\
& \quad (3.53)^a \qquad\qquad\qquad\qquad\qquad\qquad\qquad (1.36)^c \qquad (1.14) \\[6pt]
& - 8.23 \text{ AFFEXP} + 9.91 \text{ AFFIMP} + U_i. \qquad R^2 = 0.38 \qquad F = 4.48^a \\
& \quad (-2.00)^b \qquad\quad (1.69)^b
\end{aligned}$$

(5.14.3)

Note: The symbol WCR4 is the Weibull function transformation of the four–firm concentration ratio, CR4, but the parameters of the transformation function are different: WCR4 $= 1 - \exp[-(\frac{\text{CR4}}{60})^{\frac{1}{2}}]$. Again, the parameters were chosen after experimentation with a wide range of values. Unlike the WCR4 used for the Brazilian nonlinear equations (5.13.1 to 5.13.3), this outcome for WCR4 is not S–shaped (Figure 5.2). Rather, the function describes a curve that rises continuously over the whole range of CR4 and approaches an upper horizontal asymptote at a height denoted by the estimated regression coefficient of WCR4 (for example in equation 5.14.1, the asymptote is 24.95). The a, b, and c superscripts indicate that the regression coefficient is significantly different from zero at the 1, 5, and 10 percent confidence levels, respectively, using a one–tailed "t" test or an F test. For this sample the mean of WCR4 is 0.6381.

Source: Compiled by the author.

198

FIGURE 5.2

Predicted Relationship of Profits to Four-Firm Concentration
in Mexican Manufacturing, 1972

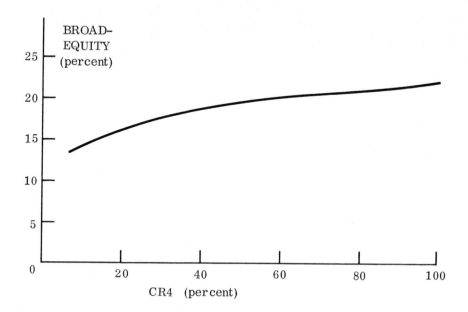

Note: Based on equation 5.14.3 of Table 5.14, holding all other variables constant at their sample means.

Source: Special survey of the U.S. Senate Subcommittee on Multinational Corporations.

weak in all three equations. The market structure-performance relationships predicted by industrial organization theory, while not contradicted by these Mexican regression results, do not receive as strong statistical support as in Brazil. Moreover, there are no ready explanations for this outcome.

Most of the control variables in the basic nonlinear equations behave as predicted. The cubic expression for LEVER is highly sig-

---

broad profits over equity was predicted. This implies that a number of firms in highly differentiated Mexican markets are making very large payments to their U.S. parents for technology or trademark rights.

nificant in both models, and its net effect on profits is negative over
most of LEVER's range. The estimated coefficients for LEVER describe an S-shaped curve.

Capital intensity is again strongly negative; its coefficient is
even larger in absolute value than in the Brazilian estimates. Hence,
capital underutilization or high marketing profits may be present in
Mexico as well. Another indication of this is given by the positive
and consistently very significant coefficient on SIZE. (This is one of
the few differences of this kind between Brazil and Mexico.) Thus,
in Mexico in 1972 there is evidence pointing to both untapped economies
of scale and unused physical plant capacity. Another difference between Brazil and Mexico is the great explanatory power of the SUPPLY
variable. The positive and highly significant coefficient of this control variable suggests that U.S. MNCs are transferring profits vertically backward between two linked Mexican subsidiaries. On average, an affiliate selling 10 percent of its output to a sister affiliate in
Mexico earned an additional four percentage points of profit on equity.
In Brazil, SUPPLY was also consistently positive, but its significance
level was so low as to not warrant inclusion in the reported regressions.

The Mexican data also reveal a systematic tendency for major-
industry growth rates to affect profit rates positively. There is a
slight downward bend in the curve, but over the observed growth-
rate range, the effect is nearly linear.

In Mexico, the four controls for international and intrafirm
trade play a generally more important explanatory role than they did
in Brazil. The two simple trade intensities, EXP and IMP, are uniformly positive in sign, though only EXP is significantly so. These
signs are just the opposite of those existing in Brazil. However, at
average export and import intensities, the effect on profits is considerably less than one percentage point. The two affiliate trade ratios
also present a different prospect in Mexico than in Brazil. In both
the nonlinear equations, AFFEXP is negative, AFFIMP is positive,
and both are statistically significant. If those variables are good
proxies for the extent of transfer pricing, then in the Mexican case
the parent corporations have evidently decided to pass profits vertically forward through the corporate system; that is, exporting affiliates
tend to underprice intermediate goods shipped internationally to their
sister affiliates. Because the mean of AFFEXP exceeds that of
AFFIMP, the net marginal "transfer pricing" effect on profits is about
-0.5 percentage points on equity.

In general, these Mexican results do not support the industrial
organization explanation of supranormal profits as strongly as did the
Brazilian regressions. While the overall fit is highly significant,
it does not "explain" nearly as much of the variation in firm profit
rates. However, the structural variables are all of the correct sign
and either statistically significant or close to it.

Throughout this section I have provided the reader with occasional examples of the estimated numerical impacts that changes in the explanatory variables will have on profit rates. The great virtue of the multiple-regression method of analysis is its ability to yield reliable estimates of the individual effects of each independent variable in the analysis, while simultaneously separating the influences of other causal factors. It is also possible, however, to illustrate the joint effect of varying the levels of two variables at the same time; that is, if two causal factors have significantly positive effects on profits, increasing both by a certain percentage will yield an expected increase in profits that is greater than that from increasing only one of them by the same amount.

Jointly varying two structural variables is illustrated for Brazil in Tables 5.15 and 5.16 and for Mexico in Tables 5.17 and 5.18. In Table 5.15 predicted BROADEQUITY rates are shown for a range of values in both CR4 and FRMS. Increasing CR4 from the lowest level shown (CR4 = 30 percent) to the highest (CR4 = op percent) results in a 13 percentage point increase, though most of this effect is exhausted by the time CR4 reaches 70 percent; the same exercise for FRMS effects an 18 percentage point increase. But a change of both CR4 and FRMS from their lowest calculated value to their highest brings about a 31 percentage point increase in profits. Thus, a U.S. MNC's affiliate both in a concentrated industry and in a clear leadership position can expect to enjoy decidedly supranormal profits. Alternatively, membership in a highly concentrated market can compensate an affiliate that is small relative to the largest market leaders, and vice versa.

Table 5.16 demonstrates for the 70 Brazilian manufacturing subsidiaries the compound effect on expected profits of different combinations of concentration and product differentiation. Where both exceed their average levels (CR4 > 60 and AD > 2.0), profits are above 20 percentage points.

Tables 5.17 and 5.18 provide parallel estimates for the 125 Mexican subsidiaries. Both tables indicate that most of the effect of CR4 on profits occurs at the lower ranges (say, CR4 < 70 percent). Table 5.17 also illustrates the relatively weak impact of the firm's relative market share on profits, and Table 5.18 shows the relatively strong influence of product differentiation on affiliate profitability.* However-

---

*Note that one can also read off the effects of different combinations of AD and FRMS levels, at any given level of CR4, by combining Tables 5.15 and 5.16 (or 5.17 and 5.18). For example, in the Brazilian case, the increase in profits associated with an increase in FRMS from 0.1 to 0.5 plus an increase in AD from 0.0 to 2.0 percent is 20.6 percentage points, holding CR4 constant at 60 percent.

TABLE 5.15

Estimated Net Income as Percentage of Equity Capital of Affiliates
of U.S. MNCs in Brazil Associated with Different Levels of
Concentration and Firm Relative Market Share, 1972
(net income as percentage of equity[a])

Four-Firm Concentration Ratio (CR4)[b] (percent)	Firm Relative Market Share (FRMS)[c] (percent)			
	10	30	50	70
30	-1.1	8.0	14.5	16.9
40	5.8	14.9	21.4	23.8
50	9.5	18.6	25.2	27.5
60	11.1	20.1	26.7	28.0
70	11.5	20.6	27.2	29.5
80	11.7	20.8	27.4	30.1
90	11.7	20.8	27.4	30.1

[a]The profit rates shown are net 1972 revenues after Brazilian
corporate income taxes plus technology payments ("broad profits")
expressed as a percentage of stockholders' equity and predicted by
equation 5.13.3, holding all other independent variables at their respective sample means.
[b]The estimated five-digit SIC product class, minimum, four-
firm concentration ratio, weighted by the affiliates' local sales.
[c]The FRMS is the ratio of the weighted (by five-digit SIC sales
levels) firm market share to the firm's weighted concentration ratio
(CR4).

Source: Special survey of the U.S. Senate Subcommittee on
Multinational Corporations.

ever, had these tables for Mexico been based on equation 5.14.1 instead, the effect of CR4 would have been correspondingly greater
and that of AD weaker.

WEIGHTED REGRESSION RESULTS

Up to this point only unweighted regressions have been employed;
that is, each firm, no matter what its size, has been given equal
weight in the least-squares method. Previous studies have shown that
the variability of profit rates across firms is not constant in a given

year; rather, it is inversely correlated with firm size. This, in turn, implies that one of the basic assumptions of the classical least-squares method has been violated, namely, that the random disturbance term has a constant variance among observations.

There are several methods of overcoming this econometric problem, called heteroskedasticity. One way of imposing homoskedasticity, and thereby obtaining estimates of the regression coefficients that are both unbiased and efficient (estimation under conditions of heteroskedasticity yields unbiased but inefficient estimates), is to use generalized least squares (as do, for example, Imel and Helmberger 1971). A special case of generalized least squares is to weight the observations according to some a priori scheme suggested by theory.

TABLE 5.16

Estimated Net Income as Percentage of Equity Capital of Affiliates of U.S. MNCs in Brazil Associated with Different Levels of Concentration and Industry Advertising-to-Sales Ratios, 1972 (net income as percentage of equity[a])

Four-Firm Concentra- tion Ratio (CR4)[b] (percent)	Advertising-to-Sales Ratio (AD)[c] (percent)					
	0	1.0	2.0	3.0	4.0	5.0
30	4.3	6.7	9.1	11.6	14.1	16.5
40	12.2	14.6	17.1	19.5	22.0	24.4
50	16.4	18.8	21.3	23.7	26.2	28.6
60	18.1	20.8	23.2	25.7	28.1	30.5
70	18.7	21.3	23.7	26.2	28.6	31.0
80	18.8	21.4	23.8	26.3	28.7	31.1
90	18.9	21.5	23.9	26.4	28.8	31.2

[a]The profit rates shown are net 1972 revenues after Brazilian corporate income taxes plus technology payments ("broad profits") expressed as a percentage of stockholders' equity and predicted by equation 5.13.3, holding all other independent variables at their respective sample means.

[b]The estimated five-digit SIC product class, minimum, four-firm concentration ratio, weighted by the affiliates' local sales.

[c]The AD is the total advertising outlays divided by the total sales of the principal product class of the affiliate.

Source: Special survey of the U.S. Senate Subcommittee on Multinational Corporations.

TABLE 5.17

Estimated Net Income as Percentage of Equity Capital of Affiliates of
U.S. MNCs in Mexico Associated with Different Levels of
Concentration and Firm Relative Market Share, 1972
(net income as percentage of equity[a])

Four-Firm Concentration Ratio (CR4)[b] (percent)	Firm Relative Market Share (FRMS)[c] (percent)			
	10	30	50	70
30	16.0	16.9	17.8	18.7
40	17.0	17.9	18.8	19.7
50	17.8	18.7	19.6	20.5
60	18.4	19.3	20.2	21.1
70	19.0	19.9	20.8	21.7
80	19.4	20.3	21.2	22.1
90	19.8	20.7	21.6	22.5

[a]The profit rates shown are net 1972 revenues after Mexican corporate income taxes plus technology payments ("broad profits") expressed as a percentage of stockholders' equity and predicted by equation 5.14.3, holding all other independent variables at their respective sample means.
[b]The estimated five-digit SIC product class, minimum, four-firm concentration ratio, weighted by the affiliates' local sales.
[c]The FRMS is the ratio of the weighted (by five-digit SIC sales levels) firm market share to the firm's weighted concentration ratio (CR4).

Source: Special survey of the U.S. Senate Subcommittee on Multinational Corporations.

Sales, employment, or asset size is suggested in the present case. Such a procedure amounts to giving greater weight to larger firms. This procedure may be viewed as treating large firms as composites of several small firms; weighting then simply treats large firms as multiples of several small firms, with the result that extreme observations are averaged out in the weighting process. *

---

*An empirical approach was taken in the present analysis. Plots were examined that graphed on the veritcal axis the residuals of some nonlinear regressions; on the horizontal axis were the predicted values

The results of the weighting procedure are not shown here but appear in appendix Tables I.1 and I.2 of Connor and Mueller (1977), and are merely summarized verbally.

Weighting the nonlinear regression models has the effect of increasing the statistical significance level of the regressions.* In Brazil, however, weighting also had the effect of reducing the confidence level of all three main structural variables (CR4, FRMS, and AD). Both CR4 and AD remain highly significant, but FRMS is generally only weakly significant. Another change is the increase in statistical significance of the R&D expression; formerly never quite significant, in the weighted equations it is significant in three of four cases. The explanatory power of the LEVER and GRO groups of terms also increases by weighting, and the SIZE variable indicates diseconomies of firm size even more strongly than before. The trade and K/S terms seem relatively unaffected by weighting. All in all, the weighted regressions tend to affirm clearly the positive influence of concentration, market leadership, and (two forms of) product differentiation upon profit performance in Brazil in 1972.

Examination of the effects of weighting regressions in Mexico indicates only a marginal improvement, if any. However, the overall F test shows a considerable increase over levels obtaining in the unweighted regressions. Two of the three structural variables increase markedly in explanatory power. The relative market share is positive and statistically significant in all the regressions; the confidence levels on AD also increase considerably over what they were in the unweighted regressions. But the significance levels on CR4 drop slightly in all

---

of the dependent variable and also certain independent variable values, especially asset size. If no heteroskedasticity were present in the data, these plots would lead to a pattern of points that is symmetrical about the horizontal axis and roughly rectangular; in other words, for large- or small-value segments on the horizontal there are about as many positive as negative residuals and they are of about the same size. When heteroskedasticity is present, however, these plots lead to horn-shaped patterns (Draper and Smith 1964: Figure 3.4[1]). These patterns were indeed observed, though the expected horn-shaped pattern was more clearly visible in the Brazilian case than in Mexico. Four different weights were applied ($A^{1/2}$, $A^{1/4}$, $A^{1/8}$, and $A^{1/16}$, where A is total assets), and the plots were reexamined. The fourth root of assets was found to correct best for the heteroskedasticity in both countries, though some subjective judgment may enter at this stage.

*In Brazil the minimum F statistic was 6.4 and the maximum 10.7; in Mexico the respective figures were 5.8 and 8.5.

TABLE 5.18

Estimated Net Income as Percentage of Equity Capital of Affiliates of
U.S. MNCs in Mexico Associated with Different Levels of
Concentration and Industry Advertising-to-Sales Ratios, 1972
(net income as percentage of equity[a])

Four-Firm Concentration Ratio (CR4)[b] (percent)	Advertising-to-Sales Ratio (AD)[c] (percent)					
	0	1.0	2.0	3.0	4.0	5.0
30	14.5	16.0	17.4	18.9	20.4	21.9
40	15.5	17.0	18.4	19.9	21.4	22.8
50	16.3	17.8	19.2	20.7	22.1	23.6
60	16.9	18.4	19.8	21.3	22.8	24.2
70	17.5	19.0	20.4	21.9	23.4	24.8
80	17.9	19.4	20.8	22.3	23.8	25.2
90	18.3	19.8	21.2	22.7	24.2	25.6

[a]The profit rates shown are net 1972 revenues after Mexican
corporate income taxes plus technology payments ("broad profits")
expressed as a percentage of stockholders' equity and predicted by
equation 5.14.3, holding all other independent variables at their respective sample means.
[b]The estimated five-digit SIC product class, minimum, four-firm concentration ratio, weighted by the affiliates' local sales.
[c]The AD is the total advertising outlays divided by the total sales
of the principal product class of the affiliate.

Source: Special survey of the U.S. Senate Subcommittee on
Multinational Corporations.

four models. Among the control variables affected by the weighting
scheme, only LEVER unequivocally rises in significance. Both
SUPPLY and GRO decrease in explanatory ability. Finally, SIZE is
affected in a most curious manner: In two equations its "t" statistic
increases and the coefficient of SIZE remains highly significant and
positive; in the two remaining models, though the coefficient of SIZE
remains positive, its confidence level drops from above the 1 percent
level to below the 10 percent threshold. Thus, an element of uncertainty is introduced as to the existence of firm economies of scale in
the Mexican case. The capital-intensiveness and trade controls remain substantially unaltered by these transformations.

SPECIAL TESTS INVOLVING OTHER VARIABLES

Several special tests were performed involving slight variations upon the nonlinear regressions reported above. In each of these special tests at least one causal variable was added to the more basic nonlinear models, though occasionally one of the independent variables was removed because the new causal variable was a very close conceptual substitute for the omitted variable. Here we shall only discuss the results of the analysis. Copies of the tables displaying most of these results, which are too large to include here, may be found in Connor (1976).

The first set of special tests dealt with several alternative measures of product differentiation. One experiment replaced the "market advertising-intensity variable AD with an expression containing the individual firm's advertising-to-sales ratio, AD/S.* In Brazil, AD/S performs rather poorly compared to AD, while in Mexico the statistical strength of AD/S is at least as high as AD; in both countries its effect on profits is positive. Thus, both the level of the individual firm's advertising efforts and the average advertising intensities of all firms in an industry appear to be positively related to firm profits in Brazil and Mexico.

In a related special test, a variable intended to provide evidence of economies of scale in advertising was devised. This variable, the ratio of firm to market advertising intensities, is called the relative advertising index (RELAD). If smaller firms are at a disadvantage relative to average-sized firms in a given market because they must advertise more intensely, it is reasoned that this will be reflected by lower profit rates. Therefore, high relative advertising indexes are expected to result in lower profits. While a consistent relationship of this sort was not discovered for the Mexican data, the expectation was modestly supported in some Brazilian regressions.

To investigate whether the concept of the extent of firm leadership was sensitive to the definition of the chosen variable, FRMS, the simple firm market share, FMS,[†] was introduced into the function in its stead. In Brazil this surrogate performed even better than FRMS, but because it was collinear with them, tended to depress the effects of the other structural variables in the equation. In Mexico, on the other hand, the weakness of FRMS was again replicated by its near relative FMS.[‡]

---

*In both countries' data sets AD and AD/S are, of course, highly correlated because the first is largely derived from the second.

[†]This statistic was weighted by the sales of the firm's different product classes.

[‡]In Mexico, however, a variable representing the average rank position, RANK, of the affiliate in its top five product markets was

Another set of special experiments attempted to refine our knowledge of the effects on profits of long-term lending relationships of the sample affiliates. To that end, two additional variables were designed to distinguish intrafirm from "arm's length" or extrafirm lending. Every affiliate's long-term debt was divided into that originating from the parent, PARDEBT, and that from "outside" financial institutions such as banks, BANKDEBT, both expressed as ratios of total assets. Neither of these indexes was significant in the Mexican tests. On Brazil the results were inclusive.

Another experiment, also related to the degree of integration of MNCs, introduced the percentage of voting stock held by the parent corporation, directly and indirectly. This variable, OWN, not only represents the extent of "foreign" control"* and possibly the inherent advantages of global planning but also may be systematically reflective of differences in accounting methods.[†] Many observers expect the reported (as distinct from real) profits of overseas affiliates to be higher in the presence of joint-venture partners. The data are not consistent with this last hypothesis. In both Brazil and Mexico, the degree of parental control is positively associated with high profit rates, though the relationship is consistently significant only in Brazil. In Brazil, wholly owned affiliates of U.S. MNCs (OWN = 100 percent) were found to earn about five percentage points more in profits over equity than affiliates with 25 percent other ownership (OWN = 75 percent).

Several additional variables were examined. None had any systematic influence on profits. For example, in both countries, the measures developed for the analysis of the absolute capital cost, ABSCOST, and economies of plant scale barriers to entry, PLANT, failed to affect profits in the expected positive manner. Either these barriers fail to operate in conditions like those of Brazil and Mexico or, more likely, the measures themselves are deficient. Likewise, various tests intended to distinguish subsidiaries according to their form or timing of entry generally proved insignificant, though there was some tendency for older subsidiaries to have lower profits. The

---

found to have the expected effect on profits; that is, the higher the rank, the higher the predicted profits. The same result was discovered in Brazil, but it was somewhat weaker.

*Some U.S. MNCs are in partnership with other U.S. or European firms, but most of the remaining ownership was in local hands.

[†]Another possibility is that greater control is preferred by MNCs producing technologically complex goods or by MNCs whose competitive advantage lies in process secrecy. (See Stopford and Wells 1972: 119-23.)

extent of vertical integration, measured by the ratio of value added to sales, VERTICAL, is positive in both cases and is very significant in the Mexican case, but the interpretation of this ratio is not clear.* Product diversification, DIVERSE, on the other hand, as represented by the proposition of a subsidiary's sales outside of its principal product's industry, had no uniform impact on profits.

A final, and especially interesting, test involved the insertion into the nonlinear model of additional terms representing rates of either nominal, NOMINAL, or effective, EFFECTIVE, rates of protection from imports. (See Appendix F.) A theory often propounded by writers on MNCs is that foreign direct investment often takes place because of the extraordinary profits induced by the generally high tariff (or other trade) barriers imposed in the LDCs on manufactures; that is, MNCs are held to cease exporting and substitute local production abroad largely in order to "jump over" and get behind high tariff walls (Robertson 1971). However, in regressions of rates of protection (see Appendix equations F3.1 to F3.6), on profits little or no effect was discovered; in fact, higher rates of protection are much more often negatively related to profits than positively related. Thus, the analysis provided no evidence that trade protection exerts an independent influence on profits when structural and other variables are included in the analysis. Of course, trade protection may have influenced some of these other variables, such as the number of firms, especially MNCs, in a market and the rate of domestic industry growth.

POOLED REGRESSIONS OF BRAZILIAN AND MEXICAN DATA

The preceding analysis has found many similarities in both the market structure and performance of manufacturing enterprises of MNCs in Brazil and Mexico. To this point, however, the statistical tests have examined the structure-profit relationships in the two countries separately. This procedure has been followed to avoid any potential loss of detail that may have depended on country-specific economic conditions. Moreover, in order to accommodate apparent

---

*Do firms operating in semi-industrialized settings opt for developing backward of forward linkages, or are they forced to do so because of conditions in the input or wholesaling sectors? Perhaps this result indicates that mere "final assembly" operations are relatively costly methods of local entry.

structure-performance relationships in the two nations, the nonlinear models were "tailored" slightly for the data for each nation.*

To determine whether or not the observed relationships were influenced by economic forces unique to each nation, I tested a model using pooled data for both countries (Table 5.19); that is, individual affiliates of U.S. MNCs located in Brazil and Mexico are combined in a single analysis that tests the hypothesis that the profit rates of affiliates, irrespective of their location, are influenced by the same basic market structure variables, after adjusting for differences in industry growth rates in the two nations. In order to determine whether any strong country-specific differences exist between Brazilian and Mexican affiliate performance, a new variable is introduced: DCOUNTRY. This variable takes a value of 1 if the observation is in Brazil and takes a value of 0 if it is in Mexico (37 percent of the observations being located in Brazil). Other than the inclusion of DCOUNTRY, the three regression equations shown below are identical to the fullest linear models presented for Brazil and Mexico separately (compare Tables 5.5-5.12).[†]

The analysis uses four measures of profit performance (equations 5.19.1 to 5.19.3).[‡] Each is statistically significant, though, as expected, the overall closeness of fit of these three regressions is somewhat lower than for the nonlinear equations applied to Brazil separately and somewhat higher than when applied to Mexico separately. As before, the fits are better when profit rates over assets are

---

*In the "linear" formulations, however, the forms of the equations were identical for both countries. An example of the differences between the two countries is the inclusion of the SUPPLY variable for the Mexican nonlinear models, which was omitted in the Brazilian models.

[†] More complex models using the pooled data can be found in Appendix H of Connor and Mueller (1977). In these equations, a Weibull function is substituted for the linear CR4 term and a few additional terms are introduced to account for possible nonlinear effects on profits. Thus, the regression functions appearing in Appendix H of Connor and Mueller (1977) correspond closely to the nonlinear models used for Brazil (equations 5.13.1 to 5.13.3) and Mexico (equations 5.14.1 to 5.14.3). In general, these nonlinear, pooled data regressions are better fitted to the data and reinforce the interpretations given in this section. Also, in Table H.1 in Appendix H of Connor and Mueller, one can find a list of descriptive statistics for all variables used in these pooled data regressions.

[‡] The regression equation employing BROADASSET is not, however, shown here, because it is very similar to equation 5.12.9 with one major exception: The coefficient of AD is much higher (0.50) and is significant at the 1 percent level.

TABLE 5.19

Results of Pooled Data Regressions of Profit Rates on Market Structure Variables, 206 Brazilian and Mexican Manufacturing Affiliates of U.S. MNCs, 1972

EQUITY PROF $=$ (5.19.1)

$8.18 + 0.114$ CR4 $+ 8.29$ FRMS $+ 0.42$ AD $+ 0.51$ R&D
$(1.02)\ (2.97)^a$ $(2.27)^b$ $(1.30)^c$ $(1.47)^c$

$- 20.38$ K/S $+ 0.69$ SIZE $+ 13.34$ EXP $- 1.91$ IMP
$(-5.73)^a$ (0.95) (1.25) (-0.25)

$- 0.59$ GRO $+ 0.44$ LEVER $+ 2.85$ DCOUNTRY $+ U_i$.
$(-1.87)^b$ (0.09) (1.04)

$R^2 = 0.23$ $F = 5.19^a$ n = 206

ASSETPROF $=$ (5.19.2)

$-4.70 + 0.049$ CR4 $+ 3.91$ FRMS $+ 0.17$ AD $+ 0.054$ R&D
$(-1.23)\ (2.68)^a$ $(2.27)^b$ (1.12) (0.33)

$- 11.25$ K/S $+ 0.56$ SIZE $+ 8.82$ EXP $- 2.12$ IMP
$(-6.68)^a$ $(1.62)^c$ $(1.74)^b$ (-0.60)

$- 0.22$ GRO $+ 14.87$ LEVER $+ 1.60$ DCOUNTRY $+ U_i$.
$(-1.50)^c$ $(6.60)^a$ (1.23)

$R^2 = 0.35$ $F = 9.67^a$ n = 206

BROADEQUITY $=$ (5.19.3)

$8.93 + 0.123$ CR4 $+ 8.38$ FRMS $+ 1.15$ AD $+ 0.42$ R&D
$(0.94)\ (2.69)^a$ $(1.94)^b$ $(3.05)^a$ (1.02)

$- 23.20$ K/S $+ 1.31$ SIZE $+ 10.15$ EXP $+ 1.69$ IMP
(-5.50) $(1.52)^c$ (0.80) (0.19)

$- 0.70$ GRO $+ 0.06$ LEVER $- 2.08$ DCOUNTRY $+ U_i$.
$(-1.88)^b$ (0.01) (-0.64)

$R^2 = 0.22$ $F = 5.09^a$ n = 206

Source: Compiled by the author.

used as the dependent variable. Similarly, the rates of profit performance employing the broad earnings concept reveal a much higher
significance level for the market advertising-to-sales ratio (AD) than
is the case with the narrow earnings definition. Otherwise, the outcomes for all three "pooled" data regressions shown are quite compatible.

All four structural dimensions have positive impacts on firm
profits, as predicted (Figure 5.3). The three main structural variables (CR4, FRMS, and AD) are all highly significant, except AD in
equations 5.19.1 and 5.19.2. But R&D, though also positive, is generally insignificant.

There are several interesting results for the control variables.
Capital-intensiveness has its usual strong negative effect on profits,
but affiliate size is consistently positive in its impact on profits and
is significant in all equations except 5.19.1. This parallels the results for Mexico but is at variance with the regressions using Brazilian data only. Also major industry growth has a uniformly negative
influence on profit rates. This is also somewhat contrary to previous
results and appears to at least partially reflect differences between
the two countries; that is, the generally lower profit rates and higher
industry growth rates in Mexico lead to the negative coefficient on
GRO.* Among the trade ratios, only the simple export intensity,
EXP, has a significant impact on performance; affiliates exporting
10 percent of their output earn slightly over 1 percentage point more
in profits on equity than nonexporting subsidiaries. Finally, a most
important result is that when differences in industry growth rates are
accounted for, affiliates of U.S. MNCs in both Brazil and Mexico that
are in similar market environments earn roughly similar profits.

The statistical tests presented in this section lend strong support to the preceding findings. Not only, as was demonstrated in Chapter 3, are the market structures of Brazil and Mexico quite similar,
but those structural elements generate essentially the same kinds of
profit performance in both countries. This indicates that the fruits
of market power transcend national boundaries and are similar despite

---

*In other regressions not shown here, GRO was omitted from equa-
equations 5.19.1 to 5.19.3. The main effect was to change the sign
and significance level of DCOUNTRY: It became positive and highly
significant when narrow rates of profit were used and positive but insignificant when broad rates were used. This outcome is consistent
with the special survey's finding that when royalties and fees are added
to net revenue, the profit configurations of Brazil and Mexico are
highly similar. The positive sign on DCOUNTRY in equations 5.19.1
and 5.19.2 and its negative sign in equation 5.19.3 carry the same
meaning.

FIGURE 5.3

Predicted Relationship of Profits to Four-Firm Concentration in
Brazilian and Mexican Manufacturing, 1972

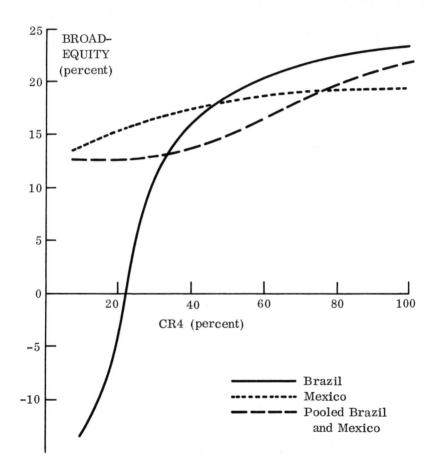

Note: Based on Figures 5.1 and 5.2, and equation H-3 in Appendix H of Connor and Mueller (1977)

Source: Special survey of U.S. Senate Subcommittee on Multinational Corporations.

differences in the cultural and institutional environments in which MNCs operate. These findings confirm Newfarmer and Mueller's (1975) report to the U.S. Senate Subcommittee on Multinational Corporations that the structural roots of MNCs' power in Brazil and Mexico are deep and confer substantial power on many MNCs. The fruits of power may enable its holders to engage in a variety of practices, including the restructuring of industries in which they operate. The ultimate uses of such power, however, will depend on the public policies of both the host nations and the United States. In Chapter 6, therefore, I conclude with an extensive discussion of public policy options for nations acting alone and nations acting in concert, focusing especially on decisions related to the empirical findings of the present chapter.

6

This book has had three primary objectives. First, a comprehensive data base was developed for the manufacturing operations of U.S. MNCs in Brazil and Mexico. In addition to data on the affiliates themselves, it was also considered desirable to know as much as possible about the host country market structures. Much of this descriptive material was originally collected for a pair of U.S. Senate subcommittee reports (Newfarmer and Mueller 1975; Connor and Mueller 1977). Further original statistical data were expressly generated for the present work subsequent to publication of those reports and these appear in tables in Chapter 3 or the appendixes. All these data are valuable in themselves because they give the first reliable measures of several elements of market structure available for any less developed country.

But development of this data base was also essential for our second main objective, positive economic analysis. The analysis, which accounts for a major part of this work, sought to identify the determinants of market power among the manufacturing affiliates of U.S. MNCs in Brazil and Mexico in order to test the industrial organization model of foreign direct investment. The means toward this end was multiple regression analysis, a statistical tool that allows the investigator to sort out the relative strength that several, theoretically promising aspects of market and firm structure are likely to have upon a given index of a firm's market power. The results of the analysis, in other words, permit the researcher to test which of many factors are the causes of economic power operating among a group of firms in a given economic setting.

If it is established that there are market imperfections giving rise to market failures in some manufacturing industries, there is sufficient justification for some form of public intervention ("theory of the second best" arguments aside). My third main purpose, then, is an evaluation (at the end of this chapter) of feasible policy options and their relative effectiveness, particularly in the light of the preceding empirical findings. Because the phenomenon is transnational, not only domestic but also intergovernmental policies will be considered.

SUMMARY

This brief section is intended to aid the reader in recalling the main points made in the body of the work. The several parts of this section will parallel the exposition in Chapters 1 through 5. From Chapter 2 I will reiterate the primary and peculiar characteristics of FDI and the MNC and contrast the five alternative theoretical approaches that have been used to explain the origins and flows of FDI. Chapters 2 and 3 consisted of four parts: a description of the basic macroeconomic and trade conditions in postwar Brazil and Mexico, an analysis of those countries' basic industrialization and trade policies, a recounting of those government policies more specifically designed to control or facilitate inward foreign direct investments, and finally, an examination of conditions affecting the state of competition in the industrial sectors of Brazil and Mexico. This last topic emphasized the many striking parallelisms in the industrial structures of not only Brazil and Mexico but the United States as well. Chapter 4 consisted of a review of previous statistical market structure–performance studies, and a section of the chapter addressed itself to the special problems associated with the application of such a test against data from a less industrialized economy. Finally, I recapitulate the empirical test results contained in Chapter 5 and present some new tabular and graphic material based on the estimated functions.

The Special Features of FDI

I isolated six essential characteristics of private foreign direct investment that need to be incorporated into any valid explanatory theory of FDI.

First, almost all FDI is the work of corporations, unlike portfolio investments, which are made by individuals operating through intermediate financial institutions. These corporations provide continuing management services to their foreign affiliates and eventually develop highly complex methods of internal control and communication.

A second crucial feature of FDI is its geographic, industrial, and aggregate concentration. There is a strong tendency for FDI to

originate in only a few high-income, generally larger countries and
to flow from a given country to only a few recipient countries. Since
1900, more than 80 percent of the stock of all FDI has been owned by
firms in five countries or fewer; since 1945, the United States has
held more than 50 percent of the world's FDI. In the 1960s, more
than 70 percent of all U.S. FDI flowed to only seven countries, and
this pattern was also characteristic of the other prominent investor
countries. Manufacturing FDI is also highly "industry-specific"; investing firms (and thus their affiliates) tend to be largely located in
only a few major industries: transportation equipment, machinery,
and chemicals. Finally, in any given investor or receptor country,
the ownership and control of FDI are concentrated among the very
largest companies, out of proportion to their overall asset size (that
is, the greater the total assets of an MNC, the greater its ratio of
foreign to total assets). There is evidence that since 1960 or so, the
distributions of the geographic and aggregate dimensions of FDI concentration have been becoming less skewed. The trend with respect
to the industry concentration of FDI is more mixed, however.

Third, the nature of FDI has changed. Since the interwar period, except for petroleum, both backward and forward vertical in-
tegrations via FDI have declined relative to total FDI. Since the
1930s, the share of petroleum investments overseas has remained
fairly constant. Thus, raw-materials ventures and trading subsidiaries
have been continuously supplanted by manufacturing operations over
the last few decades. This pattern holds for U.S. direct foreign investment worldwide, in Latin America in the aggregate, and in both
Brazil and Mexico.

Fourth, the more FDI-prone industries exhibit many of the structural characteristics associated with oligopoly: high seller concentration, extensive product differentiation, substantial barriers to entry,
and evidence of socially undesirable levels of profit performance.
These features persist whether one measures them at the major industry or individual product level.

A fifth property of FDI is the cross-hauling of industrial capital
among the capital-exporting makret economies. Unlike portfolio
flows, which were unidirectional, FDI has interpenetrated even the
same narrowly defined industries between pairs of highly developed
countries. Between two countries with highly disparate income levels,
however, FDI flows only from the richer to the poorer (with reverse
income flows occurring after a lag of a few years).

A final, universal trait of FDI is that it typically takes the form
of a highly differentiated bundle of complementary inputs: Not only
money capital is transferred but also technical and managerial services, intermediate inputs, legal rights to intangible property, and
sometimes new or used capital equipment. Even the financial capital

itself may be a package put together from such diverse sources as
the parent's own resources, home-country financial institutions, home-
country official aid agencies, and local private or public sources.
The bundle of factors is often cemented by contractual agreements
with highly restrictive conditions affecting affiliate operations and
trade.

Alternative Theories of FDI

Five fairly distinct theoretical approaches exist in the body of
orthodox economic literature.* Some of these offer useful insights
and draw instructive parallels with other economic phenomena. But
it was concluded that the last, the "industrial organization" model,
was most in accord with the empirical findings surrounding FDI; that
is, because so few empirical studies on the origins of FDI are available for comparison of their relative predictive accuracies, the different models were assessed on the basis of the "realism" of their assumptions. Moreover, only the industrial organization approach offers some explanation of the continued growth and preeminence of
MNCs in the host countries; that is, the other theories primarily focus
on the determinants of initial flows of capital from investing countries
and have little to say concerning the continuing denationalization of the
host country industries.

The first, and most clearly faulty, approach suggests that FDI
is closely analogous to flows of portfolio capital. Under this line of
reasoning, FDI flows from capital-rich to capital-poor countries
strictly in response to expected profit-rate differentials. The portfolio capital theory, as originally propounded, has proved to be a poor
predictive device and fails to explain the industrial pattern of FDI.
However, later versions of this approach do throw some light on the
choice of an MNC among alternative foreign investments in different
geographic areas as a means of reducing cyclic earnings instability.
While by no means a comprehensive explanation of the determinants
of FDI, the portfolio selection emphasis on risk aversion as an element of decision making by MNCs may be usefully incoporated with
other theories of FDI.

The second theoretical avenue taken in recent years is via adaptations of formal, general equilibrium models of pure international
trade. While these models are appealing for their great rigor, they
also impose strict limitations on the researcher. In particular, the

---

*After writing Chapter 1, I discovered a paper by John Dunning
(1973) that analyzes the literature on FDI in a similar manner.

models must assume that trade occurs through competitive markets (though they may be segmented) and that states of technology are independently determined across countries. The dynamic "product life cycle" theory, on the other hand, offers a plausible framework for many forms of FDI, though in this case the mechanisms governing the transition between stages remains rather obscure.

The third strand of economic writings distinguished is an offshoot of the basic neoclassical theory of the firm and especially of the fixed investment decisions of firms. Models of this type attempt to predict levels of investment in terms of output, lagged capital stock, prices, wages, and rental rates. Criticism of this approach is raised because of the narrowness of its focus: Only one of the many components of FDI is explained, only competitive markets and prices are employed, and only investing-country factors have been generally included in tests. While it may eventually shed light on the total domestic fixed capital levels decided upon by MNCs for new investment overseas, it is unlikely to be valuable for decisions regarding geographic distribution or reinvestment in foreign operations.

The fourth and fifth schools of thought on FDI base their reasoning on the existence of market failures. The first group maintains that the movement of firms abroad is due to the firms' possession of some unique, intangible, and rent-yielding asset that is virtually freely transferable within the firms. The second group agrees with, but goes farther than, the first group in that it proposes to explain FDI as a mode of conduct arising from a multiplicity of interrelated market failures; that is, FDI is essentially a mode of rivalry among firms in oligopolistic markets that recognize their mutual dependence internationally. The MNCs initially invest abroad in order to gain or maintain market shares; they continue to reinvest and outperform host country firms because of the imperfect market structures they find or create. In addition to the three standard market structure elements, ownership denationalization and international conglomeration may be additional sources of MNCs' market power.

I concluded that this last approach, the industrial organization theory, though largely untested, is the most consistent with the six distinctive features of FDI. Moreover, it is the only approach that explains both the origin and the maintenance of foreign investments. *

---

*I adopt the industrial organization approach in order to examine the continuing denationalization of the LDCs by MNCs, and not the causes of the initial investment decisions. High profit performance due to market imperfections provides only one out of possibly many motives for MNCs' reinvestment and expansion abroad. It also suggests why MNCs' initial advantages are simply not eroded over time by the rivalry of locally owned firms.

The Economic Setting

Some basic data on macroeconomic, demographic, and trade conditions were gathered, partly to place the case studies in perspective and partly to provide some bases of comparison for the empirical tests.

Compared with other regions of the world, Latin America is not densely populated, but it is among the fastest growing. The region's level of development is low, but it is the most developed of the three least developed continents, as measured by either per capita incomes or industrial activity. Excluding Japan, Latin America's regional industrial growth has been the fastest over 1960-72. Latin American commodity trade has grown more slowly than its domestic industry as a whole, more slowly than that of the developed countries, and except for the oil-exporting countries, has led to recurring trade-balance deficits.

Brazil and Mexico have half of Latin America's population and originate almost half of its gross economic product. Brazil is almost twice as large as Mexico in population, but its GDP is only about 25 percent higher. Both the population and income distributions are quite uneven. During the 1960s, general and industrial growth was very rapid in both countries but much more erratic in Brazil than in Mexico. When measured at world prices, the sectoral shift from agriculture to industry has been more rapid in Mexico than in Brazil. Brazil experienced chronic inflation and Mexico practically none during the 1960s. Import substitution took place in both countries since 1950, primarily by restricting consumer goods imports. Export diversification has also occurred, especially in Mexico and particularly since the late 1960s. Much of the recent export diversification has been into partially processed or manufactured goods.

Industrialization and Trade Policies

Since the 1950s, rapid industrial growth has been a prime target of economic policies in both countries. Large public sector investment, fiscal and monetary reforms, and government planning have all had important impacts on industrialization. But perhaps the prime form of public intervention aimed at fostering industrial growth was protectionist policies, supplemented later by tax credits or foreign exchange controls. In the 1960s, Brazil manipulated imports mainly via tariffs, while Mexico relied on quantitative controls.

In both countries a new emphasis was placed on the promotion of manufactured exports after the mid-1960s. In both countries also there is renewed concern for employment generation, income redis-

tribution, and regional disparities, none of which has been alleviated
to any great extent by recent industrialization.

With respect to policies specifically designed to apply to inward
foreign direct investment, the overall impression is one of considerably greater regulation in Brazil than in Mexico. Both countries prohibit foreign investment in some sectors or limit the degree of foreign
participation, restrict the introduction of some kinds of technology,
and offer investment incentives in certain industries to foreign investors. However, only Brazil has had comprehensive and formal means
of enforcing local content standards, a progressive withholding tax
on foreign profit remittances, and has the authority to set limits on
repayment of loans or interest.

Patterns of FDI in Brazil and Mexico

The sources and amounts of FDI, its industrial distribution, and
some of the microeconomic characteristics of MNCs in Brazil and
Mexico were reviewed in Chapter 3.

The total stake of FDI in Mexico is slightly less than half of that
in Brazil, and in Mexico a far higher proportion comes from U.S.
sources (about 80 percent versus 35 percent of manufacturing investment in recent years). In both countries, however, almost three-
fourths of all FDI has occurred in the manufacturing sector during the
most recent period.

U.S. FDI in manufacturing in Mexico increased at an average
annual rate of about 11 percent during 1950-72; it was slower in Brazil before 1966 but during 1966-72 rose at an annual rate of about 12
percent. More than half of all U.S. manufacturing FDI in both nations
has gone into only four major industry groups in recent years: transportation equipment, chemicals, and electrical and nonelectrical machinery. Thus, U.S. manufacturing investment has followed a pattern
of locating in the most technology- and capital-intensive industries
and also the ones that received the greatest import protection in the
post-1945 period.

The affiliates of all MNCs in Brazil and Mexico dominate many
of their manufacturing sectors in the sense that more than 150 of the
largest 300 manufacturing firms are foreign-controlled, and these
foreign subsidiaries tend to be larger than their local counterparts.
The extent of aggregate denationalization in manufacturing appears to
be increasing in Mexico while remaining roughly constant in Brazil.

Subsidiaries of U.S. MNCs in Brazil and Mexico grew on average at an annual rate exceeding 15 percent during 1960-72, generally
faster than their industries' rates of growth. At least one-fifth of the
growth of U.S. subsidiaries can be attributed to the takeovers of pri-

marily locally owned firms. Moreover, the rate of acquisition (as a proportion of all market entries by U.S. MNCs) has been increasing, at least as recently as 1972.

The extent of multinational centralization and integration ("multinational conglomeration") of their affiliates is extraordinary. In both countries, the parent organization owns on average more than 80 percent of the voting stock of its subsidiaries. In addition to voting rights, some subsidiaries are controlled by the ownership of long-term debt and by a high degree of intrafirm real trade (especially subsidiary imports of raw or intermediate inputs). Subsidiaries make a large proportion of their returns to the parent company in the form of technology payments; hence, technological dependence is also high.

Brazilian, Mexican, and U.S. Market Structures Compared

A major finding of this work is the uncanny structural similarities of the product markets in which U.S. MNCs are most prominent, both in the home economy (the United States) and in two typical host countries (Brazil and Mexico). The analysis made use of highly detailed statistics provided by U.S. MNCs themselves in a special survey conducted at the behest of the U.S. Senate Subcommittee on Multinational Corporations. These parallelisms were discovered in manufacturing-sector markets that were defined in a finer manner (that is, at the four- or five-digit level) than has heretofore been possible in investigations of this type. Strong associations were found for several aspects of market structure: market shares of affiliates, changes in market shares over time, seller concentration ratios, and advertising-to-sales ratios of firms. The only feature of these markets that is not being replicated in the host countries is the technological capacity of the MNCs' affiliates, as measured by their R&D expenditures.

With respect to market shares, it was found that about one-fourth of all manufacturing affiliates of U.S. MNCs were dominant firms in their principal product markets (that is, they controlled more than 50 percent of the sales of those markets). Furthermore, roughly one-half of the firms reported shares of at least 25 percent for their principal products—in both Brazil and Mexico. In general, industries with exceptionally high average market shares are the ones that are the most heavily denationalized by MNCs: transportation equipment, chemicals (except drugs), food processing, rubber products, nonelectrical machinery, and electrical equipment. There is also a narrative discussion of the position of U.S. MNCs vis-a-vis other MNCs in those six major industry groups.

Another indicator of competitive conditions is the stability of market shares over time. The changes in market shares of U.S. MNCs over 1966-72 were computed for several hundred products. Because of new market entries and diversification during 1966-72, market shares generally increased quite markedly. However, when the market shares of only products made throughout the six-year period were checked, far greater stability was found, particularly in those industry groups most heavily denationalized by U.S. MNCs, such as chemicals, tires, and machinery. This finding provides strong, albeit indirect, evidence of oligopolistic forbearance in Brazil and Mexico. Exceptions to the rule can often be explained by the entry into the market of uncooperative Japanese MNCs or state-owned enterprises.

Minimum, four-firm concentration ratio estimates averaged 65 percent for Brazil and 69 percent for Mexico. The cross-industry distributions of these concentration indexes were highly and positively correlated between the two Latin American countries. Most interesting, however, was the highly significant correlation of U.S. concentration ratios with matched industries in both Brazil and Mexico. Thus, for whatever reason, MNCs are drawn to or create compatible industry structures in all countries in which they operate. Again, as with market shares, high concentration is characteristic of the most heavily denationalized industries. In both Latin American countries, more than 80 percent of all manufactures sales by U.S. subsidiaries occur in highly concentrated markets (four-firm sales concentration in excess of 50 percent).

Another crucial dimension of market structure is the variation in levels of product differentiation across markets. Taking as the measure of product differentiation efforts the firms' average advertising-to-sales ratios, the relative levels of advertising intensity were found to be highly positively correlated between matched Brazilian and Mexican markets in which U.S. MNCs sold products. Moreover, U.S. patterns of advertising outlays were also found to be highly correlated with the Latin American expenditures, whether measured by national or firm-level data. Thus, U.S. MNCs are transferring those forms of consumer marketing rivalry with which they are the most familiar. To the extent that their non-U.S. competitors abroad are induced to counter with similar advertising campaigns, yet another relatively inflexible trait of those markets is being imposed. Because advertising is likely to raise barriers to new market entry, stable market shares and high levels of concentration will be fostered and maintained by this means of interfirm rivalry.

The final structural characteristic investigated was the intensity of firm and industry R&D expenditures. Though very low on average, in the LDCs, R&D capacity is thought to be an important factor in the transfer of advanced technologies and in the adaptation of product designs of the parent by its subsidiaries. Unlike the case with all the elements of market structure mentioned above, here there was no statistical tendency for subsidiaries producing the same products as their parents to have relatively similar levels of R&D expenditures. However, like advertising, R&D ratios of MNCs' subsidiaries were found to be distributed among the affiliates in a highly skewed fashion. Finally, the royalty payments of affiliates of U.S. MNCs in Mexico were found to be weakly related to their parents' levels of R&D outlays, but in many cases these technology payments were far in excess of the parent corporations' R&D intensities.

In conclusion, these findings suggest that the observed structural parallelisms among the Brazilian, Mexican, and U.S. markets under study are results of similar underlying forces. While some of these similarities may be due to the inexorable forces of technological determinism, a more likely force is the restructuring of host country industries that occurs during the denationalization process and later when MNCs engage in all the familiar and time-tested modes of oligopolistic conduct common in their home markets.

The Theory and Statistical Study
of Market Power

Previous empirical studies of the relationship of profit performance to the elements of market structure were reviewed both in order to establish prior expectations concerning the strength and direction of the causal variables and to examine how conceptual models of market power have been operationalized.

Most statistical studies have omitted the conduct link of the basic industrial organization model, instead relating structure directly to performance. Rather than being based on any specific oligopoly model with a particular mode of behavior, empirical tests have relied upon an array of such models, almost all of which predict similar performance outcomes from given structural configurations of the market. Empiricism has also outdistanced theory because many investigators were primarily interested in policy questions, rather than the traditional orientation toward hypothesis verification. I concluded that an extension of tests of the industrial organization theory to the markets of LDCs would be a manifestation of the exploratory spirit evidenced in this field of investigation in the past two decades or so.

Most of the empirical review considered the choice of variables for empirical tests of market power and the various interpretations given them.

Profit rates have been used as an indirect index of market power in most econometric tests. With proper controls, after-tax net in-

comes as a proportion of sales, of equity, and of assets have all been
considered relatively interchangeable measures. The "price-cost
margin" and "valuation ratio" have also been employed in statistical
tests. Numerous difficulties can be anticipated if one uses reported
accounting profits as a proxy for economic or "pure" profit. The
level and period of analysis covered will also affect the statistical
results.

Seller concentration indexes are the most widely used set of independent variables employed in statistical market structure-performance studies, and four-or eight-firm sales concentration ratios the
most popular variants. Concentration is most often interpreted as
a measure of the ease of sellers' collusion whose aim is joint profit
maximization for the oligopolists. Several other variables have been
suggested to help control for biases in publicly available concentration
data or to use in interaction terms with concentration.

Another set of variables can measure market structure by indi-
cating the leadership potential of firms. The distribution of firms
in a market can be quantified by using raw firm rank, market share,
or relative market share. These variables may also capture some
"firm differentiation" variance as well, that is, the ability of some
consumer product firms to develop buyer loyalty to the firm itself,
the whole array of its products, or the firm's image. A firm's entrenchment in the producer goods industries may, on the other hand,
be more related to innovations or production efficiencies.

The best measure of product differentiation in market structure
is rarely used, namely, the cross-elasticity of demand. Low elasticities imply the ability of producers to charge higher prices than for
homogeneous products that are close substitutes. High advertising-
to-sales ratios have, however, been taken to be good proxies for the
existence of product differentiation.

In addition to being symptomatic of product differentiation, high
advertising intensities may restructure the industry by raising barriers to entry. This will occur if brand switching is more costly for
consumers than the maintenance of loyalty or if significant real or
pecuniary economies of scale exist in the dissemination of appropriate
forms of advertising. The argument was also made that the R&D intensities of industries may, particularly in the LDCs, be proxies for
product differentiation and likewise raise barriers to entry.

Another barrier to entry is the absolute-cost advantage in production, usually measured by the outlay required for one efficient-
sized plant, though several aspects of the absolute cost barrier have
not been operationalized. Still another barrier has received more attention—the economies of large-scale plants or firms. It is normally
represented by the output of one efficient-size plant expressed as a
proportion of a national or regional market. Some researchers have

also tried to measure the diseconomies of smaller scale because the minimum efficient scale variable is usually highly correlated with concentration. Both diversification and trade barriers have also been proposed as additional factors raising the condition of entry.

All three types of market-structure dimensions—concentration, product differentiation, and barriers to entry—are expected to have separate and positive influences on a firm's market power, but several other control variables have been employed in previous studies in order to correct for biases in the performance or market structure variables or in order to adjust for factors that would affect even the profits of purely competitive firms. These control variables were grouped into three broad categories: technological and cost-related, organizational or managerial, and miscellaneous.

Among the more commonly proposed supply factors were capital intensiveness, geographic market dispersion, trade ratios, degree of vertical integration, a consumer/producer goods dichotomy, and the durability of a product. Most of these variables have no certainly predicted effect on profits, except the dispersion index, which should be positive because it picks up some of the effect of concentration when national ratios are used.

Organizational variables are important when firm level data are employed. Considered under this category were a firm's risk orientation, debt structure, and levels of management control. The first two aspects have been measured by the variance in profit deviations or by firm leverage ratios; the traditional theory expects high financial risk and high debt-to-equity ratios to be compensated by higher profits. Several empirical studies have found opposite results, however. The question of management control arises in the context of tests based on data from subsidiary firms only partially owned by the parent corporation; the effect on profits is not established by theory.

Two types of miscellaneous variables were discussed. The weight of the evidence is in favor of a positive effect of absolute firm size on profit performance when a sufficiently detailed model is employed. The effect of industry growth on profits is more ambiguous a priori, but most empirical tests have shown a positive effect on profits when growth is specified in a linear, additive fashion. Growth may interact with concentration, and its influence may not be simply linear.

No insurmountable difficulties are anticipated with similar empirical studies on the LDCs, but data limitations must be overcome and new control variables introduced to handle the special features of LDC economies.

Profitability of Affiliates of U.S. MNCs

The relative profitability of firms is the most common measure of competitive performance in an industry. High and persistent profits are indicative of the market power of a firm and thus of poor performance. In the last two decades, an activity that has absorbed much of the energy of economists studying the industrial organization of the United States has been the estimation of market structure-profitability functions. The overwhelming evidence from these studies is that concentration, product differentiation, and the various barriers to entry into markets are the sources of industrial market power. An important and largely unanswered question is whether these structure-profit relationships also persist in less industrialized economies.

Two different profit ratios were presented for the manufacturing subsidiaries of U.S. MNCs operating in Brazil and Mexico in 1972. The first measure was the ratio of simple, after-tax profits to stockholders' equity; the second index added technology payments to net profits and was called broad profits. The second index of profitability is thought to be closer to true economic profits for the parent corporation.

By both measures, U.S. MNCs earn very high profits. In 1972, average broad profits as a proportion of net worth were nearly identical in both countries—about 17 percent. Eliminating unprofitable affiliates from the calculations raises average profit rates to 22 percent in Brazil and 18 percent in Mexico. These rates were well above any competitive standard ever proposed, such as the interest rate charged by central banks to the largest corporate borrowers.

Generally speaking, in both countries the highest profits are found in the most extensively denationalized industry groups. With the possible exception of transportation equipment in Mexico, clearly supranormal returns were found in the food-processing, "consumer" and "other" chemicals, rubber, machinery, electrical equipment, transportation equipment, and instruments industries. Therefore, like the market structures, the distributions of performance levels among manufacturing industries were quite similar in both Brazil and Mexico. This suggests, and the econometric tests establish, that the underlying causal mechanisms linking the structural conditions of markets to the economic power of firms was also quite similar in both countries.

Market Structure-Profit Relationships in Brazil and Mexico

The major portion of Chapter 5 attempted to identify and measure the structural determinants of market power of manufacturing

affiliates of U.S. MNCs in Brazil and Mexico. This involved the use
of multiple regression analysis, a statistical tool that allows the investigator to sort out the relative impact that various market structure
characteristics have on a given index of market power. The analysis
uses firm profitability as the index of power, because economic
theory and industrial experience suggest that the less competitive an
industry (that is, the closer it approaches monopoly), the greater are
its profits. Although many studies have confirmed this theory in the
developed capitalistic economies, it has received no formal verification in less developed countries.

The statistical analysis confirms the expectation that the profitability of MNCs' affiliates is determined in large part by the competitive environment in which they operate. Three key determinants of
the degree of competition in a market are the level of market concentration, the relative market position of the individual firm, and the
barriers facing new competitors wishing to enter the market. The
analysis confirmed that each of these factors had a significant impact
on profitability of MNCs in both Brazil and Mexico. The profits of
MNCs' affiliates were higher when they operated in markets where a
few firms dominated the market. This is consistent with the theory of
oligopoly that states that firms compete less vigorously in markets
with few sellers than in markets with many sellers. Similarly, profits were higher for firms holding dominant positions in the market
(as measured by their share of the market compared to the shares of
their leading rivals) than for those holding lesser positions. Finally,
profits were higher for firms when entry barriers created by product
differentiation (as measured by advertising-to-sales ratios) were
larger than when they were low.

In both countries, each of the above barometers of competition
exerted an independent influence on profits; in other words, when all
other variables were held constant, each of these factors was positively
related to profit rates. Profit rates were highest for those firms
that occupied favorable positions with respect to each of these variables, that is, profits for firms that held a leading position in a highly
concentrated market in which there was substantial product differentiation.

One of the most important findings of the study is that when
MNCs' affiliates in Brazil and Mexico were combined in a single
analysis, the relationship between market structure and profits was
not influenced by country-specific characteristics. This means not
only that the overall competitive market structures in the two countries
are quite similar but also that the competitive forces result in essentially the same kinds of relative profit performance when other variables are taken into account. This represents an important confirmation
of the part of industrial organization theory that attempts to explain the

profit performance of private corporations in capitalistic market
economies. It supports the proposition that the sources and fruits of
market power are universal phenomena displaying remarkable similari
ties in different nations despite variations in the cultural and institutional environment in which private corporations operate.

The structure-profit relationships estimated by the combined
Brazil-Mexico analysis are illustrated in Tables 6.1 and 6.2. These
tables show the estimated independent influence on profits of three
measures of competition: (1) market concentration as measured by
the share of the market held by the four leading firms (CR4), (2)
the relative dominance of individual firms, as measured by a firm's
share relative to that of the four leading firms (FRMS), and (3) the
height of entry barriers created by product differentiation as measured
by industry advertising-to-sales ratios (AD). The illustration uses
the regression equations estimated from data "pooled" from both the
Brazilian and Mexican samples.

The separate influence of each factor may be estimated statistically by holding other factors influencing profits constant. Table 6.1
shows the predicted net income (net income after corporate taxes
plus technology payments) of affiliates at various levels of market
concentration (CR4) and firm relative market share (FRMS) where
other variables are held constant. When CR4 is 20 and FRMS is 10,
estimated net income is 10.9 percent of equity. Other values in the
second column show the estimated net income at various levels of CR4
when FRMS is held constant at 10 and other variables are held constant
at their means. The table shows that net income is nearly twice as
great when CR4 is 100 than when it is 20. On the other hand, the estimated net effect of FRMS on profitability is shown by changes in net
income across the top row when CR4 is held constant at 20 and FRMS
varies: an FRMS of 10 results in net income of 10.9 percent of equity,
whereas an FRMS of 90 results in net income of 18.2 percent.

Net income is highest, of course, when CR4 and FRMS both have
high values. Net income is 27.4 percent when CR4 is 100 and FRMS
is 90. This represents a near monopoly situation.

Table 6.2 shows the estimated net income of affiliates operating
in markets with various levels of CR4 and advertising-to-sales ratios
(AD). In this case all other variables, including FRMS, are held constant at their means. When CR4 is 20 and AD is 0, estimated net income is 11.4 percent of equity. The estimated net impact of AD on
net income is shown by the net income associated with various levels
of AD when CR4 is held constant. When CR4 is 20 and AD is 0, net
income is 11.4 percent; whereas when CR4 is 20 and AD is 5, net income is 17.4 percent. Again, net income is greatest when both CR4
and AD have high values. When CR4 is 100 and AD is 5, estimated
net income is 26.6 percent.

TABLE 6.1

Estimated Net Income as Percentage of Equity Capital of Affiliates of
U.S. MNCs in Brazil and Mexico Associated with Different Levels
of Industry Concentration and a Firm's Relative Market Share, 1972
(net income as percentage of equity[a])

Four-Firm Concentra-tion Ratio (CR4)[b] (percent)	Firm Relative Market Share (FRMS)[c] (percent)				
	10	30	50	70	90
20	10.9	12.7	14.5	16.4	18.2
30	11.4	13.2	15.0	16.9	18.7
40	12.4	14.2	16.0	17.9	19.7
50	13.7	15.5	17.3	19.2	21.0
60	15.3	17.1	18.9	20.8	22.6
70	17.0	18.8	20.6	22.5	24.3
80	18.4	20.2	22.0	23.9	25.7
90	19.4	21.2	23.0	24.9	26.7
100	20.1	21.9	23.7	25.6	27.4

[a]The profit rate used is broad profits (net income after Mexican
or Brazilian corporate income taxes plus technology payments to the
parent corporation) expressed as a percentage of stockholders'
equity, as predicted by equation G.3 in Appendix G and holding all
other independent variables at their respective sample means.
    [b]The variable CR4 is the estimated minimum, four-firm concen-
tration ratio for five-digit SIC products, weighted by the affiliates'
five-digit SIC sales levels.
    [c]The variable FRMS is the ratio of the affiliate's weighted (by
its five-digit SIC sales levels) market share to its weighted concentration ratio (CR4), expressed as a percentage.

Source: Special survey of the U.S. Senate Subcommittee on
Multinational Corporations.

    Tables 6.1 and 6.2 permit examination of the net effect of only
two variables at a time. It is possible, however, to estimate from
the statistical equations the combined effect of high values for all
three variables. For example, when CR4 is 20, FRMS is 10, and AD
is 0, estimated net income is 8.5 percent of equity. At the other extreme, when a firm operates in a market with a CR4 of 100 and has
an FRMS of 90 and an AD of 5, its estimated net income would be 31.0
percent. This situation would represent a firm holding a virtual monop-

oly in the sale of a highly advertised product. A few firms in Brazil and Mexico, in fact, hold such market positions.

It is significant for public policy that the relationship between CR4 and net income is not linear; that is, net income does not increase at the same rate over the entire range of CR4s. Between CR4 at 20 and CR4 at 40, net income rises only slightly, from 11.4 percent to 12.8 percent. (See second column of Table 6.2.) Thereafter, net income increases at an increasing rate until CR4 reaches 70, after which it begins increasing at a declining rate. This particular non-

TABLE 6.2

Estimated Net Income as Percentage of Equity Capital of Affiliates of U.S. MNCs in Brazil and Mexico Associated with Different Levels of Industry Concentration and Industry Advertising-to-Sales Ratios, 1972

(net income as percentage of equity[a])

Four-Firm Con-centration Ratio (CR4)[b] (percent)	Advertising-to-Sales Ratio (AD)[c] (percent)					
	0.0	1.0	2.0	3.0	4.0	5.0
20	11.4	12.6	13.8	15.0	16.2	17.4
30	11.9	13.1	14.3	15.5	16.7	17.9
40	12.8	14.0	15.2	16.4	17.6	18.8
50	14.2	15.4	16.6	17.8	19.0	20.2
60	15.8	17.0	18.2	19.4	20.6	21.8
70	17.5	18.7	19.9	21.1	22.3	23.5
80	18.9	20.1	21.3	22.5	23.7	24.9
90	19.9	21.1	22.3	23.5	24.7	25.9
100	20.6	21.8	23.0	24.2	25.4	26.6

[a]The profit rate used is broad profits (net income after Mexican or Brazilian corporate income taxes plus technology payments to the parent corporation) expressed as a percentage of stockholders' equity, as predicted by equation G.3 in Appendix G and holding all other independent variables at their respective sample means.

[b]The variable CR4 is the estimated minimum, four-firm concentration ratio for five-digit SIC products, weighted by the affiliates' five-digit SIC sales levels.

[c]The variable AD is the total advertising outlay divided by the total sales of the principal product class of the affiliate, expressed as a percentage.

Source: Special survey of the U.S. Senate Subcommittee on Multinational Corporations.

linear relationship suggests that market concentration does not confer significant market power until after CR4 reaches about 40.* Thus, until CR4 reaches about 40, no serious market power problem arises from concentration alone. Thereafter, however, firms have the capacity to achieve noncompetitive net income on invested capital.

The other two structural variables appear to have an essentially linear impact on net income; that is, net income rose at the same rate over the entire range of observations for RFMS and AD.[†]

Other Variables That Influence Profits

In addition to the basic structural variables discussed above, several other variables were examined.[‡] Three of these were designed to capture the barriers to entry created by economies of scale: absolute capital requirements, economies of scale of plant, and firm size. Both the capital requirements and plant economies variables generally were statistically insignificant and did not have the predicted positive impact on profits. At best the results were inconclusive. Although these findings suggest that economies of scale do not have a significant impact on profits, the findings may be due entirely to the crude measures used. This inference is supported by the finding that affiliate size was positively related to profits and was statistically significant in the analysis based on pooled data of both nations.

Several alternative measures for product differentiation were tried. In some regressions, particularly those using Brazilian data, the relative advertising intensity of the firm exerted a negative influence on profitability; that is, the more intensely a firm advertised relative to typical levels in its major product market, the more of a competitive disadvantage it suffered. In some formulations R&D intensity was found to affect profits positively; a term allowing for interaction between advertising and R&D was always positive but never very strong.

Substitute indexes for relative firm market share were also devised. Although not as satisfactory in many respects, weighted absolute market share and the simple rank of a firm both behaved in the

---

*This is consistent with the findings of some studies of U.S. industries (FTC 1969).

[†]This conclusion is based on the statistical analysis presented in the text that found that nonlinear statistical functional forms were not superior to linear ones for these variables.

[‡]In the interests of brevity, these experiments are not repeated here, but they are all shown in Connor (1976).

expected manner. Roughly speaking, affiliates ranked in the nth position in their main market found their profits enhanced by one percentage point over the next lower firm position.

A variable measuring the degree of a parent firm's control over
its affiliates was positively related to affiliate profits, though the variable was consistently significant only in Brazil. This finding means
that when all other variables are held constant, a 100 percent U.S.-
owned Brazilian affiliate's estimated net profits over equity were five
percentage points greater than those of an affiliate that was 75 percent
owned. This finding is contrary to the expectations of those who believe that reported profits of affiliates are higher for joint ventures
than for wholly owned affiliates. Other proxies for multinational conglomeration, such as long-term debt holding by the parent firm, did
not fare so well.*

Several attempts were made to adjust for the effects of international trade on profits of MNCs' subsidiaries. While high export intensity of the firm (reflecting export propensities of the entire industry to some extent) generally raised profits as expected, this result
is not significant in the Brazilian analysis or the pooled regressions.
Import propensities are practically randomly related to profits.
These export and import propensities include trade by MNCs' affiliates
to both related and unrelated companies.

Several variables representing trade within MNCs were examined to test the hypothesis that MNCs engage in "transfer pricing" in
sales to, and purchases from, their affiliates so as to reduce affiliates'
reported profits. These variables measured the relative importance
of an affiliate's imports from, and exports to, other members of its
corporate family. Although one or the other of these variables was
sometimes strongly influential, the general results of these tests
were ambiguous, providing no clear-cut support for the hypothesis
that MNCs engage in transfer pricing so as to reduce reported affiliate
profits. This finding, which conflicts with some studies of MNCs operating in other countries, may be challenged on grounds that the measures did not accurately capture the transfer pricing phenomenon.
Another explanation for this finding, and equally plausible, is that the
general environment within which MNCs operated in Brazil and Mexico
in 1972 provided no strong incentive to reduce artificially their reported profits in these nations.[†]

---

*However, in Brazil only, we found that the proportion of assets
in the form of long-term loans from the parent organization had a significant (positive) effect on profits that was the opposite of funding
from third parties (Connor 1976: 334-35).

[†]Several "control" variables also were used in the analysis to account for differences in (1) financial leverage of firms, (2) capital in-

In conclusion, this study provides strong confirmation that the relative profitability of firms is influenced by the competitive environment in which they operate. Because the analysis has not identified all the causes of the market structures found in Brazil and Mexico, I have not demonstrated the extent to which technological or other imperatives make it inevitable that certain firms have considerable market power. It seems probable that the relatively small size of these markets makes high concentration inevitable in many industries. Other industries are inexorably structured by business practices peculiar to the multinational corporation or to groups of such firms acting in concert, but irrespective of the origins of existing market structures in these nations, such structures clearly confer great economic power on many MNCs operating within them. This is an indisputable fact of life in Brazil and Mexico, and very probably in many other industrializing LDCs.

Although the origins of Brazil's and Mexico's industrial market structures are not certain, the social effects are. Orthodox economic theory distinguishes several undesirable outcomes in industries exhibiting supranormal returns on capital. Resources are misallocated, and the distribution of income and wealth becomes more unequal. Moreover, innovation and growth are likely to be held below the rates attainable under more competitive conditions.

The United States has responded to its own market power problem by employing a diverse blend of public policies: antitrust laws, regulatory commissions, price controls, and occasional public ownership. Because this study provides persuasive evidence that structural conditions and their consequences are very similar in both the more developed and less developed industrialized nations, there may exist sufficient shared interests to justify similar but multilateral forms of action directed at the social control of MNCs, but at the very least, my empirical analysis ought to alert national decision makers to the possibility of policies that, extending beyond the traditional fiscal and trade prescriptions, will increase the benefits of foreign direct investment.

PUBLIC POLICY ALTERNATIVES

A panoply of policies directed at the MNC have been suggested by writers on the subject. In this section, I limit my discussion pri-

---

tensiveness of industries, and (3) industry growth rates. As shown in the text, these variables were often useful in controlling for nonstructural differences among firms.

marily to public policies designed specifically to alter foreign direct
investments or certain inalienable characteristics associated with
FDI. Therefore, many general policies relating to industrialization,
trade, growth, and taxation are specifically omitted here.* Moreover, the policy changes suggested by many private interest groups,
such as labor unionization, land reform, the granting of minority
rights, or environmental protection, are also largely ignored, important though they may be. Finally, the discussion will be somewhat
more extensive where the empirical results of this work provide support for one view or other on specific policy measures.

        This section is organized into two broad policy groupings. First,
it considers those policies generally held to "facilitate" or "promote"
the flow of FDI among nations. These options are believed to increase
the level of FDI over what it would have been had not the policy been
enacted or the institution come into being. Second, it discusses policies that are likely to constrain, regulate, or control the latitude of
the decision making of MNCs. Within each of these two broad categories, it initially examines national (including bilateral) initiatives
and secondarily international (including regional) policy options. An
underlying assumption in this discussion is that the countries involved
generally prefer to leave most management decision making at the
firm level and to eschew comprehensive economic planning.

Policies Facilitating FDI

        Many of the policies that have directly or indirectly promoted
FDI grew out of the desire of the developed countries to practice free
trade and follow freely convertible monetary policies. Then, after
World War II, FDI was thought to be valuable as a means of stimulating
growth, first in Western Europe and later in the LDCs (Pearson 1969).
Many development benefits have been ascribed to FDI: balance-of-
payments infusions, an increased tax base, the transfer of more productive technology, employment generation, labor training, and other
important vertically related external economies. But, starting with

---

*For discussions of policies relating to these matters, see John-
son (1967), Little (1970), Balassa (1971), Helleiner (1973), Parry
(1973), and Pearson (1969). Most suggestions involve lower trade
barriers, trade preferences for LDCs' exports, increased official aid
or technical assistance, the formation of cartels for LDCs' primary
products, or tax incentives for foreign direct investment. These discussions often assume that LDCs require much more FDI to attain
their development goals.

balance-of-payments concerns and doubts about the appropriateness
of the transferred technologies, there has been more and more rethink-
ing about the net development contributions of FDI (Streeten 1971).
Many LDCs still wish to create a favorable "investment climate" for
a variety of strategic, economic, and political considerations.*
Among the recipient countries in Latin American and other less developed regions, there has been a clear trend away from FDI-facilitating
policies and toward "increasing intervention and control in some or
all of the activities of foreign investors" (Vaitsos 1973: 622).   This
has paralleled an increasing awareness among LDCs of the self-defeating results of competitive bidding by means of concessions for MNCs'
investments (Parry 1973).   Thus, other than the general industrialization policies of LDCs (trade protection, tax holidays, credit and other
subsidies, investment credits, and others), most of the FDI-promot-
ing policies currently under way or under consideration receive their
main support in the capital-exporting countries.

Most national and international policies promoting FDI have had
as their aim the construction of a consistent and predictable legal infrastructure (Keohane and Ooms 1975).   Some existing bilateral arrangements include the U.S. treaties of "friendship, commerce, and
navigation," more than 130 of which have been signed since the eight-
eenth century.   There are also bilateral tax treaties that deal especially with the question of double taxation.   Of growing importance in
recent years have been bilateral agreements on investment protection.
Other diplomatic activities provide informal protection, information
exchange, liaison, or persuasion, often through officially sponsored
seminars, tours, or trade fairs.

In addition, source countries regularly provide financial incentives for FDI by corporations based in their territory.   The U.S. tax
code allows tax credits for corporate income taxes paid to foreign
governments; it also permits the deferred payment of taxes on income
not remitted from subsidiaries located in most LDCs.[†]   The U.S.
government also makes available loans to MNCs through its EXIM
Bank (or the Inter-American Development Bank, which it largely controls), "coordinates" private investment with official U.S. aid grants
and loans, and offers insurance against expropriation of MNCs' properties through its Overseas Private Investment Corporation (Behrman

---

*Cohen (1973), for example, attributes South Korea's openness
to foreign direct investment, most of which comes from the United
States, to an attempt to forge both military and economic ties with a
powerful, protective ally.

[†]Many of these loopholes for MNCs in the U.S. tax code were
severely curtailed in 1976 tax reforms.   In addition, several bills are
pending in the U.S. Congress making bribery by U.S. corporations
abroad a crime.

1974b). Other FDI-source countries offer similar arrangements for
"their" MNCs.

Most of these unilateral and bilateral measures are intended to
benefit the corporations of the investor country by creating a stable
investment milieu. Many of the institutions established for this purpose could, however, become instruments of cooperation between the
investing and recipient countries. For example, information on taxes
and subsidies paid by MNCs could be exchanged on a regular, formal
basis to ensure fairness in tax payments. Such information could also
be shared among host countries as a means of avoiding "concession
wars." Similar data also could be jointly collected and distributed on
prevailing prices and the registration in both countries of international
technology contracts (Vernon 1975). Likewise, both national and international accounting standards boards could encourage firms to reveal
more details on their operations by insisting on the highest common
denominator of reporting standards across national boundaries.

There are also multilateral arrangements promoting FDI.* In
1961, the Organization for Economic Cooperation and Development
(OECD) adopted its Code of Liberalization of Capital Movements, which
is still in force. This code requires member countries to abolish pro-
gressively restrictions on movements of capital among member states.
More recently, the International Bank for Reconstruction and Development (IBRD) adopted a convention that created the International Center
for Settlement of Investment Disputes (ICSID) located at its headquarters. By 1973, the convention had 68 signatories, but most Latin
American governments (and those of Canada, Australia, and India as
well) refused to sign (Keohane and Ooms 1975). The ICSID's arbitration rulings are binding only if both parties have consented in writing
beforehand, yet most Latin American governments resist such arrangements on the grounds that they would represent a loss of national sovereignty (Vaitsos 1973). Up through mid-1974, only five cases had
been brought before the ICSID.

The oldest multinational institutions facilitating FDI are conventions regarding the protection of industrial property rights, namely, in
patents and trademarks. Most commentators have concluded that
patent protection is a necessary condition for the international transfer of most technology (other than that already embodied in final products, of course), but there are few hard empirical data on this point.

---

*Unlike the basically unilateral policies of the investor countries
just mentioned, the LDCs often have the option of "passive resistance"
to some of these multilateral arrangements. Examples of international
agreements offering scope for host country noncooperation are codes
of conduct, provisions for binding arbitration, and the patent system.

Vaitsos (1975) claims that many acquisitions by MNCs have occurred because of a threat of withdrawal of patent rights of licensors, but Penrose (1973) is of the opinion that patent protection has neither induced nor prevented any FDI in the LDCs. Many observers recognize that the patent system is a strong, potentially anticompetitive force in the LDCs today (Vernon 1974b; Newfarmer and Mueller 1975), though industrial secrecy may be a more important source of competitive advantage than the patent system per se. Several UN-sponsored studies have found numerous restrictive clauses in technology contracts applying to LDC firms; export prohibitions, price maintenance, and tying clauses are especially common in licenses written for MNCs' own subsidiaires or for joint ventures (UNCTAD 1975a, 1975b). In a recent survey of the topic, Penrose concludes that the international patenting system brings few advantages to the LDCs, while "the danger is great that foreign companies seeking patents will not assist industrialization nor benefit local industry . . . but will be used primarily to enhance the monopoly position of the foreign patentees in the local market or as a means of transferring funds or facilitating restrictive practices" (1973: 783). Even Vernon admits that the LDCs require special treatment in this regard: "Whatever the appropriate scope and terms of the patent monopoly may be in the advanced countries, wholly different criteria seem relevant in the developing countries" (1975: 39).

While the empirical data in this book did not explicitly recognize or test this particular conduct dimension (except insofar as R&D may have led to patent ownership), such a strategy is entirely consistent with its findings on the competitive positions of MNCs' affiliates in Brazil and Mexico. Some host countries have resisted full participation in the international patent system. Only about 50 of the 100 or so LDCs have signed the Convention of the International Union for the Protection of Industrial Property, and only 8 of the 25 Latin American countries adhere to it. Those that are members should consider "compulsory licensing" rules if after a few years the patents lie unused in the granting country (Penrose 1973). Other countries may be able to follow the Brazilian practice of refusing to recognize drug and food product patents; Vaitsos (1973) claims that this has kept drug prices relatively low in Brazil (compared with, for example, Columbia).

International agencies have a role to play in facilitating mutually beneficial flows of FDI. One activity, recently begun by the UN Centre on Transnational Corporations, consists of operating a clearinghouse for knowledge of the producers or owners of certain types of technology. Similar data are being collected on the activities of individual affiliates. The existence of such a centralized source should make the search for particular investments more efficient, which may encourage entry by new, perhaps smaller or less powerful MNCs. Another useful UN service is the training of LDCs' officials involved in bargaining with MNCs (Vernon 1975).

Policies Regulating FDI

In this section we consider policies directed toward the control or redirection of foreign direct investments. For most countries in Latin America this will mean a reduction but not a stoppage of inward FDI (Diaz-Alejandro 1970). The problem is not only to aim for some optimal aggregate amount of FDI but also to alter the industrial mix and the institutional forms of the investments. Donor countries must also consider new regulations in the light of their domestic invest- ment, growth, and employment objectives (for example, Grubel 1974; Musgrave 1975).

Generally speaking the United States has had no policy toward MNCs; except with respect to the aerospace and nuclear power indus- tries, it cannot be said to have even an industrialization policy. How- ever, it has had policies at least tangential to MNCs: special tax rules regarding foreign corporate income, some disclosure require- ments on foreign holdings, balance-of-payments controls in effect since the mid-1960s, the Trading with the Enemy Act, and antitrust policy. Most writers have considered U.S. foreign income taxation rules "neutral" to FDI. However, depletion allowances have undoubt- edly encouraged the use of foreign branches (rather than subsidiaries) in the extractive industries (Business International 1963). Intracom- pany sales are reviewed by the Internal Revenue Service (IRS) to at- tempt to ensure that "arm's length" prices are being recorded; further, MNCs are no longer allowed to make as full use of tax havens as they once were (before 1962). Tax deferrals are not permitted on technol- ogy payments, and personal income tax payments for MNCs' managers abroad have been somewhat higher in recent years (Behrman 1962b). But with these possible exceptions, U.S. (and most other donor coun- try) tax laws are neutral toward FDI.

The U.S. requirements for MNCs to make disclosures to the Department of Commerce (DOC) or the Securities and Exchange Com- mission (SEC) are stricter than those of most other countries. (Only Behrman [1974b] apparently believes the burden to be excessive.) Yet data limitations, particularly at the firm level, are considered woefully inadequate by most researchers (Vernon 1971; Stevens 1974; Reuber 1973; Vaitsos 1973; Newfarmer and Mueller 1975; Church 1973—all people with privileged access to bodies of data, at times, in their careers). Newfarmer and Mueller go farther in advocating in- creased disclosure to both government and stockholders and federal chartering combined with public directors for the largest MNCs.

Based on the discovered underreporting of some quantities in the DOC data and the satisfactory econometric results in this thesis, I can only concur on this point. A useful additional disclosure method might be a requirement for public corporations akin to that for holders of public archival materials: automatic declassification and public access to all stored records after a stipulated number of years (but much less than the usual 25-year period for U.S. foreign relations documents). Naturally, personal and census documents may be exempted, but today invaluable materials on sales by lines of business, feasibility studies, costs of production, and marketing surveys are being destroyed by firms that view them more as outdated than as damaging to their competitive positions.

The balance-of-payments restrictions on capital transfers in effect for ten years or more have not been very effective (Robbins and Stobaugh 1973), and the restrictions on technology transfers to "enemy" countries have proved so embarrassing that they have been largely lifted (Behrman 1974b). More apropos of the empirical findings here are unilateral antitrust regulations.

Although the United States was the first country to institute such laws, many others have followed, and it is clear that MNCs feel that their freedom of decision making is threatened by their strict enforcement. Greenhill (1975), chief of the Restrictive Practices Section of the United Nations Conference on Trade and Development (UNCTAD), has recently detailed some of the trends in "restrictive business practices" (a term that in UN parlance covers many of the conduct aspects of oligopolistic behavior, especially market allocations, price-setting policies, and mergers). He cites the increasing concern over the apparently enormous market power of MNCs and the rising realization in both the more developed and less developed countries (MDC-LDC) of a need to curb such behavior. Although little action has been taken against market allocations via cartelization, most MDCs (at least 25) have restrictive practices legislation, but very few LDCs have any. Even some centrally planned economies such as Hungary and Yugoslavia have the beginnings of a national antitrust law (Günther 1975). Moreover, Vaitsos claims that the drafting of antimonopoly legislation "is spreading rapidly in Latin America as the result of demonstration effects within the region" (1973: 644). Reinforcing the already comprehensive anticombines act in Canada has been suggested as a means of enhancing the national benefits from FDI (Task Force on the Structure of Canadian Industry 1968).

Many pricing abuses have become illegal with the formation of common markets, because they tend to inhibit intramarket free trade. Some transfer-pricing practices have been checked by many MDCs; this is especially evident in Europe since the highly publicized Hoffman-LaRoche drug-pricing revelations (Greenhill 1975). Only a few countries have systematic controls over per se dominant firms (Austria, Denmark, Finland, Norway),* but many other MDCs have taken action restricting takeovers by MNCs. Data are scanty in this area outside the United States, but Günther (1975) notes that in Europe and Canada in recent periods from 10 to 36 percent of all mergers have been carried out by international corporations. These acquisitions are regarded as especially pernicious by many because, though national concentration remains unchanged, global or regional concentration necessarily rises. In the European Economic Community (EEC), for example, aggregate industrial concentration has risen dramatically in recent years: The top hundred companies' sales have risen from only 26 percent in 1953 to 50 percent in 1970. Greenhill (1975) strongly asserts that mergers by MNCs inevitably lead to reduction in competition by the newly acquired subsidiaries, not only because international concentration has increased but also because price fixing and market allocation practices become perfectly legal after merger. Günther (1975) and others, on the other hand, believe that MNCs' entry into markets may sometimes upset prior stable oligopolistic arrangements. At the very least, countries need some disclosure mechanism for large mergers, such as that in the United States and Germany, coupled with the power to prohibit entry. Because it is much more difficult to design a divestiture plan that maintains economic efficiency than it is to prohibit a planned merger, a prior notification requirement is to be greatly preferred to an after-the-fact announcement.

The antipathy expressed by managers of MNCs is a clear signal of the potential effectiveness of national antitrust measures directed toward MNCs' actions. A survey of managerial opinion in 46 large U.S. MNCs found that antitrust strictures ranked among the two top U.S. constraints on FDI (Root 1973). In the United States over the last 80 years, the reach of the Sherman and Clayton acts has been continually extended through judicial interpretation to cover parties and acts outside U.S. territories. Since the United States v. National Lead Company (1947) case, the courts have held that any conspiracy to restrain trade that "substantially" affects U.S. commerce could be deemed unlawful, even though the act may occur extraterritorially. Similarly, Section 7 of the Clayton Act has been interpreted to apply to mergers within and without the United States that substantially lessen competition between firms (Finance Committee, U.S. Senate 1973b).[†]

---

*These countries impose additional reporting and regulatory constraints on any companies that are dominant, or nearly so, by some numerical, structural definition.

[†]A very interesting application of the extraterritorial feature of U.S. antitrust law was an FTC investigation of an alleged attempt by

There is little doubt that the U.S. enforcement of its competition laws has put U.S. MNCs at some slight disadvantage relative to European MNCs. As Edwards (1970) points out, there are three main areas in which U.S. MNCs may face antitrust curbs that their rivals do not: (1) cartel agreements, (2) restrictive licensing of patents or processes, and (3) joint ventures that may restrict U.S. trade. In general he does not consider these restraints so severe as to seriously limit the success of U.S. business ventures abroad. Moreover, U.S. laws can also be applied to foreign MNCs, as they were in the ICI-DuPont and General Electric-Phillips conspiracy cases, just as U.S. firms are potentially liable to extraterritorial prosecution by some European laws (such as those of West Germany, Austria, and the United Kingdom). The purported fear that MNCs have of entering into foreign joint ventures is particularly overplayed (Behrman 1974b). There is no doubt that joint foreign ventures are an effective means of ensuring oligopolistic discipline; this form of conduct is especially well documented in the case of petroleum by Blair (1976). I again concur with Newfarmer and Mueller (1975) in their call for a strengthening of national antitrust laws, including those that have as their aim the selective deconcentration of domestic industry. In the LDCs, a procompetition policy could be designed to complement present movements toward mandatory divestiture, the registration and review of technology contracts, and prior approval of entry by MNCs into certain industries.

The LDCs have also taken various unilateral actions to regulate and control the activities of MNCs. Many of these policies were reviewed in the Brazilian and Mexican cases in Chapter 2. Some policies affected FDI indirectly and were intended to be nondiscriminatory among national and foreign-owned firms; import substitution and export promotion policies were cited in this regard.

But other policies were overtly discriminatory, having been designed specifically to apply to foreign investment or foreign-owned firms. As I pointed out, one of the most common constraints is a list of prohibited industries, ones reserved either for a government monop-

---

the General Tire and Rubber Company to prevent the Goodyear Tire and Rubber Company from building a factory in Morocco. Before 1971 General Tire and Rubber was the sole producer of tires in Morocco. In order to keep its monopoly and discourage Goodyear from entering the market, General Tire and Rubber may have bribed a Moroccan official to obtain permission to expand its existing plant. Even though U.S. trade was not affected by the incident, the FTC believes it has jurisdiction under its enabling act because bribery is a form of unfair competition (Wall Street Journal, April 28, 1976, p. 4).

oly or for only nationally owned firms. The number of proscribed
sectors is especially large under the terms of the Andean Common
Market (ANCOM) agreement. Many policy analysts are quite concerned about the development implications of allowing MNCs to determine the product mix of host country manufacturing sectors. As I
have shown, many U.S. MNCs are engaged in the production of highly
differentiated consumer goods, or inputs used in their production.
Referring to Brazil during 1966-72, for example, Bacha perceives
two important consequences of official policies that adapt "the pattern
of domestic final demand to the expansion needs of the MNCs" (1976:
28). One is the continued necessity for high income concentration;
the other is a demand twist from traditional to "international" consumer goods (the so-called international demonstration effect). He
cites consumer budget surveys that show Brazilian working class
families spending much more over the period 1958-70 on consumer
durables, in spite of falling real incomes. As Vaitsos (1973) points
out, the main power that LDCs' governments have in their manufacturing sectors is to refuse MNCs entry into their markets; the situation
is like that of a bilateral monopoly in that the outcome of bargaining
is determinate only within a broad range. He argues that negotiations
ought to be carried out with a multiplicity of alternatives in mind, not
just "FDI" versus "no FDI" (Vaitsos 1974).

Among these alternatives are licensing of local firms, joint ventures (including those with the host government as partner), and co-
production agreements.* There is ample evidence that most U.S.
MNCs, especially those in the technology-intensive industries, have
strong preferences for closely held foreign subsidiaires, but it is
equally clear that countries such as India, Mexico, and Japan with
stated policies favoring joint ventures have been successful in imposing ownership restrictions on MNCs that normally prefer wholly owned
subsidiaries (Stopford and Wells 1972: 151-53). It is also true, however, that some of those companies will simply avoid investing in countries that insist on joint ownership; Stopford and Wells (1972) may well
be correct that only host countries with quite large markets may be
able to bear this cost of avoidance by MNCs (pp. 153-56). However,

---

*A related policy is that of planned disinvestment, or "fade out"
provisions, an agreement made between the host government and an
MNC before the approval of entry that specifies a certain schedule of
sale of equity capital on local markets. This policy is already being
implemented, though not entirely uniformly across member states,
in ANCOM as a result of the well-known "Decision 24." For an early
debate on the merits of planned disinvestment, see the seminal paper
by Hirshman (1969) and a rebuttal by Behrman (1972).

as Vernon (1975) points out, the value of total control over subsidiaries
by MNCs tends to decline over time, particularly in the case of subsidiaries producing fairly standardized or heavily advertised products
aimed at the local market, and concurrently the benefits of local ownership increase. Thus, even in smaller markets, selectively applied
fade-out requirements may be a viable policy. Co-production agreements have been used primarily in centrally planned economies; there
the land, labor, and most physical capital are provided by the state,
but long-term management control and a claim on a share of the profits are retained by the MNC. Along with technical assistance contracts, these alternatives may be difficult to obtain in negotiations because of the MNCs' preferences for control, and their possible losses
of information about the local market (Vernon 1972).

Besides policies affecting the ownership forms of MNCs' affiliates in host LDCs, there are other restrictions that a country may
impose during the entry phase. These entry negotiations generally
should not be on a case-by-case basis but, rather, more like reviews
or clearances based on regularly published and fairly consistent guidelines. Otherwise, the opportunity for corruption on a grand scale
presents itself. Even an honest, highly competent agency is likely to
become mired in details if the approval procedures were based merely
on precedent. For example, one desirable guideline might cover
MNCs' entry via takeover. "If some single decision rule were needed
to govern all cases of acquisitions [by MNCs], the present widespread
tendency to frown on such operations is probably as good a rule as
any" (Vernon 1975: 33). The development costs are likely to be especially high if the transaction is by means of a stock transfer or if the
local firm is dynamic, dominant, or profitable.

A fairly basic requirement common in most host countries is
that of prior registration of the ownership and capital structure of
firms. This is followed in Brazil along with de facto insistence upon
the submission of the production plans of new ventures to the planning
agency. In countries with competent planning agencies, approval of
the venture may hinge on a schedule of increasing domestic vertical-
integration requirements.* Procedures along these lines ought to be

---

*Increasing linkages is only one means of maximizing the local
value added of a given foreign investment project. Moreover, a more
comprehensive set of objectives should be specified in any cost-benefit
analysis of a project. It should be noted that merely increasing "local"
value added does not automatically lead to increased purchases from
domestically owned firms. To meet the requirements, MNCs may induce their traditional home country suppliers to set up a "local" operation.

coupled with regular, comprehensive submissions of financial and
trade data as well as merger plans to a local, central data collection
agency. Monitoring of the performance of MNCs' affiliates is an important check on changes in structure, on efficiency and innovation,
on taxation (especially for losses being carried forward), and on depreciation and interest payment schedules—all very sensitive issues
directly affecting the performance of MNCs' affiliates. Neither planning
nor a competition policy can be rationally designed without an adequate local data base (Vaitsos 1973; Vernon 1975; Church 1973).

In addition to placing various social controls on incoming MNCs,
recipient nations can also take steps to encourage entry by their own
domestic firms. A first step, already a long-standing practice by
Mexico's National Financiera, is selectively to favor nationally owned
private enterprises in the disbursement of investment capital. This
could help counteract the advantage MNCs have in the international
capital market. Unfortunately, government lending practices of this
sort often tend to favor only the largest, best-established firms.
More useful perhaps would be government programs that provide subsidized engineering services or that aid in the global search for productive licensing opportunities (Dunning 1974d). These are all programs
that can aid in "depackaging," or untying the benefits of foreign direct
investment, while improving domestic competition.

In line with these government actions are policies that encourage the formation of public or cooperative enterprises as a counter-
vailing force against foreign economic domination. In Mexico and
Brazil, state-owned industrial firms have been established in basic
metals, petrochemicals, and petroleum.* Public enterprises can be
justified on both efficiency and equity grounds, but historically the
equity benefits (such as correcting regional disparities, creating employment, or making subsidized mass-consumption necessities) of
public enterprises have tended to disappear rather soon after the firm
begins operation (Shepherd 1976). In addition to the infant industry
benefits of state enterprise, the most important efficiency benefits
are likely to be in the area of stimulating growth and competition in
highly oligopolistic industries. To play the role of a "maverick firm,"
the public enterprise must be a credible threat; that is, it needs suffi-

---

*A variant on the state ownership of firms is worker participation
in management. In Brazil and Mexico, labor unions have played no
positive roles in recent industrialization, but extensive experimentation with worker participation has gone on in Algeria, Peru, Tanzania,
and above all, Yugoslaiva. Many of the most advanced Western European nations (for example, West Germany, Sweden) have also mandated
labor union participation.

cient scale to attain most economies and a large enough market share to affect the profits of rival firms substantially. Both the Brazilian state petroleum company and the Mexican steel firm are in this position. On the whole, this policy of "mixed oligopoly" seems preferable to the policy of designating wide areas of industry as off limits to private enterprise (as in India). When workable competition is established in one industry, the government should consider selling the state firm to the public (as Japan did) and investing in another "problem" industry.

Another policy option concerns restrictions on profit repatriation or other international flows of funds. The Brazilian rule has been so generous as to be ineffectual for all practical purposes. Even lower limits may ultimately have detrimental effects because the upper limit on repatriation may become a target for foreign companies whereas without such certainty many firms may be willing to settle for higher reinvestment rates and lower remissions. This seems to have happened with respect to the "fair" limits on technology payments (about 3 percent on gross sales is allowed) recently instituted by the Mexican government. The Brazilian law disallowing excessive interest payments on international (especially intrafirm) loans is also in this category.

My own position is that restrictions on rates of return merely relieve the symptoms of the problem and fail to remedy its source; that is, rather than disallow excessive profits as a general policy, the conditions giving rise to these supranormal profits should be altered. As the empirical tests have shown, high profits are largely due to the prevalence of certain market structures in the host countries that encourage noncompetitive conduct. The resulting inefficiencies and redistribution of income are well established. Even the high rates of growth of MNCs' affiliates, and the national income generated, may have been quite low relative to their potential. Although industrial restructuring may be premature in some industries because of scale economies, strong consideration should be given to the encouragement of entry (White 1974).* The specter of "overcompetition" is hardly as credible as Behrman (1974b: 31) makes it out to be, though in smaller nations economies of scale may be an overriding consideration.

---

*Although I have focused primarily on the fostering of entry by domestic firms, competitive benefits also devolve through encouragement of more extensive market entry via importation. As has been pointed out, the relatively lower levels of market power in Mexico as contrasted to Brazil can be partially attributed to the former's freer trade policies.

An area of public policy making that is still at an experimental stage in the developed market economies is rule making on the product differentiation activities of manufacturers, advertising in particular. Many policies in this area are popular with consumers and simple to administer. For example, rules on weights, packaging, grading, and labeling of products can be inexpensively instituted. Requiring a somewhat more elaborate bureaucratic effort are various consumer protection laws covering the truthfulness of advertising claims and the safety levels of some types of consumer goods. Laws that insist on the provision of price information in all advertising (as in Argentina) may be difficult to enforce, but certainly organizations that aid in the maintenance of collusive pricing do consumers a disservice. A new (February 1976) Mexican law that requires generic terms to be given prominence over trademarks for some product classes "in the public interest" is another step that could aid consumers in making rational decisions. Any measure that helps provide buyers with objective price and quality information eventually lowers the barriers to new market entry. Finally, a highly controversial topic, but one that I have shown applies to Brazil and Mexico at least, is that of self-canceling advertising. While it is admittedly somewhat arbitrary to distinguish the informational from the purely emotive content of advertising messages, advertising carried on strictly in response to rival advertising is a luxury even rich nations cannot afford (Comanor and Wilson 1974).*

Many LDCs have begun registering and reviewing technology contracts (Aguilar 1975). When tied to a scrutiny of restrictive practices, the exercise can be especially beneficial (Andean Group 1970). By all means, public R&D programs should eventually be instituted, but an intermediate stage, along Japanese lines, of searching for existing technology before trying to generate new basic inventions is likely to have a greater payoff for most LDCs. Highly competitive markets in

---

*An alternative course, less satisfactory to "liberal" economic thinking, is simply banning advertising meant to increase consumer demand for some goods or through certain media. Perhaps the strongest case for this action can be made in regulated or nationalized industries that produce commodities generated largely from irreplaceable natural resources. Where a consensus exists, countries may wish to prohibit certain types of advertising of potentially harmful products; tobacco products, alcoholic beverages, some drugs, guns, and unnutritious foods targeted at children have been cited in this regard in some of the more developed countries. Many countries have advertising councils with regulatory powers over members.

themselves are a potent force for innovation and technological adaptation, but pressuring MNCs to perform local R&D will yield few external benefits (Vernon 1975: 38-40).

In addition to national initiatives to control FDI, some multilateral efforts or suggestions have been put forward. In contrast to the other major functional areas of international economic relations (finance, trade, and aid), there is no important set of international institutions concentrating primarily on FDI (comparable to the IMF,* GATT,[†] UNCTAD, or the IBRD). This institutional hiatus partially derives from the present lack of agreement on the net value of FDI itself (Keohane and Ooms 1975). "In a period of rising national regulation of multinational firms, the relative underdevelopment of international measures is striking" (Vernon 1975: 191).

Yet there appears to be considerable support for regional or international agencies or conventions on such topics as the harmonization of data collection, accounting rules, merger guidelines, and competition policies. Testimony before the U.S. Senate Antitrust Subcommittee of the Judiciary Committee (1973), for example, saw favorable opinions expressed concerning such harmonization by representatives of international business and the MNCs' governments. Moreover, a UN Economic and Social Council (ECOSOC 1974) report by a "Group of Eminent Persons" largely sympathetic to the view of the LDCs similarly advocates the adoption of an international antitrust agreement similar to the stillborn Havana Charter.

The emergence of the EEC and other economic unions (LAFTA, the CACM,[‡] and ANCOM in Latin America) may signal an especially ripe moment for the formulation of coordinated policies toward FDI. Larger markets mean a better bargaining position vis-a-vis the MNCs over conditions and forms of entry. They also open the way for increased cooperation in basic R&D, harmonization of fiscal and monetary policies, and the creation of a unionwide companies law, as in the EEC (Keohane and Ooms 1975). Economic unions will help avoid self-defeating rivalry among members over investment concessions, and may even engender the formation of unionwide mergers of national firms to countervail against MNCs (Diaz-Alejandro 1970). The secretariat of a common market may find it easier to impose more stringent standards of disclosure and technology transfer than any of the member states would individually.** Finally, if the EEC experience is any

---

*The International Monetary Fund.
[†] The General Agreement on Tariffs and Trade.
[‡] The Central American Common Market.
**The adoption and maintenance of fade-out provisions by common markets have been particularly difficult in Latin America of late.

guide, surprisingly strong antitrust rules may emerge, even in states with no prior tradition of such laws, though their initial purpose may be to make intraunion trade as free as possible (Timberg 1972).

But such discussion on multilateral approaches to the regulation of FDI has revolved around international harmonization of FDI policies on a global (or at least among market economies) scale. Dunning and Gilman (1975) provide an incisive theoretical argument for the superiority of multilateral policies toward MNCs, based on the crucial assumption that MNCs " are often more response-elastic than indigenous firms in respect to policies taken to affect their behavior" (p. 18). A multilateral approach can compensate for the footloose characteristics of MNCs, and the benefits from the conversion of MNCs' profits into additional taxes could in theory be shared internationally in a Pareto-improving fashion.

One approach along these lines envisions a convention spelling out in some detail the rights and obligations of both MNCs and their host governments in their relations with each other, possibly linked with the establishment of an arbitration commission (Reuber 1973). Business groups would like guarantees concerning earnings repatriation, import duty schedules, and compensation for nationalization of property. Host countries would like disclosure on affiliate operations, limits to local borrowing (expressed perhaps as maximum debt-to-equity ratios), assurances on future R&D activities, and assent to local laws and business customs (Behrman 1974b). Voluntary codes of behavior of this kind are unlikely to be accepted, nor would they serve any useful purpose unless the provisions were highly operationalizable and supervised by some international organization such as the United Nations or OECD (Günther 1975). Very general guidelines for "good corporate behavior" are very likely useless (Dunning 1971b). Binding, enforced codes in relatively homogeneous regions might be more successful (Newfarmer and Mueller 1975: 155).

The most comprehensive proposal to date has been the General Agreement for the International Corporation (GAIC), a convention structurally very similar to GATT. The agency supervising the GAIC would deal with five important areas involving FDI: taxation, antitrust policy, foreign exchange controls, export controls, and securities regulation (Keohane and Ooms 1975). Opinion varies widely on whether a consensus exists that would be strong enough to lead to successful negotiations. Edwards (1970) believes there is, except among business interests; Behrman (1974b) is of the opinion that some functional areas

---

Stress between Chile and ANCOM has led to the provision's relaxation in Chile, and the Caribbean Common Market has initially declined to adopt one (Wall Street Journal, May 24, 1976, p. 6).

(incorporation laws, accounting principles, dispute settlement) are more likely to come to agreement than others (such as competition policy). Dunning (1971b) takes the opposite view in some respects, suggesting that the curtailment of monopoly behavior and harmonization of antitrust policies would be the most likely areas for the attention of an international authority.

Of all the proposed functions for the proposed GAIC, my empirical findings apply most directly to antitrust harmonization. The primary reasons for standardization of rules are a solution to the dilemma of the national versus global concentration effects of mergers by MNCs and a resolution of the extraterritoriality aspects of many national antitrust codes (ECOSOC 1974). Furthermore, stricter enforcement by developed countries' governments of competitive standards will externally benefit the host countries whose own bureaucracies may not be equal to the enforcement task. National antitrust policies may effectively alter domestic market structures, but an international antitrust agency may usefully specialize in international market structures and conduct from which the power of MNCs derives. Harmonization will not be easy; some concepts, such as the U.S. idea of a per se antitrust violation, may have to be dropped (Vernon 1974). But the benefits of international antitrust harmonization are demonstrably great.

This protrait of policy options has been executed with a decidedly broad brush—and the end result may resemble an artist's palette more than a finished canvas. Nevertheless, the point has been made that the range of policies, both facilitative and restrictive, is wide for both donor and recipient nations. Perhaps the main theme that emerges, flowing inevitably from my theoretical stance and empirical findings, is that a concern for the competitive, and especially structural, consequences of foreign direct investment can well serve as a unifying principle in the formation of the relevant public policies. The more traditional tools of government control—taxes, subsidies, tariffs, quotas, and suasion—are best reserved for the broader macroeconomic goals of a country. Channeling the patently magnificent energies of the modern multinational enterprise into tracks that parallel sovereign social goals will test the mettle of the most resourceful bureaucracies. The less industrialized countries have much to learn from the experiences of Brazil and Mexico, not the least of which is that once MNCs have been firmly implanted in a country's soil, their growth patterns may make pruning more expensive than uprooting. Therefore, standards governing MNCs' activities are best applied during bargaining at the point of entry. Because individual host countries are understandably reluctant to lose tempting foreign investments, these criteria are often best designed and implemented by international organizations. And finally, I hope to have demonstrated the extent to which there is an empirical basis for the construction of uniform or harmonized international policies on multinational industrial organization.

APPENDIX A
THE U.S. SENATE
SUBCOMMITTEE ON
MULTINATIONAL
CORPORATIONS
SPECIAL SURVEY

THE SAMPLING METHOD

The special survey was designed with a view to selecting only the largest industrial corporations in the United States with substantial interests in Brazil and Mexico. Reporters were initially chosen from among the 500 largest industrial firms in 1972 appearing in the May 1973 issue of Fortune magazine. Questionnaires were then sent by the Subcommittee on Multinationals staff to the 296 firms among the "Fortune 500" that owned at least one subsidiary (or branch) in either Brazil or Mexico. Information on ownership and country of location of affiliates was obtained from Who Owns Whom 1972 (New York: Oxford University Press, 1973).

A "substantial interest" in an affiliate was defined for the purposes of the special survey to be at least 25 percent ownership in 1972 (direct plus indirect) of all outstanding voting stock. The questionnaire instructions also directed reporters to respond only if their affiliates had 1972 total assets or total revenue of at least $250,000. Thus, U.S. corporations that did not have at least 25 percent ownership of one affiliate in Brazil or Mexico of sufficient size were excluded. Both the questionnaire and its instruction sheet can be found in Newfarmer and Mueller (1975).

THE RESPONSE

Of the 296 U.S. multinational corporations receiving the questionnaire, 27 were exempted for the reasons given above. Of the remaining 269 qualified companies, 197 (73 percent) returned completed questionnaires. A complete list of the 197 respondents, 27 exempted firms, and 45 nonrespondents can be found in Newfarmer and Mueller (1975: 191-93).

With a few exceptions, the nonrespondents were generally among the smaller companies on the Fortune 500 list or owned relatively small affiliates in Brazil or Mexico.* This can be ascertained by

---

*Fifteen companies among the top hundred in 1972 did not respond. They were Allied Chemicals, Aluminum Company of America, American Can, American Home Products, Bethlehem Steel, Coca-Cola, Con-

comparison with the universe figures compiled by the U.S. Department of Commerce. The 197 respondents reported owning more than $42 billion in foreign direct investment in 1972 (or 45 percent of all U.S. FDI in that year). The 179 predominantly manufacturing MNCs held more than $24 billion (or 62 percent) of the total U.S. foreign direct investments in manufacturing. However, these two totals somewhat underestimate the actual holdings of these reporters. The difference arises from the two methods used by firms to evaluate their foreign holdings. The first accounting method, the "cost basis" procedure, includes only the values of the equity or debt investments at the time they were initially transferred. Although instructed to do otherwise, about 15 percent of the reporters used this accounting procedure. The second, "equity basis" method (the one that has been advocated by the major accountancy board for some time) adds annual increases in the parents' shares of equity in affiliates due to retained earnings to the initial costs. Thus, the "carrying value" of foreign investments on the books of the parent corporations is closer to the market value when the equity method is employed.

The 197 U.S. MNCs also owned at least 74 percent of all U.S. foreign direct manufacturing investment in Latin America in 1972 (compare Survey of Current Business, August 1973). This investment was spread out over approximately 1,300 Latin American manufacturing affiliates.

In Brazil, the affiliates of reporting U.S. MNCs accounted for $1.7 billion (68 percent) of the total of $2.5 billion of the 1972 net book value of U.S. foreign direct investment. In Brazilian manufacturing investment, the special survey encompassed $1.4 billion of the $1.7 billion (or 82 percent) of the U.S. total. In Mexico, the special survey respondents held about $1.1 billion (82 percent) of the $1.4 billion in net book value of U.S. manufacturing investment.

Official data for the sales of majority-owned subsidiaries of U.S. MNCs at a disaggregated, major industry level are available only for 1972 (Survey of Current Business, August 1974). A comparison of the majority-owned subsidiaries of firms in the special survey provides a picture of coverage across industries. In Brazil, manufacturing coverage is 80 percent of sales.* The survey response was significantly below average in the food manufacturing, primary metals, and fabricated metals industries. On the other hand, coverage was almost complete in the paper, chemicals, and rubber industries.

---

solidated Foods, Greyhound, International Harvester, Minnesota Mining and Manufacturing, Occidental Petroleum, Rapid-American, TRW, U.S. Steel, and Warner-Lambert.

*By the same criterion, the response rate for petroleum affiliates was 94 percent in Brazil and 68 percent in Mexico.

In Mexican manufacturing, the special survey accounted for 86 percent of the 1972 sales of majority-owned affiliates of U.S. MNCs. The response rate led to underrepresentation in the food manufacturing, chemicals, and metals industries. However, coverage was high for the rubber, electrical machinery, and transportation equipment industries.

INDUSTRIAL CODING SYSTEM

In every case, both the parent reporters and their affiliates were classified according to the Standard Industrial Classification (SIC) System formulated by the U.S. Bureau of the Census. Each MNC was given the three-digit SIC number found in Baldwin H. Ward, ed., 25,000 Leading U.S. Corporations (New York: News Front, 1970). This SIC designation represents the industry of the primary activity of the reporter.

Each Brazilian and Mexican affiliate was also classified according to its primary three- and four-digit industry. These codes were derived from the U.S. Bureau of the Census's manual Numerical List of Manufactured Products, 1972 (New Basis) (Washington, D.C.: U.S. Department of Commerce, 1972). The affiliates' industrial codes were based on the responses to the five-digit product-sales data on lines 18-22, page B-2 of the questionnaire. Each product was grouped into its three- (and four-) digit SIC category, and the sales of these products were summed. The largest single three- (or four-) digit industry by sales provided the code number for the whole subsidiary. The product and firm code numbers were checked against the verbal descriptions provided by the respondents. In ambiguous cases, telephoned or written inquiries were made to corporate officers.

DERIVATION OF CONCENTRATION RATIOS

Concentration estimates were prepared for this book by combining information in the Senate Subcommittee on Multinational Corporations's special survey questionnaires on market shares with that on the affiliate's market position. For example, if a certain U.S. affiliate reported a market share of 15 percent and was the third-ranked firm in that particular product market, then the minimum four-firm concentration ratio (hereafter CR4) was calculated to be 45 percent. This estimate is an understatement on two accounts. First, it fails to capture the sales share of any firm ranked lower in the market than the reporting affiliate. In my example the fourth-ranked company in the market could have a market share of up to 15 percent, raising the CR4 to 60 percentage points. Second, this method fails to account for the likely fact that competitors in positions above the reporting subsidiary have market shares substantially larger than the reporting subsidiary. Conceivably, an affiliate reporting itself in third place in a given market could also be the smallest of the only three producers of that product; in that case, the true CR4 would be 100 percent. In a few cases, it was apparent from the questionnaire that there were only four or fewer companies producing a particular product.

Two procedures were used to improve the estimates of CR4 in Brazil and Mexico. The first method involved a cross-checking of market share and competitor information given by two or more subsidiaries of U.S. MNCs marketing the same product in the same country. This procedure yielded a more complete profile of certain product markets and allowed us to revise the original estimates upward. For example, if two rivals ranked themselves in the second and fourth places, it was assumed that the third-ranked firm had a market share equal to the fourth-ranked firm's and that the leading firm had a market share at least as large as the second-ranked affiliate. It was possible to cross-check about one-third of the more than three hundred different manufactured product classes represented in the special survey. In addition, cross-checking was often facilitated by reporters who gratuitously provided the market shares of all their competitors. In well-defined markets, better CR4 estimates could also sometimes be made from the five-digit SIC sales data of competing firms, even if only one rival gave us its market share.

The second method of adjustment used the Brazilian and Mexican concentration data computed by Fajnzylber (1970, 1975). Because the Fajnzylber data are for the top four <u>plants</u> rather than <u>firms</u>, it too provides a conservative (downward) estimate of the true CR4. However, because of the size of the market, even leading firms often produce all of their output in a single plant. Therefore, where the Fajnzylber plant CR4 was larger than our estimated firm CR4, we used the former. Comparisons were made only when the industry definitions were the same. These data were highly complementary to the special survey derivations because the Brazilian and Mexican industry-classification codes are generally best developed (that is, have more specific categories) in those major industry groups with a traditionally high population of domestic firms (for example, food manufacturing, nonmetallic metals). These industries tended to be those where often only one U.S. affiliate was present and, hence, the ones for which "cross-checking" was impossible.

TABLE B.1

Estimates of Minimum, Four-Firm, Five-Digit SIC-Level Concentration Ratios, Brazilian, Mexican, and U.S. Manufacturing Industries, 1972

SIC Industry Group	Industry	Brazil		Mexico		Brazil and Mexico,	United States,[c]
		Number of Five-Digit Products[a]	Mean CR4 (percent)	Number of Five-Digit Products[a]	Mean CR4 (percent)	Number of Five-Digit Products[b]	Mean CR4 (percent)
201	Meat products	0	—	1	76	0	—
202	Dairy products	2	94	3	60	1	69
203	Preserved fruits and vegetables	3	100	10	89	3	74
204	Grain products	3	67	5	81	3	58
205	Baking	1	20	1	100	0	—
206	Candy	2	71	6	65	0	—
207	Oils	0	—	2	30	0	—
208	Beverages	5	67	2	62	2	52
209	Other food processing	0	—	7	91	0	—
211	Cigarettes	1	88	1	98	1	84
221	Cotton-weaving mills	1	59	0	—	0	—
222	Synthetic-weaving mills	3	86	0	—	0	—
224	Narrow fabric mills	0	—	1	60	0	—
225	Knitting mills	1	27	0	—	0	—
228	Thread and yarn	1	36	0	—	0	—
234	Brassieres, corsets, and so forth	0	—	1	37	0	—
238	Raincoats, and so forth	0	—	1	37	0	—
251	Wood furniture and mattresses	1	45	6	40	1	34
261	Pulp mill products	2	91	1	35	1	39
262	Paper mill products	2	68	5	70	2	31
263	Paperboard products	2	52	1	73	0	—
264	Converted paper products	4	75	1	68	1	15
265	Paper containers	1	50	3	74	1	19
273	Book publishing	0	—	3	58	0	—
276	Business forms	0	—	2	49	0	—
281	Industrial inorganic chemicals	7	60	11	70	5	46
282	Plastics and synthetic cloths	5	70	6	67	3	46
283	Drugs, medicinals, biologics	14	32	13	26	12	42
284	Soaps and cosmetics	6	54	12	76	6	54

Code	Industry						
285	Paints and finishes	2	74	2	46	2	24
286	Industrial organic chemicals	8	52	9	65	6	41
287	Agricultural chemicals	5	69	6	64	3	56
289	Other chemical preparations	4	80	8	60	3	35
291	Gasoline, and so forth (except 29117)	6	68	0	—	0	—
295	Asphalt	1	71	1	71	1	30
299	Lubricants (including 29117)	2	65	5	90	5	67
301	Tires	5	97	1	33	1	48
304	Hoses and belting	1	88	3	84	3	22
306	Rubber goods	1	80	4	79	2	23
307	Plastics articles	3	58	1	90	1	19
313	Footware cut stock	1	93	2	73	1	—
322	Glass containers	1	76	0	—	0	—
324	Cement	1	48	2	85	0	—
325	Clay tiles and refractories	0	—	1	70	2	64
326	Plumbing fixtures	0	—	2	66	1	—
327	Gypsum products	4	73	6	92	2	64
329	Abrasives	2	40	2	72	6	46
331	Primary steel	1	100	0	—	2	—
332	Steel foundries	1	87	9	90	0	54
333	Primary nonferrous metals	5	41	1	100	2	—
335	Nonferrous rolling and drawing	0	—	1	45	1	33
336	Nonferrous foundries	1	41	5	99	2	23
341	Metal cans	1	100	2	50	1	43
342	Tools and hardware	1	100	2	100	1	24
343	Plumbing and heating fixtures	1	62	1	100	2	30
344	Structural metalwork	1	94	2	100	1	—
345	Fasteners	1	84	1	86	2	18
346	Metal stampings	5	76	6	91	6	96
348	Arms and ammunition	2	98	2	63	0	81
349	Other fabricated metals	1	100	6	75	4	49
351	Internal combustion engines	8	92	2	100	4	—
352	Farm machinery	0	—	5	81	2	33
353	Construction machinery	5	74	7	67	6	31
354	Power machinery and hand tools	0	—	2	100	2	—
355	Special industry machinery	5	74	5	81	5	33
356	Other industry machinery	6	78	7	67	7	31

(continued)

TABLE B.1 (continued)

SIC Industry Group	Industry	Brazil		Mexico		Brazil and Mexico	United States
		Number of Five-Digit Products[a]	Mean CR4 (percent)	Number of Five-Digit Products[a]	Mean CR4 (percent)	Number of Five-Digit Products[b]	Mean[c] CR4 (percent)
357	Office and computer	5	96	10	82	5	69
358	Service-industry machinery	3	81	1	45	0	—
361	Electric-power transmission equipment	3	31	0	—	0	—
362	Electric motors and industrial equipment	2	54	3	82	1	61
363	Household appliances	6	73	4	91	3	78
364	Lighting and wiring devices	2	62	1	56	1	26
365	Radio, television, and phonographs	4	71	3	49	3	57
366	Telephonic and communications equipment	4	100	4	97	3	80
367	Electronic components	3	97	4	98	3	75
369	Batteries and other electrical equipment	3	77	5	72	3	69
371	Motor vehicles and parts	2	96	3	72	2	79
372	Aircraft	0	—	1	100	0	—
374	Railroad equipment	1	100	0	—	0	—
382	Measuring and controlling devices	3	63	6	65	3	39
384	Surgical and dental equipment	3	65	1	70	1	32
386	Photography and photocopying	2	78	3	99	1	100
394	Toys and games	0	—	2	100	0	—
396	Clotying fasteners	0	—	2	94	0	—
399	Miscellaneous manufactures	1	60	0	—	0	—
	Total	201	69.5	267	73.1	130	50.3
	Total for same products	130	69.4	130	71.1	130	50.3

[a]Number of different five-digit SIC products in each three-digit industry group that are affiliates of U.S. MNCs in special survey produced and for which data on concentration are available.

[b]Number of different five-digit SIC products in three-digit SIC industry group common to both countries.

[c]Simple average of four-firm, five-digit SIC concentration ratios of product classes common to both Latin American countries. They are census, not minimum, ratios.

Sources: Special survey of the U.S. Senate Subcommittee on Multinational Corporations, Fajnzylber (1970, 1975); and 1972 Census of Manufactures.

TABLE C.1

Weighted Average Advertising-to-Sales Ratios in Brazilian and Mexican Manufacturing Industries, 1972

SIC	Industry	Brazil		Mexico	
		Advertising-to-Sales Ratio (percent)	Sales[c] ($ millions)	Advertising-to-Sales Ratio (percent)	Sales[c] ($ millions)
201-02	Meat and dairy	2.29	43.4	0.53	36.1
203	Canning, fruit and vegetable			4.72	29.2
2043, 2046, 205	Cereals, corn, and baking products	3.84	53.8	4.06	55.5
2048	Animal feeds	0.42	29.2	0.43	96.7
206	Candy and chocolate	—	0	8.74	28.0
208	Liquor and soft drinks	2.94	64.1	17.64	41.3
209	Other food processing	—	0	4.76	33.7
211	Cigarettes	H[a]	H	8.96	52.1
221-27	Cloth and carpets	—	0	0.66	35.7
234	Brassieres, and so forth	—	0	H	0
243	Veneer	L[b]	L	—	H
251	Mattresses	—	0	H	H
26211-13, 26216	Writing paper	—	0	3.35	37.5
2643	Specialty bags	0.13	26.9	—	0
26214, 2631, 2653	Book paper, paperboard, and cartons	0.05	56.8	0.03	61.9
273, 276	Books and business forms	L	L	0.14	11.4
281	Industrial inorganic chemicals	0.15	80.9	0.97	38.9
282	Plastics and synthetics	0.89	112.7	0.57	193.5
2833	Bulk medicinals	—	0	1.00	22.4
28340-48	Pharmaceuticals, human	5.19	164.3	8.59	139.2
28349	Veterinary drugs	—	0	1.68	0.6
2841	Soaps and detergents	13.74	55.9	16.30	121.4
2844	Toiletries			12.43	55.3
2851	Paints	1.08	41.2	1.41	17.2

(continued)

259

TABLE C.1 (continued)

SIC	Industry	Brazil Advertising-to-Sales Ratio (percent)	Brazil Sales[c] ($ millions)	Mexico Advertising-to-Sales Ratio (percent)	Mexico Sales[c] ($ millions)
286	Industrial organic chemicals	0.06	34.9	0.02	36.7
2873-74	Fertilizers	0.53	45.9	0.00	6.8
2879	Agricultural chemicals, n.e.c.	—	0	0.35	16.4
289	Other chemicals	0.37	60.2	0.34	33.4
29111-16	Gasoline, and so forth	0.22	1,182.7	—	0
29117, 2992	Lubricating oils	1.61	57.5	1.52	20.9
2951	Paving mixtures	L	L	—	0
301	Tires	0.69	226.9	1.28	98.2
306	Other rubber products	—	0	0.77	5.9
307	Plastic products	25.53	15.4	5.40	17.7
313	Leather products	L	L	—	0
322	Glass products	L	L	0.00	9.9
324	Cement	0.45	18.1	—	0
3255	Clay refractories	—	0	0.45	2.4
3291	Abrasives	0.61	17.5	0.81	3.3
326, 3292-97	Other nonmetallic-minerals products	H	H	0.68	34.4
331-35	Primary metals	0.14	41.5	0.16	34.1
3423	Metal hand tools	—	0	1.50	2.4
3494	Valves	1.15	3.0	0.54	6.9
341, 343, 344, 348, 3496-99	Other fabricated metal products	0.38	22.9	0.16	59.0
352, 3531	Tractors and road-building machinery	0.38	87.2	0.66	22.5
3532-37	Other construction machinery	0.54	32.6	0.29	14.0
3546	Power hand tools	—	0	0.90	6.2
355	Special industrial machinery	1.09	4.2	0.11	5.7
3561	Pumps	—	0	0.33	16.3
3562-69	Other mechanical power transmission equipment, including bearings	1.09	12.8	0.60	5.3

SIC code	Industry				
3573	Electronic computers	0.42	126.8	0.40	47.0
3572, 3574, 3579	Office equipment	0.51	72.2	0.27	26.0
3585	Air-conditioning equipment	—	0	0.31	20.4
3519, 3586, 3589, 359	Other machinery, nonelectrical	0.53	9.8	0.00	2.3
363	Household appliances	3.05	50.9	1.08	102.8
3643	Wiring devices	—	0	0.99	2.5
361–62, 366, 3694	Other electrical equipment	0.17	56.8	0.30	44.6
365	Radio, television, and phonographs	2.99	158.3	2.26	115.6
367	Electronic components	0.00	14.3	0.00	9.3
3691, 3692	Batteries	n.a.	47.6	2.80	54.7
3711	Motor vehicles	1.06	750.1	0.31	547.8
3714	Motor vehicle parts, n.e.c.	0.35	55.3	0.27	46.0
3713, 3715, 374, 375	Other motor vehicle parts	0.46	6.5	0.23	8.9
382	Control and measuring devices	0.22	1.4	0.20	4.0
384	Medical instruments	4.71	55.0	5.97	17.5
3861	Photographic and photocopying equipment	2.13	54.7	2.14	72.6
394–96	Toys, zippers, and so forth	—	0	2.01	22.9
3999	Miscellaneous manufacturing, high, H	2.14	61.5	2.07	6.5
	Miscellaneous manufacturing, low, L	0.08	58.3	—	0

n.a. = not available.

[a] Industries with advertising-to-sales ratios above 2 percent, included in "miscellaneous" below.

[b] Industries with advertising-to-sales ratios below 2 percent, included in "miscellaneous" below.

[c] Sales of reporting firms.

Note: Table includes all active subsidiaries selling manufactures, whether a manufacturing or distribution operation. The advertising-to-sales ratios are weighted by the sales levels of the firms in that industry, classified according to their largest-selling five-digit SIC product. Affiliates not reporting their advertising expenditures are omitted, as are purely "service" sector operations (holding companies, hotels, repair shops, and so forth). A few adjustments were made. Each industry or product class listed in the table has at least three affiliates of U.S. MNCs selling at least one of its products in that category, with the unavoidable exception of two or three "other" industry categories.

Source: Special survey of the U.S. Senate Subcommittee on Multinational Corporations.

TABLE D.1

Average Research-and-Development Intensities of 175 U.S. Multinational Corporations and Their Brazilian and Mexican Manufacturing Subsidiaries, 1972

SIC	Primary Industry of U.S. MNC	Brazil		Mexico		United States	
		Number[a]	R&D/Sales[c] (percent)	Number[a]	R&D/Sales[c] (percent)	Number[b]	R&D/Sales[c] (percent)
20	Grain products (204)	4	0.08	7	0.01	5	0.92
	Beverages (208)	3	0.00	7	0.00	3	0.67
	Other food	1	L[e]	13	0.16	11	0.53
21	Tobacco	0	—	2	L	1	0.77
22	Textiles	1	L	4	0.00	4	0.44
23	Apparel	0	—	1	L	1	1.39
24	Wood	2	L	0	—	1	0.00
25	Furniture	0	—	1	L	1	n.a.
26	Paper	2	L	4	0.05	2	1.17
27	Printing	1	L	1	L	1	n.a.
28	Industrial chemicals (281)	16	0.56	23	0.65	10	3.33
	Drugs (283)	24	0.62	29	0.86	17	5.70
	Soaps and cosmetics (284)	3	0.07	4	0.39	4	1.92
	Other chemicals	6	0.10	9	0.29	5	2.37
29	Petroleum[d]	13	0.00	7	0.21	9	0.59
30	Rubber	4	0.00	4	0.05	4	2.29
31	Leather	0	—	0	—	0	—
32	Stone, clay, and glass	7	1.57	17	0.25	7	2.11
33	Primary metals	3	0.00	8	0.00	7	1.21
34	Fabricated metals	1	L	4	0.00	4	1.16

35	Industrial machinery	9	0.16	14	0.03	10	2.65
	Office and computer (357)	4	0.04	5	0.00	8	5.39
	Other nonelectrical	1	H	3	0.38	3	3.53
36	Household appliances (363)	4	1.10	6	0.00	5	1.29
	Other electrical	5	0.46	5	0.27	9	3.37
37	Motor vehicles (3711)	3	1.56	3	0.96	3	2.84
	Motor vehicle parts (3714)	6	0.63	16	0.20	10	1.49
38	Instruments	3	0.00	5	0.04	3	6.47
39	Miscellaneous and conglom- erates	8	2.26	16	0.24	12	1.49
	Total	134	0.52	218	0.31	158	2.46

[a]These are the Latin American manufacturing operations of U.S. MNCs producing products in the same industry group as the primary industry of the parent corporation and for which 1972 R&D data were given.

[b]These are all U.S. MNCs with at least one manufacturing subsidiary in Brazil or Mexico and for which data were available on their R&D in 1972.

[c]These data are the simple averages of the weighted R&D-to-sales ratios of each consolidated Latin American unit.

[d]Some of the subsidiaries in this industry group are involved in only marketing activities and none distills crude petroleum.

[e]L means there are fewer than three observations available for this industry in this country, but the average is no higher than that of the parent corporation's; H means there are fewer than three observations, but the average is higher than that of the parent corporation's.

[f]Although only 158 MNCs are   in this table, data from the subsidiaries of 17 other MNCs were also employed, for a total of 175. The total averages include data suppressed because of disclosure considerations.

Sources: U.S. data from Moody's COMPUSTAT; Latin American data computed from the special survey of the U.S. Senate Subcommittee on Multinational Corporations.

APPENDIX E
MATRICES OF
SIMPLE CORRELATION
COEFFICIENTS

The three matrixes of simple correlation coefficients given below are based on the 1972 samples. (See Appendix A.) For Brazil, 70 active, "full data" manufacturing affiliates are included; the Mexican basic sample consists of 125 such subsidiaries; the pooled data set comprises 206 affiliates. Only some of the most commonly used variables are included in the matrixes; for definitions of their symbols, see Table 5.4. The symbol WCR4 stands for the Weibull transformation of CR4 with the parameters as given in footnotes in Chapter 5.

TABLE E.1

Matrix of Simple Correlation Coefficients for the (n = 70) Brazilian Sample, 1972

	CR4	FRMS	AD	R&D	LEVER	K/S	GRO	EXP	IMP	SIZE	WCR4	
CR4	1.00	0.14	−0.49^a	0.01	−0.11	0.05	0.37^a	0.01	0.02	0.05	—	CR4
		1.00	−0.32^a	−0.12	0.06	0.20^c	0.08	0.11	0.06	0.09	0.18	FRMS
			1.00	−0.07	−0.00	−0.25^b	−0.19^c	−0.12	−0.14	−0.13	−0.62^a	AD
				1.00	−0.12	−0.06	−0.01	0.15	−0.04	0.22^c	0.04	R&D
					1.00	0.19	−0.25^b	−0.13	−0.14	0.07	−0.11	LEVER
						1.00	−0.06	0.11	0.10	0.29^b	0.20^c	K/S
							1.00	0.23^b	0.00	0.08	0.30^a	GRO
								1.00	−0.05	0.16	0.14	EXP
									1.00	−0.02	0.05	IMP
										1.00	0.10	SIZE
											1.00	WCR4

[a]Significance from zero at the 1 percent level.
[b]Significance from zero at the 5 percent level.
[c]Significance from zero at the 10 percent level.

TABLE E.2

Matrix of Simple Correlation Coefficients for the (n = 125) Mexican Sample, 1972

	CR4	FRMS	AD	R&D	LEVER	K/S	GRO	EXP	IMP	SIZE	WCR4	
	1.00	0.22^b	-0.03	-0.03	-0.15	-0.08	0.09	-0.33^a	0.13	-0.08	—	CR4
		1.00	-0.15	-0.12	0.01	0.31^a	0.07	-0.06	0.06	0.08	0.24^b	FRMS
			1.00	0.04	0.03	0.02	0.29^a	-0.03	-0.16^c	0.14	-0.04	AD
				1.00	-0.06	-0.04	-0.09	0.13	-0.07	0.04	-0.02	R&D
					1.00	-0.14	-0.20^b	0.05	-0.00	-0.09	-0.15	LEVER
						1.00	-0.14	0.09	0.01	0.18^c	-0.11	K/S
							1.00	-0.01	0.23^b	0.13	0.12	GRO
								1.00	-0.06	0.10	-0.48^a	EXP
									1.00	0.03	0.12	IMP
										1.00	-0.04	SIZE
											1.00	WCR4

[a]Significance from zero at the 1 percent level.
[b]Significance from zero at the 5 percent level.
[c]Significance from zero at the 10 percent level.

TABLE E.3

Matrix of Simple Correlation Coefficients for the (n = 206) Pooled Sample, 1972

	CR4	FRMS	AD	R&D	LEVER	K/S	GRO	EXP	IMP	SIZE	DCOUNTRY	WCR4
CR4	1.00	0.22b	-0.20b	-0.01	-0.11	-0.01	0.15c	-0.09	0.09	0.04	0.00	0.99
FRMS		1.00	-0.20b	-0.10	0.04	0.23b	0.10	-0.03	0.06	0.07	-0.07	0.20b
AD			1.00	0.02	0.02	-0.10	-0.20b	-0.05	-0.16c	0.05	-0.01	-0.17c
R&D				1.00	-0.05	-0.05	-0.01	0.12	-0.06	0.06	-0.08	-0.01
LEVER					1.00	0.02	-0.11	-0.00	-0.04	-0.07	-0.08	-0.10
K/S						1.00	-0.19b	0.07	0.10	0.26a	0.18b	-0.01
GRO							1.00	0.04	0.10	-0.06	-0.63a	0.15c
EXP								1.00	-0.07	0.09	-0.03	-0.07
IMP									1.00	0.03	0.06	0.10
SIZE										1.00	0.22b	0.04
DCOUNTRY											1.00	-0.00
WCR4												1.00

[a]Significance from zero at the 1 percent level.
[b]Significance from zero at the 5 percent level.
[c]Significance from zero at the 10 percent level.

These data on nominal and effective rates of protection are taken from Balassa et al. (1971). The Brazilian rates are based on tariffs in force in the year 1967 (Balassa et al. 1971: Table 6.6). The Mexican rates are based on differences between observed domestic and world prices due to import quotas and refer to the year 1960 (Balassa et al. 1971: Table 8.7). For both countries, net effective protection was calculated according to the "Corden" rather than the "Balassa" formula. See Appendix C for details on the Brazilian and Mexican industrial nomenclatures.

The regression estimates simply take the nonlinear formulations of Chapter 3 and append either the nominal rates of protection (symbolized by NOMINAL) or by the effective rates of protection (EFFECTIVE). The results are presented for Brazil in equations F3.1 to F3.4 and for Mexico in equations F3.5 to F3.8.

TABLE F.1

Import Protection for Brazil

SIC	Industry	Nominal Protection (percent)	Effective Protection (percent)
201–07, 209	Food products	10	23
208	Beverages	59	139
21	Tobacco	55	96
32	Nonmetallic minerals	22	22
33, 34	Metallurgy	17	19
35	Machinery, nonelectrical	17	16
36	Electrical equipment	37	73
37	Transport equipment	37	53
24	Wood products	7	10
25	Furniture	46	96
26	Paper	29	39
30	Rubber	55	89
31	Leather	44	62
281, 285–89	Chemicals	17	25
283	Pharmaceuticals	19	18
284	Soaps and cosmetics	69	3,210
282	Plastics	29	39
22	Textiles	57	130
23	Clothing	77	112
27	Printing and publishing	38	46
38, 39	Miscellaneous	37	51

TABLE F.2

Import Protection for Mexico

SIC	Industry	Nominal Protection (percent)	Effective Protection (percent)
201–02	Meat and dairy	47	166
204–05	Grain mill and bakery	4	–21
203, 206, 207, 209	Other processed food	21	16
208	Beverages	28	40
21	Tobacco	31	52
29	Petroleum	6	–8
324	Cement	–10	–2
323, 325–29	Other nonmetallic minerals, excluding glass	9	2
241, 242	Lumber	14	25
31	Leather	20	27
287	Agricultural chemicals	9	9
282	Synthetic fibers	22	16
33	Primary metals	24	61
321, 322	Glass	11	17
281, 286	Basic chemicals	23	42
220, 221, 228, 229	Cotton textiles	12	14
223	Wool textiles	43	85
222	Artificial-fiber textiles	56	164
224, 226, 227	Other textiles	25	46
243–49, 25	Wood products	18	45
26	Pulp and paper	35	75
30	Rubber	33	48
285, 288, 289	Other chemicals	26	63
34	Fabricated metals	31	44
2841	Soaps	10	1
283	Pharmaceuticals	12	9
2844	Cosmetics	22	58
225	Knitwear and hosiery	51	103
23	Clothing	10	3
27	Printing	13	8
38, 39	Other manufactures	32	64
363–69	Electrical appliances	45	54
375	and bicycles	25	48
371	Motor vehicles	52	212
35	Nonelectrical equipment	30	43
361–62	Electrical machinery	25	32
374	Railroad equipment	26	37

Regression Results for Brazil and Mexico, 1972

Brazil

(F.3.1)

EQUITYPROF = $-27.40 + 29.62$ WCR4 + 47.49 FRMS $- 31.82$ FRMS^3 + 2.06 AD
$(-1.33)^c$ $(3.22)^a$ ——————$(6.11)^a$——————— $(2.56)^a$

+ 2.29 R&D $- 0.63$ R&D^2 + 50.40 LEVER $- 47.46$ LEVER^3 $- 13.00$ K/S
——————(1.12)—————— ——————$(2.68)^c$———————— $(-2.05)^b$

$- 30.65$ EXP + 0.37 IMP + 18.69 DAFFEXP $- 2.72$ DAFFIMP
(-1.03) (0.03) $(3.47)^a$ (-0.62)

$- 3.45$ SIZE + 3.91 GRO $- 0.017$ GRO^3 $- 0.019$ NOMINAL + U$_i$.
$(-2.06)^b$ ——————(1.13)———————— (-0.84)

$R^2 = 0.528$ $F = 3.42^a$

(F.3.2)

ASSETPROF = $-31.42 + 15.78$ WCR4 + 18.40 FRMS $- 11.90$ FRMS^3 + 1.09 AD
$(-3.56)^a$ $(4.00)^a$ ——————$(5.24)^a$——————— $(3.15)^a$

+ 1.61 R&D $- 0.36$ R&D^2 + 44.24 LEVER $- 32.48$ LEVER^3 $- 7.79$ K/S
——————(1.29)—————— ——————$(14.12)^a$———————— $(-2.86)^a$

$- 16.54$ EXP + 0.59 IMP + 8.53 DAFFEXP $- 1.16$ DAFFIMP
(-1.29) (0.10) $(3.70)^a$ (-0.61)

$- 1.56$ SIZE + 3.72 GRO $- 0.014$ GRO^3 $- 0.014$ NOMINAL + U$_i$.
$(-2.18)^b$ $(3.28)^b$ $(-1.48)^c$

$R^2 = 0.658$ $F = 5.90^a$

(F.3.3)

EQUITYPROF = $-29.63 + 28.57$ WCR4 + 49.17 FRMS $- 34.29$ FRMS^3 + 2.18 AD
$(-1.44)^c$ $(3.09)^a$ ——————$(6.09)^a$——————— $(2.28)^a$

+ 2.54 R&D $- 0.66$ R&D^2 + 50.02 LEVER $- 49.94$ LEVER^3 $- 13.32$ K/S
——————(1.09)—————— ——————$(2.55)^c$———————— (-2.09)

$- 27.92$ EXP $- 2.31$ IMP + 18.45 DAFFEXP $- 2.30$ DAFFIMP $- 3.46$ SIZE
(-0.94) (0.16) $(3.39)^a$ (-0.51) $(-2.05)^b$

+ 4.29 GRO $- 0.018$ GRO^3 $- 0.001$ EFFECTIVE + U$_i$.
——————$(6.09)^a$———————— (-0.25)

$R^2 = 0.522$ $F = 3.34^a$

(F.3.4)

ASSETPROF = $-32.69 + 14.45$ WCR4 + 19.28 FRMS $- 13.40$ FRMS^3 + 1.02 AD
$(-3.64)^a$ $(3.60)^a$ ——————$(4.97)^b$——————— $(2.46)^a$

+ 2.01 R&D $- 0.41$ R&D^2 + 44.60 LEVER $- 34.85$ LEVER^3 $- 8.10$ K/S
——————(1.40)—————— ——————$(12.85)^a$———————— $(-2.92)^a$

$- 14.55$ EXP $- 0.96$ IMP + 8.52 DAFFEXP $- 1.04$ DAFFIMP
(-1.12) (-0.16) $(3.60)^a$ (-0.53)

$- 1.62$ SIZE $- 4.10$ GRO $- 0.015$ GRO^3 + 0.000 EFFECTIVE + U$_i$.
(-2.20) ——————$(3.42)^b$———————— (0.28)

$R^2 = 0.645$ $F = 5.55^a$

Mexico, 1972

(F.3.5)

$$EQUITYPROF = 22.71 + 28.97\ WCR4 + 2.21\ FRMS + 0.51\ AD$$
$$\quad\quad\quad\quad (1.21)\quad (2.22)^b \quad\quad (0.58) \quad\quad (1.59)^c$$

$$- 259.3\ LEVER + 407.4\ LEVER^2 - 194.9\ LEVER^3 - 19.56\ K/S$$
$$\underline{\quad\quad\quad\quad\quad\quad (7.07)^a \quad\quad\quad\quad\quad\quad} \quad (-4.06)$$

$$+ 2.56\ SIZE + 0.37\ SUPPLY + 20.34\ EXP + 4.61\ IMP$$
$$(2.87)^a \quad\quad (3.88)^a \quad\quad\quad\quad (1.84)^b \quad\quad (0.55)$$

$$- 6.91\ AFFEXP + 6.44\ AFFIMP + 0.58\ GRO - 0.0016\ GRO^3$$
$$(-2.16)^b \quad\quad\quad (1.40)^c \quad\quad\quad\quad\underline{\quad (2.39)^c \quad}$$

$$- 0.06\ NOMINAL + U_i.$$
$$(-0.69)$$

$R^2 = 0.40$ $F = 4.52^a$

(F.3.6)

$$ASSETPROF = -15.01 + 9.54\ WCR4 + 1.74\ FRMS + 0.19\ AD$$
$$\quad\quad\quad\quad (1.50)^c (1.37)^c \quad\quad (0.85) \quad\quad\quad (1.13)$$

$$-36.65\ LEVER + 71.28\ LEVER^2 - 27.20\ LEVER^3 - 9.78\ K/S$$
$$\underline{\quad\quad\quad\quad\quad\quad (11.47)^a \quad\quad\quad\quad\quad\quad} \quad (-3.79)^a$$

$$+ 1.35\ SIZE + 0.18\ SUPPLY + 12.05\ EXP + 0.49\ IMP - 3.65\ AFFEXP$$
$$(2.84)^a \quad\quad (3.44)^a \quad\quad\quad\quad (2.04)^b \quad\quad (0.11) \quad\quad (-2.13)^b$$

$$+ 3.44\ AFFIMP + 0.99\ GRO - 0.0017\ GRO^3 - 0.00\ NOMINAL + U_i.$$
$$(1.39)^c \quad\quad\quad\underline{\quad (2.85)^c \quad}\quad (-0.11)$$

$R^2 = 0.46$ $F = 5.67^a$

(F.3.7)

$$EQUITYPROF = 21.46 + 30.06\ WCR4 + 2.08\ FRMS + 0.43\ AD$$
$$\quad\quad\quad\quad (1.15)\quad (2.32)^b \quad\quad (0.55) \quad\quad (1.33)^c$$

$$- 259.2\ LEVER + 405.8\ LEVER^2 - 193.3\ LEVER^3 - 19.79\ K/S$$
$$\underline{\quad\quad\quad\quad\quad\quad (7.27)^a \quad\quad\quad\quad\quad\quad} \quad (-4.12)$$

$$+ 2.64\ SIZE + 0.38\ SUPPLY + 19.10\ EXP + 3.76\ IMP - 6.42\ AFFEXP$$
$$(3.00)^a \quad\quad (3.95)^a \quad\quad\quad\quad (1.73)^b \quad\quad (0.45) \quad\quad (-1.99)^b$$

$$+ 6.41\ AFFIMP + 0.61\ GRO - 0.0017\ GRO^3 - 0.03\ EFFECTIVE + U_i.$$
$$(1.40)^c \quad\quad\quad\underline{\quad (2.94)^c \quad}\quad (-1.21)$$

$R^2 = 0.41$ $F = 4.62^a$

(F.3.8)

$$ASSETPROF = -15.22 + 9.88\ WCR4 + 1.69\ FRMS + 0.18\ AD$$
$$\quad\quad\quad\quad (-1.52)^c (1.42)^c \quad\quad (0.83) \quad\quad\quad (1.03)$$

$$- 37.02\ LEVER + 71.62\ LEVER^2 - 27.19\ LEVER^3 - 9.82\ K/S$$
$$\underline{\quad\quad\quad\quad\quad\quad (11.90)^a \quad\quad\quad\quad\quad\quad} \quad (-3.81)^a$$

$$+ 1.39\ SIZE + 0.18\ SUPPLY + 11.81\ EXP + 0.28\ IMP - 3.54\ AFFEXP$$
$$(2.93)^a \quad\quad (3.47)^a \quad\quad\quad\quad (1.99)^b \quad\quad (0.06) \quad\quad (-2.04)^b$$

$$+ 3.41\ AFFIMP + 0.99\ GRO - 0.0017\ GRO^3 - 0.00\ EFFECTIVE + U_i.$$
$$(1.38)^c \quad\quad\quad\underline{\quad (3.14)^b \quad}\quad (-0.40)$$

$R^2 = 0.46$ $F = 5.68^a$

The regression results reported here extend the tests performed in Chapter 5 using data from both Brazil and Mexico (see equations 5.19.1 through 5.19.3). In designing the regression equations used for this appendix, an F test was used to determine the significance of adding a second- or third-degree term for FRMS, R&D, LEVER, and GRO—terms that had been justified when only the individual country data were employed. However, these tests indicated that in no case was significant improvement in fit obtained by such additional terms. However, replacing the straight-line CR4 term with a Weibull function did prove useful. A wide range of parametric values was experimented with, but a function of the following form was discovered to fit best:

$$WCR4 = 1 - \exp\left(-\left[\frac{CR4}{70}\right]^3\right)$$

In addition to this substitution, three more terms were included: AFFEXP, AFFIMP, and SUPPLY. As before, the "t" statistic is given in parentheses below the relevant coefficient, and statistical significance at the 1, 5, and 10 percent levels is again represented by a, b, and c superscripts, respectively. Leverage terms are omitted from the equity-capital rate-of-return regressions.

(G.1)

$EQUITYPROF = 6.20 + 9.12 \ WCR4 + 8.87 \ FRMS + 0.45 \ AD + 0.51 \ R\&D + 1.27 \ SIZE$
$(0.82) \ (3.00)^a \qquad (2.44)^a \qquad (1.40)^c \quad (1.49)^c \qquad (1.55)^c$

$-21.88 \ K/S + 15.94 \ EXP - 4.38 \ IMP - 2.73 \ AFFEXP + 2.99 \ AFFIMP$
$(-5.60)^a \quad (1.37)^c \quad (-0.56) \qquad (0.94) \qquad (0.79)$

$+ 0.09 \ SUPPLY - 0.59 \ GRO + 2.28 \ DCOUNTRY + U_i.$
$(1.30)^c \qquad (-1.90)^b \qquad (0.83)$

$R^2 = 0.24 \qquad F = 4.76^a \qquad n = 206$

(G.2)

$ASSETPROF = -6.23 + 4.06 \ WCR4 + 4.16 \ FRMS + 0.18 \ AD + 0.06 \ R\&D + 0.78 \ SIZE$
$(-1.52)^c(2.79)^a \qquad (2.40)^a \qquad (1.18) \qquad (0.34) \qquad (1.99)^b$

$-11.90 \ K/S + 17.34 \ LEVER - 2.80 \ LEVER^3 + 9.48 \ EXP - 3.73 \ IMP$
$(-6.83)^a \ \text{———} (13.52)^a \text{———} \quad (1.71)^b \quad (-1.00)$

$-0.91 \ AFFEXP + 2.16 \ AFFIMP + 0.04 \ SUPPLY - 0.24 \ GRO$
$(-0.64) \qquad (1.20) \qquad (1.25) \qquad (-1.57)^c$

$+ 1.22 \ DCOUNTRY + U_i.$
(0.93)

$R^2 = 0.37 \qquad F = 7.46 \qquad n = 206$

273

(G.3)

$$BROADEQUITY = 5.50 + 9.97 \ WCR4 + 9.11 \ FRMS + 1.20 \ AD + 0.42 \ R\&D + 2.03 \ SIZE$$
$$(0.62) \quad (2.77)^a \qquad (2.12)^b \qquad (3.17)^a \quad (1.03) \qquad (2.10)^b$$

$$-25.26 \ K/S + 12.20 \ EXP - 2.36 \ IMP - 2.83 \ AFFEXP + 5.20 \ AFFIMP$$
$$(-5.86)^a \qquad (0.89) \qquad (-.25) \qquad (-0.82) \qquad (1.16)$$

$$+ 0.13 \ SUPPLY - 0.71 \ GRO - 2.97 \ DCOUNTRY + U_i.$$
$$(1.54)^c \qquad (-1.94)^b \qquad (-0.92)$$

$$R^2 = 0.24 \qquad F = 4.78^a \qquad n = 206$$

In addition to the more complex functional specifications above, the linear regressions with the pooled data (equations 5.19.1 to 5.19.3) were examined for graphic evidence of heteroskedasticity. There was some evidence in the pattern of residual plots to suggest that the variability of profits increased with height of predicted profits and with total asset size. Therefore, regressions were run weighting all observations by functions of their total assets and reexamining their patterns of residual plots. Weighting by the square root of assets resulted in markedly higher fits (R^2 of 0.53 to 0.60) and an increase in the "t" statistics of all the structural variables except CR4 (though it remained highly significant in all four equations), but this particular weight seemed to accentuate the flared pattern characteristic of heteroskedastic models. Weighting by the eighth root of total assets produced estimates much closer to the unweighted pooled regressions, as would be expected; though the overall fit improved considerably and the statistical strength of the CR4 term rose in all cases, the pattern of residuals was little altered. Some noticeable amelioration in the scatter did, however, result when the fourth root of total assets was the chosen weight. In general, the regression estimates under the fourth-root-of-total-assets weighting scheme improved the R^2 by 8 to 12 percentage points and increased the statistical level of confidence of all the structural terms save CR4. I show these last results in equations G.4 to G.6, below:

(G.4)

$$EQUITYPROF = 15.18 + 0.09 \ CR4 + 9.07 \ FRMS + 0.41 \ AD + 0.40 \ R\&D + 3.60 \ LEVER$$
$$(0.64) \quad (2.26)^b \qquad (2.63)^a \qquad (1.43)^c \quad (1.16) \qquad (0.79)$$

$$- 18.44 \ K/S + 1.22 \ SIZE + 11.35 \ EXP - 2.06 \ IMP - 0.47 \ GRO$$
$$(-6.13)^a \qquad (2.28)^b \qquad (1.16) \qquad (-0.29) \qquad (-1.68)^b$$

$$+ 2.81 \ DCOUNTRY + U_i.$$
$$(1.11)$$

$$R^2 = 0.35 \qquad F = 9.58^a$$

(G.5)

$$ASSETPROF = -13.18 + 0.04 \ CR4 + 4.60 \ FRMS + 0.15 \ AD + 0.06 \ R\&D + 15.50 \ LEVER$$
$$(-1.13) \quad (2.29)^b \qquad (2.73)^a \qquad (1.06) \quad (0.35) \qquad (6.98)^a$$

$$-11.43 \ K/S + 0.18 \ SIZE + 7.84 \ EXP - 3.51 \ IMP - 0.20 \ GRO$$
$$(-7.78) \qquad (0.68) \qquad (1.64) \qquad (-1.01) \qquad (-1.47)^c$$

$$+ 1.72 \text{ DCOUNTRY} + U_i.$$
$$(1.39)^c$$

$$R^2 = 0.46 \qquad F = 14.88^a$$

$$(G.6)$$

$$\text{BROADEQUITY} = 23.62 + 0.10 \text{ CR4} + 8.70 \text{ FRMS} + 1.35 \text{ AD} + 0.29 \text{ R\&D} + 4.70 \text{ LEVER}$$
$$(0.81) \ (2.11)^b \qquad (2.07)^b \qquad (3.89)^a \quad (0.70) \qquad (0.85)$$

$$-19.40 \text{ K/S} + 1.45 \text{ SIZE} + 6.90 \text{ EXP} - 0.02 \text{ IMP} - 0.46 \text{ GRO}$$
$$(-5.29)^a \qquad (2.22)^b \qquad (0.58) \qquad (-0.00) \qquad (-1.36)^c$$

$$-1.33 \text{ DCOUNTRY} + U_i.$$
$$(-0.43)$$

$$R^2 = 0.33 \qquad F = 8.87^a$$

As I reported, the size range of U.S. MNCs' affiliates included in the pooled sample is enormous: from \$100,000 to \$294.3 million in 1972 total assets. In the belief that the very smallest of these companies may seriously distort the regression estimates, the linear model was rerun, eliminating those 18 affiliates with total assets of less than \$1 million. The general effect was to increase the closeness of fit and to lower slightly the impact of the structural variables on profit performance. An example of one of the regression estimates is provided below, in equation G.7 (corresponding to equation 5.19.3 in the text).

$$(G.7)$$

$$\text{BROADEQUITY} = 8.73 + 0.11 \text{ CR4} + 6.78 \text{ FRMS} + 1.17 \text{ AD} + 0.37 \text{ R\&D} + 1.37 \text{ LEVER}$$
$$(0.82) \ (2.26)^b \qquad (1.54)^c \qquad (3.02)^a \quad (0.94) \qquad (0.24)$$

$$-22.66 \text{ K/S} + 1.60 \text{ SIZE} + 9.90 \text{ EXP} - 2.76 \text{ IMP} - 0.77 \text{ GRO}$$
$$(-5.34) \qquad (1.58)^c \qquad (0.80) \qquad (-0.28) \qquad (-2.07)^b$$

$$-3.06 \text{ DCOUNTRY} + U_i.$$
$$(-0.92)$$

$$R^2 = 0.24 \qquad F = 5.07^a$$

TABLE G.1

Basic Descriptive Statistics of Selected Variables Used in the Profit Performance–Market Structure Re–gressions, Pooled Data, 1972

Variable	Symbol	Mean	Standard Deviation
Four-firm, minimum concentration ratio, weighted by product sales, percent	CR4	68.9	25.6
Relative firm market share, weighted	FRMS	0.410	0.275
Market advertising-to-sales ratio, percent	AD	1.95	3.15
Research-and-development intensity, percent	R&D	0.84	2.77
"Leverage," the equity-to-assets ratio	LEVER	0.536	0.202
Net fixed assets-to-sales ratio	K/S	0.308	0.287
Total asset size, in natural log units	SIZE	8.64	1.38
Sales growth per year of firm's major–industry growth, 1966– 70 or 1962–70, percent	GRO	11.37	4.24
Exports-to-sales ratio	EXP	0.031	0.089
Imports-to-sales ratio	IMP	0.072	0.128
Country of location, dummy variable	DCOUNTRY	0.345	0.475
Net income/stockholders' equity, percent	EQUITYPROF	15.24	14.71
Net income/total assets, percent	ASSETPROF	8.13	7.61
Net income plus technology payments/equity, percent	BROADEQUITY	19.39	17.39
Net income plus technology payments/assets, percent	BROADASSET	10.37	9.31

ABBREVIATIONS USED

AER	American Economic Review
GPO	U.S. Government Printing Office
J.	Journal
JEL	Journal of Economic Literature
JPE	Journal of Political Economy
NBER	National Bureau of Economic Research
QJE	Quarterly Journal of Economics
RES	Review of Economics and Statistics
UN	United Nations
U.P.	University Press

Adler, Michael, and Guy V. G. Stevens
  1974   The Trade Effects of Direct Investment. J. of Finance 29:
         655-76.
Aguilar, Enrique M.
  1975   The Transfer of Technology in Mexico and the Multinational
         Corporation. Queretaro, Mexico: CONACYT-CIDE Sympo-
         sium on Transnational Enterprises and the Host Countries.
Aharoni, Yair
  1966   The Foreign Investment Decision Process. Boston: Har-
         vard Graduate School of Business Administration.
  1971   On the Definition of a Multinational Corporation. Quarterly
         Review of Economics and Business, Autumn: 27-37.
Aliber, Robert Z.
  1970   A Theory of Direct Foreign Investment. In The Interna-
         tional Corporations. Ed. Charles P. Kindleberger. Cam-
         bridge, Mass.: MIT Press.
  1972   Comments on "The Internationalization of Capital." J. of
         Economic Issues 6: 112-15.
Andean Group.
  1970   Common Treatment on Foreign Capital, Trademarks,
         Patents, Licensing Agreements, and Royalties (Decision 24).
         Lima: Comision del Acuerdo de Cartegena.
Antitrust and Monopoly Subcommittee, Committee on the Judiciary,
U.S. Senate.
  1973   International Aspects of Antitrust. Washington, D.C.: U.S.
         GPO.

Apter, David E., and Louis Wolf Goodman, eds.
  1976   The Multinational Corporation and Social Change. New
          York: Praeger.
Asch, Peter, and J. J. Seneca
  1976   Is Collusion Profitable? RES 58: 1-12.
Bacha, Edmar L.
  1976   Issues and Evidence on Recent Brazilian Economic Growth,
          Development Discussion Paper No. 12. Cambridge, Mass.:
          Harvard Institute for International Development.
Baer, Werner
  1965   Industrialization and Economic Development in Brazil.
          Homewood: Irwin.
Bain, Joe S.
  1951   Relation of Profit Rate to Industry Concentration: Ameri-
          can Manufacturing, 1936-1940. QUE 65: 293-324.
  1954   Economies of Scale, Concentration, and the Condition of
          Entry in Twenty Manufacturing Industries. AER 44: 15-39.
  1960   Price Leaders, Barometers, and Kinks. J. of Business
          33: 193-203.
  1966   International Differences in Industrial Structure. New
          Haven: Yale U.P.
  1968   Industrial Organization. New York: Wiley.
  1970a   Changes in Concentration in Manufacturing Industries in
          the United States, 1954-1966. RES 52: 411-16.
  1970b   The Comparative Stability of Market Structures. In Indus-
          trial Organization and Economic Development. Ed. Jesse
          Markham and Gustav Papanek. Boston: Houghton Mifflin.
Balassa, Bela, et al.
  1971   The Structure of Protection in Developing Countries. Bal-
          timore: Johns Hopkins Press.
Baldwin, Robert E.
  1970   The International Firm and Efficient Economic Allocation:
          International Trade in Inputs and Outputs. AER Proceed-
          ings 60: 435-40.
Ball, George W.
  1970   Cosmocorp: The Importance of Being Stateless. In World
          Business: Promise and Problems. Ed. Courtney C. Brown.
          New York: Macmillan.
Baran, Paul
  1957   The Political Economy of Growth. New York: Monthly
          Review Press.
Baranson, Jack
  1970   Technology Transfer Through the International Firm. AER
          Proceedings 60: 435-40.

Barnet, Richard J., and Ronald E. Müller
  1974   Global Reach: The Power of the International Corporations.
         New York: Simon & Schuster.
Basche, James R.
  1970   Measuring Profitability of Foreign Operations. New York:
         Conference Board.
Baumol, William J.
  1959   Business Behavior, Value, and Growth. New York: Mac-
         millan.
Behrman, Jack N.
  1962a Foreign Associates and Their Financing. In U.S. Private
         and Government Investment Abroad. Ed. Raymond F.
         Mikesell. Eugene: University of Oregon Books.
  1962b Foreign Investment and the Transfer of Knowledge and
         Skills. In ibid.
  1969   Some Patterns in the Rise of the Multinational Enterprise.
         Chapel Hill: University of North Carolina Press.
  1972   International Disinvestment: Panacea or Pitfall? In The
         Multinational Enterprise in Transition. Ed. A. Kapoor and
         Phillip Grub. Princeton, N.J.: Darwin Press.
  1974a Decision Criteria for Foreign Direct Investment in Latin
         America. New York: Council of the Americas.
  1974b Conflicting Constraints on the Multinational Enterprise:
         Potential for Resolution. New York: Council of the Ameri-
         cas.
Behrman, Jack N., and Harvey W. Wallender
  1976   Transfers of Manufacturing Technology within Multinational
         Enterprises. Cambridge, Mass.: Ballinger.
Belli, R. David, and Leo C. Maley
  1974   Sales by Majority-Owned Foreign Affiliates of U.S. Com-
         panies, 1966-72. Survey of Current Business 54, no. 8:
         10-24.
Benoit, Emile
  1972   Comment. J. of Economic Issues 6: 116-23.
Bergsman, Joel
  1970   Brazil: Industrialization and Trade Policies. London: Ox-
         ford U.P.
Bergsten, C. Fred, Thomas Horst, and Thomas Moran
  1977   American Multinationals and American Interests. Wash-
         ington, D.C.: Brookings (forthcoming).
Bergsten, C. Fred, and Lawrence B. Krause, eds.
  1975   World Politics and International Economics. Washington,
         D.C.: Brookings Institution.

Bertin, Gilles Y., ed.
    1973a La croissance de la grande firme multinationale, Colloques
           Internationaux No. 549. Paris: Centre Nationale de la
           Recherche Scientifique.
    1973b Multinational Growth, Oligopoly, and Competition. In ibid.
Bhagwati, Jagdish, et al., eds.
    1971 Trade, Balance of Payments, and Growth. North-Holland.
Blair, John M.
    1972 Economic Concentration: Structure, Behavior, and Public
          Policy. New York: Harcourt Brace Jovanovich.
    1976 The Control of Oil. New York: Pantheon.
Blalock, Hubert M.
    1961 Causal Inferences in Nonexperimental Research. New York:
          Norton.
Bloch, Harry
    1971 Advertising, Competition, and Market Behavior. Ph.D.
          dissertation, University of Chicago.
Bos, H. C., Martin Sanders, and Carlo Secchi
    1974 Private Foreign Investment in Developing Countries. Dor-
          drecht, Netherlands: Reidel.
Branch, Ben
    1974 Research and Development Activity and Profitability: A
          Distributed Lag Analysis. JPE 82: 999-1012.
Brooke, Michael A., and H. Lee Remmers
    1970 The Strategy of Multinational Enterprise. London: Long-
          mans.
Brown, Courtney C., ed.
    1970 World Business: Promise and Problems. New York: Mac-
          millan.
Brozen, Yale
    1974 Entry Barriers, Advertising, and Product Differentiation.
          In Industrial Concentration: The New Learning. Ed. Har-
          vey J. Goldschmidt. Boston: Little, Brown.
Business International
    1963 Foreign Branch vs. Subsidiary, Management Monograph
          No. 13. New York: Business International.
Caves, Richard E.
    1971 International Corporations: The Industrial Economics of
          Foreign Investment. Economica 38: 1-27.
    1974a Industrial Organization. In Economic Analysis and the
           Multinational Enterprise. Ed. John H. Dunning. London:
           Allen & Unwin.
    1974b Causes of Direct Investment: Foreign Firms' Shares in
           Canadian and United Kingdom Manufacturing Industries.
           RES 56: 279-93.

1974c   Multinational Firms, Competition, and Productivity in
          Host-Country Markets. Economica 41: 176-93.
Caves, Richard E., J. Khalilzadeh-Shirazi, and M. E. Porter
  1975   Scale Economies in Statistical Analyses of Market Power.
          RES 57: 133-40.
Caves, Richard E., and Masu Uekusa
  1976   Industrial Organization in Japan. Washington, D.C.:
          Brookings Institution.
Chamberlin, Edward
  1962   The Theory of Monopolistic Competition. Cambridge,
          Mass.: Harvard U.P.
Chipman, J.
  1971   International Trade with Capital Mobility. In Trade, Bal-
          ance of Payments, and Growth. Ed. Jagdish Bhagwati,
          et al. North-Holland.
Church, Frank
  1973   Multinational Corporations: Will They Usher in a New
          World Order? Center Magazine, May-June: 15-18.
Clevenger, Thomas S., and Gerald R. Campbell
  1977   Vertical Organization: A Neglected Element in Market
          Structure-Profit Models. Industrial Organization Review
          (forthcoming).
Cohen, Benjamin I.
  1973   Comparative Behavior of Foreign and Domestic Export
          Firms in a Developing Country. RES 55: 190-97.
  1975   Multinational Firms and Asian Exports. New Haven, Conn.:
          Yale U.P.
Collins, Norman R., and Lee E. Preston
  1969   Price-Cost Margins and Industry Structure. RES 51: 271-86.
Comanor, William S.
  1967   Market Structure, Product Differentiation, and Industrial
          Research. QJE 81: 639-57.
  1971   Comments. In Frontiers of Quantitative Economics. Ed.
          Michael D. Intrilligator. Amsterdam: North-Holland.
Comanor, William S., and Thomas A. Wilson
  1974   Advertising and Market Power. Cambridge, Mass.: Har-
          vard U.P.
Connor, John M.
  1976   A Quantitative Analysis of the Market Power of United
          States' Multinational Corporations in Brazil and Mexico.
          Ph.D. dissertation, University of Wisconsin at Madison.
Connor, John M., and Willard F. Mueller
  1977   Market Power and Profitability of Multinational Corpora-
          tions in Brazil and Mexico, a report to the U.S. Senate Sub-
          committee on Multinational Corporations. Washington,
          D.C.: GPO.

Cook, Hugh
  1974   Big Food Processors in Rural Development, Inaugural Lecture Series No. 11. Ile-Ife, Nigeria: University of Ife Press.
Corden, W. M.
  1967   Protection and Foreign Investment. Economic Record 43: 209-32.
  1974   The Theory of International Trade. In Economic Analysis and the Multinational Enterprise. Ed. John H. Dunning. London: Allen & Unwin.
CTU (UN Commission on Transnational Corporations)
  1976   Research on Transnational Corporations (E/C.10/12). New York: UN.
Dalton, James A., and David W. Penn
  1971   The Quality of Data as a Factor in Analysis of Structure-Performance Relationships. Washington, D.C.: Federal Trade Commission.
DeJong, Frits J.
  1973   Multinational Enterprises and the Market Form. In La croissance de la grande firme multinationale, Colloques Internationaux No. 549. Ed. Gilles Y. Bertin. Paris: Centre Nationale de la Recherche Scientifique.
Demsetz, Harold
  1974   Two Systems of Belief about Monopoly. In Industrial Concentration: The New Learning. Ed. Harvey J. Goldschmidt. Boston: Little, Brown.
de Vries, Henry P.
  1970   Legal Aspects of World Business. In World Business: Promise and Problems. Ed. Courtney C. Brown. New York: Macmillan.
Diaz-Alejandro, Carlos F.
  1970   Foreign Direct Investment in Latin America. In The International Corporations. Ed. Charles P. Kindleberger. Cambridge, Mass.: MIT Press.
  1975   North-South Relations: The Economic Component. In World Politics and International Economics. Ed. C. Fred Bergsten and Lawrence B. Krause. Washington, D.C.: Brookings Institution.
DOC (See U.S. Department of Commerce)
Draper, Norman, and Harry Smith
  1966   Applied Regression Analysis. New York: Wiley.
Duerr, Michael G.
  1970   R&D in the Multinational Company. New York: Conference Board.

Duerr, Michael G., and James Greene
  1968   Foreign Nationals in International Management. New York:
          Conference Board.
Dunning, John H.
  1970   Studies in International Investment. London: Allen & Un-
          win.
  1971a   The Multinational Enterprise. London: Allen & Unwin.
  1971b   The Multinational Enterprise: The Background. In ibid.
  1973   The Determinants of International Production. In La crois-
          sance de la grande firme multinationale, Colloques Inter-
          nationaux No. 549. Ed. Gilles Y. Bertin. Paris: Centre
          Nationale de la Recherche Scientifique.
  1974a   Economic Analysis and the Multinational Enterprise. Lon-
          don: Allen & Unwin.
  1974b   The Distinctive Nature of the Multinational Enterprise. In
          ibid.
  1974c   Conclusions. In ibid.
  1974d   Multinational Enterprises, Market Structure, and Industrial
          Policy. J. World Trade Law 8: 575-613.
Dunning, John H., and Martin Gilman
  1975   Alternative Policy Prescriptions and the Multinational En-
          terprise. Queretaro, Mexico: CONACYT-CIDE Symposium
          on Transnational Enterprises and the Host Countries.
ECAT (Emergency Committee for American Trade)
  1972   The Role of the Multinational Corporation in the United
          States and World Economies.
ECLA (UN Commission for Latin America)
  1969   Second United Nations Development Decade: Latin Ameri-
          ca's Foreign Trade Policy. New York: UN.
ECOSOC (UN Economic and Social Council)
  1974   Impact of Multinational Corporations on the Development
          Process and on International Relations. New York: UN.
Edwards, Corwin D.
  1951   Public Policy and Business Size. J. of Business of the
          University of Chicago 24: 280-92.
  1970   The World of Antitrust. In World Business: Promise and
          Problems. Ed. Courtney C. Brown. New York: Macmil-
          lan.
Esposito, Louis, and Frances Esposito
  1971   Foreign Competition and Domestic Industry Profitability.
          RES 53: 343-53.
Fajnzylber, Fernando
  1970   Sistema Industrial y Exportacion de Manufacturas. Rio de
          Janeiro: ECLA-UN.

Fajnzylber, Fernando, and Trinidad Martinex Tarrago
   1975   Transnational Enterprises, Their Global Expansion and Their
          Influence on Mexican Industry (2 vols). Queretaro, Mexico:
          CONACYT-CIDE Symposium on Transnational Firms and
          the Host Countries.
Fayerweather, John
   1972   Nationalism and the Multinational Firm. In The Multina-
          tional Enterprise in Transition. Ed. A. Kapoor and Phillip
          Grub. Princeton, N.J.: Darwin Press.
Finance Committee, U.S. Senate
   1973a Implications of Multinational Firms for World Trade and
          Investment and for U.S. Trade and Labor. Washington,
          D.C.: GPO.
   1973b Legal Implications of Multinational Corporations. Washing-
          ton, D.C.: GPO.
Fisher, R. A.
   1948   Statistical Methods for Research Workers. New York:
          Hafner.
Fishlow, Albert
   1973   Some Reflections on Post-1964 Brazilian Economic Policy.
          In Authoritarian Brazil. Ed. Alfred Stephan. New Haven,
          Conn.: Yale University Press.
Foreign Economic Policy Subcommittee, Joint Economic Committee,
U.S. Congress
   1970   Hearings. Washington, D.C.: GPO.
Frank, A. G.
   1969   Capitalism and Underdevelopment in Latin America. New
          York: Monthly Review Press.
Freidlin, J. N., and L. A. Lupo
   1974   U.S. Direct Investment Abroad in 1973. Survey of Current
          Business 54, no. 8: 10-24.
FTC (Federal Trade Commission)
   1966   Economic Report on the Structure and Competitive Behavior
          of Food Retailing. Washington, D.C.: GPO.
   1969   Economic Report on the Influence of Market Structure on
          the Profit Performance of Food Manufacturing Companies.
          Washington, D.C.: GPO.
   1974   Statistical Report on Mergers and Acquisitions. Washing-
          ton, D.C.: GPO.
Fuchs, Victor R., ed.
   1972   Policy Issues and Research Opportunities in Industrial Or-
          ganization. New York: NBER.
Furtado, Celso
   1965   Diagnosis of the Brazilian Crisis. Berkeley: University
          of California Press.

1970   Obstacles to Development in Latin America. Garden City,
        N.Y.: Anchor.
Gale, Bradley T.
1972   Market Share and Rate of Return. RES 54: 412-23.
Gambeles, G.
1969   Structural Determinants of Profit Performance in the United
        States Manufacturing Industries 1947-1967. Ph.D. disser-
        tation, University of Maryland.
Gaston, J. Frank
1973   Why Industry Invests Abroad. In Office of International
        Finance and Investment, U.S. Department of Commerce.
        The Multinational Corporation. Washington, D.C.: GPO.
Goldschmidt, Harvey J.
1974   Industrial Concentration: The New Learning. Boston:
        Little, Brown.
Goldsmith, Raymond W.
1969   Financial Structure and Development. New Haven, Conn.:
        Yale U.P.
Gordon, Lincoln, and Englebert Grommers
1962   United States Manufacturing Investment in Brazil 1946-
        1960. Boston: Graduate School of Business, Harvard Uni-
        versity.
Gorecki, Paul K.
1977   The Determinants of Entry by Domestic and Foreign Enter-
        prises in Canadian Manufacturing Industries. RES 59:
        485-88.
Gouveneur, J.
1971   Productivity and Factor Proportions in Less Developed
        Countries. London: Oxford U.P.
Grabowski, Henry G.
1968   The Determinants of Industrial Research and Development.
        JPE 76: 292-306.
Grabowski, Henry G., and Nevins Baxter
1973   Rivalry in Industry Research and Development. J. of In-
        dustrial Economics 21: 209-35.
Greene, James, and Michael G. Duerr
1970   Intercompany Transactions in the Multinational Firm. New
        York: Conference Board.
Greenhill, Colin
1975   Restrictive Business Practices in the Context of the Opera-
        tions of the Transnational Corporations. Queretaro, Mexi-
        co: CONACYT-CIDE Symposium on Transnational Enter-
        prises and the Host Countries.
Greer, Douglas
1971   Advertising and Market Concentration. Southern Economic
        J. 38: 19-32.

Griffen, Keith
1977   Multinational Corporations and Basic Needs Development. Development and Change 8: 61–76.
Grubel, Herbert G.
1974   Taxation and the Rates of Return from Some U.S. Asset Holdings Abroad, 1960–1969. JPE 82: 469–88.
Gruber, W., D. Mehta, and R. Vernon
1967   The R&D Factor in International Trade and International Investment of United States Industries. JPE 75: 20–37.
Günther, Eberhard
1975   Multinational Enterprises and Competition. Queretaro, Mexico: CONACYT-CIDE Symposium on Transnational Enterprises and the Host Countries.
Hall, Marshall, and Leonard Weiss
1967   Firm Size and Profitability. RES 49: 423–40.
Hansen, Roger D.
1971   The Politics of Mexican Development. Baltimore: Johns Hopkins U.P.
Hastings, N. A. J., and J. B. Peacock
1975   Statistical Distributions. New York: Halsted Press.
Heggestad, Arnold A., and Stephen A. Rhoades
1976   Concentration and Firm Stability in Commercial Banking. RES 58: 443–52.
Helleiner, G. K.
1973   Manufactured Exports from Less-Developed Countries and Multinational Firms. Economic J. 83: 21–47.
Heller, Robert
1973   International Trade. Englewood Cliffs, N.J.: Prentice-Hall.
Helmberger, Peter
1976   What Do Statistical Structure–Profit Relationships Show? Unpublished manuscript.
Hirsch, Seev, and Lev Hirsch
1971   Sales Stabilization through Export Diversification. RES 53: 270–77.
1973   Multinational Corporations: How Different Are They? In La croissance de la grande firme multinationale, Colloques Internationaux No. 549. Ed. Gilles Y. Bertin. Paris: Centre Nationale de la Recherche Scientifique.
Hirshman, Albert O.
1969   How to Divest in Latin America and Why, Essays in International Finance No. 76. Princeton, N.J.: Department of Economics, Princeton University.

Horst, Thomas
  1971   The Theory of the Multinational Firm: Optimal Behavior
          under Different Tariff and Tax Rates. JPE 79: 1059-72.
  1972a   Firm and Industry Determinants of the Decision to Invest
          Abroad: An Empirical Study. RES 54: 258-66.
  1972b   The Industrial Composition of U.S. Exports and Subsidiary
          Sales to the Canadian Market. AER 62: 37-45.
  1974a   The Theory of the Firm. In Economic Analysis and the Mul-
          tinational Enterprise. Ed. John H. Dunning. London: Al-
          len & Unwin.
  1974b   At Home Abroad. Cambridge, Mass.: Ballinger.
  1975   Reply. AER 65: 235.
House, W. J.
  1973   Market Structure and Industry Performance: The Case of
          Kenya. Oxford Economics Papers 25: 405-19.
Hufbauer, G. C.
  1974   Multinational Corporations and the International Adjustment
          Process. AER Proceedings 64: 271-75.
Hurdle, Gloria
  1974   Leverage, Risk, Market Structure, and Profitability. RES
          56: 478-85.
Hymer, Stephen H.
  1960   The International Operations of National Firms: A Study of
          Direct Investment. Ph.D. dissertation, Massachusetts In-
          stitute of Technology.
  1970a   The Multinational Corporation and Uneven Development. In
          Foreign Economic Policy Subcommittee, Joint Economic
          Committee, U.S. Congress. Hearings. Washington, D.C.:
          GPO.
  1970b   The Efficiency (Contradictions) of Multinational Corpora-
          tions. AER Proceedings 60: 441-48.
  1972   The Internationalization of Capital. J. of Economic Issues
          6: 91-111.
Hymer, Stephen H., and S. Resnick
  1969   Interactions between the Government and Private Sector.
          In Economic Development and Structural Change. Ed. J.
          G. Stewart. Edinburgh: Edinburgh U.P.
Imel, Blake, and Peter Helmberger
  1971   Estimation of Profit-Structure Relationships with Applica-
          tions to the Food Processing Sector. AER 61: 614-27.
Intrilligator, Michael D., ed.
  1971   Frontiers of Quantitative Economics. Amsterdam: North-
          Holland.
Jalée, Pierre
  1968   The Third World in the World Economy. New York:
          Monthly Review Press.

Jenkins, Rhys
  1976   The Dynamics of Dependent Industrialization in the Latin
         American Motor Industry. Unpublished manuscript.
Johnson, Harry G.
  1967   Economic Policies toward Less Developed Countries. New
         York: Praeger.
  1970   The Efficiency and Welfare Implications of the International
         Corporation. In The International Corporations. Ed.
         Charles P. Kindleberger. Cambridge, Mass.: MIT Press.
Johnston, J.
  1963   Econometric Methods. New York: McGraw-Hill.
Jones, Ronald W.
  1967   International Capital Movements and the Theory of Tariffs
         and Trade. QJE 81: 1-38.
  1970   The Role of Technology in International Trade. In The
         Technology Factor in International Trade. Ed. Raymond
         Vernon. New York: Columbia U.P.
Jorgenson, Dale
  1971   Economic Studies of Investment Behavior: A Survey. JEL
         9: 1111-47.
Kamien, Morton I., and Nancy Schwartz
  1975   Market Structure and Innovation: A Survey. JEL 13: 1-37.
Kapoor, A., and Phillip Grub, eds.
  1972   The Multinational Enterprise in Transition. Princeton,
         N.J.: Darwin Press.
Keegan, Warren J.
  1970   Multinational Pricing Is a Complex Task: The Case of the
         U.S. In World Business: Promise and Problems. Ed.
         Courtney C. Brown. New York: Macmillan.
Kemp, M. C.
  1962   Foreign Investment and the National Advantage. Economic
         Record 38: 56-62.
  1966   The Gain from International Trade and Investment. AER
         56: 788-809.
  1969   The Pure Theory of International Investment. Englewood
         Cliffs, N.J.: Prentice-Hall.
Keohane, Robert O., and Van Doorn Ooms
  1975   The Multinational Firm and International Regulation. In
         World Politics and International Economics. Ed. C. Fred
         Bergsten and Lawrence B. Krause. Washington, D.C.:
         Brookings Institution.
Khalilzadeh-Shirazi, Javad
  1974   Market Structure and Price-Cost Margins in United King-
         dom Manufacturing Industries. RES 56: 67-76.

Kindleberger, Charles P.
 1969   American Business Abroad: Six Lectures on Direct Invest-
        ment. New Haven, Conn.: Yale U.P.
 1970   The International Corporations. Cambridge, Mass.: MIT
        Press.
 1974   Size of Firm and Size of Nation. In Economic Analysis and
        the Multinational Enterprise. Ed. John H. Dunning. Lon-
        don: Allen & Unwin.
King, Timothy
 1970   Mexico: Industrialization and Trade Policies since 1940.
        London: Oxford U.P.
Klein, R. W.
 1973   A Dynamic Theory of Comparative Advantage. AER 63:
        173-84.
Kmenta, Jan
 1971   Elements of Econometrics. New York: Macmillan.
Knickerbocker, Frederick
 1973   Oligopolistic Reaction and the Multinational Enterprise.
        Boston: Harvard Graduate School of Business Administra-
        tion.
Kopits, George F.
 1972   Dividend Remittance Behavior within the International Firm:
        A Cross-Country Analysis. RES 54: 339-42.
Lall, Sanjaya
 1975   Foreign Private Manufacturing Investment and Multinational
        Corporations: An Annotated Bibliography. New York:
        Praeger.
Landes, David S.
 1969   The Unbound Prometheus: Technological Change and In-
        dustrial Development in Western Europe from 1750 to the
        Present. Cambridge, England: Cambridge U.P.
Ledogar, Robert J.
 1975   Hungry for Profits: U.S. Food and Drug Multinationals in
        Latin America. New York: IDOC-North America.
Leff, Nathaniel H.
 1968a Economic Policy-Making and Development in Brazil, 1947-
        1964. New York: Wiley.
 1968b The Brazilian Capital Goods Industry 1929-1964. Cam-
        bridge, Mass.: Harvard U.P.
 1977   Multinational Corporate Pricing Policies in the Developing
        Countries. J. of International Business 8: 1-22.
Leibenstein, Harvey
 1966   Allocative Efficiency vs. X-Inefficiency. AER 56: 392-415.
Lim, David
 1976   Capital Utilization of Local and Foreign Establishments in
        Maylasian Manufacturing. RES 58: 209-17.

Lintner, J.
  1965   The Valuation of Risk Assets and a Selection of Risky In-
          vestments in Stock Portfolios and Capital Budgets. RES
          47: 13-37.
Little, Ian, Tibor Scitovsky, and Maurice Scott
  1970   Industry and Trade in Some Developing Countries: A Com-
          parative Study. London: Oxford U.P.
Lustgarten, Stephen H.
  1975   The Impact of Buyer Concentration in Manufacturing Indus-
          tries. RES 57: 125-32.
MacDougall, G. D. A.
  1960   The Benefits and Costs of Private Investments from Abroad.
          Bulletin of the Oxford University Institute of Statistics 22:
          189-211.
McGee, John S.
  1974   Efficiency and Economies of Size. In Industrial Concentra-
          tion: The New Learning. Ed. Harvey J. Goldschmidt.
          Boston: Little, Brown.
McKie, James W.
  1972   Industrial Organization. In Policy Issues and Research Op-
          portunities in Industrial Organization. Ed. Victor R. Fuchs.
          New York: NBER.
Machlup, Fritz, W. S. Salant, and L. Tarshis, eds.
  1972   International Mobility and Movements of Capital. New York:
          Columbia U.P.
Manchester, Alden C.
  1974   Market Structure, Institutions, and Performance in the
          Fluid Milk Industry, Agricultural Economics Report No.
          248. Washington, D.C.: ERS-USDA.
Mancke, Richard B.
  1974   Causes of Interfirm Profitability Differences: A New Inter-
          pretation of the Evidence. QJE 88: 181-93.
Mann, H. Michael
  1974   Advertising, Concentration, and Profitability. In Industrial
          Concentration: The New Learning. Ed. Harvey J. Gold-
          schmidt. Boston: Little, Brown.
Mansfield, Edwin
  1968   Industrial Research and Technological Innovation. New
          York: Norton.
  1974   Technology and Technological Change. In Economic Analy-
          sis and the Multinational Enterprise. Ed. John H. Dunning.
          London: Allen & Unwin.
  1975   International Technology Transfer: Forms, Resource Re-
          quirements, and Policies. AER 65: 372-76.

Marion, Bruce, et al.
  1977   The Profit and Price Performance of Leading Food Chains,
          1970-74, a report to the Joint Economic Committee, U.S.
          Congress. Washington, D.C.: GPO.
Markham, Jesse, and Gustav Papanek
  1970   Industrial Organization and Economic Development. Boston:
          Houghton Mifflin.
Markowitz, H.
  1959   Portfolio Analysis. New York: Wiley.
Mason, R. Hal
  1973   Some Observations on the Choice of Technology by Multi-
          national Firms in Developing Countries. RES 60: 349-55.
May, Herbert
  1970   Effects of United States and Other Foreign Investment in
          Latin America. Washington, D.C.: Council for Latin
          America.
Means, Gardiner C.
  1931   The Large Corporation in American Economic Life. AER
          21: 10-42.
Meissner, Charles F.
  1969   Foreign Owned Food Processing Firms in Five Latin Ameri-
          can Countries. Ph.D. dissertation, University of Wiscon-
          sin.
Melvin, James R., and Robert D. Warne
  1973   Monopoly and the Theory of International Trade. J. of In-
          ternational Economics 3: 117-34.
Mikesell, Raymond F.
  1962   U.S. Private and Government Investment Abroad. Eugene:
          University of Oregon Books.
Miller, Richard A.
  1967   Marginal Concentration Ratios and Industrial Profit Rates.
          Southern Economics J. 84: 259-67.
Miracle, Gordon E.
  1972   International Advertising Principles and Strategies. In
          The Multinational Enterprise in Transition. Ed. A. Kapoor
          and Phillip Grub. Princeton, N.J.: Darwin Press.
Morley, Samuel A., and Gordon W. Smith
  1971   Import Substitution and Foreign Investment in Brazil. Ox-
          ford Economic Papers 23: 120-35.
  1974   The Choice of Technology: Multinational Firms in Brazil.
          Houston: Rice University Program of Development Studies.
Morley, Samuel A., and Jeffery G. Williamson
  1974   Demand, Distribution, and Employment: The Case of Bra-
          zil. Economic Development and Cultural Change 23: 33-60.

Mueller, Willard F.
  1974   Industrial Concentration: An Important Inflationary Force:
           In Industrial Concentration: The New Learning. Ed. Har-
           vey J. Goldschmidt. Boston: Little, Brown.
  1975   Antitrust in a Planned Economy: An Anachronism or an Es-
           sential Complement? J. of Economic Issues 9: 159-79.
  1977   Conglomerates: A "Nonindustry." In The Structure of
           American Industry, 5th ed. Ed. Walter Adams. New York:
           Macmillan.
Mueller, Willard F., and Larry G. Hamm
  1974   Trends in Industrial Market Concentration, 1947 to 1970.
           RES 56: 511-20.
Mueller, Willard F., Larry Hamm, and Hugh Cook
  1976   Public Policy toward Mergers in the Dairy Processing In-
           dustry. Monograph 3 of N.C. Project 117. Madison:
           University of Wisconsin.
Müller, Ronald, and Richard D. Morgenstern
  1974   Multinational Corporations and Balance of Payments Impacts
           in LDCs: An Econometric Analysis of Export Pricing Be-
           havior. Kyklos 27: 304-21.
Multinational Corporations Subcommittee, Committee on Foreign Relations, U.S. Senate
  1973   Multinational Corporations and U.S. Foreign Policy. Wash-
           ington, D.C.: GPO.
Musgrave, Peggy B.
  1974   Direct Investment Abroad and the Multinationals: Effects
           on the United States Economy. A report to the Subcommit-
           tee on Multinational Corporations of the Committee on For-
           eign Relations, U.S. Senate. Washington, D.C.: GPO.
Nam, W. H.
  1975   The Determinants of Industrial Concentration: The Case
           of Korea. Maylasian Economics Review 20: 37-48.
National Academy of Sciences
  1973   U.S. International Firms and R, D, and E in Developing
           Countries. Washington, D.C.: National Academy of
           Sciences.
NCFM (National Commission on Food Marketing)
  1966   The Structure of Food Manufacturing, Technical Study No.
           8. Washington, D.C.: GPO.
Negandhi, Anant R., and S. Benjamin Prasad
  1975   The Frightening Angels: A Study of U.S. Multinationals in
           Developing Nations. Kent, Ohio: Kent State U.P.
Ness, Walter L., Jr.
  1974   Financial Markets Innovation as a Development Strategy:
           Initial Results from the Brazilian Experience. Economic
           Development and Cultural Change 22: 453-72.

Newfarmer, Richard S.
   1977   Multinational Conglomerates and the Economics of Dependent
           Development: A Case Study of the International Electrical
           Oligopoly and Brazil's Electrical Industry. Ph.D. disser-
           tation, University of Wisconsin at Madison.
Newfarmer, Richard S., and Willard F. Mueller
   1975   Multinational Corporations in Brazil and Mexico: Structural
           Sources of Economic and Noneconomic Power. A report
           to the Subcommittee on Multinational Corporations of the
           Committee on Foreign Relations, U.S. Senate. Washing-
           ton, D.C.: GPO.
Nikaido, Hukukane
   1975   Monopolistic Competition and Effective Demand. Princeton,
           N.J.: Princeton U.P.
Ohara, Yoshinori
   1974   Brazilian Economic Development since 1956: A Study on
           Policies Reflecting the Stages of Growth. Developing
           Economies 12: 133-54.
Olizar, Marynka
   1972   A Guide to the Mexican Markets. Mexico City.
Onitsuka, Yusuke
   1974   International Capital Movements and the Patterns of Eco-
           nomic Growth. AER 64: 24-36.
Orr, Dale
   1974   The Determinants of Entry: A Study of the Canadian Manu-
           facturing Industries. RES 56: 58-66.
   1975   The Industrial Composition of U.S. Exports and Subsidiary
           Sales to the Canadian Market: Comment. AER 65: 230-34.
Parry, Thomas G.
   1973   The International Firm and National Economic Policy: A
           Survey of Some Issues. Economic J. 83: 1201-21.
Pavitt, Keith
   1971   The Multinational Enterprise and the Transfer of Technol-
           ogy. In The Multinational Enterprise. Ed. John H. Dun-
           ning. London: Allen & Unwin.
Pearson, Lester B.
   1969   Partners in Development. A report of the Commission on
           International Development. New York: Praeger.
Penrose, Edith
   1971   The State and Multinational Enterprises in Less-Developed
           Countries. In The Multinational Enterprise. Ed. John H.
           Dunning. London: Allen & Unwin.
   1973   International Patenting and the Less-Developed Countries.
           Economics J. 83: 768-86.

Perlmutter, Howard V.
  1970   The Tortuous Evolution of the Multinational Corporation.
          In World Business: Promise and Problems. Ed. Courtney
          C. Brown. New York: Macmillan.
Phillips, Almarin
  1976   A Critique of Empirical Studies of Relations between Mar-
          ket Structure and Profitability. J. of Industrial Economics
          24: 241-49.
Porter, Michael E.
  1974   Consumer Behavior, Retailer Power and Market Perfor-
          mance in Consumer Goods Industries. RES 56: 419-36.
Prachowny, M. J.
  1972   Direct Investment and the Balance of Payments in the
          United States. In International Mobility and Movements of
          Capital. Ed. Fritz Machlup, W. S. Salant, and L. Tarshis.
          New York: Columbia U.P.
Prebisch, Raul
  1959   Commercial Policy int he Underdeveloped Countries. AER
          Proceedings 49: 253-57.
Pryor, Frederick L.
  1972   An International Comparison of Concentration Ratios. RES
          54: 25-35.
Ragazzi, G.
  1973   Theories of the Determinants of Direct Foreign Investment.
          IMF Staff Papers, July: 471-98.
Reuber, Grant L.
  1973   Private Foreign Investment in Development. London: Ox-
          ford U.P.
Rhoades, Stephen A.
  1973   The Effect of Diversification on Industry Profit Performance
          in 241 Manufacturing Industries: 1963. RES 55: 146-55.
  1974   A Further Evaluation of the Effect of Diversification on In-
          dustry Profit Performance. RES 56: 557-59.
Rhodes, Robert I.
  1970a   Mexico: A Model for Capitalist Development in Latin
          America? Science and Society 34: 61-77.
  1970b   Ed. Imperialism and Underdevelopment. New York:
          Monthly Review Press.
Robbins, Sidney M., and Robert B. Stobaugh
  1973   Money in the Multinational Enterprise. New York: Basic
          Books.
Robertson, David
  1971   The Multinational Enterprise: Trade Flows and Trade Pol-
          icy. In The Multinational Enterprise. Ed. John H. Dun-
          ning. London: Allen & Unwin.

Robock, Stefan H.
   1975   Brazil: A Study in Development Progress. Lexington,
          Mass.: Heath
Robock, Stefan H., and Kenneth Simmonds
   1972   International Business: How Big Is It? In The Multinational
          Enterprise in Transition. Ed. A. Kapoor and Phillip Grub.
          Princeton, N.J.: Darwin Press.
Rodriguez, Carlos Alfredo
   1975   Trade in Technological Knowledge and the National Advan-
          tage. JPE 83: 121-35.
Root, Franklin R.
   1973   Public Policy Expectations of Multinational Managers.
          MSU Business Topics, Autumn: 5-12.
Rosenthal, Gert
   1975   The Expansion of the Transnational Enterprise in Central
          America: Acquisition of Domestic Firms. Queretaro,
          Mexico: CONACYT-CIDE Symposium on Transnational En-
          terprises and the Host Economies.
Rowthorn, Robert
   1971   International Big Business 1957-1967: A Study of Compara-
          tive Growth. Cambridge, England: Cambridge U.P.
Safarian, A. E.
   1968   Country of Ownership and Performance of the Firm. Eco-
          nomic Record 44: 82-96.
Sato, Kazuo
   1961   Price-Cost Structure and Behavior of Profit Margins. Yale
          Economic Essays 1: 361-425.
Scherer, F. M.
   1965   Firm Size, Market Structure, Opportunity, and the Output
          of Patented Inventions. AER 55: 1097-1125.
   1970   Industrial Market Structure and Economic Performance.
          Chicago: Rand McNally.
   1974   Economies of Scale and Industrial Concentration. In Indus-
          trial Concentration: The New Learning. Ed. Harvey J.
          Goldschmidt. Boston: Little, Brown.
Scherer, F. M., et al.
   1975   The Economics of Multiplant Operation. Cambridge, Mass.:
          Harvard U.P.
Schmitz, Andrew, and Peter Helmberger
   1970   Factor Mobility and International Trade: The Case of Com-
          plementarity. AER 60: 761-67.
Schollhammer, Hans
   1972   The Compensation of International Executives. In The Mul-
          tinational Enterprise in Transition. Ed. A. Kapoor and
          Phillip Grub. Princeton, N.J.: Darwin Press.

Severn, Alan K., and Martin M. Lawrence
  1974   Direct Investment, Research Intensity, and Profitability.
         J. of Finance and Quantitative Analysis 9: 181-90.
Shepherd, William G.
  1964   Trends of Concentration in American Industries, 1947-1958.
         RES 46: 400-12.
  1972   The Elements of Market Structure. RES 54: 25-35.
  1976   Public Enterprise: Economic Analysis of Theory and Prac-
         tice. Lexington, Mass.: Lexington Books.
Siegfried, John J., and Leonard Weiss
  1974   Advertising, Profits, and Corporate Taxes Revisited. RES
         56: 195-200.
Södersten, Bo
  1970   International Economics. New York: Harper & Row.
Stern, Joseph J.
  1977   The Employment Impact of Industrial Investment, Develop-
         ment Discussion Paper No. 20. Cambridge, Mass.: Har-
         vard Institute for International Development.
Stevens, Guy V. G.
  1969   U.S. Direct Manufacturing Investment to Latin America:
         Some Economic and Political Determinants. Washington,
         D.C.: Agency for International Development.
  1972   Capital Mobility and the International Firm. In Interna-
         tional Mobility and Movements of Capital. Ed. Fritz Mach-
         lup, W. S. Salant, and L. Tarshis. New York: Columbia
         U.P.
  1974   The Determinants of Investment. In Economic Analysis and
         the Multinational Enterprise. Ed. John H. Dunning. Lon-
         don: Allen & Unwin.
Stigler, George J.
  1964   A Theory of Oligopoly. JPE 72: 44-61.
  1968   The Organization of Industry. Homewood, Ill.: Irwin.
Stobaugh, Robert B.
  1972   Where in the World Should We Put That Plant? In The Mul-
         tinational Enterprise in Transition. Ed. A. Kapoor and
         Phillip Grub. Princeton, N.J.: Darwin Press.
Stopford, John, and Louis Wells
  1972   Managing the Multinational Enterprise. London: Longmans.
Streeten, Paul
  1971   The Costs and Benefits of Multinational Enterprises in Less-
         Developed Countries. In The Multinational Enterprise.
         Ed. John H. Dunning. London: Allen & Unwin.
  1974   The Theory of Development Policy. In Economic Analysis
         and the Multinational Enterprise. Ed. John H. Dunning.
         London: Allen & Unwin.

Sweezy, Paul
    1942   The Theory of Capitalist Development. New York: Monthly
           Review Press.
Syvrud, Donald E.
    1974   Foundations of Brazilian Economic Growth. Stanford,
           Calif.: American Enterprise Institute and Hoover Institution.
Task Force on the Structure of Canadian Industry
    1968   Foreign Ownership and the Structure of Canadian Industry
           (the Watkins Report). Ottawa: Privy Council Office.
Tavares, Conceicao
    1975   Latin American Industrial Development and the Present
           Crisis of Transnationalism. Queretaro, Mexico: CONACYT-
           CIDE Symposium on Transnational Enterprises and the Host
           Countries.
Telser, Lester G.
    1972   Competition, Collusion, and Game Theory. Chicago: Al-
           dine.
Timberg, Sigmund
    1972   Antitrust in the Common Market: Innovation and Surprise.
           Law and Contemporary Problems 37: 1027-38.
Torre, Jose de la
    1974   Foreign Investment and Export Dependency. Economic
           Development and Cultural Change 23: 133-50.
Tsurumi, Yoshi
    1976   The Japanese Are Coming: A Multinational Interaction of
           Firms and Politics. Cambridge, Mass.: Ballinger.
Tyler, William G.
    1973   Manufacturing Export Promotion in a Semi-Industrialized
           Economy: The Brazilian Case. J. of Development Studies
           10: 3-15.
UN
    1974   The Acquisition of Technology from Multinational Corpora-
           tions by Developing Countries (ST/ESA/12). New York:
           UN.
UNCTAD (UN Conference on Trade and Development)
    1972   Transfer of Technology. Santiago, Chile (third session).
    1974   Restrictive Business Practices in Relation to the Trade
           and Development of Developing Countries (TD/B/C.2/119/
           Rev.2). New York: UN.
    1975a The Role of the Patent System in the Transfer of Technol-
           ogy to Developing Countries (TD/B/AC.11/19/Rev.1). New
           York: UN.
    1975b Major Issues Arising from the Transfer of Technology to
           Developing Countries (TD/B/AC.11/10/Rev.2). New York:
           UN.

U.S. Department of Commerce
  1974   Input-Output Structure of the U.S. Economy: 1967. Wash-
          ington, D.C.: GPO.
Vaitsos, Constantine V.
  1973   Foreign Investment Policies and Economic Development in
          Latin America. J. of World Trade Law, November-Decem-
          ber: 619-65.
  1974   Intercountry Income Distribution and Transnational Enter-
          prises. London: Oxford U.P.
  1975   Power, Knowledge, and Development Policy: Relations
          between Transnational Enterprises and Developing Countries.
          Queretaro, Mexico: CONACYT-CIDE Symposium on Trans-
          national Enterprises and the Host Countries.
Vaupel, James W., and Joan P. Curhan
  1969   The Making of Multinational Enterprise. Boston: Division
          of Research, Graduate School of Business, Harvard Univer-
          sity.
Vernon, Raymond
  1959   The American Corporation in Underdeveloped Areas. In
          The Corporation in Modern Society. Ed. Edward Mason.
          Cambridge, Mass.: Harvard U.P.
  1963   The Dilemma of Mexico's Development. Cambridge, Mass.:
          Harvard U.P.
  1966   International Investment and International Trade in the Prod-
          uct Cycle. QJE 80: 190-207.
  1970   The Technology Factor in International Trade. New York:
          Columbia U.P.
  1971   Sovereignty at Bay: The Multinational Spread of U.S. En-
          terprises. New York: Basic Books.
  1972   Conflict and Resolution between Foreign Direct Investors
          and Less Developed Countries. In The Multinational Enter-
          prise in Transition. Ed. A. Kapoor and Phillip Grub.
          Princeton, N.J.: Darwin Press.
  1974a   The Location of Economic Activity. In Economic Analysis
          and the Multinational Enterprise. Ed. John H. Dunning.
          London: Allen & Unwin.
  1974b   Competition Policy toward Multinational Corporations.
          AER Proceedings 64: 176-82.
  1975   Multinational Enterprises in Developing Countries: An An-
          alysis of National Goals and National Policies, Development
          Discussion Paper No. 4. Cambridge, Mass.: Harvard In-
          stitute for International Development.
Victor, A. Paul
  1973   Multinational Corporations: Antitrust Extraterritoriality
          and the Prospect of Immunity. J. of International Law and
          Economics 8: 11-29.

Ward, Barbara, et al., eds.
    1971   The Widening Gap: Development in the 1970s. New York:
            Columbia U.P.

Weiss, Leonard
    1966   Business Pricing Policies and Inflation Reconsidered. JPE
            74: 177-87.
    1974   The Concentration-Profits Relation and Antitrust. In
            Industrial Concentration: The New Learning. Ed. Harvey
            J. Goldschmidt. Boston: Little, Brown.

Wells, Louis T.
    1972a   Economic Man and Engineering Man: Choice of Technology
            in a Low Wage Country, Economic Development Report No.
            226. Cambridge, Mass.: Development Research Group,
            Center for International Affairs, Harvard University.
    1972b   The Product Life Cycle and International Trade. Cambridge,
            Mass.: Harvard U.P.

White, Lawrence J.
    1974a   Industrial Organization and International Trade: Some
            Theoretical Considerations. AER 64: 1013-20.
    1974b   Industrial Concentration and Economic Power in Pakistan.
            Princeton, N.J.: Princeton U.P.

Wilkins, Mira
    1970   The Emergence of Multinational Enterprise: American
            Business Abroad from the Colonial Era to 1914. Cambridge,
            Mass.: Harvard U.P.
    1974   The Maturing of Multinational Enterprise. Cambridge,
            Mass.: Harvard U.P.

Wilson, J. S. G., and C. Scheffer, eds.
    1974   Multinational Enterprises: Financial and Monetary Aspects.
            Leiden, Netherlands: Sijthoff.

Wolf, Bernard M.
    1971   Internationalization of U.S. Manufacturing Firms: A Type
            of Diversification. Ph.D. dissertation, Yale University.

Wright, Harry K.
    1971   Foreign Enterprise in Mexico: Laws and Policies. Chapel
            Hill: University of North Carolina Press.

Zeitlin, Maurice
    1974   Economic Concentration, Industrial Structure, and National
            and Foreign Capital in Chile in 1966. Industrial Organiza-
            tion Review 2: 195-205.

Zenoff, David B.
    1970   Slicing the Financial Pie. In World Business: Promise and
            Problems. Ed. Courtney C. Brown. New York: Macmil-
            lan.

5-8, 13, 16, 18, 30, 216-18; distribution, 6, 13, 29, 216-17; effects, 1, 6, 19, 20, 23, 26, 28,
59-60, 235-36; government policies, 10, 61-65, 234-50; horizontal, 7, 26, 30-31, 217; and imperfect competition, 5, 6-8, 17, 18-
19, 22, 24-32, 217-18, 219-20;
package of inputs, 7-8, 13, 22,
24, 217, 245; risk, 5, 6, 11, 13,
32, 218; theory, 11-32, 217-20;
theory of firm, 19-22, 219; vertical, 7, 26, 31, 217
Frank, A. G., 11
FTC (Federal Trade Commission),
120, 129, 147, 149, 155
Fuchs, Victor, 141
Furtado, Celso, 63

Gale, Bradley, T., 145, 147, 148,
149, 152, 172
Gambeles, G., 129, 143, 148
Gaston, Frank, 10
GATT (see, General Agreement
on Tariffs and Trade)
General Agreement for the Inter-
national Corporation, 249
General Agreement on Tariffs and
Trade (GATT), 248, 249
Gilman, Martin, 248
Gordon, Lincoln, 62
Grabowski, Henry G., 130
Greenhill, Colin, 240, 241
Greer, Douglas, 130
growth, 128-29, 147-48, 152, 172-
73, 235, 246
Grubel, Herbert, 238
Gruber, Mehta, 17
Gruber, Vernon, 17
Günther, Eberhard, 240, 241, 249

Hall, Marshall, 127, 133, 143,
145, 147, 149, 171
Hamms, Larry G., 122, 130
Hansen, Roger, 57

Heller, Robert, 15
Herfindahl index, 131
Hirschman, Albert, 243
Horst, Thomas, 11, 13, 19, 20,
150
House, W. J., 153
Hurdle, Gloria, 145, 155
Hymer, Stephen, 3, 6, 7, 11,
17, 25

IBRD (see, International Bank
for Reconstruction and Development)
Imel, Blake, 110, 134, 136, 141,
204
IMF, 248
India, 151, 243
industrial organization (IO) theory,
12, 26-32, 117-23, 219-20 (see
also, oligopoly models)
industrialization, 36-39, 50-52,
59-60, 239
instruments industry, 87-90, 95
Inter-American Development
Bank, 236
International Bank for Reconstruction and Development (IBRD),
237, 248
International Center for Settlement of Investment Disputes
(ICSID), 237
International Monetary Fund
(IMF), 248
international trade, 38-39, 65;
theory, 5, 8, 12-13, 14-19,
32, 143
intrafirm trade, 8, 16, 77-78,
173, 233
investment climate, 236-37
IO (see, industrial organization
theory; oligopoly models)

Jalée, Pierre, 11
Japan, 4, 26, 36, 39, 151, 243,
247

ABOUT THE AUTHOR

JOHN M. CONNOR is an assistant professor in the Department of Agricultural Economics of the University of Wisconsin at Madison. During 1975 and 1976, he served as a consultant to the Subcommittee on Multinational Corporations of the U.S. Senate Committee on Foreign Relations. In that capacity he collaborated in the research for, and writing of, two substantial monographs published by the subcommittee on the operation of U.S. multinational corporations in Brazil and Mexico.

Dr. Connor holds an A.B. degree from Boston College, master's degrees from the University of Florida and the University of Wisconsin, and a Ph.D. degree from the University of Wisconsin at Madison.

DEPENDENT INDUSTRIALIZATION IN LATIN
AMERICA: The Automotive Industry in Argentina,
Chile, and Mexico
                    Rhys Owen Jenkins

ECONOMIC NATIONALISM IN LATIN AMERICA:
The Quest for Economic Independence
                    Shoshana B. Tancer

*MANAGING MULTINATIONAL CORPORATIONS
                    Arvind V. Phatak

MARKETING MANAGEMENT IN MULTINATIONAL
FIRMS: The Consumer Packaged Goods Industry
                    Ulrich E. Wiechmann

THE NATIONALIZATION OF VENEZUELAN OIL
                    James F. Petras
                    Morris Morley
                    Steven Smith

THE USE OF INDEXATION IN DEVELOPING
COUNTRIES
                    G. Donald Jud

*Also available in paperback as a PSS Student Edition